Glimpses of the Supernatural
Volumes I & II
Originally Edited by the Rev. Frederick George Lee, D.C.L.
This Edition Edited by Anthony Uyl

Woodstock, Ontario, 2017

Glimpses of the Supernatural Volumes I & II
Glimpses of the Supernatural Volumes I & II
The Other World; Being Facts, Records, and Traditions Relating to Dreams, Omens, Miraculous Occurrences, Apparitions, Wraiths, Warnings, Second-Sight, Witchcraft, Necromancy, etc.
In Two Volumes

Originally Edited by the Rev. Frederick George Lee, D.C.L.
Vicar of All Saints', Lambeth.
This Edition Edited by Anthony Uyl

Originally Published by:
Henry's, King and Co., London. 1875.

Originally Printed by:
Chiswick Press: - Printed by Whittingham and Wilkins, Tooks Court, Chancery Lane

The text of Glimpses of the Supernatural Volumes I & II is all in the Public Domain. The layout and Devoted Publishing logo are Copyright ©2017 Devoted Publishing. This edition is published by Devoted Publishing a division of 2165467 Ontario Inc.

**What kind of stories do you have?
Let us know!**

Visit our website: www.devotedpublishing.com
Contact us at: devotedpub@hotmail.com
Visit us on Facebook: @DevotedPublishing

Published in Woodstock, Ontario, Canada 2017

For bulk educational rates, please contact us at the above email address.

ISBN: 978-1-77356-096-0

Rev. Frederick George Lee, D.C.L.

Table of Contents

VOLUME I 4
DEDICATION 5
   PREFACE 6
   CHAPTER I - INTRODUCTORY - MATERIALISM OF THE PRESENT AGE 7
   CHAPTER II - THE MIRACULOUS IN CHURCH HISTORY 12
   CHAPTER III - SPIRITUAL POWERS AND PROPERTIES OF THE CHURCH ... 18
      APPENDIX TO CHAPTER III - THE FORM OF EXORCISING THE POSSESSED 39
   CHAPTER IV - WITCHCRAFT AND NECROMANCY 44
   CHAPTER V - DREAMS, OMENS, WARNINGS, PRESENTIMENTS, AND SECOND SIGHT 55
      FOOTNOTES: 76
VOLUME II 89
   CHAPTER VI - SPECTRAL APPEARANCES 90
   CHAPTER VII - HAUNTED HOUSES AND LOCALITIES 108
   CHAPTER VIII - MODERN SPIRITUALISM 120
   CHAPTER IX - MODERN SPIRITUALISM (CONTINUED) 128
      APPENDIX TO CHAPTER IX - SPIRITUALISM AND SCIENCE 135
   CHAPTER X - SUMMARY AND CONCLUSION 139
      APPENDIX TO CHAPTER X - THE CLAIMS OF SCIENCE AND FAITH 147
      FOOTNOTES: 148

VOLUME I

Rev. Frederick George Lee, D.C.L.

DEDICATION

To the Right Honourable Augusta, Countess of Stradbroke of Henham Hall, in the County of Suffolk, These Volumes are, by her Ladyship's Kind Permission, Very Respectfully Dedicated

"It is often asked--Do you believe in Prophecies and Miracles? Yes and no, one may answer; that depends. In general, yes; doubtless we believe in them, and are not of the number of those who 'pique themselves,' as Fénelon said, 'on rejecting as fables, without examination, all the wonders that God works.' But if you come to the particular, and say--Do you believe in such a revelation, such an apparition, such a cure?--here it is that it behoves us not to forget the rules of Christian prudence, nor the warnings of Holy Writ, nor the teaching of Theologians and Saints, nor, finally, the decrees of Councils, and the motives of those decrees. Has the proper Authority spoken? If it has spoken, let us bow with all the respect due to grave and mature ecclesiastical judgments, even where they are not clothed with infallible authority; if it has not spoken, let us not be of those who reject everything in a partizan spirit, and want to impose this unbelief upon everybody; nor of those who admit everything lightly, and want alike to impose their belief; let us be careful in discussing a particular fact, not to reject the very principle of the Supernatural, but neither let us shut our eyes to the evidence of testimony; let us be prudent, even to the most careful scrutiny--the subject-matter requires it, the Scriptures recommend it--but let us not be sceptics; let us be sincere, but not fanatical: that is the true mean. And let us not forget that most often the safest way in these matters is not to hurry one's judgment, not to decide sharply and affirm absolutely--in a word, not to anticipate, in one sense or the other, the judgment of those whose place and mission it is to examine herein; but to await, in the simplicity of faith and of Christian wisdom, a decision which marks out a wise rule, although not always with absolute certainty."--Dupanloup, Bishop of Orleans, "On Contemporary Prophecies."

PREFACE

These volumes have been compiled from the standing-point of a hearty and reverent believer in Historical Christianity. No one can be more fully aware of their imperfections and incompleteness than the Editor; for the subjects under consideration occupy such a broad field, that their treatment at greater length would have largely increased the bulk of the volumes, and indefinitely postponed their publication.

The facts and records set forth (and throughout, the Editor has dealt with facts, rather than with theories) have been gathered from time to time during the past twenty years, as well from ordinary historical narrations as from the personal information of several friends and acquaintances interested in the subject-matter of the book. The materials thus brought together from so many quarters have been carefully sifted, and those only made use of as would best assist in the arranged method of the volume, and suffice for its suitable illustration.

The Editor regrets that, in the publication of so many recent examples of the Supernatural (about fifty), set forth for the first time in the following pages, the names of the persons to whom those examples occurred, and in some cases those likewise who supplied him with them, are withheld.

The truth is, there is such a sensitive dislike of publicity and of rude criticism consequent upon publicity, that very many persons shrink from the ordeal. However, it may be sufficient to state that the Editor holds himself personally responsible for all those here recorded, which are not either details of received History, or formally authenticated by the names and addresses of those who have supplied him with them.

Many examples of the Supernatural in modern times and in the present day are here published for the first time, in an authoritative and complete form.

By the kind courtesy of Lord Lyttelton, the family records of a remarkable apparition, which is said to have been seen by his noble ancestor, were placed at the Editor's disposal, and, by his Lordship's permission, are in the following pages now first set forth in detail and at length.

The Editor is also indebted to the following, either for obliging replies to his inquiries, or for information which has been embodied in the succeeding pages:--The late Lady Brougham, the late Rev. W. Hastings-Kelke, of Drayton Beauchamp; A. L. M. P. de Lisle, Esq., of Garendon Park; the Very Rev. A. Weld, S.J.; the Right Rev. Monsignor Patterson, D.D., of S. Edmund's College, Ware; the Rev. J. Jefferson, M.A., of North Stainley Vicarage, near Ripon; the Very Rev. E. J. Purbrick, S.J., of Stonyhurst College; the Rev. John Richardson, B.A., of Warwick; Henry Cope Caulfeild, Esq., M.A., of Clone House, S. Leonard's; the Rev. Theodore J. Morris; Mrs. George Lee; the Rev. H. N. Oxenham, M.A.; Miss S. F. Caulfeild; Dominick Browne, Esq. (Dytchley); Captain Lowrie, of York; Mr. C. J. Sneath, of Birmingham; and many others.

If there be anything set forth in this volume, in ignorance or misconception, contradictory to the general teaching of the Universal Church, the Editor puts on record here his regret for having penned it, and his desire altogether to withdraw such error.

F. G. L.
All Saints' Vicarage, York Road, Lambeth.

Rev. Frederick George Lee, D.C.L.

CHAPTER I - INTRODUCTORY - MATERIALISM OF THE PRESENT AGE

"In some sense of the Supernatural, in some faith in the Unseen, in some feeling that man is not of this World, in some grasp on the Eternal God, and on an eternal supernatural and supersensuous life, lies the basis of all pity and mercy, all help, and comfort, and patience, and sympathy among men. Set these aside, commit us only to the Natural, to what our eyes see and our hands handle, and, while we may organize Society scientifically, and live according to 'the laws of Nature,' and be very philosophical and very liberal, we are standing on the ground on which every savage tribe stands, or indeed on which every pack of wolves gallops."

To any sincere and hearty believer in Historical Christianity the advance of Materialism and the consequent denial of the Supernatural must be the cause both of alarm and sadness. The few lead, the many follow; and it is frequently the case that conclusions contrarient to the idea of the Supernatural are arrived at, after a course of reasoning, which conclusions appear to many wholly unjustified, either by the premisses adopted, or from the argument that has ensued.

It has been stated, in a serial of some ability,[1] that the final issue of the present conflict between so that things are necessarily different to what they would have been if he had not thus acted, and no disturbance nor dislocation of the system around him ensues as a consequence of such action, surely He Who contrived the system in question can subsequently interpose both in the natural and spiritual order of the world. For to deny this possibility is obviously to place God on a lower level than man; in other words, to make the Creator of all things weaker and less free than His own creatures.

Now, to go a step further, all human efforts to find out God have been the result of the combination of ideas gleaned from human experience. These ideas have often enough been grotesque, fanciful, and distorted--a judgment which will be admitted to be accurate by all Christian people; whether the gross conceptions of Pagan mythology or the nebulous speculations of modern "thinkers" are brought under consideration. That man, the created, cannot understand God the Creator--that the thing made cannot compass the Maker--is not only perfectly certain, but necessary. The being of God cannot be grasped by a finite intellect; nor can such an intellect conceive the mode of an existence absolutely and utterly removed from created conditions. Such knowledge is too wonderful and excellent: we cannot attain unto it.[2]

But though it may be, and is, utterly impossible to conceive Almighty God, it is anything but impossible to conceive the fact and reality of His being. For, as is well known, the general thought and conscience of mankind have believed in a God, semper et ubique, everywhere and at all times. Thus a thing may exist, and its existence may be perfectly patent to the understanding; and furthermore its existence may be worthy of implicit belief; while, at the same time, the thing itself may be found to transcend and overpass the limited powers of man's intellect. Take, for example, the ideas conveyed by the terms "eternal"[3] and "infinite." Who can comprehend them? Who can explain them? Ordinary popular conceptions make them mere indefinite extensions of duration and space; yet these conceptions need not and do not appear absurd, but, on the contrary, enable ideas, at once definite, distinct, and recognizable, to be conveyed from man to man.

Thus, by a simple process of thought, we may see for ourselves the place and propriety of a Revelation, and appreciate the truth of the Supernatural. Here, in the province of a Revelation, not man's conception of God, but God Himself is set forth. Not so unlike ourselves is He that we find Him, with will, actions, and purposes, unintelligible; but, using analogies gathered and systematized by experience, we learn, at the same time, that our Creator is beyond the range both of thought and language--never to be fully known, until, with divinely-illuminated faculties in a higher state, we see Him face to face.

And when we have attained to this point in our course of thought, the first leading fact of God's revelation meets us. Here it is: "There is but one living and true God, everlasting, without body, parts, or passions; of infinite power, wisdom, and goodness; the Maker and Preserver of all things, both visible and invisible. And in unity of this Godhead there be three Persons, of one substance, power, and eternity: the Father, the Son, and the Holy Ghost."[4]

Now in this revelation, given in its fullness by the Eternal Word, and bequeathed to the Christian Church, to be preserved and handed down for future generations, all is Supernatural. That body of doctrine which Christians believe, divinely guarded by the Church, was announced beforehand, centuries ere it was actually delivered, by a wisdom above nature--the divine light of prophecy. When it was set forth by the Eternal Word, its truth was attested in the face of a hostile people by a power above nature, whose word Creation obeyed, as in regularity, so in marked and palpable change. This body of doctrine or gospel put forth a supernatural power in the strange rapidity and manifest success with which it subdued hearts to itself. Ancient Rome owned the Crucified as a Monarch conquering and to conquer. His Revelation, of the truth of which there shall be witnesses unto the end, is above nature, in that it alone provides adequate remedies for the manifold infirmities of the human race. The life it produces here is supernatural, as are also the means by which that life is created, and the efficient gifts by which it is being constantly renewed. Supernatural, too, is the work of the Holy Ghost, wrought out by human agents and human instrumentality; changing, sanctifying, illuminating; shadowing forth by its action the reunion of earth with heaven, of man with God, only to be completed and made perfect in the life to come.

Now the purport of this volume is to show by examples of supernatural intervention--examples many of which have been gathered from quite recent periods--that Almighty God, from time to time, in various ways and by different human instruments, still condescendingly reveals to man glimpses of the world unseen, and shows the existence of that life beyond the grave, in which the sceptic and materialist of the present restless age would have us disbelieve, and which they themselves scornfully reject.

From the sure and solid standing-point of Historical Christianity, believing Holy Scripture to be the Word of God, and the Christian Church to be the divinely-formed corporation for instructing, guiding, and illuminating mankind, remarkable examples of the Supernatural, miracles, spectral appearances of departed spirits, providential warnings by dreams and otherwise, the intervention and ministry of good angels, the assaults of bad, the certain power and efficacy of the gifts of Holy Church, the sanctity of consecrated places, and the persevering malignity of the devil and his legions, are gathered together, and set forth in the pages to follow. For it may reasonably be believed that, as Almighty God has graciously vouchsafed to intervene in the affairs of mankind in ages long past, so there has never been a period in which such merciful intervention has not from time to time taken place. Granted that in the days of Moses and Aaron, and of Elijah and Elisha, man owned miraculous powers, and wrought wonders by the gift of God; granted that in dreams and visions the will of the Most High was sometimes made known to favoured individuals of the Jewish Dispensation; remembering the miracles of our Lord's apostles and disciples, and bearing in mind the divine and supernatural powers which were first entrusted to, and have been ever since exercised by, the Catholic Church, it is at once unreasonable and unphilosophical to deny the existence in the world of the supernatural and miraculous. As will be abundantly set forth, their presence and energy are in perfect accord and harmony with the universal experience of mankind. Sceptics may contemn and object, materialists may scoff; but numerous facts as well as a very general sentiment are against their conclusions and convictions.

Floating straws show the direction and force of a current. As an example of the lengths to which an adoption of the materialistic principle will lead some persons, who regard themselves as "philosophers," and as a specimen of the dangers which threaten us, it may be well to refer briefly to the proposal which has recently been formally and publicly made, viz., that in certain cases of hopeless disease or imbecile old age, physicians should be legally authorized to put an end to such patients by poison.

Thus, when the head of a family becomes old or borders on childishness, the son, by going through the proposed legal formality, may stand by and witness the poisoning of his father, and so enter on the possession of his property. When a mother becomes old, the daughter may assist in a similar manner at her mother's death. A crippled child, a weak-minded relation, an infirm member of the family, according to the "philosophers," should have a poisonous drug efficiently administered; that so the weak, crippled, or imbecile might be murdered and put out of the way. Thus these philosopher-fanatics assure us that "the natural law of the preservation of the fittest," propounded by them, will come into active and unchecked operation. Having warned us that the penalty we endure for ignoring this "law" is a population largely composed of weak, unhealthy, poor and suffering people, they now earnestly recommend a "scientific method," by which the lame, the blind, the weak, and the imbecile should be cleared off from the stage of life.[5] "Natural selection," would, unchecked and never opposed, have preserved alive only the best and noblest types; and as, they tell us in their infallible wisdom, this principle or law has developed us so far from the mollusk to the man, it might by this time, had it been carefully and faithfully applied, have developed us, if not into angels, at least into nineteenth-century savages of great muscular power. This is the odious message to mankind which naturalistic Materialism announces. And if we

Rev. Frederick George Lee, D.C.L.

confine ourselves to what is sometimes called "science"--that is, exclusive knowledge of things material--such a conclusion as that arrived at, and such degrading principles as those propounded for acceptance and practice, may not be altogether unreasonable.[6] In this kind of "science" there is little else but coldness, cruelty, and savagery. Only the strong have a right to live. The weak were born to have their life trampled out, and, according to this newly-revived theory, the sooner it is done the better. The murder of the lame, the halt, and the blind, therefore, becomes thoroughly scientific, and follows as a matter of course. Its practice is based upon laws which the materialists have been for some time proclaiming to be "supreme." If there be no supernatural basis of life, if the supernatural have no real existence, if man be of the earth earthy, if he be only an outgrowth of the dumb forces of matter (the first article of the creed of these "philosophers"), if he be governed solely and altogether, absolutely and completely by an inexorable material law (the highest and the only law, as they would have us believe), then, of course, their conclusion inevitably follows--that it is both merciful and wise to put a man out of his misery when he becomes a burden both to himself and his friends. There is no place in the lofty and elevating system of Naturalism for a being who cannot take care of himself.

Again: while Scepticism is rampant, and some are endeavouring to bring back the Pagan notions of ancient nations, to galvanize into new life the corrupt imbecilities of the past, men of science are making assertions and assumptions of the boldest, if not of the wildest nature. One such recently maintained the following proposition:--"Taking our earth, we know that millions of years have passed since she began to be peopled." Now, the maintainer of this assertion notoriously holds some peculiar theories about the means by which the solar system (and consequently other systems) was made, or rather grew. These theories, in some of their details, are or may be founded upon certain more or less well-ascertained facts. But when he uses the term "know," we are bold to point out that such an assertion rests on mere assumption.[7] We need facts,--facts which could stand the careful investigation of persons skilled in taking and measuring evidence; and secondly, we require to be reasonably convinced that no other possible explanation of a difficulty be forthcoming, except that on which his assumption is founded and his inevitable conclusion (as he regards it) deduced. But how often with scientific people the phrase "We know" stands for "This is our theory," or rather "This is our present theory;" for scientific theories change very frequently; and points which have been most dogmatically laid down at one period have been with equal dogmatism condemned and repudiated at another, by those who apparently strain every nerve and exercise every gift bestowed upon them, to deny and cast out the Supernatural from amongst mankind.

From the introduction to a volume of great interest ("The Maxims and Examples of the Saints"), the following extract is taken, both because of its inherent truth, and also because the Christian instinct in defence of the Supernatural is so prominently and forcibly expressed in every line. Mr. de Lisle's words stand thus:--

"In these days of shallowness and scepticism, men pride themselves on calling everything into question, as if they proved their claim to wisdom according to the measure of their unbelief. But those who dive a little deeper into things will not be so ready to admit the claims of modern insolent writers. They will find that our ancestors had heads as sound, judgments as cool and unprejudiced, at least, as any of these moderns; and the more they examine, the more reasons will they find for attaching weight to their testimony. In my intercourse abroad with divers holy priests and religious monks, I have seen and heard enough to convince me that many things take place in this world of a supernatural order. Nor do I believe there ever has been a period in the history of the Church, when our Lord has not borne testimony to her divine truth, and to the admirable sanctity of many of her children, by evident and glorious miracles. This is the faith of the Church; and who shall gainsay the teaching of that society that carries with it the experience of eighteen centuries, the immutable promises of God, the attestations of innumerable martyrs, and the consent of nations? To him who believes the words of the holy Gospel, 'The works that I do shall they do also, and greater than these,' &c. (speak not now to the unbeliever), the conclusion will be clear, and humble faith will bow with submission. Keeping this promise in view, the Christian will not find it difficult to believe even the most wonderful histories in the lives of the Saints; at all events, his spirit will not be that which loves to question everything, still less that which treats the testimony of devout writers with levity or scorn. To the humble observer of the ways of Divine Providence, enough occurs every day to prepare him for any manifestation of the Power of God: not to say that there is not a state in Christendom in which, even in our own times, many wonderful miracles have not taken place. Witness the glorious appearance of a vast cross of fire in the heavens at Migné, near Poictiers in France, in the year 1826, in the month of December, an event which was attested on oath before the bishop of the diocese by several thousand eye-witnesses.[8] Josephus relates the prodigies that appeared in the heavens before the downfall of Jerusalem: and who shall say that this sublime apparition in France did not portend the approaching calamities that have since fallen upon that kingdom and upon Europe? In the years 1830 and 1831, blood miraculously flowed from the arms of S. Nicholas, at Tolentino in Italy, and the circumstance was solemnly attested by the bishop, the clergy, and the magistrates of that city. History records similar prodigies to have taken place at Tolentino whenever any calamities were about to befall Christendom. S. Nicholas has been dead above 500 years. I myself had the consolation to visit his shrine; and I heard from several individuals, with tears in their eyes, the affecting recital of the miracle. Who does not call to mind the wonderful manifestations of God's power at Rome and at Ancona during the period of the French Revolution, in the year 1792? Innumerable images of our Blessed Redeemer, and of his Virgin Mother, were seen to move their eyes, and some even to weep. Nor were these events seen only by a few, they were beheld and attested by thousands.[9] The miracles that God has performed by means of the holy Prince Hohenlohe are known to all, and some of them have been wrought even in England. These are facts so notorious, that no one can call them in question; nor is it in the power of profane ridicule to throw doubt over their authenticity. At the same time, it will always be true that the Catholic Church does not oblige her children to believe any miracles but those recorded in the sacred Scriptures; she leaves it to the discretion of each individual to ground his conviction on the evidence which has come before him; though it would not be an act of piety, or worthy of praise for anyone to speak lightly of such miracles as have been honoured by the approbation of the Holy See."

***

As a mark of rapid theological decline, it may here be put on record, that a recent writer, the author of "Supernatural Religion: an Inquiry into the Reality of Divine Revelation" (Longman: 1874), sets forth his "views" (not his "opinion," least of all his faith, but his "views") as follows:--

"The importance which has been attached to theology by the Christian Church, almost from its foundation, has been subversive of Christian morality. In surrendering its miraculous element and its claims to supernatural origin, therefore, the religion of Jesus does not lose its virtue, or the qualities which have made it a blessing to humanity. It sacrifices none of that elevated character which has distinguished and raised it above all human systems: it merely relinquishes a claim which it has shared with all antecedent religions, and severs its connection with ignorant superstition. It is too divine in its morality to require the aid of miraculous attributes. No supernatural halo can heighten its spiritual beauty, and no mysticism deepen its holiness. In its perfect simplicity it is sublime, and in its profound wisdom it is eternal.

"We gain infinitely more than we lose in abandoning belief in the reality of Divine revelation. Whilst we retain pure and unimpaired the treasure of Christian morality, we relinquish nothing but the debasing elements added to it by human superstition. We are no longer bound to believe a theology which outrages reason and moral sense. We are freed from base anthropomorphic views of God and His government of the universe; and from Jewish theology we rise to higher conceptions of an infinitely wise and beneficent Being, hidden from our finite minds, it is true, in the impenetrable glory of Divinity, but whose laws of wondrous comprehensiveness and perfection we ever perceive in operation around us. We are no longer disturbed by visions of fitful interference with the order of Nature, but we recognize that the Being who regulates the universe is without variableness or shadow of turning. It is singular how little there is in the supposed revelation of alleged information, however incredible, regarding that which is beyond the limits of human thought; but that little is of a character which reason declares to be the 'wildest delusion.' Let no man, whose belief in the reality of Divine Revelation may be destroyed by such inquiry, complain that he has lost a precious possession, and that nothing is left but a blank. The revelation not being a reality, that which he has lost was but an illusion, and that which is left is the truth."

In another volume recently written by Mr. Congreve, the Positivist, the author maintains in the plainest possible language, what is the immediate and practical object of the small sect to which he has allied himself:--"The professed servants of Humanity must lead in the struggle to eliminate God; and that this is the essential element in the whole existing perplexity is forcing itself upon all." Again, man's duty is said to be "openly and avowedly to take service in one or the other of the opposing camps; to bring face to face the two beliefs; the belief in the Past, the belief in God, and the belief in the Future, the belief in Humanity; and to choose deliberately between them." Furthermore, he avers: "We contemplate the Trinity of our religion, Humanity, the World, and Space." A Christian critic has made the following terse comments on Mr. Congreve's book:--

"The chief feeling which possesses us in reading these Essays is one of sorrow for the writer. It is really sad that a man of education should lend himself to such a delusion. The 'Religion' itself is ridiculous; indeed it has not so much as a theory. Not even on paper can its doctrines be stated,

Rev. Frederick George Lee, D.C.L.

for the simple reason that it has no doctrines whatever. But it is always melancholy to watch a naturally good intellect under the sway of a fantastic idea, or to see an educated gentleman writing 500 pages on the 'Worship' of what does not exist. The sensation of the reader, as he turns page after page, is expressed in such an inquiry as this: Since the writer himself believes in nothing whatever, how can he invite my conversion?"

CHAPTER II - THE MIRACULOUS IN CHURCH HISTORY

"And He said unto them, Go ye into all the World, and preach the Gospel to every creature. He that believeth and is baptized shall be saved; but he that believeth not shall be damned.
"And these signs shall follow them that believe: In My Name shall they cast out devils; they shall speak with new tongues; they shall take up serpents; and if they drink any deadly thing, it shall not hurt them; they shall lay hands on the sick and they shall recover." - S. Mark xvi. 15-18.

The important subject of the Miraculous in Church History sufficiently well known to students of it, involves the existence of a religious principle of universal application. This will be apparent, in due course, from the following preliminary considerations:--"A miracle," writes Hume, "is a violation of the laws of Nature; and, as a firm and unalterable experience has established these laws, the proof against a miracle is as entire as any argument from experience can possibly be imagined."[10] Further on, he declares "that a miracle supported by any human testimony is more properly a subject of derision than of argument."[11] On these statements, definite and precise as they appear, and yet not sufficiently definite, it may be remarked in the first place that no human experience is unalterable: it may to a certain person or certain persons have been hitherto unaltered. But this is all. Are there then no facts beyond our experience--no natural positions or states with which we are unacquainted? When a man writes of "unalterable experience," he obviously means so much of that experience, as either mediately or immediately has come to his knowledge; in other words his own past experience.[12] And this Hume declares sufficient to enable him to determine what are the unvarying laws of Nature, and, by consequence, what are miracles. But surely here is something akin to arrogance. For what modest person would venture to maintain his own experience to be altogether and absolutely firm and unalterable? Who would declare of a witness, who testified, for example, what was contrary to that experience, that such a man was worthy only of disbelief and derision? And yet many, in the present day, adopt and put into practice this unstable and imperfect theory of Hume.

What has been set forth above in opposition to that theory is still more pointedly expressed in the following remarkable passage:

"The natural philosopher when he imagines a physical impossibility which is not an inconceiveability, merely states that his phenomenon is against all that has been hitherto known of the course of Nature. Before he can compass an impossibility, he has a huge postulate to ask of his reader or hearer, a postulate which Nature never taught: it is that the Future is always to agree with the Past. How do you know that this sequence of phenomena always will be? Answer, Because it must be. But how do you know that it must be? Answer, Because it always has been. But then, even granting that it always has been, how do you know that what always has been always will be? Answer, I see my mind compelled to that conclusion. And how do you know that the leanings of your mind are always towards truth? Because I am infallible, the answer ought to be; but this answer is never given."[13]

Of course no Christian will deny the following elementary propositions here briefly stated, before the general subject is further discussed. First that man consists of body and soul, the nobler and more important part being the soul, which is spiritual, immortal, and eternal. God, the Creator of all things, is a Spirit; and, in this particular, man is made in the image of God. Destined to dwell on the earth for a while, during an appointed period of probation, man passes by death, which is a temporary separation of soul and body, to the life beyond the grave. Man's duty here, therefore, ought to fit and prepare him for a future state, and teach him better the value of his soul and the reality of the Supernatural.

Now the Almighty, in calling man into being here, and making him "lord of the whole earth," giving him, in fact, dominion over the beasts of the field, the fowls of the air, and the fishes of the sea, has established in connection with him a two-fold order, the natural, which relates to the visible world, and the Supernatural or miraculous, which concerns the spiritual and invisible. The natural order comprises the law of nature, by which the World created by God is governed, and concerns man in his dealings with nature. But the Supernatural concerns him in his relations with God and

Rev. Frederick George Lee, D.C.L.

the world of spirits. Both orders are alike from God, and each has its appointed sphere. The Author of both is the controller of each. And, as if to indicate to man from time to time that God has something to say in His own creation, and will not be totally excluded from it by man's forgetfulness, the Supernatural is wisely and mercifully interwoven with the natural, to remind man, by the Glimpses occasionally vouchsafed of the former, that, though the World has been made for his use and advantage, many things in it speak eloquently of a continued existence in the future, though now the same World's fashion most surely passeth away. How prone man becomes, by constantly contemplating the natural, to thrust the Supernatural aside, is the experience of many. And this being so, how merciful is God to remind us of the next world, not only by the ordinary modes and channels appointed for so doing, by change, by revelation, by death; but occasionally by suddenly, strangely, and abruptly breaking in upon the usual order of events, and the ordinary course of nature, to let us see with our natural eyes, and hear with our ears, that He is. Thus the Supernatural indicates the tracing of the Finger of God. Freely, and for a lofty purpose, to set forth His glory, power, and mercy, He created the laws of nature; freely, and for a like lofty purpose, He sometimes suspends them. Such intervention on His part, such a suspension, is a miracle, which may be defined as "a record and evidence of the Supernatural manifesting itself in the midst of the natural order;" or, as S. Thomas Aquinas so clearly and ably defined it of old, "A miracle is an act performed by God out of the ordinary course of nature." In accepting this, we do but maintain that God alone is the Author and Controller of all laws, whether natural or supernatural. Historical Christianity calls upon us to believe, firstly, the great principle that miracles are possible; and, secondly, that those recorded in Holy Scripture, ranging from the time of Moses to that of S. John the Divine, are true. Other miracles or miraculous interventions rest upon the value, purport, and character of the evidence and testimony forthcoming for their authenticity. They are all equally possible, because all are acts of the Almighty; but they are not all equally credible, because the evidence of their authenticity may be of a less precise, definite, and well-authenticated character.

To assert, as some do, that a miraculous intervention implies change or contradiction in God, is inaccurate; for in His works surely He may exercise that liberty which is one of His perfections. Were man's range of vision wider than it is, the working of a miracle might be found to be, after all, only the realization and carrying out of God's original design and primary purpose. Again, from the point of view of another objection, to maintain that we cannot know what a miracle is, or whether any miracle has been ever wrought, without being acquainted with all the laws of nature, is likewise inaccurate; for we know enough, both of the natural and supernatural, to be perfectly certain that it is out of the ordinary course of nature for a dead man to come to life again. While, then, such a miracle teaches us to acknowledge the power of God, it may, at the same time, serve to let the Materialist realize his own possible ignorance of the laws of nature. For after all there may be some hidden law, as yet unknown, which may contradict a known law, and so modify it--a probability which is at least deserving of the consideration of those who altogether deny the Supernatural.

As regards miracles, let the well-known argument of the great S. Augustine of Hippo be considered: "Christianity," he writes, "was either founded by miracles, or it was not. If it was, then miracles exist. If it was not, then this is the greatest of all miracles, viz. that a religion so radically contrarient to all human prejudices, and so much resisted by all human influence, should, without the aid of miracles, have made its place and assured its progress in the world." If, again, the only evidence that a person will admit is that of his own personal experience, that he must himself witness a miracle; that, like S. Thomas, he will maintain, "Except I shall see ... I will not believe," has he not power of mind enough to appreciate the fact that he is in every way unreasonable, by demanding for himself that which he altogether refuses to admit in others?

But, in truth, the miracles of our Blessed Lord, and more particularly the miracle of His Resurrection, were so striking and convincing, being testified to, both as regards their act and consequences, by so many, that they produced both conviction and triumph. Not universally, but with a sufficient number of persons to ensure the steady increase of the infant Church--though the very miracles which wrought such a vast moral and religious change, were rejected by the unbelievers of the day.

In the Church of the primitive, as well as in later, ages, the Supernatural was being constantly manifested. The apostles proved the divinity of their mission by the power of their works. The miracles recorded in the "Acts of the Apostles" were followed by others equally marvellous and remarkable in succeeding periods--a feature that might have been most reasonably looked for in the history of Christianity, for the very life and spirit of the Church are supernatural.[14] Persecuted in every age, she has risen again. After being cast down, driven from this place in one century, she has made still greater progress elsewhere in another. For the first three hundred years of her existence, and in the very heart of the world's civilization, Rome, every patriarchal primate of that Holy See died a witness to the truths of Christianity. The ordinary supernatural powers of our Lord's first followers were duly inherited by those formally set apart to fill their place and office. Men freely testified to what they had seen and heard. As occasion seemed to need it, the divine power was duly manifested in outward, notable, and noted acts,--to the truth and reality of which even Profane History has abundantly witnessed.

While in the records of the Christian Church there is an almost constant tradition of miraculous facts. The tale of every century is rife with them. They were to have been anticipated, because He had spoken Whose Word shall never fail, and His promise seems to have been always remembered: "Verily, verily I say unto you, He that believeth on Me, the works that I do he shall do also; and greater works than these shall he do; because I go unto My Father."[15] Consequently it is found that many of the later miracles, those termed "ecclesiastical," in distinction to scriptural, are even more remarkable than those wrought by our Blessed Lord Himself--a fact which, instead of deserving ridicule and contempt, merits, from persons of a Christian habit of mind, patient consideration, and a careful, if not a ready, acceptance. For in such the faithful will only perceive a perfect realization of their Master's divine pledge.

To take a notable example of the miraculous occurring towards the close of the second century (A.D. 174), testified to, as far as the fact of the miracle is concerned, by at least four independent Pagan writers, Dionysius Cassius, Julius Capitolinus, Ælius Lampridius, and Claudian.

Eusebius, in his "Ecclesiastical History,"[16] puts on record the following account of a most remarkable event:[17]--"It is said that when Marcus Aurelius Cæsar was forming his troops in order of battle against the Germans and Sarmatians, he was reduced to extremities by a failure of water. Meanwhile the soldiers in the so-called 'Melitene legion,' which for its faith remains to this day, knelt down upon the ground, as we are accustomed to do, in prayer, and betook themselves to supplication. And whereas this sight was strange to the enemy, another still more strange happened immediately--thunderbolts which caused the enemy's flight and overthrow; and upon the army to which the men were attached, who had called upon God, a rain, which restored it entirely when it was all but perishing by thirst." This fact had been previously put on record by Claudius Apollinaris,[18] Bishop of Hierapolis, in his "Apology for Christianity," addressed about the year 176 to the Emperor Marcus. Tertullian, about fifteen years later, affirms the truth of the same fact when addressing the Proconsul of Africa. Each of these writers gives point to the narrative, the first by recording that henceforth the term "Thundering Legion" was applied to that in which the Christian soldiers had prayed: the second by his statement that the Emperor had, in consequence, promulgated an edict in favour of the Christians. It is clear from Eusebius, likewise, that the Pagans acknowledged the miracle, as they could not fail to do, wrought as it was in the presence of so many; but, of course, they denied that it was to be attributed to the prayers of the Christians. Julius Capitolinus attributed it to the prayers of the Emperor;[19] Dionysius Cassius to the operations of Arnuphis, an Egyptian magician.[20] A record of the unquestioned fact, however, is sculptured on the Antonine column at Rome;[21] a medal, struck the very year of the occurrence, likewise commemorates the event. Here, then, we find on record an occurrence which ordinary people will call a miracle; here we obtain a distinct example of the Supernatural. In answer to the prayers of certain Roman soldiers, sons and servants of the Crucified, palpable benefits are vouchsafed, and marvellous deliverances effected. The foe is destroyed, and they are rescued. And this fact is testified to by Pagans worthy of credit as well as by Christians, and is put on record in the modes already set forth.

Another example, the appearance of a luminous Cross to Constantine (A.D. 312), must here be given, because of its inherent importance; because the testimony to its having occurred before so many is very general; and because the moral and religious changes consequent upon it, results that both immediately and eventually followed, have been at once great and notorious:--

The conversion of the Roman empire, in the person of its head, was the most remarkable event in the early pages of Christian history. "Constantine's submission of his power to the Church," writes Dr. Newman, "has been a pattern for all Christian monarchs since, and the commencement of our state establishment to this day; and, on the other hand, the fortunes of the Roman Empire are in prophecy apparently connected with her in a very intimate manner, which we are not yet able fully to comprehend. If any event might be said to call for a miracle it was this; whether to signalize it, or to bring it about. Thus it was that the fate of Babylon was written on the wall of the banqueting-hall; also portents in the sky preceded the final destruction of Jerusalem, and are predicted in Scripture as forerunners of the last great day. Moreover our Lord's prophecy of 'the Sign of the Son of Man in Heaven' was anciently understood of the Cross. And further, the sign of the Cross was at the time, and had been from the beginning, a received symbol and instrument of Christian devotion, and cannot be ascribed to a then rising superstition. Tertullian speaks of it as an ordinary rite for sanctifying all the ordinary events of the day; it was used in exorcisms; and, what is still more to the point, it is regarded by S. Justin, Tertullian, and Minucius as impressed with a providential meaning upon natural forms and human works, as well as introduced by divine

Rev. Frederick George Lee, D.C.L.

authority into the types of the Old Testament."[22]

The supernatural manner in which the Emperor's conversion was accomplished may be thus recorded. Marching from the border of the Rhine, through Gaul and part of Italy by Verona to Rome, against the tyrant Maxentius, who had declared war against him, and was already near Rome with a largely superior force, Constantine solemnly and earnestly invoked the One True God, the God of the Christians, for assistance and victory. At that period he was not a Christian himself, though he had no doubt accurately enough measured the true character of Roman paganism. A short time after midday, upon his march, there appeared in the heavens[23] a large luminous Cross in sight of himself and the whole of his army, with the inscription surrounding it, "In this conquer." On the following night it is recorded that our Blessed Lord appeared to him in a dream, or, as some say, a vision, and commanded him to have a representation of the sign made, and to use it henceforth as his chief standard in battle. The Emperor, rising early the next morning, announced this vision and message to his confidential friends, and at once gave orders for the making of the imperial standard.[24] This being done, fifty men of the stoutest and most religious of his guards were chosen to carry it. And, surrounded by these, it was borne immediately before the Emperor himself. The Christian soldiers were full of faith and hope. They saw the Finger of God, and looked for victory.

On the other hand the army of Maxentius, consisting of three divisions of veteran soldiers, esteemed the most efficient in the empire, engaged Constantine in the Quintian fields near the bridge Milvius. The attack was fast and furious. But the aggressors were at all points met with vigour and bravery, and soon succumbed and were in retreat. Constantine, with far fewer numbers than those opposed to him, was completely victorious; the legions of Maxentius were scattered or slain, and on the same day, with the sacred Labarum (as the imperial standard in question was termed) borne before him, he entered Rome in triumph. His conversion to Christianity soon followed upon his victory. In his triumph he dropped the old customs of his Pagan predecessors. He neither mounted the Capitol, nor offered sacrifices to the deities of Rome, but by suitable inscriptions recorded his belief in the power of Christ's saving Cross. In his palace at Constantinople, as well as in the chief square of that city, the sacred sign was at once set up; and medals were struck, with representations of the symbol in question upon them, to commemorate both the victory and his own religious change. This occurred about A.D. 312.

Here then we find the record of a distinctively supernatural intervention. No known physical cause could have formed a sentence of Greek or Latin in the air. Nor could a whole army have mistaken a Cross, with its corresponding and appropriate inscription, for a halo of light, or a mere natural phenomenon. Moreover: three years after the event, Constantine erected his triumphal arch at Rome, with an inscription, which still remains, testifying that he had gained the victory "instinctu divinitatis, mentis magnitudine." Lactantius, likewise, in his treatise "De mortibus Persecutorum" (if it be his book, though some attribute it to Cæcilius), asserts the main facts of the case as regards the dream, describing the "heavenly sign of God;" and this in a treatise certainly written within two years of its occurrence. Seven years later, Nazarius, a Pagan orator, in a panegyric on the Emperor, also puts upon record his solemn conviction that celestial aid was miraculously rendered to Constantine in his defeat of Maxentius. Thus far those who were not Christians testify to the fact under consideration. On the other hand, Eusebius, who received the account from Constantine himself (who is known to have confirmed it with an oath), gives that record of the occurrence which has been already set forth--and he was notoriously an historian who had small leaning towards over-belief. While the reasonable conclusion, therefore, is that so many independent writers and records of the fact could not have been made to conspire in disseminating a falsehood; the action of the Emperor which followed the event was in perfect harmony with that which might have been looked for under the circumstances narrated--the supernatural appearance of a luminous Cross, heralding a change, even the triumph of the Religion of Christ over the effete systems of a decaying and decayed idolatry.

The principle which was manifested in these cases is, through the study of history, likewise seen to have existed and energized in every part of the Church. Everywhere, from time to time, the proximity of the unseen world and the existence of the Supernatural were made manifest: while, here and there, examples of special miraculous interventions evidently stood forth to show that neither the Arm of the Most High was shortened nor the faith of the followers of our Blessed Lord stunted in its growth. In fact miracles of the most remarkable character have been performed from the age of the apostles to the present time: while Glimpses of the Supernatural have been granted to many as partially unfolding the mysteries of the Unseen World to those who longed and prayed for the same; by which glimpses or visions their faith has been deepened and their conviction of the truths of Christianity most surely strengthened. Just as our Blessed Saviour, following Moses, constantly appealed to the prodigies He wrought in attestation of His divine mission and in support of His doctrine; so was it with His followers who came after Him. For to them He had promised as much. So far therefore from confining the power of working miracles to His own person and time,

He expressly pledged himself and promised that His servants and ambassadors should receive power to work still greater works.[25] Just as under the laws of Nature and the written law given by Moses, the Almighty was pleased to illustrate the society of His chosen servants with frequent miracles, so we are led to expect that the One Family of God should be for ever distinguished by occasional miracles wrought in and through her, as a standing proof of her divine origin and as a guide to the wanderers beyond the confines of her fold. And thus it comes to pass that the Fathers and Teachers of the Church, amongst other proofs of her favour, have constantly appealed to the miracles by which she is illustrated as a proof of her heavenly mission, and as marking her off, at the same time, from the various heretics and schismaticks who, going out from her, were not of her. For example S. Irenæus, a disciple of S. Polycarp, himself a disciple of S. John the Evangelist, reproaches the Hereticks against whom he writes in his well-known treatise,[26] that they could neither give sight to the blind, hearing to the deaf, cast out devils, nor raise the dead to life again, as he maintains was frequently done in the Church. Tertullian, a contemporary of his, writing of the hereticks, asks, "I wish to see the miracles which they have worked." S. Pacian, in the fourth century, opposing Novatus, and considering his claims, scornfully inquires, "Has he the gift of tongues, or of prophecy? Has he restored to life the dead?" S. Augustine of Hippo, in numerous passages of his works, refers to the miracles wrought by and through and in the Church as most important if not conclusive evidence of her heavenly character and veracity.

Again: In the middle of the fourth century occurred that most wonderful miracle, when the Emperor Julian deliberately attempted to rebuild the Temple at Jerusalem, with the express intention of disproving the prophet Daniel's[27] utterance concerning it. Then tempests, whirlwinds, earthquakes, and fiery eruptions convulsed the scene of the undertaking, maiming and alarming the persistent workmen, throwing down buildings in the neighbourhood, as Rufinus testifies, and rendering the carrying on of the work a sheer physical impossibility. A luminous Cross surrounded by a circle, indicating that to the Crucified was given all power in heaven and earth, and showing that the Word of God could never fail, nor be brought to nought by the vain determinations of men, appeared in the sky,--a portent witnessed by thousands, and testified to both by Pagan and Arian, as well as by Christian writers.[28]

Furthermore, in the following century, another miracle took place at Typassus or Typasa in Africa, where a large congregation of Christians, being assembled in divine worship, in opposition to the decree of the Arian tyrant Hunneric, they were collected in the Forum, in the presence of the whole province, their right hands were chopped off, and their tongues cut out to the roots by his command; yet, nevertheless they continued to speak as plainly and perfectly as they had done before the barbarous mutilation in question.

This is vouched for by Victor, Bishop of Vite, in the following words:--"The king in wrath sent a certain count with directions to hold a meeting in the Forum, of the whole province, and there to cut out their tongues by the root, and to cut off their right hands. When this was done, they so spoke and speak, by the gift of the Holy Ghost, as they used to speak before. If, however, anyone will be incredulous, let him now go to Constantinople, and there he will find one of them, Reparatus a subdeacon, speaking like an educated man without any impediment whatsoever. On which account he is regarded with exceeding great veneration in the court of the Emperor Zeno, and specially by the Empress."[29]

Now, this miracle is remarkable for various reasons. The witnesses to its authenticity are varied, both as to their persons and the details of their testimony, which testimony is both consistent and at one on all important and material points. Moreover, the evidence on behalf of the miracle is very complete: the number of persons upon whom it was wrought was more than considerable; thus, at the same time, increasing the occasion of valid testimony in its favour, and preventing the interposition of what some persons term "chance." Furthermore, the miracle is entire; for, as Dr. Newman remarks, "it carried its whole case with it to every beholder:" it is also permanent, that is, it continued to indicate its effects before thousands, whose inquiries, public investigations, and conclusions must have exercised considerable weight with those who were prepared to accept it.[30]

In this brief survey of the miraculous, it is impossible even to touch on the more remarkable evidences of the Supernatural as set forth in the History of the Christian Church. Numerous miracles are recorded by S. Basil, S. Gregory Thaumaturgus, S. Athanasius, S. Jerome, S. Chrysostom, S. Ambrose, and S. Augustine, as well as by other illustrious Fathers and Church Historians who adorned the fourth, fifth, and sixth centuries of the Christian era. One, however, related by both the last-named, by S. Ambrose and S. Augustine, deserves notice, because both those holy bishops were eye-witnesses of it. A cloth in which the relics of SS. Gervasius and Protasius had been wrapped was applied to the eyes of a blind man, who thereupon received his sight.[31] S. Augustine likewise gives an account of numerous miracles wrought in his own diocese of Hippo,--some through the instrumentality of the sacred remains of S. Stephen, others in answer to earnest prayer: while three of the miracles so recorded by him are the raising of three dead bodies to life.

The miracles recorded to have been wrought by S. Basil, S. Athanasius, S. Jerome, S. John Chrysostom, S. Ambrose, and S. Augustine (and, in this particular, he who runs may read) testify clearly and sufficiently to the Divine power which existed in the Church Universal in the times of those holy saints, and the rich fruits of which were both seen and tested by the faithful. One of the most remarkable was the verification of the Wood of the Cross, after its discovery by S. Helena, A.D. 326, through the convincing miracle wrought upon a dead man, who, on being touched by it, was immediately restored to life.

And so soon as the Religion of Christ was brought to Britain by our great Apostle and Archbishop S. Augustine, "greater works than these" followed, as a matter of course, when the banner of the cross was unfurled upon the coasts of Kent. That this was so, that many miracles were wrought, we learn from a Letter written by S. Gregory the Great to S. Augustine, embodied in the well-known "History" of the Venerable Bede, and preserved amongst S. Gregory's "Works," in which the Archbishop is duly and lovingly cautioned against becoming too much elated with vain glory, because of these marked manifestations of Divine power and favour; and is reminded that God Almighty had, no doubt, bestowed the gift of working them, not on the Archbishop's own account, or for his own merit, but for the conversion of the English nation.[32]

So, through every succeeding age, were Glimpses afforded of the Supernatural. For example, S. Bernard, perhaps the most illustrious saint of the twelfth century, in the "Life of S. Malachi of Armagh," records the miraculous cure of the withered hand of a youth, by the dead hand of his holy friend S. Malachi. But nothing can exceed the splendour and publicity of the miracles of S. Bernard himself,--to the reality of which the faithful of France and Switzerland, as well as those of Germany and Italy, bore abundant testimony. Princes and prelates, kings and priests were witnesses of his supernatural power; for, like his Lord and Master, he wrought instantaneous cures on the lame, the halt, and the blind, in the presence of multitudes, and to the great spread and triumph of the Faith. Of those worked at Cologne, Philip, Archdeacon of Liége, who was formally commissioned to inquire and report upon them by Lampeon, Archbishop of Rheims, declared as follows: that "they were not performed in a corner, but the whole city was witness to them. If anyone," he adds, "doubts or is curious, he may easily satisfy himself on the spot, more especially as some of the miracles were wrought upon persons of no inconsiderable rank and reputation."[33] Moreover, S. Bernard himself distinctly refers to them in one of his most celebrated treatises, "De Consideratione," addressed to Pope Eugenius III., and maintains that the evidence of God's special graces and exceptional blessings thus resting upon him, enabled him to feel sufficient confidence of the Divine aid and benediction to enter upon the grave and laborious task of preaching the Second Crusade.

And if we proceed onward to the sixteenth century, where in some places, and especially amongst the northern nations of Europe, Faith began to wax cold, and Charity was not, we find, from History, that the miracles of Francis Xavier, the saintly apostle of India, may almost vie with those of the great S. Bernard, for they were as numerous and as inherently remarkable; while the testimony as to their truth, reality, and influence[34] was generally acknowledged by the faithful, as well as by Protestants.

In truth, wherever the Catholic religion has been taught and accepted, wherever the Name of Jesus has been loved and venerated, wherever faith in the Unseen has been active and daring, there the Finger of God has sometimes been manifested. And this, of course, was to have been expected. Our Blessed Saviour's glorious and unfailing promise, that His disciples, with whom He pledged Himself to remain unto the end of the world, should do even "greater works" than He Himself had wrought, was thus, from time to time, as man's faith merited God Almighty's intervention, literally and strictly fulfilled.

CHAPTER III - SPIRITUAL POWERS AND PROPERTIES OF THE CHURCH

"When a man holds up to my conscious eye the page of futurity; or when, at the mandate of a mortal, I clearly perceive Nature to listen and to suspend her laws, I rationally conclude that such a man is indeed employed by God. These miraculous and prophetical tests, produced by the ancient seer to the Israelites, appealed to by Christ in His own sacred cause, and made over by Him to His ministers for ever in the work of conversion, have been a means to guide the enquiring soul to that Authority divinely-commissioned to teach the World. This power to deliver the dictates of the Holy Spirit, this society of continued apostles, or in other words, the Holy Catholic Church in every age, has proved by the evidence of actual miracles her possession of this gift presented to her by her Divine Founder."

It is allowed on all hands by Catholic Christians that liberty has been sometimes permitted to the devil or his angels to enter into the bodies of men (just as of old Satan was allowed to try the patriarch Job), and to obtain such an absolute command over their powers and faculties as to incapacitate them, more or less, for any of the common duties of life. On this point, those who accept the Written Word of God as a portion, and a very important portion, of His Divine Revelation to mankind, through Christ, can have no doubt. In the New Testament, numerous instances of possession by evil spirits are recorded.

The case of the daughter of the woman of Canaan, who cried out to our Blessed Saviour, "Have mercy upon me, O Lord, Thou Son of David, my daughter is grievously vexed with a devil,"[35] and obtained from Him the gracious and merciful reply, "Be it unto thee even as thou wilt," is familiar to all.

So likewise is that of the man with an unclean spirit, recorded in the first chapter of the Gospel according to S. Mark. Here the spirit acknowledging that Christ was the "Holy One of God," received the rebuke of Jesus Christ. "And when the unclean spirit had torn" the man suffering, "and cried with a loud voice, he came out of him. And they were all amazed, insomuch that they questioned among themselves, saying, What thing is this? What new doctrine is this? for with authority commandeth He even the unclean spirits, and they do obey Him."

Again we read, "Unclean spirits, when they saw Him, fell down before Him, and cried saying, Thou art the Son of God."[36] And when His apostles were called and formally ordained, it is written that they were "to have power to heal sicknesses, and to cast out devils," power which in due course both the Gospels and the recorded History of the Church assure us was duly exercised.

Another miraculous intervention, by which our Blessed Saviour manifested His divine power over evil spirits, and freed suffering men from their frightful influence, is here given from S. Mark's Gospel at length: "When He was come out of the ship, immediately there met Him out of the tombs a man with an unclean spirit, who had his dwelling among the tombs; and no man could bind him, no not with chains: because that he had often been bound with fetters and chains, and the chains had been plucked asunder by him, and the fetters broken in pieces: neither could any man tame him. And always, day and night, he was in the mountains and in the tombs, crying and cutting himself with stones. And when he saw Jesus afar off, he ran and worshipped Him, and cried with a loud voice, and said, What have I to do with Thee, Jesus, Thou Son of the Most High God? I adjure Thee by God that Thou torment me not. For He said unto him, Come out of the man, thou unclean spirit. And He asked him, What is thy name? And he answered, saying, My name is Legion, for we are many. And he besought Him much that He would not send him away out of the country. Now there was nigh unto the mountains a great herd of swine feeding. And all the devils besought Him, saying, Send us into the swine, that we may enter into them. And forthwith Jesus gave them leave. And the unclean spirits went out, and entered into the swine; and the herd ran violently down a steep place into the sea (they were about two thousand), and were choked in the sea. And they that fed the swine fled, and told it in the city and in the country. And they went out to see what it was that was done. And they came to Jesus, and see him that was possessed of the devil, and had the legion, sitting and clothed and in his right mind."[37]

With these solemn and awful facts before us, it is impossible to doubt either of the power or

Rev. Frederick George Lee, D.C.L.

influence of the devil and his angels. That such power had been known amongst the ancient nations, and that certain persons had entered into compacts or alliances with evil spirits, seems to be generally admitted. And although the fact of the Incarnation had sorely crippled the influence of the enemy of souls, it is clear from the last promise given by our Lord to His apostles, "In My Name they shall cast out devils," that such authority and action would still be needed. For possessions were not to cease, as a reference to the Acts of the Apostles shows: where it is recorded that the very authority bestowed by our Blessed Saviour was actually and efficiently exercised; and there is no reasonable evidence to show that such divinely-bestowed powers have ever ceased. All through the History of the Church, here and there, from time to time, as man needed and as God willed, such direct supernatural powers as those referred to, appear to have been put into operation. For the Church can bless and the Church can curse. The Church can bind and can loose. She can commend to the protection of God Almighty and His holy angels, and she can deliver over to Satan. She can bestow light and peace on her true and faithful children, and send out the disobedient and impenitent beyond the consecrated confines of her spiritual powers and graces. As effects of Christ's most gracious promise, such ordinary and extraordinary works were wrought; for the glory of His great Name, and as a testimony of the truth of the Church Universal.

For generations, up to the very earliest age of Christianity, there have been officers of the Church duly set apart and ordained for the particular work of exorcism. Amongst the minor orders of Western Christendom the exorcist has always found a place; and although, in later years, this special work, when undertaken, has been more frequently done by persons in the higher or sacred orders, yet the very office itself, and its title, as well as the existing forms for casting out evil spirits, abundantly attest the Church's divine and spiritual powers.

In countries which are specially and eminently Christian, where churches, sanctuaries, and religious houses are numerous; where, by the road-side and on the hill-top, stand the signs and symbols of the Faith of Christendom; where the Sacrament of Baptism is shed upon so many; where post-baptismal sin is remitted by those who have authority and jurisdiction to bind and loose in the Name of their Master; and where the Blessed Sacrament of the Altar, God manifest in the Flesh, reposing in the tabernacle, or borne in triumph through aisle and street and garden, hallows and feeds the faithful--there the power and influence of the Evil One is circumscribed and weakened. Sacred oil for unction, and holy water and the life-giving power of the Cross, and the relics of the beatified as well as of the favoured and crowned servants of the Crucified, make the devils flee away, and efficiently curb their power. Hence it is found that in countries where the Catholic Faith has been halved or rejected, Superstition has taken the place of the first theological virtue, Faith; and the Prince of the Powers of the air comes back again with his evil and malignant spirits to vex mankind anew,[38] and mar and stay the final triumph of Him to Whom all power is given in heaven and in earth.

A remarkable case of the Supernatural will here be put on record, which occurred in the diocese of Exeter during the seventeenth century. Preliminary inquiries and comments concerning the various incidents would be obviously out of place; for the well-authenticated story itself is unfolded with a simplicity and yet with a power which efficiently serve to stamp it as true.

"About 152 years since," writes Mr. Fortescue Hitchins, in his "History of Cornwall," "a ghost is said to have made its appearance in this parish[39] (Little Petherick[40]), in a field about half a mile from Botaden or Botathen (in that county). In the narrative which is given of this occurrence, it is said to have been seen by a son of Mr. Bligh, aged about sixteen, by his father and mother, and by the Rev. John Ruddle, master of the grammar school of Launceston, and one of the prebendaries of Exeter, and vicar of Alternon. The relation given by Mr. Ruddle is in substance as follows:--

"Young Mr. Bligh, a lad of bright parts and of no common attainments, became on a sudden pensive, dejected, and melancholy. His friends observing the change, without being able to discover the cause, attributed his behaviour to laziness--an aversion to school--or to some other motive which they suspected he was ashamed to discover. He was, however, induced after some time to inform his brother that in a field through which he passed to and from school he was invariably met by the apparition of a woman whom he personally knew while living, and who had been dead about eight years. Ridicule, threats, and persuasions were alike used in vain by the family to induce him to dismiss these absurd ideas. Mr. Ruddle was however sent for, to whom the lad ingenuously communicated the time, manner, and frequency of this appearance. It was in a field called 'Higher Bloomfield.' The apparition, he said, appeared dressed in female attire, met him two or three times while he passed through the field, glided hastily by him, but never spoke. He had thus been occasionally met about two months before he took any particular notice of it: at length the appearance became more frequent, meeting him both morning and evening, but always in the same field, yet invariably moving out of the path when it came close by him. He often spoke, but could never get any reply. To avoid this unwelcome visitor he forsook the field, and went to school and returned from it through a lane, in which place between the quarry-park and nursery it always met

Glimpses of the Supernatural Volumes I & II
him.

"Unable to disbelieve the evidence of his senses, or to obtain credit with any of his family, he prevailed upon Mr. Ruddle to accompany him to the place. 'I arose,' says this clergyman, 'the next morning, and went with him. The field to which he led me I guessed to be about twenty acres, in an open country, and about three furlongs from any house. We went into the field, and had not gone a third part before the spectrum, in the shape of a woman, with all the circumstances that he had described the day before, so far as the suddenness of its appearance and transition would permit me to discover, passed by.

"'I was a little impressed at it, and, though I had taken up a firm resolution to speak to it, I had not the power, nor durst I look back; yet I took care not to show any fear to my pupil and guide; and therefore, telling him that I was satisfied in the truth of his statement, we walked to the end of the field, and returned: nor did the ghost meet us that time but once.

"'On the 27th July, I went to the haunted field by myself, and walked the breadth of it without any encounter. I then returned, and took the other walk, and then the spectre appeared to me, when about the same place in which I saw it when the young gentleman was with me. It appeared to move swifter than before, and seemed to me about ten feet from me on my right hand, insomuch that I had not time to speak to it as I had determined with myself beforehand. The evening of this day the parents, the son, and myself being in the chamber where I lay, I proposed to them our going to the place next morning; we accordingly met at the stile we had appointed; thence we all four walked into the field together. We had not gone more than half the field before the ghost made its appearance. It then came over the stile just before us, and moved with such rapidity, that by the time it had gone six or seven steps, it passed by. I immediately turned my head and ran after it, with the young man by my side. We saw it pass over the stile at which we entered, and no farther. I stepped upon the hedge at one place, and the young man at another, but we could discern nothing; whereas I do aver that the swiftest horse in England could not have conveyed himself out of sight in that short space of time. Two things I observed in this day's appearance; first a spaniel dog, which had followed the company unregarded, barked and ran away as the spectrum passed by: whence it is easy to conclude that it was not our fear and fancy which made the apparition; secondly the motion of the spectrum was not gradatim or by steps, or moving of the feet, but by a kind of gliding, as children upon ice, or as a boat down a river, which practically answers the description the ancients give of the motion of these lemures. This ocular evidence clearly convinced, but withal strangely affrighted, the old gentleman and his wife. They all knew this woman, Dorothy Durant, in her lifetime; were at her burial: and now plainly saw her features in this apparition.

"'The next morning being Thursday, I went very early by myself, and walked for about one hour's space in meditation and prayer, in the field next adjoining. Soon after five I stepped over the stile into the haunted field, and had not gone above thirty or forty paces before the ghost appeared at the further stile. I spoke to it in some short sentences, with a loud voice, whereupon it approached me but slowly, and, when I came near, it moved not. I spoke again, and it answered in a voice neither audible nor very intelligible. I was not in the least terrified, and thereupon persisted until it spoke again, and gave me satisfaction; but the work could not be finished at this time. Whereupon the same evening, an hour after sunset, it met me again near the same place, and after a few words on each side it quietly vanished, and neither doth appear now, nor hath appeared since, nor ever will move to any man's disturbance. The discourse in the morning lasted about a quarter of an hour.

"'These things are true, and I know them to be so, with as much certainty as eyes and ears can give me; and until I can be persuaded that my senses all deceive me about their proper objects, and by that persuasion deprive myself of the strongest inducement to believe in Christian Religion, I must and will assert that the things contained in this paper are true. As for the manner of my proceeding, I have no reason to be ashamed of it. I can justify it to men of good principles, discretion, and recondite learning, though in this case I chose to content myself in the assurance of the thing, rather than be at the unprofitable trouble to persuade others to believe it, for I know full well with what difficulty relations of so uncommon a nature and practice obtain belief.'"

So much as regards the record of the appearance found in the volume already referred to.

The following extract from Mr. Ruddle's MS. Diary, was taken by the Rev. R. S. Hawker, M.A., vicar of Morwenstow, the accomplished and well-known Christian poet, and appears in his interesting "Footprints of Former Men in Far Cornwall" (London, 1870), and still further amplifies and illustrates this story, the practical and eventual issue of which is now to be recorded:--

"January 7, 1665. At my own house I find by my books what is expedient to be done; and then Apage Sathanas!

"January 9, 1665. This day I took leave of my wife and family, under pretext of engagements elsewhere, and made my secret journey to our diocesan city, wherein the good and venerable bishop then abode.[41]

Rev. Frederick George Lee, D.C.L.

"January 10. 'Deo gratias,' in safe arrival at Exeter: craved and obtained immediate audience of his lordship; pleading it was for counsel and admonition on a weighty and pressing cause. Called to the presence; made obeisance; and then, by command, stated my case, the Botathen perplexity--which I moved with strong and earnest instances and solemn asseverations of that which I had myself seen and heard. Demanded by his lordship, what was the succour that I had come to entreat at his hands? Replied, license for my exorcism, that so I might, ministerially, allay this spiritual visitant, and thus render to the living and the dead release from this surprise.

"'But,' said our bishop, 'on what authority do you allege that I am entrusted with faculty so to do? Our Church, as is well known, hath abjured certain branches of her ancient power, on grounds of perversion and abuse.'

"'Nay, my Lord,' I humbly answered, 'under favour, the seventy-second of the Canons[42] ratified and enjoined on us, the clergy, Anno Domini 1604, doth expressly provide that No minister, unless he hath the license of his diocesan bishop, shall essay to exorcise a spirit, evil or good. Therefore it was,' I did here mildly allege, 'that I did not presume to enter on such a work without lawful privilege under your lordship's hand and seal.'

"Hereupon did our wise and learned bishop, sitting in his chair, condescend upon the theme at some length, with many gracious interpretations from ancient writers and from Holy Scripture, and did humbly rejoin and reply; till the upshot was that he did call in his secretary and command him to draw the aforesaid faculty forthwith and without further delay, assigning him a form, insomuch that the matter was incontinently done, and after I had disbursed into the secretary's hands certain moneys, for signitary purposes, as the manner of such officers hath always been, the Bishop did himself affix his signature under the sigillum of his see, and deliver the document into my hands.

"When I knelt down to receive his benediction, he softly said, 'Let it be secret, Mr. Rudall,--weak brethren! weak brethren!'"

Some details from the same Diary as to the exact manner in which the ghost was laid give an additional interest to the narrative.

"January 12th, 1665. Rode into the gateway of Botathen, armed at all points, but not with Saul's armour, and ready. There is danger from the demons, but so there is in the surrounding air every day. At early morning then and alone, for so the usage ordains, I betook me towards the field. It was void, and I had thereby due time to prepare. First I paced and measured out my circle on the grass. Then did I mark my pentacle in the very midst, and at the intersection of the five angles I did set up and fix my crutch of raun [rowan]. Lastly I took my station south, at the true line of the meridian, and stood facing due north. I waited and watched for a long time. At last there was a kind of trouble in the air, a soft and rippling sound, and all at once the shape appeared, and came on towards me gradually. I opened my parchment scroll, and read aloud the command. She paused and seemed to waver and doubt; stood still: and then I rehearsed the sentence again, sounding out every syllable like a chant. She drew near my ring, but halted at first outside, on the brink. I sounded again, and now at the third time I gave the signal in Syriac--the speech which is used, they say, where such ones dwell and converse in thoughts that glide.

"She was at last obedient and swam into the midst of the circle: and there stood still suddenly. I saw, moreover, that she drew back her pointing hand. All this while I do confess that my knees shook under me, and the drops of sweat ran down my flesh like rain. But now, although face to face with the spirit, my heart grew calm and my mind composed, to know that the pentacle would govern her, and the ring must bind until I gave the word. Then I called to mind the rule laid down of old that no angel or fiend, no spirit, good or evil, will ever speak until they be spoken to. N.B.--This is the great law of prayer. God Himself will not yield reply until man hath made vocal entreaty once and again. So I went on to demand, as the books advise; and the phantom made answer willingly. Questioned, wherefore not at rest? Unquiet because of a certain sin. Asked what and by whom? Revealed it; but it is sub sigillo, and therefore nefas dictu; more anon. Inquired, what sign she could give me that she was a true spirit and not a false fiend? Stated [that] before next Yule-tide a fearful pestilence would lay waste the land;[43] and myriads of souls would be loosened from their flesh, until, as she piteously said, 'Our valleys will be full.' Asked again, why she so terrified the lad? Replied, 'It is the law; we must seek a youth or a maiden of clean life, and under age, to receive messages and admonitions.' We conversed with many more words; but it is not lawful for me to set them down. Pen and ink would degrade and defile the thoughts she uttered, and which my mind received that day. I broke the ring and she passed, but to return once more next day. At evensong a long discourse with that ancient transgressor, Mr. B----. Great horror and remorse; entire atonement and penance; whatsoever I enjoin; full acknowledgment before pardon.

"January 13, 1665. At sunrise I was again in the field. She came in at once, and, as it seemed, with freedom. Inquired if she knew my thoughts, and what I was going to relate? Answered, 'Nay, we only know what we perceive and hear: we cannot see the heart.' Then I rehearsed the penitent words of the man she had come up to denounce, and the satisfaction he would perform. Then said she, 'Peace in our midst.' I went through the proper forms of dismissal, and fulfilled all, as it was set down and written in my memoranda; and then with certain fixed rites, I did dismiss that troubled ghost, until she peacefully withdrew, gliding towards the west. Neither did she ever afterwards appear; but was allayed, until she shall come in her second flesh, to the Valley of Armageddon on the Last Day."

Another example, giving with singular power and effect a very striking Glimpse of the Supernatural, from the experiences of a venerated and exemplary Roman Catholic clergyman, the late Rev. Edward Peach, of S. Chad's, Birmingham, is here given at length. The events narrated occurred in the year 1815, and Mr. Peach deliberately affirmed of the following account that it "may be relied on in every particular as being strictly true." "I," he continues, in a formal record of the successful exorcism, "was the minister of God employed on the occasion; and truth is more to me than all the boastings of pride and vain glory."

The authentic record stands as follows:--

"Some time after Easter, in the year 1815, I was informed that a young married woman of the name of White, in the parish of King's Norton, Worcestershire, a Protestant, was afflicted with an extraordinary kind of illness, and that her relations, who occupied a small farm, were convinced that her illness arose solely from the malice of a rejected admirer, who, they said, had employed the assistance of a reputed wizard at Dudley to do her a mischief. These were their terms. I paid but little attention to this story. Afterwards I was informed by a sister who frequents our markets, and supplies with butter a respectable family of my congregation, Mr. Powell, Suffolk Street, that the young woman was married in the beginning of the preceding Lent; that her former admirer repeatedly declared that, if she did marry any other, she should never have another happy day; that the day after her marriage she was seized with an extraordinary kind of mental complaint; that she became suddenly delirious; that she raved, and declared that a multitude of infernal spirits surrounded her; that they threatened to carry her away; that she must go with them. The poor sister informed my friend, with tears streaming down her cheeks, that she continued in that state, day and night, for nearly two months, and that the whole family were almost exhausted with the fatigue of constantly attending her, for, she said, they could not leave her alone, lest she should put her threats of destroying herself into execution.

"At the end of about two months, according to the relation of the same sister, the poor creature was so spent that her medical attendant (who, during the whole time of his attendance, declared that her illness arose more from a mental than corporeal cause,) declared that, in all probability, she could not survive four-and-twenty hours. The clergyman of the parish was called in to assist her in her last moments; but he found her in a state not to be benefited by his assistance, and he departed.

"Amongst the neighbours who came to make a tender of their good offices for the relief of the afflicted family was a Catholic woman. Her offers were accepted, and she was frequently with her. Finding her reduced almost to a state of inanition, and hearing her speak of these infernal spirits every time she opened her lips, the thought came into her mind of applying to her some holy water. She accordingly procured some, dipped her finger into it, and made the sign of the cross upon her forehead. Instantly the poor sufferer started, and, in a faint voice, exclaimed, 'You have scalded me.' However, she leaned upon the bosom of her attendant, and, what she had not done for a considerable time before, she fell into a gentle sleep. On awaking, she continued to hold the same language as before. The Catholic put a little holy water into her mouth. But the very instant it entered her mouth she seemed to be in a state of suffocation. She and the others who were with her were alarmed, and expected that every instant would be her last. In a short time, however, she swallowed it, and after many convulsive struggles she regained her breath, and exclaimed with violence, 'You have scalded my throat, you have scalded my throat.' In a few minutes she fell again into a comfortable sleep, and continued so for some hours. The next morning she appeared refreshed, and spoke reasonably for a short time. Being informed of what had been applied to her, she seemed to wish for more. The swallowing was attended with the same sensation of scalding, and the same convulsive struggles as before; but it seemed to give her ease. From that time the danger of death seemed to decrease by degrees. She enjoyed lucid intervals from time to time; and invariably after the application of holy water, although attended with the same sensations as before, she fell into a slumber.

"One remarkable circumstance deserves notice. In one of her paroxysms, she insisted on getting up, and going out of doors. She said that there was a large snake in front of the house, that she would go and kill it, and then one of her enemies would be removed. Nothing would satisfy her, till this same sister, who gave the account, assured her that she would go down and kill it. She went down, and, to her great astonishment, found a large snake, and succeeded in destroying it.

"This in substance is the account which the sister gave of Mrs. White's extraordinary illness. At the same time it was asked whether I could be of any assistance to her, or whether it was probable that I could be prevailed on to go and see her? My friend who related to me the whole of the above account, asked me to go. I replied that I knew nothing of them, nor they of me; but that if she would walk over, and examine into the state of the poor woman, I would go, if there appeared to her to be any probability of my being of service. She went, and, on her return, she informed me that all she had heard seemed to be true, and assured me that all the family were desirous of seeing me, and particularly the young woman herself.

"However, I still delayed, till at length, on Tuesday in Rogation Week, May 2nd, 1815, a special messenger came over to inform me that Mrs. White was in a worse state than ever, and to request me to go and see her without delay.

"I obeyed the call, and I may say with truth that it was the most awful visit I ever made during the whole course of my ministry. The distance was about six miles. No sooner had I cleared the skirts of the town than I heard the distant thunder before me. Before I had proceeded two miles, the storm was nearly over my head; and I may say the remainder of my walk, and during the time I was with her, there was hardly cessation of one minute between the claps of thunder. I do not say that in this there was anything supernatural, but, knowing the business I was upon, it was truly awful.

"When I arrived at the house, I was informed that she was in a dreadful state, and that the strength of two persons was necessary to keep her in bed. I went up-stairs, and on entering into the room, before she saw me, the curtains being drawn on the side where I entered, she turned to the other side of the bed, and struggled so violently to get away that it was with difficulty that her husband and two women overpowered her. In a few minutes, before she had lifted up her eyes to see me (for she had turned her face downwards) she stretched out her hand to me, in a convulsive manner, and fell speechless and spent upon her back.

"After a time she opened her eyes, and in a faint whisper, answered a question that was put to her, and said she knew who I was. She revived by degrees, and in a short time could speak in an audible voice. Her friends having requested me to try if I could discover what it was that weighed most upon her mind, for they said they had tried to no purpose, I requested them to withdraw. Being alone, she related to me, as far as she could recollect, the circumstances of her illness, and I found that they corresponded exactly with the accounts given by her sister. I questioned her as to the cause, but I could not discover that it was owing to anything weighing heavy on her mind. She was positive, she said, that it was the young man who had done her a mischief.

"I then proceeded to explain to her some of the articles of the Catholic Faith. She listened with every attention; and when I assured her that she must believe the Holy Catholic Church before she could obtain relief, she, without hesitation, declared that she did believe, and that she believed from the moment she knew what holy water was, and experienced its effects. From the time it was first applied, she said that the devils seemed to keep at a greater distance from her, and that the number seemed to be diminished.

"Such were the ideas on her mind at the time. She was convinced, she said, that it was not the effect of imagination--that she was not delirious--that she knew everything that was said to her, and that she could recollect everything that had passed. I asked her to tell me where the holy water was. Her voice immediately faltered; and with every endeavour, I perceived that she could not point out with her finger, nor tell me by words where it was. She was like an infant attempting to point out an object.

"I looked about and found it. I dipped my finger into it, and made the sign of the cross on her forehead. She started as soon as I touched her, and was a little convulsed. I asked her what was the matter. For a few moments she could not articulate; but as soon as she could speak, she said that it scalded her.

"After a little more conversation, I desired her to join with me in repeating the Lord's Prayer. She consented, and without difficulty repeated the first words. But when we came to the petitions, her voice faltered; she was labouring for breath, and appeared to be almost suffocated: her countenance and limbs were convulsed. The greatest stammerer could not find greater difficulty in pronouncing words than she did in pronouncing every word of the petitions. At one time I was inclined to desist, thinking that it was impossible for her to finish it; but we laboured on, and at length came to the end.

"After a short pause, she again began to converse with a free voice, without the least faltering. I explained to her the nature of exorcisms, and proposed to read them over her. She consented, and said that she would endeavour to offer up her prayers to God during the time in the best manner she could. As soon as I began the exorcisms, she fell into a state of convulsive agitation, not indeed endeavouring to get away; but every limb, every joint seemed to be agitated and convulsed, even her countenance was distorted,--it required constant attention to keep her covered.

"Now it was that I felt in a particular manner the awful situation in which I was. All alone with a person in a distressed condition,--the lightning flashing, the thunder rolling, and I with an imperative voice commanding the evil spirit to reply to my interrogatories, and to go forth from her.

I acknowledge that my flesh began to creep and my hair to stand on end. However, I proceeded on till I came to the conclusion, and nothing happened except the violent agitation of the poor sufferer, which continued uninterrupted during the whole time.

"After I had finished, she became calm, and in a few minutes began to converse with me with the same ease as before. Among other things, I asked her whether she had felt any particular sensations during the time that I was coming to see her? She said that during the whole afternoon she had felt the most determined resolution to destroy herself; that she employed every means to induce her friends to leave the room, or to make her escape from them; and that if she had succeeded, she would have laid violent hands on herself the moment she was at liberty. I explained to her the nature of baptism, the necessity of receiving it, and the effects produced by it.

"During the course of our conversation, discovering that there were strong reasons to doubt whether she had been baptized at all, or whether the essential rites had been observed in her baptism, I conceived that it would be advisable to re-baptize her conditionally. I proposed it, and she readily consented. I gave her what instructions were necessary, and repeated several acts of contrition. Finding her in dispositions the most satisfactory, I made use of the holy water, and baptized her, subject to the condition, if she was not baptized. During the time she trembled like a leaf, and the features of her countenance were distorted, like those of a person in acute pain. Upon my putting the question to her, she replied as she did before, that it gave her as much pain as if boiling water had been poured over her.

"Immediately after the ceremony was concluded, she began to speak to me with all the cheerfulness of a person in perfect health and spirits. We conversed together for a few minutes, and I took my leave, promising to see her again the next day. Her sister went to her, and her first request was that she might have a cup of tea and something to eat; and before I left the house, she eat and drank as she had done before her affliction. I went to see her the next day, and found her down-stairs in perfect health; at least, no effects of her illness were perceptible, except a weakness of body. From that time to this, she has enjoyed good health, and not the least symptom of her former complaint has been felt. It is more than a twelvemonth since."

A second example of successful exorcism, now to be narrated, is from the pen of an eminent and well-known clergyman[44] of the Church of England, whose literary labours in the early part of the Oxford movement, were recognized and rewarded by high authority in the English Church. Only a slight verbal alteration here and there to make the narrative of itself quite intelligible, has been made by the Editor.

"The subject is almost too sacred for pen; and I only put it on record to show the goodness of God, and to indicate that His powers are not withdrawn, nor His Arm shortened. It is some years, however, since the event to be related happened; and the subject of it has long gone to his last account. I must scrupulously refrain from any indication of place and person; though, in these latter days of rude and coarse unbelief, when such interpositions of the Almighty's mercy are laughed to scorn, some may find comfort and edification from its recital.

"The son of a farmer, who had just come of age, having heard a sermon of mine, which I had preached some five years previously, came a distance of more than thirty miles to seek at my hands ghostly counsel. From his childhood he had been led to indulge in breaches of the seventh commandment, and these after a while were certainly of a heinous character. He believed himself (when I saw him) to be possessed by an unclean spirit. Wherever he went, he asserted that he saw a hideous black figure, darkly draped, with a form like a man, but with the face of a beast, sitting opposite to, huddled up, and staring at him. It would appear for weeks together, at home, abroad, in his sleeping-room, in the field, in the market. Sometimes he would throw himself on to the floor in an agony of distraction, and pray God that it might be removed. For a short term he would cease to see it. But in due course it reappeared. And at last (an event which had never happened hitherto,) it would likewise haunt him in dreams. On one occasion he declared that it seemed to elongate itself into a long serpent-like figure, and, as he asserted, tried to creep down his throat. But wherever he went he almost always saw it. Thinking it might be the result of bodily ailment he consulted a physician; but with no effect.

"I am free to say that I was not long in coming to a conclusion, that it was a case of possession; though I did not arrive at that conclusion until I had taken counsel from one of the most pious and holy clergymen I ever knew,[45] and had commended the subject to God Almighty in very earnest prayer.

"The result was that I unfolded to the subject of this apparition my intention, with God's help, and his own sanction, to cast out the spirit, according to the old rule and custom of Holy Church. Prior to this he made a full and frank confession of his whole life, and resolved by God's help to amend. Having made an appointment, a fortnight hence, with him, and being resolved to consecrate my proposed act, by special deeds of fasting, self-denial, and prayer, I was alarmed to hear, by letter, of his most serious illness a few days later. His relations asserted that he was suffering from

Rev. Frederick George Lee, D.C.L.

epilepsy, and that the fits were rapid and most severe.

"The following day, taking with me a book containing an authorized form of exorcism, I went to see the sick man. His sufferings seemed to be excruciating: his fits shocking to witness. At a half-lucid interval he saw me; and, starting from his bed, tried to throw himself out of the window. When he was calmer, I knelt down and prayed for him with his relations; making several times an act of Faith.

"Then signing him with the cross on forehead, mouth, and breast, I began the authorized form. During this, his fits returned; and his violence and ravings were terrible to witness. Throughout I felt sustained in my action by a Higher Power, and completed my task in the Name of the Adorable and Ever-Blessed Trinity. Here he sank into a deep sleep; and this sleep proved to be the beginning of a complete change for the better. The fits ceased, the body was no longer tortured with writhings; and, as I heard from him afterwards, the hideous vision or apparition vanished, and was never seen again. A few years afterwards he died, as I believe in grace; and, as I commended his soul to God, so I committed his body to the dust; and have always looked upon this remarkable event as a token, to myself most unworthy, of the Almighty's power and Presence amongst us, as well as of His exceeding great mercy and goodness to this poor sufferer."

Another remarkable instance of the active and energizing powers of the Church of God, unimpaired and uncrippled, may be gathered from the record which follows of the sudden and effectual cure of Françoise-Geneviève-Philippe, which took place in the church of the Carmelites of Pontoise on the 16th of July, 1784, upon the Festival of Our Lady of Mount Carmel. The record below is a literal translation of the formal act and deed of the person cured:--

"I, the undersigned Françoise-Geneviève-Philippe, called in religion 'Sister Josephine-Mary of the Incarnation,' aged thirty years, declare that my health being disordered at Pontoise, where I resided with the Ursuline Dames for eleven years, I was advised to make a change of air; I consequently withdrew to the Dames of the Congregation of Trouvelle-les-Vernon, where I entered on the 16th of February, 1782. My health continued bad in consequence of the frequent attacks of hæmorrhage to which I became subject.

"On the 29th of December following I was seized with a violent headache, beginning with a swoon, which lasted more than two hours, and with a frightful hæmorrhage. Suitable remedies were instantly administered to me by skilful physicians, but in vain; and after this I was attacked with convulsions, and the entire suspension of all motion in my body.

"Different consultations were held at Paris; MM. Fumé and Petit sent me prescriptions which produced no effect. This sickness continued until the 13th of May, 1783, when I was removed into the town of my uncle's. All these facts have been attested by the physicians and surgeons of Vernon, by the testimony of M. Atadie, physician to his Serene Highness the Duke of Penthievre, and of M. le Noble, physician, who had employed magnetism, but without effect. These certificates, duly legalized by M. le Lieutenant-Général of the same town, attest that my disorder was deemed so violent and incurable to the period when I decided upon returning to Pontoise, hoping to recover my health by the means which it might please God to employ. I arrived there on the 5th of August, 1783; from that time my condition was precisely the same, namely habitual convulsions. I was deprived of the use of my limbs, particularly of my right arm, in which the convulsions were so violent that it was found necessary to fix and tie it with a bandage. The left was not much better, for on merely touching it, or on a change of weather, it experienced similar convulsions. Added to this I was attacked violently with gout, which I felt all over my body, but especially in my head and the extremities of my fingers. I was subject to pains in my breast and stomach, so severe as to occasion me to spit blood and to vomit up even the most liquid of my food. Sleep, of which I had in general but little till this period, now became, as it were, a stranger to me. My voice was for a month or six weeks almost extinct, and there was not a part of my body which was not in a state of suffering; the least noise became almost insupportable.

"It is moreover to be remarked, that I never discovered, although always valetudinary, what could be capable of occasioning such a malady. This is a testimony I offer to truth. The persons who could not be ignorant of what concerned their patient have made the same depositions.[46]

"Such was my condition when they were proceeding at Pontoise, by order of the Holy See, in the process of the beatification of the servant of God, Marie de l'Incarnation, whose name in the world was Madame Acarie, foundress of the Carmelites in France, who, having edified the World by the virtues which characterize great souls, and consecrated at Carmel three of her daughters, herself embraced this holy state under the humble quality of converse-sister in the Convent of Carmelites at Amiens, and died at that of Pontoise in the odour of sanctity on the 18th of April, 1618, aged fifty-two years.

"The fame of this process revived my faith. I made a Novena to her, in which the Carmelites, as well as many other pious persons, united. I not only, during this Novena, took no medicines, but I told my physician: 'Perhaps, sir, you will smile at me when I tell you that I am performing a

Novena to the venerable Sister Marie de l'Incarnation, and that I hope to-morrow to be taken to her tomb!' 'I commend your piety,' said he, 'to make a Novena to that blessed person, but I do not equally commend the step which you propose to take; I fear that none but bad consequences will result from it.' I replied, as I had done to many other of my friends, 'that I had the firmest confidence of a cure.'

"I persevered constantly in this moral and physical disposition until the moment when I was carried in a sedan chair into the church of the Carmelites. I was brought there at five o'clock in the morning. I heard mass, and communicated without quitting my chair. Towards the moment of elevation I felt severe pains throughout my whole frame, and seemed to myself to be in such a state of weakness that I then thought if I were to be communicated it would have been for the last time. A cold sweat spread itself at that time over my whole body. The priest who gave me the Holy Sacrament noticed that I was so weak that I could not hold the cloth upon my knees. He was so much afraid from the paleness of my countenance and the alteration he perceived in me, that in fear of some accident he put the sacred ciborium almost close to my lips.

"Finding me in this painful state, which announced rather a speedy dissolution than a cure, I formed acts of submission to the Will of God. I begged Him to accept the sacrifice of my life; I also thrice made the prayer of the blind man, 'Son of David, have mercy on me;' the while interiorly, having lost my power of articulation. I remained in that state till the end of the mass, and finding my strength recovering I called my nurse, and begged her to go and see if the chapel in which the precious remains of the Venerable Sister Marie de l'Incarnation were deposited was open, having the design to be carried there. But O bounty and mercy of the Lord! at the very moment the people were preparing I quitted the chair myself; my nurse came hastily upon me to stop me, imagining that this movement was a last effort of nature. I corrected her, saying that I thanked her, but that thanks be to God! I had no need of her help, and instantly after, on the steps of the altar, returned thanks after communion; for I did not as yet perceive the change that was made in me. I was not sensible of it till after having made my thanksgiving, which was near a quarter of an hour after. I then raised myself from the ground filled with joy and consolation, finding I had recovered the use of my limbs; my breast and stomach at ease and devoid of pain, enjoying tranquillity altogether wonderful. I first ascended the seven steps of the altar; and then went to the grate of the choir and thanked the community for the prayers that they had the goodness to offer up for me; requesting them to add still further their thanks to mine. I then turned towards the Blessed Sacrament, where I remained on my knees on the ground without any support during the period of three masses, which were said in succession. I afterwards heard high mass, and assisted at the entire Office of the Day, without the noise of chaunting, of the instruments, nor the great concourse of people, occasioning me the slightest inconvenience. Although I had to answer in the course of the day to more than four thousand persons attracted by the novelty of the circumstance to the church of the Carmelites, on the afternoon of the same day I went on foot to visit the Ursuline Dames.

"Done at Compiègne on the 12th of Feb. 1792.
(Signed) "Françoise-Geneviève-Philippe,
"Called in religion 'Sr. Josephine of the Incarnation,' Religious Carmelite of the Monastery of the City of Compiègne, in which I had the happiness to enter on the 20th of December, 1786, and to pronounce my holy and inviolable engagements on the 22nd of July, 1788."

Another point bearing very directly on the subject of this chapter here suggests itself for some brief consideration:--

Deeds of benediction have been so universally recognized in history, that it may be credibly maintained that the custom originated in the earliest ages of the World's existence, either by a direct revelation from Heaven or by the most elementary religious instinct of the immediate descendants of our first parents. The heads of tribes, after the Flood, blessed their children and followers. And, when the Patriarchal dispensation drew towards its close, the power of blessing was exercised by the leaders and chiefs of God's chosen people. Proof of all this is on record in the Sacred Writings. He, therefore, who runs may read. And we may gather from the same source that a form of blessing was attached to the priest's office;[47] and that such blessing was efficient. All this is of course taken for granted under the Christian dispensation; and it is evident that the various forms of sacerdotal benediction are true means of bestowing the Divine blessing and grace: and this, because of the salient principle that the Fall of man from original righteousness, having effected a loss of union with God Almighty, salvation is the renewal of that union by and through Jesus Christ and His Church. Now, a Blessing, in the Name of God, is bestowed by a superior upon an inferior.[48] Thus a bishop gives his benediction to a priest, deacon, or layman; a priest to a layman; a father or head of a family to a son or an inferior member of that same family; a patriarch or chieftain to his tribe, or to any member of it. The blessing of God is a great and mighty gift of grace, and has always been intimately conjoined with the offering of sacrifice, and so particularly and specifically with the offering of the Christian sacrifice, as also with and by a benediction, some of the most solemn services of Holy Church have been brought to an end.

Of course, if there be a power to bless, there is, as has already been pointed out, likewise a power to curse. Neither blessing nor curse may be absolute in their effect, and all acts and deeds are done under God, or with the permission of the Almighty. Of the results respectively of blessings or curses we know but little. But the glimpses which History, Revealed Religion, and Experience alike afford of those results are full of interest, and are subjects for contemplation and study. Here, as in the consideration of similar details, concerning the Supernatural, the Church Universal should be our guide. Where she leads we should go: where she directs we should follow.

As bearing on this subject, it may be suitably pointed out that Mr. Robert Southey in his "Common-Place Book" puts on record a very remarkable story of "citation" by a man unjustly and cruelly murdered:--

"The Philipsons of Colgarth coveted a field like Ahab, and had the possessor hung for an offence which he had not committed. The night before his execution the old man (for he was very old) read the 109th Psalm as his solemn and dying commination, verses 2, 3, 8, 9, 10, 12, 13, 14, 15, and 16." The verses contain a prayer for vengeance upon "the wicked and deceitful, who have spoken with a lying tongue," and whose days are to be few, and their children to be fatherless, their descendants continually vagabonds and beggars, and their posterity to be cut off. "The curse," Southey adds, "was fully accomplished; the family were cut off, and the only daughter who remained sold laces and bobbins about the country."

Two remarkable and, as may be well believed, supernatural events occurred (which may be fittingly recorded here) with regard to the cruel and shameful death of Edmund Arrowsmith, a Roman Catholic priest of the county of Lancaster, in the year 1628. He was born at Haddock in the parish of Winwick, five miles from Warrington and seven from Wigan. His father was Robert Arrowsmith, a yeoman, and his mother Margaret Gerard, of the ancient and noble family of that name. His immediate ancestors had suffered much for their religion. Edmund, their son, having been received into the College at Douay in 1605, was eventually ordained priest at Arras on December 9th, 1612. A year afterwards he was sent to England to minister to his fellow religionists. One of his flock being exasperated against him because he refused to marry him to his first cousin and had rebuked him for evil-living, informed against him to the vigilant authorities; and Arrowsmith, being apprehended, was sent to Lancaster Castle, "for not having taken the oaths, and upon vehement suspicion that he was a priest and a jesuit." The judge on circuit was Sir Henry Yelverton.

"Are you a priest, sir?" asked the judge, when the accused person was brought before him.

Arrowsmith, signing himself with the cross, replied, "My lord, I would to God I were worthy."

On the judge repeating the question Arrowsmith replied coolly, "I would I were."

When the accused, in reply to a minister on the bench, suggested a disputation regarding religion, and claimed to defend his Faith, the judge silenced him at once, and declared that he would not allow him to make any defence at all.

"I am ready, my lord, bear in mind," replied Arrowsmith, "not only to defend it in words, but in deeds, and to seal it with my blood."

The judge then told him, in an insulting and savage manner, that he should die, and see his bowels burnt before his very face.

"And you too must die, my lord, and that within a year."[49]

Two indictments were framed against him: one for being a priest and a jesuit, and the other for disparaging Protestantism; on these he was found guilty of high treason, and ordered to die according to the law. To the gaoler of the prison, the sheriff brought express commands from the judge to load him with the heaviest irons in the Castle, and to lodge him in a small cell where he could not lie down. This occurred on the 26th of August, 1628, and he suffered death on the 28th of the same month. He was dragged on a hurdle from the Castle to the place of execution, having received absolution from a fellow prisoner, Mr. Southworth, in the Castle yard. He was bound on the hurdle, and for greater ignominy with his head to the horse's tail. The gallows and boiling caldron were set up about a quarter of a mile distant from the Castle. The devotion and piety of this holy and zealous man were as remarkable as his constancy and fortitude,--graces which edified those who witnessed his sad end. He offered himself up as a sacrifice thrice: once upon his knees at the foot of the ladder, again on the ladder, which he kissed, and a third time just before the halter was fastened round his neck; and then prayed fervently, "O Sweet Jesus, I freely offer Thee my death, in satisfaction for my sins." Then he was cast off, suffered to hang until he was dead--an act of mercy, by no means ordinary or common--cut down, disembowelled, and quartered; his head being placed on a pole amongst the pinnacles of the Castle. It is recorded that the judge being vexed and annoyed with the clever and luminous answers which Arrowsmith made when under examination, in the hearing of so many, appeared to take a special pleasure in viewing the execution from his lodgings, through a perspective glass; that he had the curiosity to examine the four quarters of his body, which, by his command, being brought to his apartment, he made an unnatural and shocking comparison between them and a haunch or two of venison with which he had that day been presented; and that he deliberately kicked the right hand of the body in contempt. On leaving the town he ordered the martyr's head to be placed on a pole six yards higher than the pinnacles of the Castle.

The judge, sitting at supper at an inn on January 23, 1629, upon return from circuit, felt a heavy blow, as if someone had struck him on the back of the head; upon which he fell into a violent rage with, and severely rated, the servant who was waiting upon him; who protested that he had not struck him, nor did he see anyone strike him. A little while afterwards, the judge felt another blow like the first; and, as some records say, a third just as the meal was being ended. The blows he himself evidently thought to have come from the hand of divine justice, for he exclaimed in fear and trepidation: "That dog Arrowsmith hath killed me."[50] In great terror he was carried to bed, and dying the next morning, the prophecy of the holy priest regarding his death was exactly fulfilled.

As regards the Hand of the sufferer, it was procured and treasured up by his relatives the Gerards: and the following remarkable occurrence is connected with it.

In the year 1813 a young man named Joseph Lamb, then residing at Eccles, near Trafford Hall, about four miles from Manchester, fell from a rick of considerable height to the ground, and received a violent injury in the back. He was so injured that he could neither stand nor walk and suffered very considerable pain; but after many attempts had been made by physicians to give him relief and effect a cure, his case at a later stage was unanimously pronounced to be incurable. In religion he was a Roman Catholic, having been converted to that ancient faith from being an Anabaptist--a sect to which his father still belonged. Local circumstances had led to his investigating the martyrdom of the venerable priest, Edmund Arrowsmith, who, as already recounted, gave up his life in the cause of God at Lancaster, on the 28th of August, 1628. Of this holy man a Hand had been long and carefully preserved at Sir William Gerard's, of Garswood, near Wigan, where it was and is deservedly venerated and held in respect by all Roman Catholics. The sufferer Lamb, finding that the skill and power of man could do nothing for him, conceived a firm conviction that it would please the Almighty to restore him to health by the instrumentality of this relic, and he consequently most earnestly and systematically prayed to God that it might be so. His parents consequently, in response to his urgent entreaties, on October 2nd, 1814, had him conveyed in a covered cart from his own house near Trafford Hall to Garswood, a distance of fourteen miles.[51] In a state of considerable suffering, and quite unable to assist himself, he was lifted out of the cart and carried into the Roman Catholic chapel, where he was placed before the altar. Then the "Holy Hand," as it is termed, was brought forth; the sacred sign of the cross was solemnly made over the affected part of the poor suffering man's back; when, in an instant, he felt freedom from pain and found his former health and strength perfectly restored. He immediately rose, stood up for some time in prayer, and then walked, without any assistance whatsoever, to his relatives and friends who were gathered at the chief entrance of the chapel. He returned home quite recovered and perfectly well, and so remained, up to the 19th of September, 1816.[52] The result of this miraculous intervention was that several of his kinsmen and acquaintances became converts to the religion which he had elected to follow; and these, together with many Roman Catholics who became acquainted with Almighty God's merciful visitation of him, joined in a solemn act of thanksgiving, by assembling to sing the Te Deum in the chapel of Garswood.[53]

Thus, then, we see the prophecy of a Christian priest, who was unjustly and illegally condemned and cruelly murdered, exactly and most strikingly fulfilled; and a wonderful sign bestowed from God to man of Eternal Truth, in the supernatural cure wrought some two centuries and more afterwards upon this Lancashire farm-labourer.

Here something may be properly put on record, regarding cases in which visible marks and tokens of the Passion of our Lord and Saviour Jesus Christ have been supernaturally and miraculously impressed upon God's saints and servants, in order to set forth before the eyes of man, as a matter of sight and not as a matter of faith, the truth of the Revelation of Almighty God, through His Son Jesus Christ our Lord.

The first recorded instance of stigmatization is that of S. Francis of Assisi, in the thirteenth century. From the life of this distinguished saint, written by S. Bonaventure (chapters xii. and xv.), we gather the following particulars of these remarkable phenomena.

It was the custom of the saint, from time to time, to retire into the solitudes of Mount Alverna, in the Apennines, in order the more easily to give himself up to prayer and meditation. "While fasting there for forty days, being in prayer, on the Feast of the Exaltation of the Holy Cross, and feeling within his soul an intense desire to be crucified with his Lord, he beheld, descending from heaven towards him, a seraph, having six wings as it were of fire.[54] When the celestial messenger came near to him, there appeared between the wings the form of One crucified, with the hands and feet stretched out upon the cross. Two wings rose above the head, two were spread forth in flight, while the others veiled the whole body." Francis felt a great joy at the apparition, and yet, at the same time, a deep sorrow at beholding Him Whom his soul loved, so cruelly fastened to the Cross, the thought of which pierced his heart as with a sword of grief. It was presently revealed to him that he was to imitate the Passion of our Lord.

"The vision disappearing, his soul was filled with heavenly light, while a marvellous sign was left imprinted on his limbs. On his hand and feet were the marks of the nails, as he had beheld in the seraphic vision, and on his right side was a wound, as if made by a lance's thrust. His hands and feet appeared transfixed with the nails, their heads being seen in the upper part of the feet, and the points on the reverse sides. The heads of these nails were round and black, and the points somewhat long and bent, as if turned back; so that between them and the skin there was the space of a finger. They could be moved with ease; for on the one side they were embedded in the flesh, whilst on the other they were clear of it: yet it was not possible to draw them out, as we are assured by S. Clare, who, after the saint's death, essayed to do so, but could not succeed. The wound in the side was deep, and of the width of three fingers. It was red, and the saint's habit was often stained by the blood which flowed from it."

These stigmata were seen during his life by the reigning Pope Alexander with many of his cardinals; and after his death, by more than fifty brethren together, by S. Clare and many of her sisters, and an innumerable crowd of seculars, who came from all parts of the country to be witnesses of these wonders.

At the close of the seventeenth century, another case of stigmatization occurred to Veronica Juliana, a nun; and her examination by the bishop of her diocese, aided by several physicians, was of so strict and severe a character, that deception on her part would have been quite impossible.

In the early part of the same century, Joanna di Jesu Maria, a Spanish nun, was subjected to even a more rigorous examination, before a court composed of the Commissary of the Inquisition, the Suffragan Bishop, several of the secular and regular clergy of the district, of many learned men, and two distinguished physicians. In this case, the subject of the phenomena bore not only the wounds on her hands, feet, and side, from which blood and water frequently flowed, but also around her head, as from the crown of thorns, a deep wound, which, in the opinion of the doctors, penetrated to the skull. They, furthermore, declared by oath that the wounds were not natural, and could not possibly be the effect of fraud.

The most celebrated subjects of stigmata in our own days are Maria Mörl, the Ecstatica of Caldamo, in the Tyrol, and Maria Domenica Lazzari, a peasant girl of Capriana, whose cases were brought before the English public by that late distinguished nobleman John, Earl of Shrewsbury, A. L. M. P. De Lisle, Esq.,[55] the Rev. T. W. Allies, and others.

The following account of Maria Mörl is abridged from that of Görres, in his work on the Supernatural, entitled "Christliche Mystik," which, perhaps, is the most complete and detailed description published. After giving a brief sketch of her life, which tells us that she was a girl of great piety, also that at the age of eighteen she became a confirmed invalid, and after receiving Holy Communion she always remained in an ecstasy for several hours, we read, that "in the autumn of 1833, her Confessor, Father Capistran, had by chance noticed that the parts of her hands where the wounds afterwards appeared had begun to form in hollows, as though impressed by some external substance, the parts, at the same time, becoming the seat of considerable pain, accompanied by frequent cramps." Soon afterwards, the wounds appeared on the hands, feet, and side. On Thursdays and Fridays these places often ran with clear blood, and were covered on other days with a scar of dried blood, without showing any signs of inflammation. "In 1834, on the occasion of a solemn procession, a new phase of her ecstasy developed itself, and one day surprised her in the presence of several witnesses, when she was transfigured with an angelic beauty, radiant and glorious as a heavenly spirit, her arms extended to their extreme width in the form of a cross, and her feet barely seeming to touch the bed on which she reposed. All around could then plainly perceive the mysterious stigmata, and the matter could no longer remain a secret."

Of Maria Domenica Lazzari, who was born March 16th, 1815, and whose case is no less remarkable than the above, Mr. Allies, then a clergyman of the Church of England, wrote the following account, twenty-five years ago:--"In August, 1833, she had an illness, not in the first instance of an extraordinary nature; but it took the form of an intermittent fever, confining her completely to her bed, and finally contracting the nerves of her hands and feet so as to cripple them. On the 10th of January, 1834, she received on her hands, feet, and left side, the marks of our Lord's Five Wounds.... Three weeks afterwards, her family found her in the morning covering her face in a state of great delight,--a sort of trance. On removing the handkerchief, letters were found on it marked in blood, and Domenica's brow had a complete impression of the crown of thorns, in a line of small punctures about a quarter of an inch apart, from which the blood was flowing freshly. They asked her who had torn her so. She replied, 'A very fair lady had come in the night and adorned her.'... From the time that she first received the stigmata, in January, 1834, to the present time (account published in 1847), the wounds have bled every Friday, with a loss of from one to two ounces of blood, beginning early in the morning, and on Friday only. The above information (Mr. Allies declares) we received from Signor Yoris, a surgeon of Cavalese, the chief village of the district in which Capriana lies."

Two additional and quite recent examples of stigmatization, most perfectly and satisfactorily authenticated, demand to have the facts which are known and admitted here set forth. The first is as follows:--

On the 30th January, 1850, was born at Bois d'Haine, a village in the province of Hainaut, in Belgium, Anne Louise Lateau, the daughter of Gregory and Adèle Lateau. The family, though of humble condition, were at the time in tolerably comfortable circumstances. The father was employed as a workman in a neighbouring metal factory, and the cottage in which they dwelt, together with the land on which it stood, was their own property. But a sad change soon took place. On the 30th April, 1850, Gregory Lateau died of small-pox, leaving the mother and three children (the infant Louise and two little girls of two and three years of age) unprovided for. To add to their distress, the widow Lateau was seriously ill, and the infant had caught the small-pox. Abandoned by all, they were in danger of perishing of starvation had they not been relieved by the timely aid of a charitable neighbour. It was a long time, however, before the mother's health was sufficiently restored to enable her to better their condition by her own exertions. When eight years old, Louise was sent to take charge of an old woman confined to her bed, and almost as poor as themselves. She afterwards received five months' schooling, which is all the education she has ever had. At eleven years old, having made her first communion, she went as a servant to her aunt, with whom she remained until her death, which occurred two years later. Her next situation was with a lady at Brussels, but she was obliged to leave through illness. On her recovery, she was again employed in a farm at Manage, where she remained till called home by her mother, with whom she has since lived, working as a dressmaker. With regard to her moral character, one of its most important features is charity. During the ravages of the cholera in Belgium, in 1866, she gave examples of the most heroic devotedness--nursing the sick when their own relations had fled in dismay, laying out the dead, and, in some instances, even conveying them to the cemetery. For the rest, she is of a cheerful disposition, simple and straightforward in her manner, possessed of good sense, without smartness or enthusiasm. Owing to the small amount of instruction she has received, her education is limited, but has been much improved by her own exertions. She speaks French with tolerable fluency, but is unable to write correctly or read with ease. The mother of Louise is fifty-eight years of age, of a frank and outspoken character, upright and religious. Though poor, she refuses to receive any pecuniary assistance, and manifests great reluctance to the introduction of the numerous visitors attracted to her cottage from all parts of the world by the wonderful accounts respecting her daughter. We now come to the consideration of those phenomena which for nearly six years have been exciting such universal interest. On Friday, the 24th April, 1868, manifestations of an extraordinary character commenced with a flow of blood from the chest. The young girl, with her accustomed reserve, made no mention of the fact; but as on successive Fridays the bleeding extended to the feet and hands, concealment became no longer possible. The phenomenon, as it now appears, is thus described by Dr. Lefebvre:--

"If in the course of the week, from Saturday to Thursday morning, an inspection is made of the parts from which blood flows on the Friday, this is what is seen:--On the back of each hand there is a rather oval surface, nearly one inch in length. It is rather more pink in colour, and it is smoother than the neighbouring skin, and does not show a trace of oozing of any kind. On the palm of each hand there is also an oval surface of a light pink colour, corresponding precisely to the stigmatized surface of the back. On the upper aspect of each foot, the impress has the shape of a long square with rounded angles, the square being a little more than an inch long. To conclude, there are on the soles of the feet, as on the palms of the hands, small surfaces of pinkish white colour.

"... The first symptoms indicative of the approaching efflux of blood occur on the Thursday, generally about noon. On each of the pink surfaces already described on the hands and feet, a vesicle is seen to commence, and to rise little by little. When completely developed, it is a rounded hemispherical prominence on the surface of the skin; its base is the same size as the pink surface on which it rests--that is, nearly an inch long, by a little more than half an inch broad. This vesicle is formed by the epidermis detached from the dermis, and elevated as a half sphere by serous liquid within."

We again quote some of the medical details:--

"The phenomenon occurs thus:--The vesicle bursts, and the contained serosity escapes. This

Rev. Frederick George Lee, D.C.L.

occurs in different ways--sometimes by a rent lengthways, sometimes by a crucial or a triangular division. In the last case, the rupture of the vesicle suggests the puncture of a leech; but this is a mere resemblance, to prove which it is enough to ascertain the entire absence on the hands and feet of those three-cornered white and indelible scars which always follow leech-bites. But a still more decisive observation is that this triangular rent only divides the epidermis; in fact, if this be removed by rubbing with a cloth, the little wound is no longer seen, and the true skin is found to be quite intact. Directly after the rupture of the vesicle and the escape of the fluid, blood begins to ooze from the bare derma.

"The flow of blood always detaches the piece of scarf-skin that makes the vesicle, so that the bleeding surface of the true skin is quite bare; sometimes, however--and especially on the palms of the hands and the soles of the feet, where the epidermis is very tough--the blood collects, and forms a clot in the partly-torn vesicle."[56]

The general appearance of the wound in the side on Friday is as follows:--The blood issues from three small points of a triangular form at the distance of half an inch from each other. A vesicle has also been observed similar to those upon the hands and feet. On its bursting, the blood flowed through the derma or thick skin over a round surface of the diameter of about half an inch.

The bleeding on the forehead commenced on Friday, the 25th September, 1868, and, at the present time,[57] takes place every week, and has extended round the whole of the head. The bleeding circlet on the forehead forms a band of two fingers' breadth in width, and the blood oozes from twelve or fifteen points. There is no appearance of vesicle, nor is the skin discoloured.

The second extraordinary account of a young girl, who is now marked with the stigmata, is furnished by the Rev. F. Prendergast, of San Francisco:[58]--

"Miss Collins was born in England; both her parents are Roman Catholics. About two years and a half ago she was a pupil at the Convent of Notre Dame. On her return to this city she left her father's home, and with a friend, Miss Armer, commenced the practice of charitable acts--visiting the sick, clothing the destitute, and instructing little children. Many of the charitable persons of the city co-operate with Miss Collins, Miss Armer, and an elderly lady who keeps house for them, in their good works. The archbishop approved of this semi-religious order, and has paid the house rent of these ladies since they began this practice. Miss Collins has always been in delicate health, and has frequently received the last sacraments of the Church, given to those in a dying condition. She has had periodical attacks of heart disease, and intense pulmonary congestion. Soon after Miss Collins and Miss Armer entered upon their charitable and self-denying duties, the former was prostrated by a return of her complaint. She recovered but slowly and imperfectly, and on January 2nd, at the children's festival in the basement of S. Mary's Cathedral, she was seized with a most violent attack. She was taken to her residence; and two or three days afterwards was again seized with congestion of the lungs, followed by congestion of the brain. The attending physician, herself, and all her friends were convinced that there was no hope of her recovery. She took leave of those who stood by her bedside, and made her final preparations for death. On Wednesday, January 8th, she was all day in convulsions.... Towards six o'clock she grew better, but on the night of the third day became speechless, and was compelled to write her wants and wishes in pencil.

"At twelve o'clock that night, Miss Armer and the nurse, who watched by her bedside, believed her to be dying, if not dead. They recited the prayers for the departing soul, and held the blessed candle by her hand, according to the custom of the Church. Presently Miss Collins closed her eyes and drew a long breath. They then believed her to be dead; but to their utter amazement and bewilderment she revived, and made signs that she wished to write. They gave her the pencil and paper, and she wrote as follows: 'Put three drops of the water from the font of Our Lady of La Salette in my mouth, and say three Hail Maries with me before the crucifix.' They complied with the instructions, and perceived that she joined mentally in the recital of the prayers. As soon as ended, she reached out her hands for the crucifix, and kissed, with an expression of great devotion, the Five Wounds of our Blessed Saviour. She then intimated that she wished to have a little water. They gave her some, and she immediately rose up and declared, with a beaming and heavenly countenance, that she was cured; and she called on her companions, Miss Armer and the nurse, to join her in saying the rosary for the sick. She wished to recite the principal parts of the devotion herself, but yielding to the request of Miss Armer, only made the responses in a clear and loud voice. She then requested her companions to retire, but seeing they had some objections, told them she would set the example. She laid down quietly, and slept without motion or sign till morning, when she ate heartily, and seemed quite restored to health. Since then she has never for a moment suffered from any of those diseases to which she had been before a victim, and which had more than once brought her to death's door.

"On being questioned about her recovery, she stated to her confessor, her companions, and others of her friends, that immediately previous to her recovery the Blessed Virgin spoke to her in a voice clear and musical, but as if it were coming from afar, directing her what to do in order to obtain her health, approving her manner of life, and giving her some counsels for her own guidance. Her recovery was regarded by all conversant with the facts as being a miraculous one; and, contrasting her subsequent excellent health with her former miserable condition, there seems to be no reason to doubt but that she was saved by the merciful interposition of the Supreme Power of God.

"After some weeks she experienced, without any assignable natural cause, an intense pain in her temples, which caused her indescribable anguish. These sufferings suddenly passed away, but in the course of some days returned with equal violence. So far there were no perceptible marks on any portion of her body, but during her sufferings on the Feast of the Five Wounds of our Lord she felt an acute pain in her head, her side, in both hands, and in both feet. On the Friday before Good Friday, the Feast of the Seven Sorrows of the Blessed Virgin, she experienced pains in the same parts, and on that day the stigmata, or marks of our Saviour's Wounds, became clearly visible on the backs of her hands, and blood oozed from her left side, near the heart.

"Several persons witnessed the stigmata on this occasion, but were loth to reveal the fact, preferring to await further developments. That night the pains passed away, and her usual health returned. On Holy Thursday the same sufferings were experienced, commencing in the afternoon and becoming very intense during Thursday night. On Friday the stigmata appeared on the surfaces of both hands and on the upper surface of both feet. Blood also oozed from her side. During the day her sufferings were indescribable, and were witnessed by a large number of people.[59] The stigmata and suffering continued unabated until twelve o'clock on Friday night, when she suddenly experienced some relief, and was able, for the first time in twenty-four hours, to take a little water. On the next day she attended divine service in church, and has since been in the enjoyment of excellent health. The marks of the stigmata remain on her hands and side. She has never, at any time during her sufferings, been unconscious, except when they were so intense as to cause momentary delirium. She prayed continually, and her countenance, ordinarily indicating extreme agony, occasionally relaxed into a sweet and heavenly smile. At times her hands were extended in the form of a crucifix, and became so rigid in that position that it was impossible to move them."[60]

As serving still further to illustrate the subject of this chapter, it should be known that Dr. John Milner, F.S.A., Vicar Apostolic of the Midland District of England (a prelate eminent both for his high character and great literary ability), records a supernatural cure, the subject of which was personally known to himself.

"On March 15, 1809, Mary Wood, living at Taunton Lodge, near Taunton, in Somersetshire, in attempting to open a sash-window, pushed her left hand through a pane of glass, which caused a very large and deep transverse wound in the inside of the left arm, and divided the muscles and nearly the whole of the tendons that lead to the hand; from which accident she not only suffered at times the most acute pain, but was, from the period the bishop saw her [March 15, 1809], until some time in July, totally deprived of the use of her hand and arm."[61] What passed between the latter end of July, when, as the surgeon states, "he left his patient with no hope of her recovery or of restoring her," until the 6th of August, on the night of which she was miraculously cured, can be gathered from a Letter to Bishop Milner, dated November 19th, 1809, by her amanuensis Miss Maria Hornyold, of the ancient family of that name:

"The surgeon gave little or no hopes of the girl ever again having the use of her hand; which, together with the arm, seemed withered and somewhat contracted; only saying [that] in some years Nature might give her some little use of it, which was considered by her superior as a mere delusive comfort. Despairing of further human assistance toward her cure, she determined, with the approbation of her said superiors, to have recourse to God, through the intercession of S. Winifred by a Novena.[62] Accordingly on the 6th of August she put a piece of moss from the Saint's Well on her arm, continuing recollected and praying, &c., when, to her great surprise, the next morning she found that she could dress herself, put her arm behind her, and to her head, having regained the free use and full strength of it. In short, she was perfectly cured."

So much for this portion of Miss Hornyold's narrative. Now, reverting to Bishop Milner, his testimony to the fact of the cure having been effected is here set forth:

"In this state I myself saw her a few years afterwards, when I examined her hand; and in the same state she still continues, at the above-named place, with many other highly credible vouchers, who are ready respectively to attest these particulars."

The conclusion of Miss Hornyold's Letter is as follows:

"On the 16th of the month the surgeon was sent for, and being asked his opinion concerning Mary Wood's arm, he gave no hope of a perfect cure, and little of her ever having even the least use of it; when she, being introduced to him and showing him the arm, which he thoroughly examined and tried, he was so affected at the sight and the recital of the manner of the cure, as to shed tears, and exclaim, 'It is a special interposition of Divine Providence.'"

The case of Winifred White, a young woman of Wolverhampton, suddenly and miraculously cured, is not less important and interesting:--"The disease from which she was suffering," writes Bishop Milner, "was one of the most alarming of a topical nature of any that is known, namely a curvature of the spine, as the physician and surgeon ascertained, who treated it accordingly, by making two great issues, one on each side of the spine, of which the marks are still imprinted on the patient's back. Secondly, that besides the most acute pains throughout the whole nervous system, and particularly in the brain, this disease of the spine produced a hemiplegia, or palsy of one side of the patient, so that when she could feebly crawl, with the help of a crutch under her right arm, she was forced to drag her left leg and arm after her, just as if they constituted no part of her body. Thirdly, that her disorder was of long continuance, namely, of three years' standing, though not in the same degree till the latter part of that time, and that it was publicly known to all her neighbours and a great many others. Fourthly, that having performed the acts of devotion which she felt herself called upon to undertake, and having bathed in the fountain [at Holywell in Flintshire], she, in one instant of time, on the 28th of June, 1805, found herself freed from all pains and disabilities, so as to be able to walk, run, and jump like any other young person, and to carry a greater weight with the left arm than with the right. Fifthly, that she has continued in this state these thirteen years, down to the present time; and that all the above-mentioned circumstances have been ascertained by me in the regular examination of the several witnesses of them, in the places of their respective residences, namely in Staffordshire, Lancashire, and Wales, they being persons of different counties, no less than of different religions and situation of life."[63]

The result of a solemn Curse, made in the Name of Almighty God, by one who had been greatly and grievously wronged, is recorded and not unsuitably here, it is hoped, in the following remarkable narrative--one fresh evidence of the existence of the Supernatural amongst us, had we only eyes to see and ears to hear.

The younger son of a Nova Scotia baronet, under promise of marriage, betrayed the only surviving daughter of a Northumbrian yeoman of ancient and respectable family, nearly allied to a peer, so created in William the Fourth's reign. She was a person of rare beauty and of considerable accomplishments, having received an education of a very superior character in Edinburgh. After her betrayal she was deserted by her lover, who fled abroad. The night before he left, however, at her earnest request, he met her in company with a friend with the avowed intention of promising marriage in the future, when his family (as he declared) might be less averse to it. After-events show that this was merely an empty promise, and that he had no intention of fulfilling it. A long discussion took place between the girl and her betrayer, in the presence of the female friend in question, a first cousin of her father. High words, strong phrases, and sharp upbraidings were uttered on both sides; until at last the young man in cruel and harsh language, turning upon her fiercely, declared that he would never marry her at all, and held himself, as he maintained, perfectly free to wed whom he should choose. "You will be my certain death," she exclaimed, "but death will be more welcome than life." "Die and be ----," he replied. At this the girl, with a wail of agony, swooned away. On her recovery she seemed to gather up her strength to pronounce a Curse upon him and his. It was spoken in the Name of the One Living and True God. She uttered it with deliberation, yet with wildness and bitterness, maintaining that she was his wife, and would haunt him to the day of his death; declaring at the same time to her relation present, "And you shall be the witness." He left the place of meeting without any reconciliation or kind word, and, it was believed, went abroad. In less than five months, in giving birth to her child, she died, away from her home, and was buried with it (for the child, soon after its baptism, died likewise) in a village churchyard near Ambleside. Neither stone nor memorial marks the grave. Her father, a widower, wounded to the quick by the loss of his only daughter, pined away and soon followed her to his last resting-place.

Five years had passed and the female cousin of the old yeoman, being possessed of a competency, had gone to live in London, when, on a certain morning in the spring of the year 1842, she was passing by a church in the west end, where, from the number of carriages waiting, she saw that a marriage was being solemnized. She felt mysteriously and instinctively drawn to look in. On doing so, and pressing forwards towards the altar, she beheld to her astonishment, the very man, somewhat altered and weather-worn, who had caused so much misery to her relations, being married (as on inquiring she discovered) to the daughter of a rich city merchant. This affected her deeply, bringing back the saddest memories of the past. But, as the bridal party were passing out of the church, and she pushed forward to look, and be quite sure that she had made no mistake, both herself and the bridegroom at one moment saw an apparition of her relation, the poor girl whom he had ruined, dressed in white, with flowing hair and a wild look, holding up in both hands her little infant. Both seemed perfectly natural in appearance and to be of ordinary flesh and blood. There was no mistaking her certain identity. This occurred in the full sunshine of noon and under a heavy Palladian Porch in the presence of a crowd. The bridegroom turned deathly pale in a moment, trembled violently, and then, staggering, fell forward down the steps. This occasioned a vast stir and sensation amongst the crowd. It seemed incomprehensible. The bridegroom, said the church officials in answer to inquiries, was in a fit. He was carried down the steps and taken in the bridal carriage to his father-in-law's house. But it was reported that he never spoke again; and this fact is mentioned in a contemporary newspaper-account of the event. Anyhow his marriage and death appeared in the same number of one of the daily papers. And although the family of the city merchant knew nothing of the apparition, what is thus set forth was put on record by the lady in question, who knew the mysterious circumstances in all their details; which record is reasonably believed by her to afford at once a signal example of retributive justice and a marked piece of evidence of the Supernatural. Names, for obvious reasons, are not mentioned here. The truth of this narrative, however, was affirmed on oath by the lady in question, before two justices of the peace, at Windsor, on October 3, 1848, one of whom was a beneficed clergyman in the diocese of Oxford, well known to the Editor of this volume,--to whom this record was given, in the year 1857 (when he was assistant-minister of Berkeley Chapel), by a lady of rank who worshipped there.

Here, accounts of two cases of miraculous cure through and by the Blessed Sacrament will be suitably and fittingly introduced. The first is from the pen of a well-known mission-preacher of the Church of England, and occurred in the diocese of London: the second, equally remarkable, took place in the diocese of Metz.

The introductory remarks, so full of truth and piety, which immediately precede the first narrative, have an equal bearing on that which follows. Both are instances of God's extraordinary mercy and goodness to the children of men.

"The Blessed Sacrament of the Body and Blood of the Lord works its effects not only on the soul of man, but also on his body. We need not be surprized at this, for if the body is affected by the soul, so that a person depressed in mind often falls sick in body; and, on the contrary, if good spirits are of great use in preserving bodily health--as indeed we frequently see,--if this be the case, may we not expect that the Sacrament, which only reaches the soul through the body, will have some influence on that body through which they are transmitted. The Blessed Sacrament, then, when worthily received, affects the body in three ways. First, it tends to moderate what is called 'concupiscence,' that is those natural appetites and desires of the body which dwell in the flesh and tempt to sin. And this we learn from the words of the prayer of Humble Access in the Communion Service--that our sinful bodies may be made clean by His Body.

"Secondly, the Blessed Sacrament gives to our bodies glory in the Day of the Resurrection.

"Our Lord says, 'He that eateth My Flesh and drinketh My Blood hath Eternal Life, and I will raise him up at the last day.' Not that all men will not rise from the dead at that day, but that the wicked will rise with hideous bodies, and the righteous only with bodies like unto our Lord's own Body; whilst the glory also of those who are saved will differ one from another. And so S. Paul writes, 'One star differeth from another star in glory.'

"Thirdly, the Blessed Sacrament sometimes works the cure of sick persons who receive it with faith. Of course this is not often the case, for if miracles were common they would cease to be miracles. Moreover, there is but little faith now-a-days, and even when our Lord walked in the flesh there were some places in which He did not do many mighty works because of their unbelief. Also He worked bodily cures the rather during His earthly ministry; because when He gives these more excellent gifts it is less necessary for Him to show this power by miracles of healing. It pleases Him however, sometimes even now, to cure bodily sickness by his bodily touch, and a case of this sort we will now relate:--

"I. Two or three years ago there lived in one of our great cities a poor woman of devotion and faith. She attended a church where the Holy Eucharist was frequently celebrated, and the true faith believingly taught. She received the faith gladly, and lived up to it, communicating regularly and with devotion. It befell her, however, to be taken with sickness, which brought on lockjaw, so that she could not eat, and only small portions of nourishment could be given her through an opening in her teeth. She was in this state several days, looking forward to certain death.

"At last, thinking more of the suffering which her loss would bring upon her family than upon any fear of death in her own heart, she said to her husband, 'Surely, the Lord Jesus is very merciful and would restore me to health if we were to ask Him. For how dreadful would it be for the poor children to be left without a mother! I have heard of a woman who was cured of a sickness by our Lord when the doctors gave her up. Why should we not ask Him to cure me?' Thus she spoke, and her husband agreed with her, that they would ask this of the Lord.

"The priest of the church which they attended was visiting the poor woman, and next time he came she told him of what she had thought, and asked whether it would be wrong to pray for this object. Seeing the faith of the poor people, he could not say anything against it, only exhorting them to be ready to accept the Will of the Lord whatever it might be. 'It is not wrong,' said he, 'to pray to the Lord for restoration to health, so long as we add, "Not my will but Thine be done."'

"Accordingly he arranged that they should have a special Celebration of the Blessed

Sacrament with that intention--to ask of our Lord the cure of the poor mother. The time was fixed. The woman was to be present herself, and to communicate, and the priest promised to ask some other devout people to attend and unite in prayer for the same object.

"At the hour appointed the priest was at the altar, a little body of devout persons was gathered in the church, and the poor woman was brought there, suffering, but still with good hope. The service proceeded; the prayer of Consecration was said; the Lamb of God was upon the altar, and the priest pleaded the one true and perfect and all-sufficient Sacrifice on behalf of the poor sufferer, and prayed for her recovery, as did also herself and her friends. Having communicated himself, the priest brought the Holy Sacrament to the woman, giving her only a small particle, such as she could receive between her teeth, and then the chalice of the Lord's Blood. The faithful now communicated; the remainder of the service was said, the Priest gave the Peace and Blessing, and the last Amen was said. Then the woman fell down in a sort of swoon; but it only lasted a short time, for presently she got up, opened her mouth, and said, 'I am quite well.' Yes! The Lord had heard her. We were astonished with joy, and joined in hearty thanksgiving to God for the miracle which he had wrought. The woman walked home, to the great delight of her family, and was able to return to her ordinary work.

"A fortnight after the event, the writer of this narrative[64] saw the woman, and heard from her own lips, as well as from the Priest, the account of the miracle, which he has related as nearly as he can remember it.

"We are not to be anxious for miracles, nor to crave after signs; but when it pleases God to work such as this, it seems to be right for His glory, and for the dignity of the Most Holy Sacrament, that His mercy should be made known; and is it not joy to every faithful heart, that the Lord should manifest His power over all His works, and show to men His tender compassion of the sick and suffering?"

II. The second case is thus related. It bears a remarkable similarity to that just set forth:--

"Anne de Cléry, the subject of the extraordinary cure about to be recorded, was at school in the Convent of the Sacred Heart, at Metz, in the year 1855. She was then thirteen years of age, and her health and spirits good. Previously she had lived two years in Africa, where her father still resides,[65] and occupies the post of Notary-General to the Imperial Court at Algiers. Madame de Cléry's health having suffered from the climate, she returned to Metz with her two daughters, the youngest of whom--Anne--was very uneasy about her mother's health, and prayed fervently for her recovery, offering herself to suffer the pains of sickness in her stead. Anne's illness, which was of a very distressing nature, commenced in the Holy Week of 1856, and continued steadily to increase, in spite of the prescriptions of the first physicians at Metz, Aix in Savoy, and Paris. Remedies of every possible kind--some of them of a terribly severe character--were tried, but without the smallest result, except to increase the sufferings of the poor patient. The Paris physician, at length (in the year 1857), pronounced her case to be incurable. He says: 'Mdlle. Anne is labouring under the disease known by the name of "muscular and atrophical paralysis." I very much apprehend that no remedies can touch the disease.' The sufferings of the poor girl were continuous and severe. Her limbs were deprived of power and strength; they shrank and contracted, and the muscles under each knee produced a sort of knot which no power on earth could untie. She would be, as far as man could foresee, a cripple as long as she lived. Anne de Cléry was, however, resigned to the Will of God, and supported her heavy trial by a deep piety and constant prayer. At times her faith suggested the possibility of a miraculous cure; but she scarcely hoped or wished for such a wonderful favour. She had a particular devotion to the Blessed Sacrament; and every week the priest brought her the Holy Communion, which was her greatest support and consolation. She employed her time, when able, though in the recumbent position, and unable to lift her head, in embroidering altar-cloths, and making artificial flowers for the adornment of the sanctuary. It was while thus preparing for the devotion known as 'the Forty Hours' Adoration' in the parochial church of S. Martin at Metz, in the year 1865, that the thought sometimes crossed her mind that she might be cured by the Blessed Sacrament. But she was slow to encourage an idea which might be an illusion, and deprive her of her resignation and peace of mind. The devotion above mentioned was to take place on the 12th, 13th, and 14th of June. On the first two days it was impossible to carry her to the church (whither she had not been taken for a long while), her pains were so severe; but on the third day, with the greatest difficulty, and at the cost of much suffering, after having received Communion, she was carried to the church by her maid Clémentine, who sat on a bench and held her on her knees. Madame de Cléry and Mdlle. de Coetlosquet knelt close beside her; but neither Anne nor her friends were expecting the extraordinary event about to follow.

"After a few moments' rest Anne became absorbed in devotion, and prayed as she often did at the moment of Communion: 'Lord, if Thou wilt, Thou canst cure me.' At the same instant she felt so violent a pain in her whole body, that it was all she could do not to scream out. She prayed for strength to bear it, and resigned herself to God's will. Then, she says, she felt filled with faith and hope, and became conscious that she was cured. Anne threw herself immediately upon her knees and said to her companions, 'Pray, pray; I am cured!' Madame de Cléry overcome with emotion, in a state of bewilderment, led her daughter out of the church, scarcely believing the evidence of her senses when she saw her standing alone and able to walk. She ascertained that the knots under her daughter's knees had entirely disappeared; and then Anne returned to the church, where she remained kneeling in praise and thanksgiving before the Blessed Sacrament for three-quarters of an hour, without feeling the least fatigue.

"Her cure was complete; all the ailments that had afflicted her disappeared, leaving behind no trace of illness. Eleven days after her cure, Anne walked through the streets of Metz in a procession of the Blessed Sacrament, which lasted an hour and a quarter, to the astonishment and admiration of all who had known her former sad condition. Her physician, when he saw her rise and walk to meet him, said, 'Mademoiselle, what men could not effect, God has done.'"[66]

The Editor has been furnished with many similar accounts; some coming before him on slender testimony: others on testimony which it is impossible either to weaken or to reject. In some cases strange and supernatural events which have occurred of late years--beautiful glimpses of the unseen world--are treasured up by those who were the direct subjects of them, though considerable difficulty is experienced in obtaining such satisfactory attestations of their authentication, (owing to the fact that persons naturally shrink from publicity,) as would warrant their appearance in this volume.

Before this chapter is closed, however, it may be well to add the following, from the pen of an English clergyman well known to the Editor, which possess some inherent interest:

"This passed under my own eyes a few weeks back. A little child, three years old, daughter of highly-respectable but poor parents, was accidentally burnt to death--fell upon the grate, and lingered only some two hours, it might have been supposed in frightful tortures. Her mother, who blamed herself for leaving the child even for a moment, seemed in imminent danger of losing her reason, and was in a state of terrible despair. The little one raised herself to say, 'Mother, don't cry! I'm going to die;' and then pointing, added, 'Don't you see that Good Man who stands there and waits for me?' This from a child of three years old.

"Let those who choose, elect to believe that this was an optical delusion: those who honestly believe that the angels of little children do behold His Father's face, and doubt not that angels minister to the heirs of salvation, will probably arrive at a different conclusion."[67]

Here is another remarkable case of the Supernatural, provided by the same clergyman:--

"A lady of my acquaintance, a woman of great intellectual powers, with a keenly satirical and inquiring mind, chastened, however, by Christian faith and love--a most devout communicant--was the voucher of these facts.

"Retiring to rest some years ago, late at night, she happened, on her way to her room, to look out of a window which opened on a court behind the house. To her surprise (she was not in the least a superstitious person, nor had her mind been travelling in a ghostly direction), she saw standing beneath the window, in the full rays of the moonlight, the figure of a child in white clothing, the arms crossed in prayer, the face inclining forward, with a kind of white cowl or head-covering, from the body of which child rays seemed to pass. She was not terrified, but amazed; and after gazing fixedly some little while, during which the figure did not move, she went to her room, and sent the nurse down to fetch something, where she would be likely to see the figure, without saying anything about it to her. The nurse returned speedily, white with fear, saying, 'Ma'am, did you see that wonderful thing all shining?' The lady inquired what she meant. The servant's impressions were identical with her own. Neither of them went to look again; but the lady thought within herself, that this might be a warning sent from God to prepare her for the death of an elder child, a daughter, whose figure and bearing, she thought, resembled that of the child enshrouded in white linen in the yard; and she consequently entertained a dread that that daughter might be taken from her. This did not prove the case; but as another younger child--the very darling of the mother's heart, and an infant at the time of this singular apparition--grew older, the idea was borne in strongly upon the lady's mind, that that younger child would be taken from her about the time when it attained the apparent age and stature of the mysterious visitant, who seemed to be a little girl of about five years old. This, doubtless, might be a fancy only: she had not seen the face, only the figure; and when this dear little one--a peculiarly sweet and engaging child--actually sickened, and at last, after a long illness, died, at about this age, the mother did not dare take to herself the consolation it seemed likely to afford her, as a foreshadowing of her child's beatified rest. On the contrary, the mother's heart was distracted with doubts and fears.... There had been no direct communion with God, as far as man could judge, near the last; rather a certain fretfulness, a turning from God to man, a clinging to the mother as her all. The Christian's heart was almost paralysed by the vast and unspeakable terror which took possession of her soul. Was her dear one indeed saved?... Although she thought all day long of this child,--I knew her at the time, and she seemed consumed by grief, fast breaking, though never was God's house opened without her finding her way thither,--she had never once dreamt of her, or seen her in her dreams, much to her own surprise, and despite the constant craving of her aching heart. But at last, one night she dreamt, and thus: that she had risen from her bed, and was standing in her chamber; that the door softly opened, and her little one came and sat upon the threshold, sweetly smiling. 'What, my own darling! (she thought she said,) are you come back again to me?' 'Yes, my mamma,' replied the child. 'And are you happy, dearest?' 'Yes, quite happy; but not for anything I have done,--only for the merit of my Lord.' The mother advanced and embraced her child, and thus embracing she awoke. And now wonderfully was it borne in upon her that the midnight apparition of so many years ago and the child of her dream were one. Her dream was so real, that she could not but receive it as a divine intimation, a direct answer to her prayers. She now felt and believed that her dear one was in Paradise. For some weeks, despite her longings to renew the vision, she saw her child no more. Then she did so once again, in a dream. She was crossing a radiant garden, where she knew not; in its centre was a stately hall or cupola, and on the marble steps which led to it stood her sweet one, looking pure and blessed. The mother bounded towards her, when she espied, within the hall, at the further end of a corridor or long passage, the form of another child of hers still living! This sight terrified her; she shrieked out, and shrieking she awoke. That child lives still, and may it long be preserved to the mother's prayers! But meanwhile, it is not a little remarkable, that during nearly three years which have elapsed, despite every effort on the mother's part, she has never once dreamt of her darling! This is what contributes, with the vision of the radiant child at first, to impart a supernatural character to the whole transaction, and take these visitations out of the category of ordinary dreams. On my own mind there is not the smallest doubt that here was a two-fold supernatural intervention; firstly, vision,--seen, remember, by two witnesses; then by a most strangely corroborative dream."

Another example, shadowing forth the possible value and power of prayer,--"the effectual, fervent prayer of a righteous man,"--though briefly told, is not without its own special interest in these days of Irreligion and Unbelief.

"An English gentleman I knew well was residing in France; his only son was a barrister in the Middle Temple Chambers in London. This son suffered from disease of the heart, not known to be immediately dangerous; he was a professed unbeliever--a scoffer, even; and had, alas! spoken lightly of Revelation the day before his death. A sudden, violent attack prostrated him; and, after a few hours of suffering, he departed. That night, the father, who was not aware of any immediate danger to his child, dreamt that the spirit of his deceased wife appeared to him, and addressed him, saying, 'Rise and pray! William is dying, and there are none to pray for him!'--or words to that effect. This dream was repeated, I believe, thrice. The father did rise, and remained in earnest intercessory prayer (he was a devout Christian man,) for the greater part of the night. This is a well-authenticated fact, the certainty of which may be relied on."

This chapter is brought to its close by a most impressive account of sweet and heavenly music which was heard near the dying bed of one, whose patience and devotion during sickness were as remarkable as her earthly life had been pure and holy.

It is from the pen of one who for many years was a clergyman of the Church of England, but is now a Cistercian monk of the Monastery of Mount S. Bernard, on the Charnwood Hills, in Leicestershire, and who is known in religion as Father Augustine.

"On the last day she [Mary, daughter of A. P. de Lisle, of Garendon Park, Esq.], longed much for a cup of cold water, but it was not thought good for her; and so, when reminded of our Saviour's thirst on the Cross, she offered up her own thirst in union with His, and said she would ask for it no more.[68] Her faculties, however, continued entire and clear to the end, and by her particular request indulgenced prayers[69] were recited to her that she might frequently repeat them. Thus her life ebbed softly away; the last words on her lips being a prayer to her 'Sweet Saviour to have mercy upon her.' And are not such things as these natural grounds for having a sure hope that she died in the favour of God? It is true that we have even supernatural grounds in the fact that on the night before her decease (whilst she was receiving with devout mind the last anointing of Holy Church to prepare her for her end) there was heard distinctly and by several persons the sound of a celestial chant, proceeding from her chamber, hymned by no earthly voices. Does not this look as if the blessed spirits themselves had been assisting to prepare her that she might soon become one of their company?"

"Four men," continues the author of the Sermon from which the above is taken, in a note to it, "none of them [Roman] Catholics, heard the chanting three several times. They all agreed in their conviction as to whence it came, that it was from the chamber of the dying child. The third time it was so loud that they could distinguish, as it were, the several voices that blended in this celestial harmony, some of which sung the treble notes, while others took the deeper parts. The character of the music was indescribably beautiful; and one of the men, who had been in the habit of attending the Catholic service in S. Mary's chapel, at Grâce-Dieu, declared that the style of it was exactly like that of the solemn Plain Chant used in that chapel which he was accustomed to hear there. They described the chanting as having no air in it that they could carry away, but the effect was solemn and beautiful beyond expression. They supposed, at the moment, that it was some service, according to the Catholic rites, which was being sung in the sick chamber by the priest and his attendants. When they heard it, therefore, they were not surprised at the sound, except that its beauty exceeded that of any religious service they had ever heard; and it was not until the following morning, at the breakfast hour, when relating what they had heard to their fellow-servants, and being then informed that there had been no service chanted in the sick room, that the conviction flashed upon them, as upon all to whom these facts have been since related, that the chanting proceeded from heavenly spirits and departed saints, who had come hither on an errand of mercy, to hedge round the dying bed of the departing child."--Note, p. 13.

  The Editor prefers to leave these varied records of the spiritual powers and properties of the Church, these different examples of the presence of the Supernatural, to the consideration of the reader; himself declining either to lay down principles, frame arguments, or draw deductions from facts already set forth.

Rev. Frederick George Lee, D.C.L.

APPENDIX TO CHAPTER III - THE FORM OF EXORCISING THE POSSESSED
[TRANSLATED FROM THE "ROMAN RITUAL."]

    The Priest, having confessed, or at least hating sin in his heart, and having said Mass, if it possibly and conveniently can be done, and humbly implored the Divine help, vested in surplice and violet stole, the end of which he shall place round the neck of the one possessed, and having the possessed person before him, and bound if there be danger of violence, shall sign himself, the person, and those standing by, with the sign of the Cross, and sprinkle them with holy water, and kneeling down, the others making the responses, shall say the Litany as far as the prayers.

    At the end of the Antiphon. Remember not, Lord, our offences, nor the offences of our forefathers, neither take Thou vengeance of our sins.

    Our Father. Secretly.

℣ And lead us not into temptation.

℟ But deliver us from evil.

Psalm liv.

Deus, in Nomine.

The whole shall be said with Glory be to the Father.

℣ Save Thy servant,

℟ O my God, that putteth his trust in Thee.

℣ Be unto him, O Lord, a strong tower,

℟ From the face of his enemy.

℣ Let the enemy have no advantage of him,

℟ Nor the son of wickedness approach to hurt him.

℣ Send him help, O Lord, from the sanctuary,

℟ And strengthen him out of Sion.

℣ Lord, hear my prayer,

℟ And let my cry come unto Thee.

℣ The Lord be with you,

℟ And with thy spirit.

Let us pray.

    O God, Whose property is ever to have mercy and to forgive: receive our supplications and prayers, that of Thy mercy and loving-kindness Thou wilt set free this Thy servant (or handmaid) who is fast bound by the chain of his sins.

    O holy Lord, Father Almighty, Eternal God, the Father of our Lord Jesus Christ: Who hast assigned that tyrant and apostate to the fires of hell; and hast sent Thine Only Begotten Son into the world, that He might bruise him as he roars after his prey: make haste, tarry not, to deliver this man, created in Thine Own image and likeness, from ruin, and from the noon-day devil (dæmonio meridiano; in our version, "the sickness that destroyeth in the noon-day"). Send Thy fear, O Lord, upon the wild beast, which devoureth Thy vine. Grant Thy servants boldness to fight bravely against that wicked dragon, lest he despise them that put their trust in Thee, and say, as once he spake in Pharaoh: I know not the Lord, neither will I let Israel go. Let Thy right hand in power compel him to depart from Thy servant N. (or Thy handmaid N.) ✠, that he dare no longer to hold him captive, whom Thou hast vouchsafed to make in Thine image, and hast redeemed in Thy Son; Who liveth and reigneth with Thee in the Unity of the Holy Spirit, ever One God, world without end. Amen.

    Then he shall command the spirit in this manner.

    I command thee, whosoever thou art, thou unclean spirit, and all thy companions possessing this servant of God, that by the Mysteries of the Incarnation, Passion, Resurrection and Ascension of our Lord Jesus Christ, by the sending of the Holy Ghost, and by the Coming of the same our Lord to judgment, thou tell me thy name, the day, and the hour of thy going out, by some sign: and, that to me, a minister of God, although unworthy, thou be wholly obedient in all things: nor hurt this creature of God, or those that stand by, or their goods in any way.

    Then shall these Gospels, or one or the other, be read over the possessed.

    The Lesson of the Holy Gospel according to S. John i. 1. As he says these words he shall sign himself and the possessed on the forehead, mouth, and breast. In the beginning was the Word ... full of grace and truth.

The Lesson of the Holy Gospel according to S. Mark xvi. 15. At that time: Jesus spake unto His disciples: Go ye into all the world ... shall lay hands on the sick, and they shall recover.

The Lesson of the Holy Gospel according to S. Luke x. 17. At that time: The seventy returned again with joy ... because your names are written in heaven.

The Lesson of the Holy Gospel according to S. Luke xi. 14. At that time: Jesus was casting out a devil, and it was dumb ... wherein he trusted, and divideth his spoils.

℣ Lord, hear my prayer,

℟ And let my cry come unto Thee.

℣ The Lord be with you,

℟ And with thy Spirit.

Let us pray.

Almighty Lord, Word of God the Father, Jesus Christ, God and Lord of every creature: Who didst give to Thy Holy Apostles power to tread upon serpents and scorpions: Who amongst other of Thy wonderful commands didst vouchsafe to say--Put the devils to flight: by Whose power Satan fell from heaven like lightning: with supplication I beseech Thy Holy Name in fear and trembling, that to me Thy most unworthy servant, granting me pardon of all my faults, Thou wilt vouchsafe to give constancy of faith and power, that shielded by the might of Thy holy arm, in trust and safety I may approach to attack this cruel devil, through Thee, O Jesus Christ, the Lord our God, Who shalt come to judge the quick and the dead, and the world by fire. Amen.

Then defending himself and the possessed with the sign of the Cross, putting part of his stole round the neck, and his right hand upon the head of the possessed, firmly and with great faith he shall say what follows.

℣ Behold the Cross of the Lord, flee ye of the contrary part.

℟ The Lion of the tribe of Judah, the Root of David, hath prevailed.

℣ Lord, hear my prayer,

℟ And let my cry come unto Thee.

℣ The Lord be with you,

℟ And with thy spirit.

Let us pray.

O God, and Father of our Lord Jesus Christ, I call upon Thy Holy Name, and humbly implore Thy mercy, that Thou wouldest vouchsafe to grant me help against this, and every unclean spirit, that vexes this Thy creature. Through the same Lord Jesus Christ.

THE EXORCISM

I exorcise thee, most foul spirit, every coming in of the enemy, every apparition, every legion; in the Name of our Lord Jesus ✠ Christ be rooted out, and be put to flight from this creature of God ✠. He commands thee, Who has bid thee be cast down from the highest heaven into the lower parts of the earth. He commands thee, Who has commanded the sea, the winds, and the storms. Hear therefore, and fear, Satan, thou injurer of the faith, thou enemy of the human race, thou procurer of death, thou destroyer of life, kindler of vices, seducer of men, betrayer of the nations, inciter of envy, origin of avarice, cause of discord, stirrer-up of troubles: why standest thou, and resistest, when thou knowest that Christ the Lord destroyest thy ways? Fear Him, Who was sacrificed in Isaac, Who was sold in Joseph, was slain in the Lamb, was crucified in man, thence was the triumpher over hell. The following signs of the Cross shall be made upon the forehead of the possessed. Depart therefore in the Name of the Father ✠, and of the Son ✠, and of the Holy ✠ Ghost: give place to the Holy Ghost, by this sign of the holy ✠ Cross of Jesus Christ our Lord: Who with the Father, and the same Holy Ghost, liveth and reigneth ever one God, world without end. Amen.

℣ Lord, hear my prayer.

℟ And let my cry come unto Thee.

℣ The Lord be with you.

℟ And with thy spirit.

Let us pray.

O God, the Creator and Protector of the human race, Who hast formed man in Thine own Image: look upon this Thy servant N. (or this Thy handmaid N.), who is grievously vexed with the wiles of an unclean spirit, whom the old adversary, the ancient enemy of the earth, encompasses with a horrible dread, and blinds the senses of his human understanding with stupor, confounds him with terror, and harasses him with trembling and fear. Drive away, O Lord, the power of the devil, take away his deceitful snares: let the impious tempter fly far hence: let Thy servant be defended by the sign ✠ (on his forehead) of Thy Name, and be safe both in body, and soul. (The three following crosses shall be made on the breast of the demoniac.) Do Thou guard his inmost ✠ soul, Thou rule his inward ✠ parts, Thou strengthen his ✠ heart. Let the attempts of the opposing power in his soul vanish away. Grant, O Lord, grace to this invocation of Thy most Holy Name, that he who up to this present was causing terror, may flee away affrighted, and depart conquered; and that this Thy servant, strengthened in heart, and sincere in mind, may render Thee his due service. Through our Lord Jesus Christ. Amen.

THE EXORCISM

I adjure thee, thou old serpent, by the Judge of the quick and the dead, by thy Maker, and the Maker of the world: by Him, Who hath power to put thee into hell, that thou depart in haste from this servant of God N., who returns to the bosom of the Church, with thy fear and with the torment of thy terror. I adjure Thee again ✠ (on his forehead), not in my infirmity, but by the power of the Holy Ghost, that thou go out of this servant of God N., whom the Almighty God hath made in His Own Image. Yield, therefore, not to me, but to the minister of Christ. For His power presses upon thee Who subdued thee beneath His Cross. Tremble at His arm, which, after the groanings of hell were subdued, led forth the souls into light. Let the body ✠ (on his breast) of man be a terror to thee, let the image of God ✠ (on his forehead) be an alarm to thee. Resist not, nor delay to depart from this person, for it has pleased Christ to dwell in man. And think not that I am to be despised, since thou knowest that I too am so great a sinner. God ✠ commands thee. The majesty of Christ ✠ commands thee. God the Father ✠ commands thee. God the Son ✠ commands thee. God the Holy ✠ Ghost commands thee. The Sacrament of the Cross ✠ commands thee. The faith of the holy Apostles Peter and Paul, and of all the other Saints ✠, commands thee. The blood of the Martyrs ✠ commands thee. The stedfastness (continentia) of the Confessors ✠ commands thee. The devout intercession of all the Saints ✠ commands thee. The virtue of the Mysteries of the Christian Faith ✠ commands thee. Go out, therefore, thou transgressor. Go out, thou seducer, full of all deceit and wile, thou enemy of virtue, thou persecutor of innocence. Give place, thou most dire one: give place, thou most impious one: give place to Christ in Whom thou hast found nothing of thy works: Who hath overcome thee, Who hath destroyed thy kingdom, Who hath led thee captive and bound thee, and hath spoiled thy goods: Who hath cast thee into outer darkness, where for thee and thy servants everlasting destruction is prepared. But why, O fierce one, dost thou withstand? why, rashly bold, dost thou refuse? thou art the accused of Almighty God, whose laws thou hast broken. Thou art the accused of Jesus Christ our Lord, whom thou hast dared to tempt, and presumed to crucify. Thou art the accused of the human race, to whom by thy persuasion thou hast given to drink thy poison. Therefore, I adjure thee, most wicked dragon, in the Name of the immaculate ✠ Lamb, Who treads upon the lion and adder, Who tramples under foot the young lion and the dragon, that thou depart from this man ✠ (let the sign be made upon his forehead), that thou depart from the Church of God ✠ (let the sign he made over those who are standing by): tremble, and flee away at the calling upon the Name of that Lord, of Whom hell is afraid; to Whom the Virtues, the Powers, and the Dominions of the heavens are subject; Whom Cherubim and Seraphim with unwearied voices praise, saying: Holy, Holy, Holy, Lord God of Sabaoth. The Word ✠ made Flesh commands thee. He Who was born ✠ of the Virgin commands thee. Jesus ✠ of Nazareth commands thee; Who, although thou didst despise His disciples, bade thee go bruised and overthrown out of the man: and in his presence, having separated thee from him, thou didst not presume to enter into the herd of swine. Therefore, thus now adjured in His Name ✠, depart from the man, whom He has formed. It is hard for thee to wish to resist ✠. It is hard for thee to kick against the pricks ✠. Because the more slowly goest thou out, does the greater punishment increase against thee, for thou despisest not men, but Him, Who is Lord both of the quick and the dead, Who shall come to judge the quick and the dead, and the World by fire. ℟ Amen.

℣ Lord, hear my prayer.
℟ And let my cry come unto thee.
℣ The Lord be with you.
℟ And with thy spirit.
Let us pray.
O God of heaven, God of earth, God of the Angels, God of the Archangels, God of the Prophets, God of the Apostles, God of the Martyrs, God of the Virgins, God, Who hast the power to give life after death, rest after labour; because there is none other God beside Thee, nor could be true, but Thou, the Creator of heaven and earth, Who art the true King, and of Whose kingdom

there shall be no end: humbly I beseech Thy glorious majesty, that Thou wouldest vouchsafe to deliver this Thy servant from unclean spirits, through Christ our Lord. Amen.

THE EXORCISM

I therefore adjure thee, thou most foul spirit, every appearance, every inroad of Satan, in the Name of Jesus Christ ✠ of Nazareth, Who, after His baptism in Jordan, was led into the wilderness, and overcame thee in thine own stronghold: that thou cease to assault him whom He hath formed from the dust of the earth for His own honour and glory: and that thou in miserable man tremble not at human weakness, but at the image of Almighty God. Yield, therefore, to God ✠ Who by His servant Moses drowned thee and thy malice in Pharaoh and his army in the depths of the sea. Yield to God ✠, Who put thee to flight when driven out of King Saul with spiritual song, by his most faithful servant David. Yield thyself to God ✠, Who condemned thee in the traitor Judas Iscariot. For He touches thee with Divine ✠ stripes, when in His sight, trembling and crying out with thy legions, thou saidst: What have I to do with Thee, Jesus, Son of the Most High God? Art Thou come hither to torment us before the time? He presses upon thee with perpetual flames, Who shall say to the wicked at the end of time--Depart from Me, ye cursed, into everlasting fire, prepared for the devil and his angels. For thee, O impious one, and for thy angels, is the worm that dieth not; for thee and thy angels is the fire unquenchable prepared: for thou art the chief of accursed murder, thou the author of incest, thou the head of sacrileges, thou the master of the worst actions, thou the teacher of heretics, thou the instigator of all uncleanness. Therefore go out ✠, thou wicked one, go out ✠, thou infamous one, go out with all thy deceits; for God hath willed that man shall be His temple. But why dost thou delay longer here? Give honour to God the Father ✠ Almighty, before Whom every knee is bent. Give place to Jesus Christ ✠ the Lord, Who shed for man His most precious Blood. Give place to the Holy ✠ Ghost, Who by His blessed apostle Peter struck thee to the ground in Simon Magus; Who condemned thy deceit in Ananias and Sapphira; Who smote thee in Herod, because he gave not God the glory; Who by His apostle Paul smote thee in Elymas the sorcerer with a mist and darkness, and by the same apostle by his word of command bade thee come out of the damsel possessed with the spirit of divination. Now therefore depart ✠, depart, thou seducer. The wilderness is thy abode. The serpent is the place of thy habitation: be humbled, and be overthrown. There is no time now for delay. For behold the Lord the Ruler approaches closely upon thee, and His fire shall glow before Him, and shall go before Him; and shall burn up His enemies on every side. If thou hast deceived man, God thou canst not scoff: One expels thee, from Whose Sight nothing is hidden. He casts thee out, to Whose power all things are subject. He shuts thee out, Who hast prepared for thee and for thine angels everlasting hell; out of Whose mouth the sharp sword shall go out, when He shall come to judge the quick and the dead, and the World by fire. Amen.

All the aforesaid things being said and done, so far as there shall be need, they shall be repeated, until the possessed person be entirely set free.

The following which are noted down will be of great assistance, said devoutly over the possessed, and also frequently to repeat the Our Father, Hail Mary, and Creed.

The Canticle. Magnificat.
The Canticle. Benedictus.
The Creed of S. Athanasius.
Quicunque vult.
Psalm xci. Qui habitat.
Psalm lxviii. Exurgat Deus.
Psalm lxx. Deus in adjutorium.
Psalm liv. In Nomine Tuo.
Psalm cxviii. Confitemini Domino.
Psalm xxxv. Judica, Domine.
Psalm xxxi. In Te, Domine, speravi.
Psalm xxii. Deus, Deus meus.
Psalm iii. Domini, quid multiplicati?
Psalm xi. In Domino confido.
Psalm xiii. Usque quo, Domine?
Each Psalm shall be said with Glory be to the Father, &c.
Prayer after being set free.

Rev. Frederick George Lee, D.C.L.

We pray Thee, O Almighty God, that the spirit of wickedness may have no more power over this Thy servant N. (or Thy handmaid N.), but that he may flee away, and never come back again: at Thy bidding, O Lord, let there come into him (or her) the goodness and peace of our Lord Jesus Christ, by Whom we have been redeemed, and let us fear no evil, for the Lord is with us, Who liveth and reigneth with Thee, in the Unity of the Holy Ghost, ever one God, world without end. ℟ Amen.

CHAPTER IV - WITCHCRAFT AND NECROMANCY

"To deny the possibility, nay actual existence of Witchcraft and Sorcery, is at once flatly to contradict the revealed Word of God, in various passages both of the Old and New Testament; and the thing itself is a truth to which every Nation in the World hath in its turn borne testimony, either by examples seemingly well attested, or by prohibitory laws, which at least suppose the possibility of commerce with evil spirits." - Blackstone's "Commentaries," book iv. chap. iv. p. 61.

Witchcraft is the system of those persons who, through the direct agency of wicked spirits, perform certain acts and deeds beyond the natural and ordinary powers of mankind.[70] On the other hand, Necromancy, according to the definition of Cotgrave, is "divination by conference with dead bodies raised." In its modern and wider acceptation, the latter is a formal summoning of the spirits of the dead out of the hidden place of their abode--"the desert where they glide,"--in order to consult with them as to the present or future by unlawful means, and to secure their active assistance in supernatural things and practices which are forbidden.

The invocation and consultation of evil spirits specially summoned to earth by certain recognized incantations, would be acts of Witchcraft and Necromancy. Of these cases, abundant examples occur both in sacred[71] and profane history.[72]

To the wizard or witch were freely given by the Devil or his angels divers powers at once supernatural and uncommon, by which, when sought for, both riches and sensual pleasures could for a while be secured, even to surfeiting. Occasionally the gift of predicting certain future events was bestowed; in other cases, the power of working evil and mischief upon the lives, limbs, and fortunes of neighbours or chosen subjects. This power, as was commonly believed, was bestowed by an express and definite compact, as some declare, formally made in writing by the Devil or his agents, and sealed with the wizard's or witch's own blood. By the unvarying terms of the bond, as an essential preliminary, the Sacrament of Holy Baptism was expressly renounced by the person accepting the Devil's terms and conditions. Satan was formally worshipped, prayed to, and acknowledged as Ruler and Lord; and then, after a certain number of years, as a necessary consequence, the soul of the wizard or witch, without any chance of redemption, was irrevocably lost, and became absolutely the everlasting property of the Evil One.

The existence of this detail of the Supernatural, sometimes dimly and obscurely set forth, at others with undoubted and remarkable clearness, owns in its favour the almost universal consent of the human race[73] in all ages. Even the incredulity of the modern persons, who term themselves "philosophers" and "thinkers," cannot be reasonably alleged in contravention of so broad and general a fact; for these "philosophers" themselves admit as much when, in their great wisdom, they proceed to characterize the opposite disposition--the readiness to accept such facts--as "vulgar" and "popular."

It is impossible to point to any period when the belief in Witchcraft and Necromancy was perfectly obliterated, or to any nation which altogether repudiated it.[74] If one particular phase was removed, discredited, or discountenanced, some other form, substantially and inherently similar, eventually took its place. Holy Scripture[75] is full of references to Witchcraft and Necromancy. The dark rites and deeds involved in their practice are distinctly and unequivocally condemned. If such had not actively existed, why should their condemnation have been pronounced in the Sacred Books? Supernatural acts are there recorded, which are expressly said to have been performed by and through the system and power of Witchcraft, which is plainly declared to be a sin of a very dark dye. The practice, consequently, is directly and plainly forbidden, as being contrary to the Mind and Will of God; and laws were enacted and put on record by which those who, in the face of warnings, continued to practise such forbidden arts, were to be punished by death.

It is equally clear from certain of the Epistles of the Apostles of our Blessed Lord, that the fact of Witchcraft and Necromancy being commonly practised by Pagan nations was not only perfectly well known[76] to the guides and rulers of the Christian Church, but was again formally forbidden by those who were left to teach in the Name and on behalf of their Lord and Master. Nothing, in fact, can be more certain than that the Apostles condemned and prohibited the consultation of, or intercourse with, either the spirits of the departed or evil angels.

Here a few remarks defining and setting forth the principle on which such unlawful arts were authoritatively prohibited, may reasonably follow.

By the very act of his profession the Christian allows the co-existence in the World of two distinct and separable orders,--the Natural, which governs the physical and moral laws of the world, and the Supernatural, which, according to God's Revelation, gradually unfolded and duly developed, governs the moral laws of man. The object of man's faith is mystery, certain in itself, but above human intelligence. He yields the homage of his will not only to a God Who is the Great Creator and Preserver of the world and of all that therein is, but renders it to a God Who is the Repairer and Restorer of the human race by the Incarnation of the Eternal Word, and the Sanctifier of souls. This supernatural order, then, was not only known and established in the earth by other supernatural facts, but the visible testimony of Nature to the invisible order superior to and above Nature, was from time to time, and when necessary, abundantly made manifest. The Supernatural, then, exists in the World to lead men to God. Everything, therefore, that rises up in opposition to the Supernatural and mars the true idea of it, of necessity turns man away from God. The World, the Flesh, and the Devil, each and all (as Christian experience by temptation testifies,) effect this most successfully.

The World, which has been defined as "the rebellion of the reason against God," scorns to accept miracles and mysteries, and boldly denies the existence both of angels and fallen spirits-- scoffing at and repudiating the idea of Witchcraft or Necromancy, which it craftily characterizes as "the foolish and ignorant superstitions of a dark age." Furthermore, the World admits of no truth superior to the human intellect, of no law which restricts what is called "human liberty" or the "rights of man;" and absolutely refuses to acknowledge in the domain of facts anything which oversteps those fixed rules which it alone chooses to recognize in the government of Nature.

The Flesh tends to degrade man to the level of the beasts, with whom he has in common notable tendencies and powerful passions. To the carnal man, who is at enmity with God, the very term "Supernatural" is a word void both of meaning and efficacy. His motto is, "Let us eat and drink, for to-morrow we die:" his conviction, as far as he may be said to have any, is that his own soul is nothing more than "a force which has its origin in matter itself," and which, by consequence, shares its destruction; while his God is simply either "a stream of tendency, by which all things tend to fulfil the law of their being," or "a substance immanent in the universe."[77]

Thirdly, the Devil, through hatred both of God and man, strives in every way to substitute himself for God in this World. He is the Prince of the Powers of the air. He is stronger and more knowing than man. His intellect is clearer and finer. Moreover, his kingdom is powerful; his spiritual auxiliaries are numerous; his allies on earth, of all kinds, in the flesh, are multitudinous. The deeds which he delights that men should do are perfectly well known.[78] By counterfeiting genuine prodigies and true revelations, therefore, he draws men into the deadly meshes of a degrading and damnable superstition, by means of a delusive and lying supernaturalism. And the mischief resulting from such an active and successful policy is by no means on the wane, if they are not surely on the increase, in these dangerous latter days. True that in England the laws against Witchcraft are abolished,[79] but history, fairly consulted and faithfully read, tells us that not a century has elapsed since the commencement of the Christian era without its demoniacal apparitions and certain examples of Necromancy and Witchcraft. While this is so, of course no intention is entertained by the Editor of denying the common belief of the Universal Church, that by and through the Incarnation and Sacrifice of the Ever-Blessed Son of God the powers and influence of the Enemy of souls have been materially and efficiently crippled.[80]

Having thus digressed for an obvious purpose, it is now needful to return to the particular subject of this section, upon which some light will, in due course, be found to have been thrown, by the above brief expositions of principles; in the consideration and by the aid of which the strange facts and singular records which follow will appear in their proper place, when the important subject of the Supernatural, as brought out, incident upon incident, by historical records and authentic accounts, is under consideration.

That Witchcraft and Necromancy were publicly recognized as facts by the Fathers of the Christian Church is indisputable; while the existence of an order of ministers known as "exorcists," acting from time to time, as occasion required or necessity demanded, in casting out evil spirits, is a sufficient proof of the watchful care and beneficent action of the Universal Church, at once authoritative, indefectible, and divine.[81]

In 1484, Pope Innocent VIII. issued a Bull against Witchcraft, upon the promulgation of which, treatises were drawn up for the guidance of local bishops, chancellors, and other ecclesiastical officials, in the necessary labour of bringing hardened offenders to justice. This Bull was renewed in the latter part of the fifteenth century, by Pope Alexander VI., so that the subject of Witchcraft gained unusual attention about that period.

As a matter of fact, it is computed that in the year 1515, no less than five hundred witches were burnt in Geneva alone, and the same was the case in other parts of Christendom,--a proof at once of the craft and power of Satan, and of the demoralization of those who had deliberately elected to become his servants and slaves. The earliest statute against Witchcraft enacted in England, was passed in the reign of King Henry VI.; and additional laws of great stringency and severity, sorely needed, were enacted under the Tudors, by Henry VIII., Queen Elizabeth, and James I. In the year 1604, the great Act of Parliament against Witchcraft, drawn up by Coke and Bacon, was passed; and it is asserted that no less than twelve bishops attended the Committee of the House of Lords when the Bill was under discussion. Sir Matthew Hale and Sir Thomas Browne, men of high legal and literary rank and mark, each gave evidence at the trials which speedily followed. In this particular, as in some others, England followed Geneva. Between the years 1565 and 1700, eleven wizards or sorcerers were burnt at the stake in the Carrefour du Bordage, in Guernsey, the square devoted by the city authorities of that island to this kind of punishment. The last case of death for Witchcraft there took place in 1747.

It may here be put on record that at the period of the Reformation, and during the succeeding century, the power of casting out devils was claimed exclusively by those who remained in visible communion with the See of Rome, and many Roman Catholic writers of those periods maintained that no such power belonged either to any teacher of heresy or to schismatics.[82] But many of the Puritans, knowing that the act of exorcism, like baptism, was not essentially a sacerdotal act (for if baptism may be validly confirmed by a deacon, it may, with equal validity, be bestowed by a layman), maintained the power to be inherent in any Christian man (with right disposition and following recognized and authorized rules) of casting out evil spirits; and, in consequence, declined altogether to repudiate the clear and plain records and statements of Holy Scripture concerning Witchcraft and Necromancy. They therefore made several attempts to secure the official authorization of a form for exorcism, framed after the old and customary rite, to be printed in the "Book of Common Prayer." This, however, was never done. But in 1604 the subject was duly considered, and determined upon in the seventy-second Canon, which, as has been already pointed out, properly and stringently forbad to the clergy the practice of exorcism without a special license or faculty from the Bishop of the diocese.

As to the facts of Witchcraft and Necromancy, it is quite impossible to deny their existence. Records of the plainest character, legal evidence and literary testimony of undisputed authority,[83] may be discovered, which very luminously set forth what was believed on the subject; and this not alone by the ignorant, but by the learned and well-informed. The only difficulty is to make a suitable selection from that evidence which so abundantly exists; being careful that such selection shall not set forth merely one aspect of the subject, but several, and leaving each account to tell its own story. This it is now proposed briefly to attempt.

For example, in the year 1599, a girl named Martha Brossier, of Romorantin, in Berry, was reputed to be possessed, and excited a considerable sensation in Paris. At the suggestion of the then Bishop of Paris, the King ordered a Committee composed of the most eminent physicians, to examine and report on her case. The physicians appointed were Marescot, Ellain, Haulin, Riolan, and Duet; and their Report, which is exceedingly curious, will be found translated into English by Abraham Hartwell, and published towards the close of the sixteenth century.[84] The dedication to his Majesty proceeds thus:--

"Sire, by the commandment of Your Majestie, we have set down briefely and truly that which wee have found in our visiting of Martha Brossier.... We present the same unto Your Majestie without any art, without any painted show, without any flourish, but with a naked Simplicitie, the faithful companion of Truth, which you have desired from us in this matter and which you have always loved and curiously sought." The Report then continues: "We the undersigned Doctors Regents in the facultie of physicke in the Universitie of Paris, touching the matter of Martha Brossier, a maide of the age of two-and-twenty yeres or thereabouts, born at Romorantin in Berry, who was brought unto us in the chappel of my Lord of Saint Genefue [Geneviève], and who we saw sometimes in constitution, countenance and speech as a person sounde of bodie and minde, ... do say in our consciences, and certify that which followeth: that all which is before set down (referring to the character of her fits) must be referred to one of these three causes--sicknesse, counterfeiting, or diabolicall possession. For the opinion that it proceedeth from sicknesse, we are clerely excluded from that, for the agitations and motions we observed therein doe retain nothing of the nature of sickness, nay not of those diseases whereunto of the first sight they might have resembled; it being neither an epilepsie or falling sickness, which always supposes the loss of sense and judgment, nor the passion which we call hysterica, ... nor any of the four motions proceeding from diseases, that is to say, shivering, trembling, panting, and convulsion, or indeede if there doe appear any convulsion; and that a man will so call the turning up of her eyes, the gnashing of her teeth, the writhing of her chaps (which are almost ordinarie with this maide while she is in her fittes); the confidence which the priest hath when he openeth her mouth, and holdeth it open with his finger within it, testifying sufficiently that they doe not proceede from, nor are caused by, any disease, considering that in diseases he that hath a convulsion is not master of that part or member wherein it is, having neither any power of election or command over it, and particularly which is in the convulsion of the jawes, which is most violent of all the rest, the finger of the priest should bee no more respected nor spared than the finger of any other man. Moreover, diseases, and the motions also of diseases (especially those that are violent), leave the body feeble, the visage pale, and the breath panting. This maide, at the end of her fittes, was found to be as little moved and changed in pulse, colour, countenance, and breath, as ever she was before; yea, which is the more to be noted, as little at the end of her exorcisme as at the beginning, at evening as in the morning, at the last day as at the first. Touching the point of counterfeiting, the insensibilitie of her bodie during her extasies and furies, tried by the deepe prickings of long pinnes, which were thrust into divers parts of her hands, and afterwards plucked out againe, without any show that ever she made of feeling the same, either in the putting in of them, or the taking out of them, a griefe which, without majicke and without speech, could not, in our opinion, be indured, without any countenance or show thereof, neither by the constancie of the most courageous, nor by the stoutnesse of the most wicked, nor by the stronge conceit of the most criminall malefactores, took from us almost the suspicion of it, but much more persuaded us from that opinion, the thin and slender foam that in her mad fits we saw issue out of her mouth, which she had no means to be abel to counterfeit. And yet more than all this, the very consideration before mentioned of the little or no change at all that was seene in her person after all these most sharpe and very long pangs, (a thing which nobody in the world did ever trie in their most moderate exercises,) we are driven, even till this houre, by all the lawes of discourse and knowledge, yea, and almost forced to beleeve that this maide is a demoniacke, and the Devill dwelling in her is the Author of these effects. If wee had seen that which my Lord of St. Genefue and many others doe report,--that this maide was lifted up into the ayre more than four foote above five or six strong persons that held her,--it would have been an argument to us of an extraordinarie power, over and beyond the common nature and condition of man. But not being presente at that wonder, we doe give a testamonie of our knowledge, which is as much or rather more admirable than that force and power was, viz., that being demanded, and in her exercising commanded, my Lord of Paris furnishing the priest with questions and interrogatories, this maide divers and sundrie times, by many persons of qualitie and worthie of credit, was seene and heard to obey and answere to purpose, not only in the Latin tongue, (wherein it had not been impertinent peradventure to have suspected some collusion,) but also in Greeke and in English, and that upon the sudden. She did, we say once againe, understande the Greeke and English languages, wherein we beleeve, as it is very likely that she was never studied, so that there was no collusion used with her, neither could she invent or imagine the interpretations thereof. It resteth, therefore, even in the judgment of Aristotle in the like case, that they were inspired unto her." The Report then concludes with this solemn declaration: "By reason whereof, and considering also, under correction, that Saint Luke, who was both a physician and an evangelist, describing the persons out of whose bodies our Lord and his apostles did drive the devils left unto us, none other or any greater signes than those which wee think wee have seene in this case, wee are the more induced and almost confirmed to beleeve and to conclude as before, taking God for a Witness of our consciences in the matter. Made at Paris, this 3rd April, 1599."

On this Report, as may be gathered from the tractate referred to, it is evident and notorious that the physicians Marescot, Ellain, Haulin, Riolan, and Duet, were all men of scientific attainments and unimpeachable moral integrity; the same facts were also witnessed and formally attested by the Bishop of Paris, the Abbot of Geneviève, and other competent observers.

Another case, that of a girl named Anne Millner, or Mylner, of Chester, about the year 1564, deserves consideration. The record here given is taken from a pamphlet of considerable interest.[85] Some curious facts connected with it are attested by Sir William Calverley, Sir William Sneyd, Lady Calverley, and other persons of distinction who then lived at Chester. The description of the paroxysm is extremely graphic:--"We went," says the Report, which is signed by the above-named persons, "at about two of the clocke in the afternoone of the same 16th day of February and there found the mayden in her traunce, after her accustomed manner lying in a bed within the haule, her eyes half shut, half open, looking as she had been agast, never moving either eye or eyelid, her teeth something open, with her tongue doubling betweene, her face somewhat red, her head as heavy as leade to lift at; there she laid, still as a stone, and feeling her pulse it beat in as good measure as if she had been in perfect health." The Report then describes her becoming violently convulsed: "She lifted herself up in her bed, bending backwards in such order that almost her head and fete met, falling down on the one side, then on the other." A person of the name of Lane, who was reputed to possess great power over demoniacs, was then called in, who first, as the Report expresses it, "willed" that she should speak, and then "willed" that she should rise and dress herself, all which she did, to the astonishment of the bystanders; and a Certificate to that effect was signed by all present on March 8, 1564.

In Lancashire seven persons belonging to one family were reputed to be under the direct influence of evil spirits, or in a certain state of bewitchment, exhibiting signs of demoniacal possession. The pamphlet, the title of which is given below,[86] puts on record what in this case is reported to have occurred: "These possessed persons had every one something peculiar to herselfe which none of the rest did shew, and that so rare and straunge that all the people were obliged to confesse it was the worke of an evil spirit within them; so had they many things in common, and were handled for the most part in their fittes alike.... They had all every one very straunge visions, they heard hideous and fearful voices of spirits sundrie times and did make marveilous answers back againe ... they were in their fits ordinarilie holden in that captivity and bondage, that for an houre, two, or three, and longer time they should neither see, heare, nor taste, nor feel nothing but the divells, they employing them wholly for themselves, vexing and tormenting them so extreameley as that for the present they could feel no other paine or torture that could bee offered; no, though you should plucke an ear from the heade or an arm from the bodie. They had also a marveilous sore heaving as if their hearts would burst, so that with violent straining some of them vomitted bloude many times. They were all of them verry fierce, offering violence both to themselves and others, whereine they shewed verie greate and extraordinarie strength. They were out of their right mind, without the use of their senses, expecially voyd of feiling: as much sense in a stock as one of them, or as possible, in a manner, to quicken a dead man as to alter or chaunge them in their traunces in anything they either saide or did. They in their fittes had divers parts and members of their bodies so striffe and stretched out as were inflexible or very hard to be bended. They shewed very great and extraordinarie knowledge, as may appear by the straunge things saide and done by them, according to that which we have already set down in the particulars. They ever after their fittes were as well as might be, and felt very little or no paine at all, although they had been never so sore tormented immediately before."

The strange and singular violence of the convulsions in those who were under the influence of Witchcraft, is brought out in almost all the records of such cases, notably in those which occurred during the Great Rebellion,[87] and specially in the case of Anne Styles, who was executed at Salisbury in 1653.

The narrative states that she was so strong in her fits that six men or more could not hold her, but while suffering under most grievous hurrying and tortures of the body, the witch being only brought into the room, she fell asleep and slept for three hours, so fast that when they would have awakened her they could not.[88] The insensibility of the body in this state, we are informed by Increase Mather, led to a cruel test for demoniacal possession. There was a notorious Witchfinder, he observes, "in Scotland, who undertook by a pin to make an infallible discovery of suspected persons, whether they were witches or not. If, when the pin was run an inch or two into the body of the accused party no blood appeared nor any sense of pain, he declared them to be witches, by means of which no less than three hundred persons were condemned for witchcraft in that country."[89]

In a small but curious tractate entitled "Daimonomagia," the effects of Witchcraft are maintained to be a disease. The definition of it stands thus:--"A disease of witchcraft is a sickness that arises from strange and preternatural causes, and from diabolical power in the use of strange and ridiculous ceremonies by witches or necromancers, afflicting with strange and unaccustomed symptoms, and commonly preternaturally violent, very seldom, or not at all, curable by natural remedies." Then follow the diagnostical signs, amongst which are insensibility, convulsions, together with a preternatural knowledge both of living and dead languages, and after these the causes of witchcraft. Biernannus and Wierius, two authorities on the subject, find that aspect and contact do not necessarily bewitch; but witches sometimes try to bewitch another of the same family. Lastly, as regards the cure, directions are provided by which the wizard, witch, or necromancer is to be compelled to use certain dark ceremonies for the cure of the bewitched.

In the year 1658, a woman named Jane Brookes was tried, condemned, and executed at Chard in Somersetshire. The indictment against her was that she had bewitched Richard the son of Henry Jones, of Shepton Mallet in that county. Numberless persons of all ranks and classes, including both clergymen and physicians, witnessed his sufferings and paroxysms; while the direct influence of the woman indicted was fully apparent and abundantly proved. "The boy," as the Rev. Joseph Glanville,[90] one of the chaplains of King Charles II. writes, "fell into his fitts at the sight of Jane Brookes and lay in a man's arms like a dead person; the woman was then willed to lay on her hand, which she did, and he thereupon started and sprung out in a very unusual manner. One of the justices, to prevent all possibilities of legerdemain, caused Gibson and the rest to stand off from the boy, and then that justice himself held him. The youth being blindfolded, the justice called as if Brookes should touch him, but winked to others to do it, which two or three successively did, but the boy appeared not concerned. The justice then called on the father to take him, but had privately before desired one Mr. Geoffrey Strode to bring Jane Brookes to touch him at such a time as he should call for his father, which was done, and the boy immediately sprang out after a very odd and violent fashion. He was afterwards touched by several persons and moved not, but Jane Brookes being again caused to put her hand upon him he started and sprung up twice as before. All this while he remained in his fit and some time after, and being then laid on a bed in the same room, the people present could not for a long time bow either of his arms or legs."

It appears tolerably evident that the boy, when under the influence of his fits, owned a faculty not unlike that of clairvoyance. As regards Jane Brookes and her sister, he seems to have had the capacity to describe them accurately wherever they might have been. As the Report declares, "He would tell the clothes and habits they were in at the time, exactly as the constable and others have found them on repairing to them, although Brookes' house was a good distance from Jones': this they often tried, and always found the boy right in his description."[91]

From the same volume, the main facts of which seem to be admitted by competent authority, a woman named Elizabeth Style of Bayford was indicted for bewitching a girl named Elizabeth Hill, thirteen years of age. In this case the formal deposition of three credible witnesses attests that "during her fits, her strength was encreased beyond the proportion of nature, and the force of divers men. Furthermore, in one fit she foretold when she would have the next, which happened accordingly."

The case of the "Surey Demoniac," as he was termed, which was set forth at length in a publication issued in London towards the close of the seventeenth century,[92] is certainly worthy of being noticed here. In the year 1697 a youth of nineteen years of age, named Richard Dugdale, excited great attention; it being generally believed that he was possessed by an evil spirit, as the direct consequence of Witchcraft. His paroxysms were witnessed by numerous clergymen, physicians, and persons of respectability and rank; and caused an amount of interest and excitement which can scarcely be realized.[93] His fits commenced with violent convulsions; his sight or eyeballs turned upward and backwards; he afterwards answered questions; predicted during one fit the period of accession and duration of another fit; spoke in foreign languages, of which at other times he was ignorant, and described events passing at a distance with singular and recognized accuracy. Here again the word of narration is quoted at length:--"At the end of one fit the demoniac told what hour of the night or day his next [fit] would begin, very precisely and punctually, as was constantly observed, though there was no equal or set distance of time between his fits; betwixt which there would be, sometimes a few hours, sometimes many, sometimes one day, sometimes many days." "He would have told you," one of the deponents asserts on oath, "when his fits would begin, when they were two or three in one day, or three or four days asunder, wherein he never was, that the deponent knoweth of, disappointed." On one occasion, when the minister was addressing him, he exclaimed, "At ten o'clock my next fit comes on." "Though he was never learned in the English tongue, and his natural and acquired abilities were very ordinary, yet, when the fit seized him, he often spake Latin, Greek, and other languages very well.... He often told of things in his fits done at a distance, whilst those things were a-doing,--as, for instance, a woman being afraid to go to the barn, though she was come within a bow's length of it, was immediately sent for by the demoniac, who said, 'Unless that weak-faithed jade come, my fits will last longer.' Some said, 'Let us send for Mr. G----.' The demoniac answered, 'He is now upon the hay-cart,' which was found to be true.... On another occasion he told what great distress there was in Ireland, and that England must 'pay the piper.' Again, one going by him to a church meeting, was told by the demoniac in his fit, 'Thou needest not go to the said meeting, for I can tell thee the sermon that will be preached there,' upon which he told him the text and much of the sermon that was that day preached." Lastly, it is certified by two of the deponents that "the demoniac could not certainly judge what the nature of his distemper was; because when he was out of his fits, he could not tell how it was with him when he was in his fits."

From another publication[94] we gather that, in the case of Florence Newton, an Irishwoman, who was charged with bewitching Mary Longdon, when the sufferer and the accused were both in court, and the evidence against the person charged was being concluded, the prisoner at the bar simply looked at the woman reputed to be under her influence, and made certain motions of her hands towards her, upon which we are told that "the maid fell into most violent fits, so that all the people that could lay hands on her could scarcely hold her."

Quaint as these records are, peculiar in their literary style, singularly simple and homely in their subject-matter as to details, and tinged, it may be, not infrequently with the exaggerated superstitions of the times, it is impossible that so many persons of all ranks and classes--the highest as well as the lowest--eye-witnesses of facts, could have been so utterly mistaken as to the Supernatural character of Witchcraft, or so deluded as to its true nature and import. Some writers have hastily and erroneously asserted that at the close of the seventeenth century the arraigning and

Glimpses of the Supernatural Volumes I & II

trying of witches came to an end. But this is not so.[95] In 1712, Judge Parker (who succeeded Chief Justice Holt,) put a check upon the so-called "trial by water," by his charge at the Essex Summer Assizes of that year. Three years later, however, in 1715, Elizabeth Treslar was hung and then burnt for Witchcraft on Northampton Heath.

The following account (extracted verbatim et literatim) is taken from a rare and curious tract[96] published early in the eighteenth century, containing an account of the trial, examination, and condemnation of two witches named Shaw and Phillips in the year 1705. One or two sentences of the old narrative are two coarse for quotation; but substantially the contemporary account is reprinted, following its old typographical form:--

"On Wednesday the 7th of this Instant March 1705, being the second day of the Assizes held at Northampton: One Ellinor Shaw and Mary Phillips[97] (two notorious Witches), were brought into court and there Arraign'd at the Bar upon several Indictments of Witchcraft; particularly for Bewitching and Tormenting in a Diabolical manner, the Wife of Robert Wise of Benefield in the said County, till she Dyed; as also for Killing by Witchcraft and wicked Facination one Elizabeth Gorham of Glapthorn, a Child of about four years of Age, in the said County of Northampton; as also for Bewitching to death one Charles Ireland of Southwick in the said County; to which Indictment the two said Prisoners pleaded not Guilty and there upon put themselves upon their Tryals as followeth:--

"The first Evidence against them was one Widdow Peak, who deposed that she with two other Women, undertook to Watch the same Prisoners after they had been Apprehended; and that about Midnight there appeared in the Room a little white Thing about the Bigness of a Cat, which sat upon Mary Phillips' Lap, at which time she heard her, the said Mary Phillips, say, then pointing to Ellinor Shaw, that she was the Witch that Killed Mrs. Wise by Roasting her Effiges in Wax, sticking it full of Pinns, and till it was all wasted, and all this she affirm'd was done the same Night Mrs. Wise Dyed in a sad and languishing Condition. Mrs. Evans deposed that when Mrs. Wise first was taken Ill, that she saw Ellinor Shaw look out at the Window (it being opposite to her House), at Which time she heard her say, 'I have done her Business now I am sure; this Night Ill send the old Devil a New Year's Gift' (next day being New year's Day), and well knowing this Ellinor Shaw to be a reputed Witch, was so much concern'd at her Words that she went then to see how Mrs. Wise did, Where she found her Tormented with such Pains, as exceeding those of a Woman in Travel, which Encreased to such a terrible Degree that she Expired about 12 of the clock to the great amasement of all her Neighbours.

"Another Evidence made Oath that Ellinor Shaw and Mary Phillips being one day at her house they told her she was a Fool to live so Miserable as she did, and therefore if she was willing, they would send some thing that Night that would Relieve her, and being an ignorant Woman she consented; and accordingly the same Night two little black Things, almost like Moles came into her bed ... repeating the same for two or three Nights after, till she was almost frightened out of her Sences [sic] insomuch that she was forced to send for Mr. Danks the Minister, to Pray by her several nights before the said Imps would leave her: She also added that she heard the said Prisoners say that they would be Revenged on Mrs. Wise because she would not give them some Buttermilk.

"Mrs. Todd of Southwick deposed that Charles Ireland being a Boy of about 12 years of Age, was taken with Strange Fitts about Christmas last, continuing so by Intervals till twelf Day last, at which time he Barked like a Dogg, and when he was Recovered and come to himself, he would Distinctly describe Ellinor Shaw and Mary Phillips, affirming them two to be the Authors of his Misfortunes, though he never saw them in his Life; so that Mrs. Ireland, the Boy's mother, was advised to Cork up some ... in a stone Bottle filled full of Pins and Needles, and to Bury it under the Fire Hearth; which being done accordingly, the two said Witches could not be quiet till they came to the same House and desired to have the said Bottle taken up, which was not granted, till they had confessed the Matter, and promised never to do so again; but for all this the Next night but one, the said Boy was so violently Handled, that he Dyed in two Hours time; and this Woman's Testimoney was confirm'd by five or six other Evidences at the same time.

"The said Witches were Try'd a third time for Bewitching to Death Elizabeth Gorham of Glapthorne on the 10th of February last, as also for killing several Horses, Hogs, and Sheep, being the Goods of Matthew Gorham, Father of the said Child aforesaid. The Evidence against them to prove all this, was William Boss and John Southwel; who deposed that being Constables of the said Town, they were Charged with the said Prisoners in their Custody, who threatning them with Death if they did not Confess, and promising them to let them go if they would Confess; after some little Whineing and Hanging about one another's Necks they both made this Confession:--

Rev. Frederick George Lee, D.C.L.

"'That living in one house together they contracted with the Devil about a Year ago to sell their Souls to him, upon condition he would enable them to do what Mischief they desired against whom they pleased, either in Body, Goods, or Children; upon which the same Night they had each of them three Imps sent them as they were going to Bed, and at the same instant the Devil appeared to them in the shape of a tall black Man, and told them that these Imps would always be at their Service, either to kill Man, Woman, Child, Hog, Cow, Ship, [i.e. Sheep] or any other Creature, when they pleased to command them, provided ... which being agree'd to, the Devil came to Bed to them Both.... And that the next morning they sent four of their Imps to kill two Horses of one John Webb of the said Town of Glapthorne, because he openly said they were Witches; and accordingly the Horses were found dead in a Pond the same day; and two Days after this, they Kill'd four great Hoggs after the same manner, belonging to Matthew Gorham, because he said they both look'd like Witches, and not thinking this Revenge sufficient, the next day after, they sent two Imps a piece to destroy his Child, being a little Girle of about four years of Age, which was done accordingly in 24 Hours' time, notwithstanding all the Skill and Endeavour of able Doctors to preserve it. They further confessed that if the said Imps were not constantly imploy'd to do Mischief they had not their Healths, but when they were imploy'd they were very Healthful and Well. They further added, that the said Imps did often tell them in the Night-time in a hollow whispering low voice, which they plainly understood, that they should never feel Hell Tormēts, and they had Kill'd a Horse and two Cows of one Widow Broughton because she deny'd them some Pea-cods last year, for which they had also struck her Daughter with Lameness, which would never be cured as long as either of them Liv'd, and accordingly she had continued so ever since.'

"The above said Evidence further deposed that having thus extorted the said Confession from the prisoners, they persuaded them to set their Hands to it, which was done accordingly, tho' with very much difficulty, upon which the said Confession was produced in Court, and the Witness's to it Examin'd, who all deposed upon Oath that the said Confession was made in their Hearing, and that they saw the said reputed Witches set their Marks to it in the presence of ten Witnesses.

"Upon which the said Prisoners were desired by the Court to declare wheather they own'd the said Confession and the Marks thereunto Affixed or not, to which they both answered in the Negative; and thereupon made such a Howling and lamentable Noise as never was heard before to the amusement of the Whole Court, and Deny'd every particular that was laid to their Charge: but the Court having heard the matter of Fact so positively asserted against them by several Evidences, and above all by their own Confessions, that after having given a Larned [sic] Charge to the Jury relating to every particular Circumstance, they brought them in both Guilty of wilful Murther and Witchcraft, and accordingly the next day the Court was pleased to pronounce sentence of Death upon them, that is to say, To be Hang'd till they are almost Dead, and then surrounded with Faggots Pitch and other Combustable matter, which being set on fire their Bodies are to be consumed to Ashes."

In the month of March, 1711-12, another woman, Jane Wenham by name[98] (formally charged with bewitching Anne Thorne, Anne Street, and others), was tried at the Assizes at Hertford, and received sentence of death. The case was heard before Sir Henry Chauncey. Before the grand jury the depositions of sixteen witnesses were taken; one of whom deposed that Jane Wenham confessed to him that she had practised Witchcraft during sixteen years. On one occasion when the girl whom she had afflicted was in one of her paroxysms, we are informed that a very ingenious gentleman and able physician happened to be present, his curiosity bringing him a little out of his way to inquire into the truth of the story of this witch, which he had heard several ways told, as things of this nature generally are. When he saw her in a fit, which was one of the least she ever had, he tried whether he could bring her out of it without prayers. He took a great feather, which burning he held under the maid's nose, and though the stink was so great that we were not able to bear it in the room, yet the maid received the strong steam into her nose without being the least affected by it and without perceiving it, as far as we could perceive. The physician then felt her pulse and assured them that "it was no natural disease under which the maid laboured, that it must be counterfeit or preternatural; but," observes the author of this account, "that she should counterfeit even death itself one minute and restore herself to health the very next, and that she should put herself to all this trouble for no manner of pleasure or profit, is so very inconceivable and so wholly unaccountable, that I must needs say I shall never have faith enough to believe such a heap of absurdities." (p. 33.)

The undoubted insensibility of the girl was tested in a very practical but remarkably barbarous manner. One of the members of the Family of Chauncey "ran a pin into her arm six or seven times, and finding she never winced for it, but held her arm as still as if nothing had been done to it, and seeing no blood come, he ran it in a great many times more; still no blood came; but she stood talking and never minded it. Then, again, he ran it in several times more. At last he left it in her arm that all the company might see it, run up to the head." (p. 19.)

The record of these cases also contains the following:--

"There are also some things in which the fits of Mary Longdon and Anne Thorn agree, particularly the great strength of the afflicted when in a fit, so great that three or four men could hardly hold 'em down, but there is one very remarkable difference, which I doubt not my readers have already taken notice of, viz. that this Mary Longdon was always worse of her fits whenever Florence Newton came in the room; whereas Anne Thorn constantly recovered from hers at the touch of the witch. And yet I think these different appearances may be accounted for [in] different ways. It is not reasonable to suppose that either of those alterations in the afflicted came to pass by the consent or procurement of the witches themselves, who could not but perceive that they served as strong circumstances against them, but this was done by the overruling providence of Almighty God to convict these miserable creatures; and either of these ways might do as well as the other, since it is equally surprising to see one in perfect health fall into such terrible fits at the sight of any one person, as to see another recover out of such fits by the bare touch of the suspected witch, both of them tending only to the discovery of the criminal." (pp. 17, 18.)

As to certain of the characteristics and evidences of Witchcraft, Increase Mather in his "Cases of Conscience" writes as follows. What he sets forth, and what is now to be quoted, serves to show not only the kind of evidence as to facts which was then forthcoming, but also to afford information as to the current sentiment of his own period: "As for that which concerns the bewitched persons being recovered out of their agonies by the touch of the suspected party, it is various and fallible; sometimes the afflicted person is made sick instead of being made whole by the touch of the accused; sometimes the power of imagination is such as that the touch of a person innocent and not accused shall have the same effect. Bodin relates that a witch who was tried at Nantes was commanded by the judges to touch a bewitched person, a thing often practised by the judges of Germany in the Imperial Chamber. The witch was extremely unwilling, but being compelled by the judges, she cried out, I am undone, and as soon as ever she touched the afflicted person the witch fell down dead. I think," continues Mather, "that there is weight in Dr. Cottar's argument, viz. that the power of healing the sick and possessed was a special grace and favour of God for the confirmation of the truth of the Gospel; but that such a gift should be annexed to the touch of wicked witches, as an infallible sign of their guilt is not easy to be believed. It is a thing well known, that if a person possessed by an evil spirit is (as oft it happens) never so outrageous whilst a good man is praying with and for the afflicted, let him lay his hand on them and the evil spirit is quiet."

The cases already referred to took place in England. A brief reference may be here made to two examples which caused considerable sensation in Scotland,--a country where the belief in Witchcraft was in times past almost universal; and where, even still, the clear statements of Holy Scripture on the subject are neither explained away, scoffed at, nor disbelieved:--

In the year 1696 a commission was appointed in Scotland by the Lords of his Majesty's Privy Council, to inquire into the case of Christian Shaw, daughter of John Shaw of Bargarran, and the accused persons confronted before Lord Blantyre, the rest of the commissioners, several others gentlemen of note and ministers, the accused and in particular Catherine Campbell were examined in the presence of the commissioners. "When they [the accused] severally touched the afflicted girl, says the Report, she was seized with grevious fits and cast into intolerable agonies; others then present did also touch her, but no such effects followed, and it is remarkable that when Catherine Campbell touched the girle she was immediately seized with more grevious fittes and cast into more intolerable torments than upon the touch of other accused persons, whereat Campbell herself being daunted and confounded, though she had formerly declined to bless her, uttered these words, 'The Lord of heaven and earth bless thee and save thee both body and soul.'"[99]

During these trials we are informed that the "prisoners were called in, one by one, and placed about seven or eight feet from the justices and accusers; then, stood between the justices and them, the prisoners were ordered to stand right before the justices, with an officer appointed to hold each hand, lest they should herewith afflict them, and the prisoners' eyes must be constantly on the justices, for if they looked on the afflicted they would either fall into fitts or cry out they were much hurt by them."

"On the trial of Bridget Bishops," it is further added that, "the indictment being drawn up according to form, it was testified at the examination of the prisoner before the magistrates that the bewitched were extremely tortured. If she did but cast her eye on them they were presently cast down, and this in such a manner that there could be no collusion in the business. But upon the touch of her hand upon them when they lay in their swoones they would immediately revive, and not upon the touch of anyone else. Moreover, upon the special actions of her body, as the shaking of her head or the turning up of her eyes, they presently fell into the same postures, and many of the like accidents fell out while she was at the bar."[100]

Rev. Frederick George Lee, D.C.L.

Most curious are the various details of the trials thus far referred to. And certain of them may be regarded as trivial, if not absurd and ridiculous. Nevertheless it should be our careful aim to distinguish between those facts which were formally, regularly, and clearly established by positive evidence, and the personal fancies, superstitions, notions and wild ideas which may possibly accompany the reports of them. Of course exaggerations may have been made, and impositions not unfrequently practised; but in the forcible words of Joseph Glanville, we should remember that "frequency of deceit and fallacy will warrant a greater care and caution in examining, and a greater scrupulosity and shyness of assent to, things wherein fraud hath been practised, or may in the least degree be suspected; but to conclude that, because an old woman's fancy hath abused her, or some knavish fellow hath put tricks on the ignorant and timorous, therefore whole assizes have been deceived in judgment upon matters of fact, and that numbers of persons have been forsworn in things wherein perjury could not advantage them, I say such inferences are as void of charity as of good manners.... In things of fact the people are as much to be believed as the most subtle philosophers and speculators, since their sense is the judge, but in matters of notion and theory they are not at all to be heeded, because Reason is to be the judge of these, and this they know not how to use."[101]

It must be frankly admitted that these records of trials--of which there are such numerous examples in print--often contain principles and details of a most disagreeable and offensive nature. They have been quoted at some length, however, in order to point out exactly what for many years was currently believed with regard to Witchcraft; and whatever fanciful additions were made, or whatever superstitious garnishings were added to such accounts, by the ignorant or half-informed, there can be little doubt that, after all reasonable deductions had been made, there was a considerable substratum of truth underlying each of them, which ought not to be ignored, and which cannot, on any satisfactory theory, be reasonably explained away.

In certain cases the subject of Witchcraft had a somewhat wide and vague meaning. It not unfrequently covered the practices of all the so-called "occult sciences," just as in the "Book of Daniel," "the magicians, the astrologers,[102] the Chaldeans, and the soothsayers," classed together, were together consulted; so it seems to have been in ancient times in places, and amongst people who practised Witchcraft and Necromancy. Invocations of the dead; the use of charms; watching the flight of birds; "reading the stars;" interpreting dreams, and foretelling future events by the aid of evil spirits, were all practices which, in a somewhat vague but popular phraseology, came under the class of sins of the nature of those directly condemned in Holy Scripture.

One or two further remarks may be added upon the general subject. From the amount of evidence which exists, it is impossible to deny that such a power as Witchcraft has been frequently exercised, and consequently may be put into practice again. It is idle to assert that it is a mere moral epidemic, at least for those who take up a Christian standing-point, and do not deny both the Inspiration of Holy Scripture and the Indefectibility and Infallibility of the Church Universal, as well as, and in addition to, well-authenticated historical facts. The practice of Witchcraft has, of course, been more ordinary in countries which are not Catholic;[103] for example in Scotland, Sweden, Germany, and North America; though, of necessity it prevailed very largely with many in England from the period of the Reformation until the beginning of the eighteenth century, as has been already sufficiently shown. Thus, many who refused to hear, and abide by, the message and guidance of Holy Church; who rejected the miracles and mercies of the Almighty, were sometimes too ready to accept as true, and participate in the weird works of necromancers, and sometimes to be duped by the Prince of darkness, through the active instrumentality of his human agents.[104]

Without, at this point of our general argument, trenching unduly on a detail of the subject in its most recent developments, which is carefully considered at some length in later chapters, it may be well to give a single example perfectly accurate and most satisfactorily authenticated.

Here it is:--The friend of a distinguished Scotch peer wished for certain important and valuable information, which in any ordinary, usual, and common modes he was, it appears, altogether unable to obtain. He therefore thought it right and proper to consult a "spiritual medium," and so held a consultation, made an inquiry, and obtained a response. The following is the authenticated record of this action:--

"A friend of mine was very anxious to find the Will of his grandmother, who had been dead forty years, but could not even find the certificate of her death. I went with him to the Marshall's[105] and we had a séance; we sat at a table, and soon the raps came; my friend then asked his questions mentally; he went over the alphabet himself, or sometimes I did so, not knowing the question. We were told [that] the Will had been drawn by a man named William Walter, who lived in Whitechapel; the name of the street and the number of the house were given. We went to Whitechapel, found the man, and subsequently, through his aid obtained a copy of the draft; he was quite unknown to us, and had not always lived in that locality, for he had once seen better days. The medium could not possibly have known anything about the matter, and even if she had, her knowledge would have been of no avail, as all the questions were mental ones."[106]

The specific features of this account are so obvious and well defined, and the account itself is so remarkably clear in all its various parts, that nothing more needs to be added, than the simple remark, that if the old and false principles of Witchcraft and Necromancy are not here again present and energizing (only appropriately and properly draped in a nineteenth-century garment, and carefully adapted to the tastes of refined and educated people), it would be well to find some other principle by which this, and thousands of other similar cases may be rationally and openly explained and accounted for, and this from the standing-point of a firm belief in Historical Christianity.

From the point of view from which this book is written, it may be reasonably maintained that recent "spiritual manifestations," as they are termed, are very possibly only another mode by which in an age of superior civilization the Prince of the Power of the air, adapting his delusions to the less coarse tastes and sentiments of his anxious clients and inquiring followers, produces "lying wonders," false miracles, and delusive appearances; or unlawfully reveals secrets, affords information in the present, and gives, or pretends to give, revelations as to the future.

Many persons in the present day are ready enough (as well they may be,) to become eloquent on the trivial absurdities and vulgar (too often dark and obscene) contrivances of the Witchcraft of the seventeenth century. Be it so. But perhaps, after all, the system as then worked was both skilfully, intellectually, and well enough adapted for the purposes and aims which its author had in hand. If the coarse-minded and uneducated of those days so readily became its agents and workers, coarseness and ignorance were reasonably and suitably, and perhaps of necessity, used in its operations. Now, however, the persistent Enemy of mankind, "the Old Serpent,"[107] appears to have adopted quite another course of tactics, less coarse it may be, and less revolting (in some particulars) to the sentimental and shallow, but equally efficacious for his diabolical purposes and eventual success. Where Witchcraft was formerly practised by ten persons, its new and more attractive phase, it is to be feared, is now accepted by thousands. All this, and more, may be gathered later on, when the subject of "Modern Spiritualism" is duly considered.

Rev. Frederick George Lee, D.C.L.

CHAPTER V - DREAMS, OMENS, WARNINGS, PRESENTIMENTS, AND SECOND SIGHT

"And how will those modern wits, of which our age is so full, account for this, who allow no God or Providence, no invisible world, no angelic kind and waking spirits, who, by a secret correspondence with our embodied spirits, give merciful hints to us of approaching mischief and impending dangers; and that timely, so as to put the means into our hands to avoid and escape them?" - History and Reality of Apparitions, by Andrew Moreton, Esq., p. 218. London: 1735.

*"The Soul's dark cottage, batter'd and decay'd,
Lets in new light through chinks which Time hath made."*
Edmund Waller.

"All who read this, I exhort in the Name of the Most Sacred Majesty of our Most Blessed King, Jesus Christ, to be extremely suspicious of all such extraordinary appearances, presentiments, trances and predictions; to examine well and minutely everything; not to look upon those books, which even pious souls in such a state have written, unconditionally as a divine revelation; and not to believe their predictions, but to be persuaded, that though some things may be fulfilled, others may not." - J. H. Jung-Stilling, On Forebodings. London: 1834.

The subjects here set forth for consideration (by which no slight progress will be made in exhibiting such facts as serve to unfold and make manifest more plainly the purpose of this treatise), are very wide in their scope. A large volume might with no great difficulty be compiled upon each separate subject; for the examples of remarkable dreams and supernatural omens which are already on record, are exceedingly numerous,[108] while the warnings and presentiments of danger and death, which are still often vouchsafed, have been so notably providential in their purport, that many of the mercifully-bestowed Glimpses of the Supernatural, brought before the Editor's notice, can only be attributed generally to the goodness of Almighty God, and particularly either to the intercession of His Saints, the effectual fervent prayers of those still in the flesh, or the direct intervention of His Holy Angels, the guardians and guides of Christians.

Some dreams, especially those of an ordinary character, appear to consist of the mere revival of old memories and associations regarding persons and events which have long passed out of the mind, and seem to have been forgotten. It is often quite impossible to trace the manner in which, or the method by which, dreams arise; and certainly many of the facts connected with them do not appear referable to any coherent principle with which it may truly be said that man is perfectly acquainted. They are mysterious; they are strange; they are supernatural. At the same time it is impossible not to remember how frequently the sacred and divine writings record examples of dreams, by which the Will of God was directly made known of old to some of His favoured servants. The case of King Abimelech, warned against taking Abraham's wife (whom he had untruly called his sister), is an early instance in point.[109] So, too, are the warnings and directions given by Almighty God to Jacob and Laban. The dreams of Joseph likewise illustrate the principle which may be readily discovered and comprehended by the help of Scripture, viz. that some dreams, whatever others may be, are certainly from God, and ought not to be disregarded. For the Almighty expressly pledged Himself to make known His Will to His prophets both by dreams and in visions.[110] And it was by the former that He appeared to Solomon, graciously and mercifully offering him a response to any request he might make. "Ask what I shall give thee." The dreams and visions of Daniel, the Hebrew Prophet, likewise of S. Joseph of Nazareth, both with regard to the Blessed Virgin and the malice of Herod; the warning dreams of the Three Eastern Kings; that of Pilate's wife, and others equally remarkable, are familiar to us all. So that, whatever theories may be excogitated by some, it is impossible for Christians to hold any novel and fantastic ideas, which would sweep away those links which in dreams and visions may still bind together the natural with the supernatural, and by which, from time to time, in the present day, warnings and necessary lessons may sometimes be mercifully vouchsafed and imparted.

A considerable difficulty has been experienced by the Editor, not only in testing recent examples which have been brought before him, but in inducing those who supplied him with them, to allow the use and support of their names.[111] In the cases to be given, he has spared no reasonable trouble in their investigation; and, where they are not matters of history (received and recognized by those who are satisfied with an application of the ordinary laws of evidence), the reader may rely on the fact that they have not been embodied in this volume without the most anxious inquiry and careful sifting of their truth and accuracy.

Thus much as to his purport and intent. Now let the examples of remarkable dreams be put on record; after a brief reference has been made to the belief and expressions of opinion of certain early Christian writers, obviously formulated upon the basis of scriptural assertions and sacred examples of old.

When the body sleeps, as Tertullian remarks,[112] it takes its own peculiar refreshment, but that refreshment not being adapted to the soul, which does not rest, she during the inactivity of the bodily members employs her own. Then in his treatise "On the Soul,"[113] he proceeds to distinguish between the hallucination of dreaming and insanity. Dreaming is agreeable to the course and order of Nature, he maintains; but he rejects the doctrine of Epicurus, in which dreams are disparaged as idle and fortuitous. He further expresses his conviction that future honours, dignities, medical remedies, thefts and treasure have been revealed by dreams--testimonies to which are both numerous and strong. Many dreams, specially those which are vain, frivolous, impure, and turbulent, may be attributed to demons. Others, again, proceed from God or holy angels, as one portion of prophecy.

Lactantius, in a short passage of his well-known "Tract,"[114] expresses his conviction of divine agency in dreams. He maintains that the undoubted testimony of History presents mankind with several most remarkable verifications of dreams; and he repeats what Tertullian had already maintained, viz. that part of the economy of prophecy depends upon them. He holds that Virgil's evidence may be admitted, that dreams are neither always true nor always false.

Again, S. Cyprian states that he was divinely instructed in a dream to mix a little water with the wine for the Holy Eucharist.[115] On the general subject, S. Basil warns those who may be ready to attribute too great importance to dreams, to rest contented with the written revelation of Almighty God in Holy Scripture.[116] S. Bernard, the last of the Fathers, treats of dreams at great length in his remarkable sermon "On Sleep," which is full of sage advice of the same nature as that set forth by S. Basil; and so does S. Thomas Aquinas, who discusses the subject with singular breadth, fulness, and system, arriving at the conclusion that it is unreasonable to deny anything--the truth of which is affirmed by general experience; and he adds that general experience affirms that dreams very frequently give indications of coming events; and therefore, concludes that it is lawful to interpret and endeavour to comprehend them.[117] But at this point, he goes on to maintain that only those dreams which are suggested by angels may be investigated and interpreted, those suggested by demons and evil spirits being left alone. But unfortunately he provides no criterion by which the one class may be safely and truly distinguished from the other; nor is it easy to supply the deficiency.

From another point of view, a thoughtful modern writer[118] has remarked that "dreams are uniformly the resuscitation or re-embodiment of thoughts which have formerly, in some shape or other, occupied the mind. They are old ideas revived, either in an entire state, or heterogeneously mingled together. I doubt if it be possible," he continues, "for a person to have in a dream, any idea whose elements did not, in some form, strike him at a previous period. If these break loose from their connecting chain, and become jumbled together incoherently, as is often the case, they give rise to absurd combinations; but the elements still subsist, and only manifest themselves in a new and unconnected shape."

This, and such as this, may be quite true; but yet whatever theories the scientific may propound which seem to oppose the facts of man's experience, will not in the long run command that adhesion which for awhile they may possibly obtain. And now for examples:

The Dream of the so-called "Swaffham Tinker"[119] is singular, and may well be here reproduced, because it represents an example of the practical results of dreaming, which is quite worthy of consideration:--

"This Tinker, a hard-working, industrious man, one night dreamed that if he took a journey to London, and placed himself at a certain spot on London Bridge, he should meet one who would tell him something of great importance to his future prospects. The Tinker, on whom the dream made a deep impression, related it fully to his wife in the morning; who, however, half-laughed at him and half-scolded him for his folly in heeding such idle fancies. Next night he is said to have re-dreamed the dream; and again on the third night, when the impression was so powerful on his mind that he determined, in spite of the remonstrances of his wife and the ridicule of his neighbours, to go to London and see the upshot of it. Accordingly he set off for the metropolis on foot, reached it late on the third day (the distance was ninety miles), and, after the refreshment of a night's rest, took his station next day on a part of the Bridge answering to the description in his dream. There he stood all day, and all the next, and all the third, without any communication as to the purpose of his journey; so that towards night, on the third day, he began to lose patience and confidence in his dream, inwardly cursed his folly in disregarding his wife's counsel, and resolved next day to make the best of his way home. He still kept his station, however, till late in the evening, when, just as he was about to depart, a stranger who had noticed him standing stedfastly and with anxious look on the same spot for some days, accosted him, and asked him what he waited there for. After a little hesitation, the Tinker told his errand, though without acquainting him with the name of the place whence he came. The stranger enjoyed a smile at the rustic's simplicity, and advised him to go home and for the future to pay no attention to dreams. 'I myself,' said he, 'if I were disposed to put faith in such things, might now go a hundred miles into the country upon a similar errand. I dreamed three nights this week that if I went to a place called Swaffham in Norfolk, and dug under an apple-tree in a certain garden on the north side of the town I should find a box of money; but I have something else to do than run after such idle fancies! No, no, my friend; go home, and work well at your calling, and you will find there the riches you are seeking here.' The astonished Tinker did not doubt that this was the communication he had been sent to London to receive, but he merely thanked the stranger for his advice, and went away avowing his intention to follow it. Next day he set out for home, and on his arrival there said little to his wife touching his journey; but next morning he rose betimes and began to dig on the spot he supposed to be pointed out by the stranger. When he had got a few feet down, the spade struck upon something hard, which turned out to be an iron chest. This he quickly carried to his house, and when he had with difficulty wrenched open the lid, found it, to his great joy, to be full of money. After securing his treasure, he observed on the lid of the box an inscription, which, unlearned as he was, he could not decipher. But by a stratagem he got the description read without any suspicion on the part of his neighbours by some of the Grammar School lads, and found it to be--

'Where this stood
Is another twice as good.'

And in truth on digging again the lucky Tinker disinterred, below the place where the first chest had lain, a second twice as large, also full of gold and silver coin. It is stated that, become thus a wealthy man, the Tinker showed his thankfulness to Providence by building a new chancel to the church, the old one being out of repair. And whatever fiction the marvellous taste of those ages may have mixed up with the tale, certain it is that there is shown to this day a monument in Swaffham Church, having an effigy in marble, said to be that of the Tinker with his Dog at his side and his tools and implements of trade lying about him."

Among the various histories of singular dreams and corresponding events, the following, which occurred in the early part of the eighteenth century, seems to merit being here placed on record. Its authenticity will appear from the relation; and it may surely be maintained that a more extraordinary concurrence of fortuitous and accidental circumstances can scarcely be produced or paralleled:--

"One Adam Rogers, a creditable and decent man of good sense and repute, who kept an inn at Portlaw, a small hamlet nine or ten miles from Waterford, in Ireland, dreamed one night that he saw two men at a particular green spot on the adjoining mountain; one of them a small, sickly-looking man, the other remarkably strong and large. He then saw the latter man murder the other, upon which he awoke in great agitation.

"The circumstances of the dream were so distinct and forcible that he continued much affected by them. He related them to his wife, and also to several neighbours next morning.

"In some time he went out coursing with greyhounds, accompanied amongst others by one Mr. Browne, the Roman Catholic priest of the parish. He soon stopped at the above-mentioned particular green spot on the mountain, and calling Mr. Browne, pointed it out to him, and told him what had happened there. During the remainder of the day he thought little more about it.

"Next morning he was extremely startled at seeing two strangers enter his house at about eleven o'clock in the forenoon. He immediately went into an inner room, and desired his wife to take particular notice, for they were precisely the two men he had seen in his dream.

"After the strangers had taken some refreshment, and were about to depart in order to prosecute their journey, Rogers earnestly entreated the little man at once to quit his fellow-traveller. He assured him that if he would remain with him that day he would accompany him to Carrick the next morning--that being the town to which the travellers were proceeding. He was unwilling and ashamed to tell the cause of his being so solicitous to separate him from his companion. But as he observed that Hickey (which was the name of the little man) seemed to be quiet and gentle in his deportment, and had money about him, and that the other had a ferocious, bad countenance, the dream still recurred to him. He dreaded that something fatal would happen, and wished at all events to keep them asunder.

"However, the humane precautions of Rogers proved ineffectual, for Caulfield (such was the other's name) prevailed upon Hickey to continue with him on their way to Carrick, declaring that as they had long travelled together, they should not part, but remain together until he should see Hickey safely arrived at the habitation of his friends. The wife of Rogers was much dissatisfied when she heard they were gone, and blamed her husband exceedingly for not being absolutely peremptory in detaining Hickey.

"About an hour after they left Portlaw, in a lonely part of the mountain, just near the place observed by Rogers in his dream, Caulfield took the opportunity of murdering his companion. It appeared afterwards from his own account of the horrid transaction, that as they were getting over a ditch he struck Hickey on the back part of the head with a stone, and when he fell down into the trench in consequence of the blow, Caulfield gave him several stabs with a knife, and cut his throat so deeply that the head was observed to be almost severed from his body. He then rifled Hickey's pockets of all the money in them, took part of his clothes and everything else of value about him, and afterwards proceeded on his way to Carrick. He had not been long gone when the body, still warm, was discovered by some labourers who were returning to their work from dinner.

"The report of the murder soon reached Portlaw. Rogers and his wife went to the place and instantly knew the body of him whom they had in vain endeavoured to dissuade from going on with his treacherous companion. They at once spoke out their suspicions that the murder was perpetrated by the fellow-traveller of the deceased. An immediate search was made, and Caulfield was apprehended at Waterford the second day after.

"He was brought to trial at the ensuing assizes and convicted of the fact. It appeared amongst other circumstances that when he went to Carrick he hired a horse and a boy to conduct him--not by the usual road, but by that which runs on the north side of the river Suir--to Waterford, intending to take his passage in the first ship from thence to Newfoundland. The boy took notice of some blood on his shirt, and Caulfield gave him a half-crown to promise not to speak of it.

"Rogers proved not only that Hickey was last seen in company with Caulfield, but that a pair of new shoes which Hickey wore had been found on the feet of Caulfield when he was apprehended; and that a pair of old shoes which he had on at Rogers's house were upon Hickey's feet when the body was found. He described with great exactness every article of their clothes. Caulfield on the cross-examination, shrewdly asked him from the dock whether it was not very extraordinary that he, who kept a public-house, should take such particular notice of the dress of a stranger accidentally calling there? Rogers in his answer said he had a very particular reason, but he was ashamed to mention it. The court and the prisoner insisted on his declaring it. He gave a circumstantial narrative of his dream, called upon Mr. Browne, the priest, then in court, to corroborate his testimony, and said that his wife had severely reproached him for permitting Hickey to leave their house, when he knew that in the short footway to Carrick they must necessarily pass by the green spot in the mountain which had appeared in his dream.

"A number of witnesses came forward, and the proofs were so strong that the jury without hesitation found the prisoner guilty.

"It was remarked as a singularity that he happened to be tried and sentenced by his namesake, Sir George Caulfeild, at that time Lord Chief Justice of the King's Bench, which office he resigned in the summer of the year 1760.

"After sentence Caulfield confessed the fact. It came that Hickey had been in the West Indies two and twenty years, but falling into a bad state of health, he was returning to his native country (Ireland) bringing with him some money his industry had acquired. The vessel on board which he took his passage was, by stress of weather, driven into Minehead. He there met with Frederick Caulfield, an Irish sailor, who was poor and much distressed for clothes and common necessaries. Hickey compassionating his poverty, and finding he was his countryman, relieved his wants, and an intimacy commenced between them. They agreed to go to Ireland together; and it was remarked on their passage that Caulfield spoke contemptuously, and often said it was a pity that such a puny fellow as Hickey should have money, and he himself without a shilling. They landed at Waterford, at which place they stayed some days, Caulfield being all the time supported by Hickey, who bought some clothes for him. The assizes being held in the town during that time, it was afterwards recollected that they were both at the Court-house, and attended the whole of a trial of a shoemaker who was convicted of the murder of his wife. But this made no impression on the hardened mind of Caulfield, for the very next day he perpetrated the same crime on the road between Waterford and Carrick-on-Suir, near which town Hickey's relations lived.

"He walked to the gallows with firm step and undaunted countenance. He spoke to the multitude who surrounded him, and in the course of his address mentioned that he had been bred at a charter-school, from which he was taken as an apprenticed servant by William Izod, Esq., of the

Rev. Frederick George Lee, D.C.L.

county of Kilkenny. From this position he ran away on being corrected for some faults, and had been absent from Ireland six years. He confessed also that he had several times intended to murder Hickey on the road from Waterford to Portlaw, which, though in general not a road much frequented, yet people at that time continually coming in sight, prevented him.

"Being frustrated in all his schemes, the sudden and total disappointment threw him probably into an indifference for life. Some tempers are so stubborn and rugged that nothing can affect them, but immediate sensation. If to this be united the darkest ignorance, death to such characters will hardly seem terrible, because they can form no conception of what it is, and still less of the consequences that may follow."

The record of the following dream is certainly curious and interesting, and is perfectly well authenticated, coming as it does from the pen of the gentleman's son more immediately concerned, who testified as to its literal fulfilment:--

"In the year 1768 my father, Matthew Talbot, Esq., of Castle Talbot, in the county of Wexford, was much surprised at the recurrence of a dream three several times during the same night, which caused him to repeat the whole circumstance to his lady the following morning. He dreamed that he had arisen as usual and descended to his library, the morning being hazy. He then seated himself at his secrétaire to write; when, happening to look up a long avenue of trees opposite the window, he perceived a man in a blue jacket mounted on a white horse coming towards the house. My father arose and opened the window. The man advancing, presented him with a roll of papers, and told him they were invoices of a vessel which had been wrecked and had drifted in during the night on his son-in-law's, Lord Mountmorris's, estate close by, and signed 'Bell and Stephenson.' My father's attention was only called to the dream from its frequent recurrence: but, when he found himself seated at his desk on the misty morning, and beheld the identical person whom he had seen in his dream in the blue coat riding on the grey horse, he felt surprised, and opening the window waited the man's approach. He immediately rode up, and drawing from his pocket a packet of papers, gave them to my father, stating they were invoices belonging to an American vessel which had been wrecked, and drifted in upon his lordship's estate; that there was no person on board to lay claim to the wreck, but that the invoices were signed 'Stephenson and Bell.' I assure you that the above is most faithfully given by me as it actually occurred; but it is not more extraordinary than other examples of the prophetic powers of the mind or soul in sleep which I have frequently heard related."[120]

Another remarkable dream, exceedingly well authenticated by an aunt of the Editor of this volume, is now set forth in detail and at some length:--

"On the night of the 11th of May, 1812, Mr. Williams, of Scorrier House, near Redruth, in Cornwall, awoke his wife, and exceedingly agitated, told her that he had dreamed that he was in the lobby of the House of Commons, and saw a man shoot with a pistol a gentleman who had just entered the lobby, who was said to be the Chancellor, to which Mrs. Williams naturally replied that it was only a dream, and recommended him to be composed, and go to sleep as soon as he could.

"He did so, but shortly after again woke her; and said that he had the second time had the same dream; whereupon she observed that he had been so much agitated with his former dream that she supposed it had dwelt on his mind, and begged of him to try to compose himself and go to sleep, which he did. A third time the same vision was repeated, on which, notwithstanding her entreaties that he would be quiet, and endeavour to forget it, he arose, being then between one and two o'clock, and dressed himself.

"At breakfast the dreams were the sole subject of conversation, and in the forenoon Mr. Williams went to Falmouth, where he related the particulars of them to all his acquaintance that he met.

"On the following day, Mr. Tucker, of Trematon Castle, accompanied by his wife, a daughter of Mr. Williams, went to Scorrier House about dusk. Immediately after the first salutation, on their entering the parlour, where were Mr., Mrs., and Miss Williams, Mr. Williams began to relate to Mr. Tucker the circumstances of his dream; and Mrs. Williams observed to her daughter, Mrs. Tucker, laughingly, that her father could not even suffer Mr. Tucker to be seated before he told him of his nocturnal visitation; on the statement of which Mr. Tucker observed that it would do very well for a dream to have the Chancellor in the lobby of the House of Commons, but that he would not be found there in reality; and Mr. Tucker then asked what sort of man he appeared to be, when Mr. Williams minutely described him; to which Mr. Tucker replied: 'Your description is not at all that of the Chancellor, but is certainly very exactly that of Mr. Perceval, the Chancellor of the Exchequer, and although he has been to me the greatest enemy I ever met with through life, for a supposed cause which had no foundation in truth (or words to that effect), I should be exceedingly sorry, indeed, to hear of his being assassinated, or of any injury of the kind happening to him.'

"Mr. Tucker then inquired of Mr. Williams if he had ever seen Mr. Perceval, and was told that he never had seen him, nor had ever even written to him, either on public or private business; in short, that he never had had anything to do with him, nor had he ever been in the lobby of the House of Commons in his life.

"At this moment, whilst Mr. Williams and Mr. Tucker were still standing, they heard a horse gallop to the door of the House, and immediately after, Mr. Michael Williams of Trevince (son of Mr. Williams of Scorrier), entered the room and said that he had galloped out from Truro (from which Scorrier House is distant seven miles), having seen a gentleman there, who had come by that evening's mail from London, who said that he was in the lobby of the House of Commons, on the evening of the 11th, when a man called Bellingham had shot Mr. Perceval, and that, as it might occasion some great ministerial changes, and might affect Mr. Tucker's political friends, he had come out as fast as he could to make him acquainted with it, having heard at Truro that he had passed through that place in the afternoon on his way to Scorrier.

"After the astonishment which this intelligence had created had a little subsided, Mr. Williams described most particularly the appearance and dress of the man whom he had seen in his dream fire the pistol, as he had before done of Mr. Perceval.

"About six weeks after, Mr. Williams, having business in town, went accompanied by a friend to the House of Commons, where (as has been already observed) he had never before been. Immediately that he came to the steps at the entrance of the lobby, he said: 'This place is as distinctly within my recollection in my dream, as any room in my house,' and he made the same observation when he entered the lobby.

"He then pointed out the exact spot where Bellingham stood when he fired, and where Mr. Perceval had reached when he was struck by the ball, and where and how he fell. The dress, both of Mr. Perceval and Bellingham, agreed with the descriptions given by Mr. Williams, even to the most minute particular."[121]

The number of records in which it is believed that dreams have been the means by which murder has been discovered are so considerable; and some are so well authenticated, that it is impossible, as it certainly would be presumptuous, to endeavour to set them aside. The murder of Maria Marten of Polstead in Suffolk, by William Corder, a farmer, in May of the year 1827, is a remarkable example:--

This unfortunate woman was induced to leave her home, and having accompanied the man who, under the promise of marriage, had betrayed her, to a certain barn, was there cruelly murdered and buried under the floor. For nearly twelve months the murder was undiscovered; for Corder, who remained away, but still communicated with her parents, maintained that she had married him; that circumstances prevented his bringing her back to his father's home: but that in due course they would both come, though it was implied that they were both on the Continent.

The mother of the murdered woman, however, about ten months after her daughter's death, dreamed that her daughter had been murdered, and buried under the floor of the barn. So strong and deep an impression did this make both on her relations and the people of the village, that the girl's father and others on April 19, 1828, took up the floor of the barn, where they discovered the body of the murdered woman in a sack; and not so much decayed but that obvious marks of violence were perceptible. The body was successfully identified by the want of two teeth--one on the left side of the upper jaw, and the other on the right side of the lower. In the meantime Corder had married, and had gone to live in Essex, where he was apprehended, tried, and condemned on the strongest circumstantial evidence. He made a full confession of the murder when in prison, under sentence of death, and was executed in August, 1828.

The following sets forth how an impressive, vivid, and twice-repeated dream induced a sailor to go to the place dreamed of, and rescue three suffering fellow-creatures from a horrible death. It was related to a Cornish friend, as a matter of fact, by a native of the island of Alderney, and is quite worthy of being here recorded:--

"Some few years before the erection of those well-known lighthouses called the Caskets, near that island, an islander dreamed that a ship had been wrecked near those rocks, and that some part of the crew had saved themselves upon them. This dream he related on the quay; but the sailors (although the most superstitious people in the world) treated it as an idle fancy. Yet the next night produced the same dream, and the man would no longer be laughed out of it; so he prevailed upon a companion the next morning to take a boat and go with him to the rock, where they found three poor wretches half-starved with cold and hunger, and brought them on shore. This circumstance, and the supposed loss of the 'Victory' on this rock, the islanders give as a reason for erecting three lighthouses there."

Still more remarkable perhaps is the following, which, telling its own story, and abundantly illustrating the reality of the Supernatural, needs no comment:--

"The Rev. Mr. Perring, Vicar of a parish which is now a component part of London, though, about forty-five years ago it had the appearance of a village at the outskirts, had to encounter the sad affliction of losing his eldest Son at an age when parents are encouraged to believe their

Rev. Frederick George Lee, D.C.L.

children are to become their survivors; the youth dying in his seventeenth year. He was buried in the vaults of the church.

"Two nights subsequently to that interment, the father dreamed[122] that he saw his Son habited in a shroud spotted with blood, the expression of his countenance being that of a person enduring some paroxysm of acute pain: 'Father, father! come and defend me!' were the words he distinctly heard, as he gazed on this awe-inspiring apparition; 'they will not let me rest quiet in my coffin.'

"The venerable man awoke with terror and trembling; but after a brief interval of painful reflection concluded himself to be labouring under the influence of his sad day-thoughts, and the depression of past sufferings; and with these rational assurances commended himself to the All-Merciful, and slumbered again and slept.

"He saw his Son again beseeching him to protect his remains from outrage, 'For,' said the apparently surviving dead one, 'they are mangling my body at this moment.' The unhappy Father rose at once, being now unable to banish the fearful image from his mind, and determined when day should dawn to satisfy himself of the delusiveness or verity of the revelation conveyed through this seeming voice from the grave.

"At an early hour, accordingly, he repaired to the Clerk's house, where the keys of the church and of the vaults were kept. The Clerk after considerable delay, came down-stairs, saying it was very unfortunate he should want them just on that very day, as his son over the way had taken them to the smith's for repair,--one of the largest of the bunch of keys having been broken off short in the main door of the vault, so as to render it impracticable for anybody to enter till the lock had been picked and taken off.

"Impelled by the worst misgivings, the Vicar loudly insisted on the Clerk's accompanying him to the blacksmith's--not for a key but for a crowbar, it being his resolute determination to enter the vault and see his Son's coffin without a moment's delay.

"The recollections of the dream were now becoming more and more vivid, and the scrutiny about to be made assumed a solemnity mingled with awe, which the agitation of the father rendered terrible to the agents in this forcible interruption into the resting-place of the dead. But the hinges were speedily wrenched asunder--the bar and bolts were beaten in and bent beneath the heavy hammer of the smith,--and at length with tottering and outstretched hands, the maddened parent stumbled and fell: his son's coffin had been lifted from the recess at the vault's side and deposited on the brick floor; the lid, released from every screw, lay loose at top, and the body, enveloped in its shroud, on which were several dark spots below the chin, lay exposed to view; the head had been raised, the broad riband had been removed from under the jaw, which now hung down with the most ghastly horror of expression, as if to tell with more terrific certainty the truth of the preceding night's vision. Every tooth in the head had been drawn.

"The young man had when living a beautiful set of sound teeth. The Clerk's Son, who was a barber, cupper, and dentist, had possessed himself of the keys, and eventually of the teeth, for the purpose of profitable employment of so excellent a set in his line of business. The feelings of the Rev. Mr. Perring can be easily conceived. The event affected his mind through the remaining term of his existence; but what became of the delinquent whose sacrilegious hand had thus rifled the tomb was never afterwards correctly ascertained. He decamped the same day, and was supposed to have enlisted as a soldier. The Clerk was ignominiously displaced, and did not long survive the transaction. Some years afterwards, his house was pulled down to afford room for extensive improvements and new buildings in the village.

"As regards the occurrence itself, few persons were apprised of it; as the Vicar--shunning public talk and excitement on the subject of any member of his family--exerted himself in concealing the circumstances as much as possible. The above facts, however, may be strictly relied on as accurate."

A somewhat similar dream is recorded in the following statement, copied from the public prints, the fact of which has been authenticated by a correspondent in Scotland, who furnished the Editor with it. The paragraph, now to be quoted, appeared some years ago in the "Scotsman" newspaper, and was quoted in the "Times" of Tuesday, April 25, 1865:--

"The legal proceedings which lately took place in the Sheriff Court of Clackmannanshire, with regard to the violation of a grave in the churchyard at Alloa, and the unwarrantable exhumation of the body of James Quin, had their origin, it is stated, in a remarkable dream of the mother of the deceased. Young Quin died in September, 1863, and was buried in a lair in the churchyard, which was purchased by his father from William Donaldson, the Kirk Treasurer, it being agreed that the price was to be paid by instalments. About six months afterwards, Robert Blair, the sexton or grave-digger, took upon himself (without the authority, it would appear, of Donaldson) to sell the same lair to another person, and to inter therein a relative of the new purchaser, without, however, at the time exhuming the body of Quin, the former tenant. Some considerable time after this the mother of Quin being desirous of erecting a head-stone on the grave of her son, made some inquiries with that view, in the course of which she heard something of another person having been buried in his grave, this having, as she stated, been 'cast up' by Blair's nephew to a younger son of hers on their way from Sunday-school. But the grave-digger denied the truth of this story, and managed to pacify her. Feeling, however, that he had got into a scrape by the lair having been resold, he, some weeks after Mrs. Quin had interrogated him on the subject, dug up the body of her son during the night of Thursday, the 23rd of March last, and reinterred it in the other ground. Now, on that very Thursday night, as sworn to by Mrs. Quin, at the trial, she had this remarkable dream:--

"She dreamt that her boy stood in his nightgown, at her bedside, and said to her, 'Oh, mother, put me back to my own bed.' She then awoke her husband, and forgetting in her half-dreaming state that her son was dead, said to him, 'Jemmie is out of his bed; put him back into it;' after which she fell asleep, and again had the same dream.

"A third time, during the same night, she dreamt that her son was standing beside her bed; but on this occasion remembering that he was dead, the figure of the grave-digger was mixed up with that of the boy, and he appeared to be shoving his spade into the body. Awakening in great trepidation, and feeling certain that her boy had been taken out of his grave, she went to the grave-digger and vehemently accused him of having dug up the body, which, after prevarication, he at last admitted. Hence arose the action of damages against Donaldson, the Kirk Treasurer, and Blair, the grave-digger, which being restricted to twelve pounds was brought in the Small Debt Court. The Sheriff, after a long proof, assoilzied Donaldson, and found Blair liable in damages, which, the parties not having settled the same extrajudicially, have since been assessed at five pounds."

Another dream, equally remarkable, by which a warning was given, and in a measure attended to by the dreamer, now follows; although not so weirdly tragic as that relating to the Perring Family, yet it efficiently serves to shadow forth the proximity of the spiritual world; and, it may be, in this example, the direct intervention of a guardian-angel:--

"Some years ago a clergyman named W---- was visiting an old college friend, Canon Hutchinson of Blurton Vicarage, near Trentham, and being a good pedestrian, proposed to accomplish his journey home again from Trentham to Birmingham, which place he desired to reach by ten o'clock one morning, on foot. In order to do this he intended to leave Blurton at four o'clock a.m. on a certain day; and so retired to rest the previous evening at an unusually early hour. During the night he had a vivid and remarkable dream, which deeply impressed him. He dreamt that whilst he was on his walking journey between Tamworth and Sutton, upon a very lonely road enclosed by tall hedges, he heard a rough voice cry out, 'Ah, Jack, are you there?' and looking round saw two exceedingly ill-looking men jumping down from an elevated part of the bank under the hedge, and alighting close to him on the path below. Their countenances and suspicious bearing seemed to bespeak their evil intentions. Presently one of them all of a sudden presented a pistol at him. The clergyman imagined that he had only a moment or two in which to commend his soul to God, which he did with earnestness, when the pistol was fired and his life thus taken away. Here the dream ended and he awoke. It left an uneasy impression on his mind, but being naturally of an undaunted spirit, and a firm believer in the protection of Almighty God, he did not hesitate to leave his friend's house at the early period determined on. After walking for about an hour and a half, and when a few miles from Sutton Coldfield, where all of a sudden, as regards locality, he realized the minutest details of the dream, two men coming through the hedge suddenly overtook him. One addressed the other in the words already set forth. They were in every particular, even to features, dress, and demeanour, identical with those whom he had seen in the dream. They accompanied him, keeping close to his side, and watched him with very mysterious looks. He was deeply startled and alarmed, but lifted up his heart to God for guidance, direction, and protection. Soon they all reached a broad and dreary common, upon the extreme distant edge of which stood a small inn, whither he resolved to go for refreshment in the hope of shaking off his companions. Here for awhile they separated; but, on entering the house and asking to be supplied with tea, he found that the two men had followed him, and were asking for refreshments likewise. After waiting for some time, he determined on leaving the inn by a path at its back entrance, which, from knowing something of the locality, he believed would take him by a nearer way to Sutton Coldfield. This turned out to be the case; for by his action he successfully avoided the two tramps, who were afterwards taken up and imprisoned for some marked offence against the laws of the land."[123]

A warning of a very similar character may now be narrated, in which the curious point seems to be that it was given so many years before it was needed, though its efficiency was fully made manifest when the actual danger threatened:--

"The Housekeeper of a county family in Oxfordshire dreamt one night that she had been left alone in the house upon a Sunday evening, and that hearing a knock at the door of the chief entrance, she went to it, and there found an ill-looking tramp armed with a bludgeon, who insisted on forcing himself into the house. She thought that she struggled for some time to prevent him so doing, but quite ineffectually; and that being struck down by him and rendered insensible, he thereupon gained ingress to the mansion. On this she awoke.

"She at once mentioned her dream to some of her fellow-servants, and also, a few days later, to the Master of the House. The latter, smiling, pooh-poohed it; but remarked that 'all the greater care should be taken by the servants to see that the fastenings were secure.'

"As nothing happened for a considerable period, the circumstance of the dream was soon forgotten; and, as she herself asserts, had altogether passed away from her mind. However, many years afterwards, this same Housekeeper was left with two other servants to take charge of an isolated mansion at Kensington (subsequently the town residence of the family), when, on a certain Sunday evening, her fellow-servants having gone out and left her alone, she was suddenly startled by a loud knock at the front door.

"All of a sudden the remembrance of her former dream returned to her with singular vividness and remarkable force, and she felt her lonely isolation greatly. Accordingly, having at once lighted a lamp on the hall table--during which act the loud knock was repeated with vigour--she took the precaution to go up to a landing on the stair, throw up the window, and there, to her intense terror, she saw in the flesh the very man whom years previously she had seen in her dream, armed with a bludgeon and demanding an entrance. With great presence of mind she went down to the chief entrance, made that and other doors and windows more secure, and then rang the various bells of the house violently, and placed lights in the upper rooms. It was concluded that by these acts the intruder was scared away. It turned out afterwards that the lodge-keeper, having left two children to guard the entrance, they had been terrified into admitting the tramp into the garden; and that the latter had fastened them into the lodge, where they were found in a considerable state of alarm by the two servants on their return home."[124]

Another example of a warning attended to, which had been given in a dream, and acted upon immediately afterwards, comes to the Editor on conclusive evidence of its undoubted truth and authenticity:

A Scotch lady, a relation of the late J. R. Hope Scott, Esq., of Abbotsford, dreamt that her nephew, a promising young student of the University of Edinburgh, had been drowned with two companions with whom he had made an engagement to take an excursion by boat on the Frith of Forth. So much impressed was she by this dream, that she rose two hours earlier than usual in the morning, and sent off her man-servant at once to prevail upon her nephew to give up his engagement. On being pressed he did so. His companions (who had also been warned not to go,) went without him, and alone, that is, without an experienced sailor. The boat was capsized and they were both drowned.

In the case which is now to follow, the warning given, not having been acted upon at once, came too late. It was narrated to the Editor, vivâ voce, in 1866, by the late Dr. J. M. Neale:--

"In the autumn of the year 1845, one of the maid-servants of the then rector of Shepperton, a village on the Thames, near Chertsey, dreamed that her brother, a respectable and steady youth belonging to that place, was drowned. The dream was singularly vivid. In it she further imagined that she actually went to search for her brother's body, and that, after seeking for some time, she found it at a certain part of the river, which she knew well, near the brink, and in a particular position. This dream took place on a Saturday night. When she awoke on the Sunday morning, she at once acquainted her fellow-servant (who saw how deep an impression the dream had evidently made), and remarked that she ought at once to obtain her master's leave to go home on the morrow, and warn her brother, who was unable to swim, not to go out on to the river. The leave was given, and her home was soon reached, but alas! the warning had come too late. Her brother had gone rowing on the Sunday evening, the boat was accidentally upset, and he was drowned. The body was not recovered for some time; nor was it found near the spot where the accident had happened. But it was found by the poor youth's sister, lower down the river, and exactly in the same place and position as had been so forcibly and clearly prefigured in her impressive dream."

The following example of a dream which occurred about twenty years ago, by which the fact of a murder was made known, being likewise well authenticated and of considerable interest, is now set forth:--

"On Saturday, the 30th of July, 1853, the dead body of a young woman was discovered in a field at Littleport, in the isle of Ely. The body has not yet been identified, and there can be little doubt that the young woman was murdered. At the adjourned inquest, held on the 29th August before Mr. William Marshall, one of the coroners for the Isle, the following extraordinary evidence was given:--

"James Jessop, an elderly, respectable-looking labourer, with a face of the most perfect stolidity, and who possessed a most curiously-shaped skull, broad and flat on the top, and projecting greatly on each side over the ears, deposed--'I live about a furlong and a half from where the body was found. I have seen the body of the deceased. I have never seen her before her death.

On the night of Friday, the 29th of July, I dreamt three successive times that I heard the cry of murder issuing from near the bottom of a close called Little Ditchment Close (the place where the body was found). The first time I dreamt I heard the cry it awoke me. I fell asleep again and dreamt the same thing. I then awoke again and told my wife I could not rest, but I dreamt it again after that. I got up between four and five o'clock, but I did not go down to the close, the wheat and barley in which has been since cut.

"'I dreamt once about twenty years ago that I saw a woman hanging in a barn, and on passing the next morning the barn which had appeared to me in my dream, I entered and did find a woman there hanging, and cut her down in time to save her life. I never told my wife that I heard cries of "murder," but I have mentioned it to several persons since. I saw the body on the Saturday it was found. I did not mention my dream to any one till a day or two after that. I saw the field distinctly in my dream and the trees therein, but I saw no person in it. On the night of the murder the wind lay from that spot to my house.'

"Rhoda Jessop, wife of the last witness, stated that her husband related his dreams to her on the evening of the day that the body was found."[125]

Another case, deeply interesting, and certainly more dramatic in the nature and importance of the very practical results which followed from the action taken upon it, than even that already recorded of the Perring family (for it greatly benefited the living), is now narrated. The interesting account, which, with the greatest simplicity, and in the actual words of the persons advantaged, records the plain facts, tells its own story with considerable power. Frivolous and pointless as are so many dreams, without intelligible purpose or sequence of action, this is one which it may be reasonably held can only be explained by a firm belief in a superintending Providence, in other words in Almighty God, Who, as an old writer asserts, "sometimes warneth and instructeth in dreams," and Who mercifully uses the ministry both of angels and men for carrying out His Divine purpose:--

"A Gloucestershire gentleman in good circumstances, who for many years had lived a retired life, quite apart from his relations, some of whom in a previous year had been cast in a lawsuit with him for the recovery of certain properties, suddenly died, and, as was supposed, died intestate.

"He had long intended, at the advice of the Rector of the village in which he dwelt, and with whom alone he was on terms of intimacy, to make certain provisions by will on behalf of the relations in question, who had lost much by his successful lawsuit. However, this (as was believed by his family lawyer, residing in an adjacent country town, who proceeded to settle his affairs) had not been done; and the whole of his property consequently seemed likely to go to his heir-at-law, a man of property, almost unknown to him.

"Five months after his death, however, the Rector of the parish in which he had lived, had what he termed 'a waking dream,' in which he imagined that the deceased gentleman came to him in sorrow, and solemnly conjured him to obtain possession of a Will, which had been duly made by him in London a few months before his decease, and which was in the custody of a firm of attorneys there, which Will was so drawn as that the relations in question should greatly benefit by the just and righteous disposition therein of his property. Imagining the dream to be only a dream and nothing more, he took no notice of it, and regarded it as the mere result of his own imagination.

"In about a fortnight, however, the identical dream occurred again--with the simple difference that the deceased gentleman bore an expression of deeper grief, and appeared to urge him, in still stronger terms, to obtain the Will. The Rector was much impressed by this; but on careful reflection upon the following day, appeared indisposed, on such testimony, to interfere with arrangements which were then being made for the settlement of the deceased person's affairs, on the supposition that he had left no Will. And consequently he did nothing.

"A third time, however, about eight days afterwards, he had the same dream, with certain additional details of import and moment. The deceased person, as the Rector imagined, appearing once again, urged him most vehemently and solemnly to do as he wished, and to go and obtain the Will. A conversation took place as it were in the dream, and the clergyman set forth many cogent arguments why he should not be called upon to undertake a work, which might not only be misunderstood, but might render him liable to misrepresentations, if not to trouble and annoyance.

"However, at last he consented, and, in his dream, accompanied the deceased person to a certain lawyer's office at a certain number, on a certain floor in Staple Inn, on the south side of Holborn, where the drawer in a writing-table was opened, and he saw the packet containing the Will sealed in three places, with the deceased person's armorial bearings. The whole room was before him vividly. It was panelled in oak, picked out with white and pale green, and over the mantel-piece hung an engraving of Lord Eldon.

"The Rector awoke, and resolved without delay to do as he was enjoined. Before proceeding, he mentioned the circumstance of the thrice-repeated dream to a clerical friend, who volunteered to accompany him to London on his important errand.

Rev. Frederick George Lee, D.C.L.

"They went together. Neither had ever been to Staple Inn before; nor did they know its exact whereabouts. On inquiry, however, it was soon found. And so was the room and office, with the furniture and print of Lord Eldon, which had been seen beforehand by the Rector in the dream, to his intense awe and wonderment. Even the peculiar handles of the writing-table, which were of brass and old-fashioned, were those which had been clearly apparent. The identical drawer was opened, and the Will, secured in an envelope of stout paper and sealed with three impressions, was found, just as it had been seen in the dream. The lawyer, who at once gave every facility for inquiry, was a junior partner in the firm which had drawn it up, and had only recently come to London, from a cathedral city, where the firm in question had a branch office, on the death of the chief partner. The Will was found to be good and valid, and was in due course proved. Under it the relations, who had so suffered by the loss of their law-suit as to have been almost reduced to penury, obtained their due. The whole of these facts are vouched for by a friend of the Editor of this book."[126]

The following example of presentiment of death is also well authenticated. It occurred on board one of the ships of the Royal Navy at Portsmouth in the year 1850. From the MS. account, furnished by one thoroughly able to give an exact record, the following is taken:--

"The officers being one day at the Mess-table, a young Lieutenant R----suddenly laid down his knife and fork, pushed away his plate, and turned extremely pale. He then rose from the table, covering his face with his hands, and retired from the room. The President of the mess, supposing him to be ill, sent one of the young men to inquire what was the matter. At first Mr. R---- was unwilling to speak; but, on being pressed, he confessed that he had been seized by a sudden and irresistible impression that a brother he had in India was dead. 'He died,' said he, 'on the 12th of August at six o'clock, I am perfectly sure of it.' No argument could overthrow this conviction, which, in due course of post, was verified to the letter. The young man had died at Cawnpore at the precise period mentioned."

Under the heading of "Singular Prognostication," "The Times" of April the 17th, 1865, copies from the "Cornish Telegraph" the narrative of a then recent dream of a young clergyman of the county of Cornwall, which was almost immediately followed by the accidental death of the dreamer:--

"On Wednesday last, the Rev. Stephen Barclay Drury, an unmarried clergyman of twenty-six, who has for about twelve months acted as the curate of Phillack and Gwithian, had a conversation with the brother of the Rector of those parishes,[127] Mr. Charles Hockin, and related a dream, which he described as a very singular one, and as having made a deep impression on him.

"His words were: 'I dreamt I was to be buried, and I followed my coffin into the church, and thence to the tomb. I took no part in the service, and when we came to the tomb, I looked into it, and saw it was very nice. I then asked the undertaker who was to be buried, and he answered, "You." I then said, "I am not to be buried, I am not dead." The undertaker then said, "I must be paid for the coffin," upon which I awoke.'

"On Sunday morning and afternoon Mr. Drury officiated at Gwithian, and after the second service remained with the children to practise singing.

"Returning to his lodgings in Gwithian at half-past four, he waited a little, took with him Thomas à Kempis' 'De Imitatione Christi,' and set out for a walk, accompanied by a Newfoundland dog. He asked for a bit of cord, as he might give the dog a dip, and started in his usually cheerful and happy mood. In an hour and a half the dog returned with the cord around his neck.

"Mr. Drury was never again seen alive. His absence throughout the night occasioned no surprise, as he sometimes went to, and slept at Copperhouse, two miles off.

"On Monday morning a Gwinear miner, in quest of seaweed at low water, near the rocky shore of Godrevy, saw Mr. Drury's body in a pool seventy or eighty yards from the sea.

"An inquest, under the county coroner, Mr. John Roscoria, was held on Tuesday at Gwithian, when these circumstances were elicited, and a verdict was returned of 'Found Drowned.'

"From the facts, however, that Mr. Drury had never shown the least signs of depression, that he started with the expressed intention of giving the dog a dip, and that he was very near-sighted, the general inference is that the unfortunate gentleman slipped on the rocks, was stunned, fell into the water, and so casually and singularly fulfilled his strange dream of a few days previously."

A somewhat similar prognostication was had in the case of Captain Speer, which may properly be put on record, for, as in the case already narrated, it turned out to be a true warning of impending death:

Captain Speer, an officer of the 3rd Surrey Militia, and a magistrate for the county of Surrey,[128] lately met his death under remarkable circumstances. The "Quebec Mercury" says:-- "Captain W. D. Speer passed the last winter among us. During part of it, he had some fine sport on the north shore of the S. Lawrence, in company with Captain Knox and Lieutenant Duthie, of the

10th Royal Artillery. This spring he made a tour through the States and West Indies, with Major Leslie, R.A., returning only for a few days, to set out again on what has, alas! proved to be his last expedition.[129] Strange to say, he stated to several gentlemen, just before setting out, that he had had a dream in which he distinctly saw a coffin with the name of 'W. D. Speer, died June 17th, 1867,' on it; and in writing to a lady three weeks previously,[130] he said in a joke that one reason for addressing her was his own approaching end. The date of his death is not known,[131] but it must have been on the day he named, or very near it. It appears that he was going to his cabin on board the Mississippi steamer, which was at anchor, and somewhere in the neighbourhood of the Indian disturbances; when in the middle of the night he was shot dead by a sentry, who omitted to challenge him."

On this remarkable incident a Letter was written, from which the following extract may fittingly be put on record here:

"It seems the account of the dream was true, as Major Terry told Mr. Kempson, that he had heard the letter read in which he [Captain Speer] related the circumstance. Singular, was it not? I trust it may have taken some little effect on his mind, but I fear he was not one to attach any importance to such a warning. However, I do hope he did, for it is so awful to think of anyone in pure health and spirits being ushered into Eternity without one moment's preparation." From a Letter, dated August 10th, 1867, signed "Anne M. Kempson, Richmond Hill, Surrey, S.W."

Another example of a warning given in a dream (but neglected) may now be put on record:

A few years ago a serious accident occurred in the village of Bulmer, in Yorkshire, to a picnic party going to Castle Howard. The party made the journey in an omnibus, and it seems that the wife of one of the men hesitated to join the others, and tried to persuade her husband not to go, because she asserted that she had dreamt a week before that they were in an omnibus, and were upset on going through a village and greatly injured, the fright awakening her. The man and his wife however did go; but on reaching Bulmer, the woman became greatly excited. Not only, she remarked, was the omnibus that which she had seen in her dream, but the village was the one in which the accident she dreamt of appeared to happen. The words were scarcely uttered when the omnibus was upset and a scene of great confusion resulted. Those on the outside were thrown to the ground with great violence; one man was rendered insensible by the omnibus falling upon him, and several sustained rather serious injuries. The woman to whom the accident was revealed beforehand, was herself badly hurt; but her husband's was the worst case, he sustaining a dislocation of an ankle. Medical aid was quickly procured, the sufferers were relieved, and afterwards conveyed to their homes. Every incident of the accident seems to have been pictured in the premonitory dream.

A remarkable presentiment by means of a dream is related in the second section of the first volume of the "Museum of Wonders," and is to the following effect. Though not new, it is so exceptionally curious as to be quite worthy of reproduction here:--

"A short time before the Princess Natgotsky, of Warsaw, travelled to Paris, she had the following dream:--She dreamed that she found herself in an unknown apartment, when a man who was likewise unknown to her, came to her with a cup, and presented it to her to drink out of. She replied that she was not thirsty, and thanked him for his offer. The unknown individual repeated his request, and added that she ought not to refuse it any longer, for it would be the last she would ever drink in her life. At this she was greatly terrified and awoke.

"In October, 1720, the Princess arrived at Paris, in good health and spirits; and occupied a furnished hotel, where soon after her arrival she was seized with a violent fever. She immediately sent for the King's celebrated physician, the father of Helvetius. The physician came, and the Princess showed striking marks of astonishment. She was asked the reason of it, and gave for answer that the physician perfectly resembled the man whom she had seen at Warsaw in a dream; but added she, 'I shall not die this time, for this is not the same apartment which I saw on that occasion in my dream.'

"The Princess was soon after completely restored, and appeared to have altogether forgotten her dream, when a new incident reminded her of it in a most forcible manner. She was dissatisfied with her lodgings at the hotel, and therefore requested that a dwelling might be prepared for her in a convent at Paris, which was accordingly done. The Princess removed to the convent, but scarcely had she entered the apartment destined for her, than she began to exclaim aloud: 'It is all over with me; I shall not come out of this room again alive, for it is the same that I saw at Warsaw in my dream!' She died in reality not long afterward in the same room, in the beginning of the year 1721, of an ulcer in the throat, occasioned by the drawing of a tooth."

"This dream," observes Jung Stilling, from whose work the account of it is transcribed, "proceeded from a good angel, who wished to attract the attention of the Princess to her approaching end."

A dignitary of the Church of England, of rank and reputation, courteously furnishes the Editor

Rev. Frederick George Lee, D.C.L.

with the following remarkable Dream, which occurred to himself,--alas! so completely fulfilled. Another account of the same, almost identical in terms, was sent to him from another quarter. But he prefers putting on record the former:[132]--

"My brother had left London for the country to preach and speak on behalf of a certain Church Society, to which he was officially attached. He was in his usual health, and I was therefore in no special anxiety about him. One night my wife woke me, finding that I was sobbing in my sleep, and asked me what it was. I said, 'I have been to a strange place in my dream. It was a small village, and I went up to the door of an inn, if so it might be called, though it really was a decent public-house. A stout woman came to the door. I said to her, 'Is my brother here?' She said, 'No, sir, he is gone.' 'Is his wife here?' I went on to enquire. 'No, sir, but his widow is.' Then the distressing thought rushed upon me that my brother was dead: and I awoke sobbing.

"A few days after, I was summoned suddenly into the country. My brother returning from Huntingdon had been attacked with angina pectoris; and the pain was so intense that they left him at Caxton (a small village in the diocese of Ely), to which place on the following day he summoned his wife: and the next day, while they were seated together, she heard a sigh and he was gone.

"When I reached Caxton, it was the very same village to which I had gone in my dream. I went to the same house, was met and let in by the same woman; and found my brother dead, and his widow there."

One of the most striking and well-authenticated cases of a Warning given in a Dream and acted upon, by which a grave temporal danger was actually averted, remains to be put on record now. The case is related with great simplicity by one who has carefully investigated the circumstances of both the dreams; and nothing is required on the Editor's part, either to enlarge on any detail of it or to point its moral:--

"Knowing as I do intimately," writes the correspondent in question, "the Widow of an Irish clergyman who was warned by a dream of the railway accident which took place a few years ago at Abergele, in North Wales, I give you gladly the following particulars:--

"About a fortnight before the accident occurred, my friend, the lady in question, had a dream in which her husband, who had been dead for three years, appeared to her, as she thought. This occurred on the night which followed the day on which she had settled and arranged with some friends to make a journey by railway. She dreamed that her husband was still living, and that she and he were walking on the sea-shore of North Wales, close to which the railway to Holyhead passes, when they came to a tunnel,[133] from which, all of a sudden, volumes of the blackest smoke were pouring out, and which became so dense that the sky was quite overcast. Alarmed at this, they hastily went forward together towards its mouth, when it seemed to be all on fire; the crackling and roar of which was quite unusual. In a moment or two the sounds of frantic cries of men and women wildly shrieking seemed to come from out of the mouth of the tunnel; and then, as if to add to the horror of what had already appeared, another train, full of people and at express speed, came up and dashed through smoke and flame into the tunnel itself. Upon this the lady awoke, and so deep an impression had the dream made (for it unhinged her for some days), that she resolved to postpone her journey, which she did. Had she gone at the time appointed and arranged, she and her friends would have travelled by the very train--the passengers of which were burnt by the explosion of petroleum.

"The most curious part of this interesting record has yet to be told. On the same night upon which this lady had this dream-warning, her own daughter, a child of nine years of age, who was staying with some relations nearly sixty miles from home, had likewise a dream, in which she thought she saw two trains meeting each other on one line of railway, in one of which her mother was seated, and in the other one of her mother's friends (who was to have travelled with her). The trains seemed to be going at a great rate, when the collision actually took place, the child at once awoke. On the following morning she recounted her dream to her relations: but at the time they took no notice of it, though it formed the subject of a general conversation regarding dreams. It was only when (as was afterwards discovered) her mother had possibly escaped the frightful disaster of a railway accident, and probably a very painful death, that the fact of her child having had the dream on the night of her own warning and mentioned it, was specially remarked and noted down."

A prognostication, or rather a personal Presentiment of impending death, and that death the result of an accident, will fittingly be recorded here:--

At the village of Bloxwich, in the diocese of Lichfield, a miner resided, well known to the person who communicated the following occurrence to the Editor of this volume:--"One morning in 1872, on his way to the pit's mouth, the miner had a strong presentiment that he should be killed at his work. He returned home, communicated his impressions to his wife (who expostulated with him for being so fanciful and superstitious), and then insisted on seeing all his children. They were assembled. He took down his Prayer Book and Bible, read a chapter from the latter, and afterwards said some of his accustomed prayers. Then affectionately greeting wife and children, he went to his work, with the same strange but vivid presentiment of approaching death upon him; as his wife so clearly testifies. He had not been at work many minutes when he was suddenly crushed to death by the fall of a rock."

These facts are duly authenticated by persons who obtained the account from the man's widow on the day of his burial, and have supplied them directly to the Editor.

The following cases, equally remarkable, are taken from the "Standard" newspaper:--

"Sir,--I beg to acquaint you of a very singular event which occurred here yesterday. On Saturday night a villager named Andrew Scott dreamed of being along the coast on S. Cyrus' Sands, and finding a man among the rocks under Whitson Houses. On Sabbath morning after breakfast he cleaned himself, and told his wife he would go and see if there was anything in his dream, taking another man with him to whom he made known his errand; and on arriving at the spot where he expected to find the man, sure enough there was the drowned man, washing amongst the rocks, just as seen in his dream. He was taken ashore, reported to the S. Cyrus' authorities, and to-day he is to be interred. He is supposed to be one of the men belonging to the 'Providence,' wrecked on Dec. 19. I have the honour to be, sir, your most obedient servant,

"Daniel Hamilton.

"Johnshaven, Kincardineshire, Jan. 20."

"At an inquest held on Monday afternoon at James Bridge, near Wolverhampton, on the body of a collier named Samuel Tinley, who had been killed in a pit there by a fall of rock strata, it transpired that during the previous night he awoke, saying he had a ton of rock on his head, though he had no headache. He was convinced it boded ill, and was reluctant to go to work. Upon being urged to go by his wife, he went to his child and saying, 'Let me have my last kiss,' went to the pit and was killed. It was further shown that a cousin of his, who is a close friend, was returning home from working a night-shift, when he said he saw the deceased standing before him in the road. Instead of going home to bed he went to the deceased's house, to which place the news of the death had just been brought, but altogether unknown to the cousin.[134] At the inquest a yet more remarkable case, that had come before the same coroner in the same locality, was mentioned."

So much as to examples and records of extraordinary Dreams, Warnings by Visions, and Presentiments. The subject of Omens may now be briefly touched upon. An "omen" has been defined to be "a token or sign of good or ill;" "a boding or foreboding;" "a prognostic." Some of the following are of such a character as that they are very suitably considered both in connection with events already described and with those yet to be narrated.

It has been forcibly and appropriately remarked, though not perhaps in any marked or specific Christian spirit, that Omens constitute the poetry of history. They cause the series of events which they are supposed to declare to flow into epical unity, and the political catastrophe seems to be produced, not by prudence or by folly, but by the superintending destiny.

The case of the Tichborne Prophecy, in connection with the well-known ancient Dole of that family, is so curious (having been in part recently fulfilled), that it may not only be set forth in detail, but may reasonably find a place at this particular part of this book. For the following version the Editor is indebted to a near connection of the family:--

"The Tichbornes date their possession of the present patrimony, the manor of Tichborne, so far back as two hundred years before the Conquest. When the Lady Mabella,[135] worn out with age and infirmity, was lying on her deathbed, she besought her loving husband, Sir Roger Tichborne, as her last request, that he would grant her the means of leaving behind her a charitable bequest, in a Dole of Bread to be distributed to all who should apply for it annually on the Feast of Annunciation of the Blessed Virgin Mary. Sir Roger, her husband, readily acceded to her request by promising the produce of as much land as she could go over in the vicinity of the Park while a certain brand or billet was burning, supposing that, from her long infirmity (for she had been bedridden some years), she would be able to go round a small portion only of his property. The venerable dame, however, ordered her attendants to convey her to the corner of the Park, where, being deposited on the ground, she seemed to regain a renovation of strength; and to the surprise of her anxious and admiring lord, who began to wonder where this pilgrimage might end, she crawled round several rich and goodly acres.

"The field which was the scene of Lady Mabella's extraordinary feat retains the name of 'The Crawls' to this day. It is situated near the entrance to the Park, and contains an area of twenty-three acres.

"Her task being completed, she was re-conveyed to her chamber; and, summoning her family to her bedside, predicted its prosperity while the annual Dole existed, and left her solemn Curse, uttered in God's most Holy Name, on any of her descendants who should be so mean or covetous as to discontinue or divert it, prophesying that when such should happen the old house should fall, and the family name would become extinct from the failure of heirs male; and that this would be foretold by a generation of seven sons being followed immediately after by a generation of seven daughters and no son.

"The custom thus founded in the reign of Henry II. continued to be observed for centuries; and our Lady's Day, the 25th of March, became the annual festive-day of the family. It was not until the middle of the last century that the custom was abused; when, under the pretence of attending the Tichborne Dole, vagabonds, gipsies, and idlers of every description, assembled from all quarters, pilfering throughout the neighbourhood; and, at last, the gentry and magistrates complaining, it was discontinued in 1796. Singularly enough, the baronet of that day, Sir Henry Tichborne,[136] had seven sons, and, when he was succeeded by the eldest, there appeared a generation of seven daughters, while the apparent fulfilment of the prophecy was completed by the change of the name of the late baronet to Doughty, under the will of his kinswoman. (This allusion is to Sir Edward Doughty, ninth baronet, who inherited the 'Doughty' estate, then Mr. Edward Tichborne.)"

Here is the record of a weird and obvious Omen:--

"The Duke of Somerset, the great sacrilegious nobleman of Henry VIII.'s reign, who worked such mischief and perpetrated such robberies on God's poor, is said to have been more than once warned of his coming death upon the scaffold, by the appearance of a Bloody Hand stretched out from the panelled wall of the corridor of his mansion; and it is also reported that the Hand was visible to his duchess as well as to himself."

And here is the narrative of a remarkable Dream, as well as of a singular coincidence:--

"Sir Thomas White, Alderman of London, was a very rich man, charitable and public-spirited. He dreamed that he had founded a college at a place where three elms grew out of one root. He went to Oxford probably with that intention; and discovering some such tree near Gloucester Hall, he began to repair the building of that community, with a design to endow it. But walking afterwards by the convent where the Bernardines formerly lived, he plainly saw an elm tree with three large bodies rising out of the same root; he forthwith purchased the ground, and endowed his college there, as it is at this day; except the additions which Archbishop Laud made near the outside of the building, in the garden belonging to the President. The tree is still to be seen. He made this discovery about the year 1557."

The numerous tokens of the death of Henry IV. of France, who reigned from 1589 until 1610, are finely tragical. Mary of Medicis, in her well-known dream, saw the brilliant gems of her crown change into pearls--the recognized symbols of tears and mourning. An owl is said to have hooted until sunrise at the window of the chamber to which the King and Queen retired at S. Denis on the night preceding her coronation. During the ceremony, it was observed with dread, that the dark portals leading to the royal sepulchre beneath the choir, were gaping and expanded. The flame of the sacred taper held by Her Majesty was suddenly extinguished, and it is said that her crown twice nearly fell to the ground.

An anecdote, which was current during the reign of King Charles I., and has the support both of Archbishop Laud and Lord Clarendon, is said to have thrown a sad gloom over the spirits of the royal friends, already saddened by the fearful pestilence which inaugurated his reign. At the coronation it was found that there was not in the whole of London, nor indeed in the whole of England, sufficient purple velvet with which to make the customary royal robes and the corresponding furniture of the chair of state and throne. What was to be done? Rigid custom, coming down no doubt for long generations, possibly from the time of S. Edward, required that old traditions should be scrupulously observed and carefully followed. What was needed could not in all probability be had nearer than Genoa. To obtain it would have caused a delay of several months: and it was agreed that the solemn anointing and coronation could not be properly postponed. So it was resolved to robe His Majesty in white velvet, from which he was known afterwards as "the White King." But this was the colour in which victims were arrayed. So many persons maintained that the Council which had sanctioned such an innovation had unwittingly, perhaps, but efficiently established an agency of evil; and many more after the King's martyrdom recalled the ominous change.

Another Warning, or supposed Warning, of approaching evil vouchsafed to the King was equally striking and peculiar. It happened a short time before the disastrous Battle of Newbury, and is thus recorded:--

The King being at Oxford, went one day to see the Public Library, where he was shown amongst other books, a Virgil, nobly printed and exquisitely bound. The Lord Falkland, to divert the King, would have his Majesty make a trial of his fortune by the Sortes Virgilianæ, which everybody knows was not an unusual kind of augury some ages past. Whereupon the King opening the book, the period which happened to come up was part of Dido's imprecation against Æneas, which Mr. Dryden translated thus:--

"*Yet let a race untamed, and haughty foes,*

His peaceful entrance with dire arms oppose;
Oppress'd with numbers in th' unequal field,
His men discouraged and himself expelled,
Let him for succour sue from place to place,
Torn from his subjects and his son's embrace;
First let him see his friends in battle slain,
And then untimely fate lament in vain;
And when at length the cruel war shall cease,
On hard conditions may he buy his peace;
Nor let him then enjoy supreme command,
But fall untimely by some hostile hand,
And lie unburied on the barren sand."
"Æneid," Book iv. 88.

It is said that King Charles seemed concerned at this accident, and that Lord Falkland observing it, would likewise try his fortune in the same manner, hoping he might fall upon some passage that could have no relation to his case, and thereby divert the King's thoughts from any impression the other might have upon him. But the place that Falkland stumbled upon was yet more suited to his destiny than the other had been to the King's; being the following expressions of Evander upon the untimely death of his son Pallas, as they are translated by the same hand:--

"O Pallas! thou hast fail'd thy plighted word,
To fight with caution, not to tempt the sword;
I warn'd thee but in vain; for well I knew
What perils youthful ardour would pursue,
That boiling blood would carry thee too far,
Young as thou wert in dangers--raw in war!
O cursed essay in arms--disastrous doom,
Prelude of bloody fields and fights to come."
"Æneid," Book xi. 230.

Again, as regards the King's bust, the following record was current and commonly discussed:--

"Vandyke, having painted the King's head, in three different attitudes, a profile, a three-quarters, and a full face, the picture was sent to Rome for Bernini, the celebrated sculptor, to make a bust from it. This artist, being exceedingly dilatory over his work, and having had complaints made to him on the subject, said that there was something so unusually sad and melancholy in the royal features, that if any stress might be laid on physiognomy, he was sure that the person whom the picture represented was destined for a violent end. When the bust arrived in England, the King being anxious to see it, it was taken immediately to Chelsea and placed on a table in the garden, whither the King, attended by many, went to inspect it. While so doing a hawk, with a wounded and bleeding partridge in its talons, flew over the King's head, and some of the blood fell upon the marble neck of the bust, where it remained without being wiped off. The omen is said to have been marked by many."

On the day of the King's burial, when the coffin was borne to S. George's Chapel, Windsor, by tried and trusted subjects and servants, it was carried through a severe snow-storm, and the purple pall was covered with the whitest snow, thus adding a fresh reason for the title by which His Majesty had been known.

There were also some remarkable Warnings in the life of the great Archbishop Laud, some of which were noted down in his "Diary." For example, he was elected Head of S. John's College, Oxford, on the Feast of the Beheading of S. John the Baptist; and of course, when he as Head of that college perished by a similar death, this more than remarkable coincidence was noticed and remembered. Another likewise is certainly curious. Not long before his martyrdom, on entering his study one day, he is said to have found his own portrait, by Vandyke, at full length on the floor, the cord which fastened it to the wall having snapped. The sight of this warning, as it was regarded, is said not only to have deeply impressed that great man, whose obvious belief in the Supernatural was considerable; but also to have brought back to his memory the fact of a great disaster which occurred to one of his barges, on the very day of his translation to the See of Canterbury, which boat sank with his coaches and horses into the Thames.

There was an Omen attached to the ancient Ferrers family, of Chartley Park in Staffordshire. The large possessions of this family were forfeited by the attainder of Earl Ferrers, after his defeat at Burton Bridge, where he led the rebellious barons against Henry III. The Chartley estate having been settled in dower was alone reserved and handed down. In the Park is said to be preserved an indigenous Staffordshire cow, small in stature, of sand-white colour, with black ears, muzzle, and tips at the hoofs. In the year of the Battle of Burton Bridge a black calf was born; the downfall of the house of Ferrers happening at the same period gave rise to the tradition, which to this day is said to be commonly current through observation of past events, viz., that the birth of a parti-coloured calf from the wild herd in Chartley Park is a sure omen of death within the same year to a member of Lord Ferrers' family. By a noticeable coincidence a calf of this description has been born whenever a death has happened of late years in this noble family.[137] The decease of the late Earl and Countess, of his son Lord Tamworth, and of his daughter, Mrs. William Joliffe, as well as the deaths of the son and heir of the present nobleman, and his daughter, Lady Frances Shirley, has each been preceded by the birth of an ominous calf. In the spring of the year 1835 an animal perfectly black was calved by one of this weird tribe; and it was soon followed by the death of the amiable Countess.

The Omen connected with the ancient gentle family of Oxenham, co. Devon,[138] may now be suitably referred to. The following, describing it, is copied from a rare and ancient pamphlet:[139]--"In the parish called Sale Monachorum, in the county of Devon, there lives one James Oxenham, a gentleman of good worth and quality, who had many children, one whereof was called John Oxenham, a young man in the vigour, beauty, and flower of his age, about 22, who was of stature comely and tall, being in height of body sixe foote and a half, a very proper person.... This young gentleman fell sicke, who being visited by many of the neighbours during the time of his sickness, departed this transitory life on the 5th day of September 1635, to whom, two days before he yielded up his soul to God, there appeared the likeness of a Bird with a white breast hovering over him." The pamphlet in question states that the White Bird also appeared previously to the deaths of Thomasine, Rebecca and Thomasine the younger,[140] facts formally testified to, on the oaths of divers eyewitnesses before the Lord Bishop of Exeter (Dr. Joseph Hall).

In Howell's "Familiar Letters," a communication dated "July 3, 1632," states that the writer saw, at a stonecutter's shop in London, a marble monument commemorating several examples of this curious omen; and gives the following as the inscriptions:--

"Here lies John Oxenham, a goodly young man, in whose chamber as he was struggling with the pangs of death, a Bird with a White Breast was seen fluttering about his bed, and so vanished.

"Here lies also Mary Oxenham, the sister of the said John, who died the next day, and the same apparition was seen in the room.

"Here lies hard by, James Oxenham, the son of the said John, who dyed a child in his cradle a little after, and such a Bird was seen fluttering about his head a little before he expir'd, which vanish'd afterwards."

At the bottom of the stone there is:--

"Here lies Elizabeth Oxenham, the mother of the said John, who died sixteen years since, when such a bird with a white breast was seen about her bed before her death."[141]

Then come the following remarks:--

"To all these there be divers witnesses both squires and ladies, whose names are engraven upon the stone. This stone is to be sent to a town hard by Exeter where this happen'd. Were you here, I could raise a choice discours with you hereupon. So hoping to see you the next tirm, I rest, etc."

From an old MS. letter of the eighteenth century, written on the fly-leaf of a copy of Howell's book already referred to, it seems that the appearance of the omen was regarded as a fact at that period. The Letter dated "December 29th, 1741," contains the following statement:--

"I have received an answer from the country in relation to the strange Bird which appeared to Mr. Oxenham just before his death, and the account which Dr. Bertie gave to Lord Abingdon of it, is certainly true. It first was seen outside the window, and soon afterwards by Mrs. Oxenham in the room, which she mentioned to Mr. Oxenham, and asked him if he knew what bird it was. 'Yes,' says he, 'it has been on my face and head, and is recorded in history as always appearing to our family before their deaths; but I shall cheat the Bird.' Nothing more was said about it, nor was the Bird taken notice of from that time: but he died soon afterwards. However odd this affair may seem, it is certainly true; for the account was given of it by Mrs. Oxenham herself: but she never mentions it to anyone unless particularly asked about it; and as it was seen by several persons at the same time, I cannot attribute it to imagination, but must leave it as a phenomenon unaccounted for."

My friend, the Rev. H. N. Oxenham, of this family, writes to me A.D. October, 1874, as follows:

"The tradition about the White Bird has certainly existed for so long a time--I believe for centuries--in our family, that I have every reason to believe there are well-authenticated accounts of its appearance before the death of the head of the family; and that certainly a white Bird was seen at the window a few days before my late uncle's death (who was the head of the family) last

Christmas" [i.e. in 1873].

Here a singular account of the possession of a charm, or amulet, and of a Curse connected with it, may be fittingly set forth:--

"The family of Graham of Inchbrachie, county Perth, are said to possess a small blue, uncut stone, set in an antique ring, of which the following story is told. Some two centuries ago, as the Head of the Family was passing by a hill near or at Crieff, he discovered a large crowd, presided over by one of the Campbells of ----, preparing to execute a witch. On approaching the crowd, he found that the unhappy victim (who had for some years lived in a rocky cave, still known by her name), was none other than his old nurse, Katherine Nivens. Charged with witchcraft, she had been condemned and was about to be executed. Graham, addressing the mob, urged them to prevent Campbell from carrying out his purpose. In acknowledgment of his generous help on her behalf, the poor creature threw him a small blue stone like a bead, which she had kept in her mouth, and desired him to keep it for her sake; adding that as long as it was preserved in his family good fortune should ever attend them; while to the Campbells of ---- (whom she solemnly cursed), she predicted that there never should be born an heir male, and cited him to appear before God's judgment-bar, where justice should be done.[142] The strange feature in the story is that (as a correspondent avers) both promise and prediction have turned out to be true. The stone is said to be an uncut sapphire. Other Scotch families possess similar amulets or charms: amongst these the Macdonald-Lockharts of Lee in the county of Lanark.

The sound of the Beating of a Drum is said to betoken death to a noble Scotch family--one which has been a staunch, good old loyalist clan for centuries, and suffered sorely for having been "leal and true" to their Royal House and their own consciences. Some years ago the then head of it was paying a visit in England, when, one day, sitting outside in the garden with the lady of the house, his lordship exclaimed suddenly, "Listen! here comes a band of music."

"Music!" she replied, "oh, impossible."

"Oh, don't you hear it? it is coming this way."

"No, I hear nothing."

"Listen!" he retorted; "don't you hear the Drum?"

She assured him that there was nothing, that it was a fancy, and that no band of music could come near enough to the house to be heard, on account of the unusual extent of the grounds and park.

On this the nobleman turned pale, and becoming much agitated, remarked that he felt sure it must be the sound of the family "Drum,"--an omen that always preceded death, and feared that something had happened to one of his relations.

The next post brought him the sad and melancholy news of his wife's unlooked-for death, through giving birth prematurely to a child.

The origin of this omen, as far as the Editor can discover, appears to be unknown.

In another family of rank a female figure, dressed in brown clothes, appears as a warning of death. To the members of an old knightly family in the West of England there always comes, before the death of its chief, the sound of a heavy carriage with many horses driven round the paved courtyard of the Elizabethan mansion.

It is equally notorious that in a certain noble English family, the form of a spectral head appears as a sign of death to any member of it, and invariably so, when the chief of it dies,--a fact which the Editor has been assured of in writing (A.D. 1872) from a member of a junior branch of the same.

To another family, living in the East of England (of the rank of gentle people), appears an Omen, equally, if not more disagreeable. The appearance of a spectral Black Dog is also a portent of death. About twenty years ago, A.D. 1853, the then head of the family married, and though he himself (by no means superstitious) could not reject the tradition of the unpleasant omen, having heard so much about it on its previous appearance, he said nothing to his wife. Some years afterwards, in 1861, their eldest child was taken ill. The illness, however, (as the physician asserted,) was slight, and not at all likely to prove dangerous; so little, in truth, was this anticipated that there were several persons staying in the house at the time. Just before dinner was announced one evening, the wife of the head of the family asked to be excused for a moment or two, while she looked into the night nursery to see how the sick child was. She went, but returned almost immediately, saying, "Darling ---- is fast asleep; but there's a large black dog lying under the bed; go and drive it out." The father, at once calling to mind the omen, was sorely terrified. He went at once to the sick room. Neither under nor near the bed, nor (as was afterwards discovered) on the premises, was there, or had there been, any dog, but the poor child's sleep was found to be the sleep of death.

To revert to Omens in general. There is a widely-spread and singular prejudice, (which with many is deeply rooted,) that if thirteen people sit down to dinner one of them, at least, shall die within a year.[143] It seems to have originated from the fact of Judas having been the thirteenth at the Paschal Feast, when our Lord instituted the Holy Sacrament.

Again, Friday has from time immemorial been considered an unlucky day;[144] because the Crucifixion of our Blessed Saviour took place on that day--a day of fear and trembling, of darkness and of earthquakes--a day of awe, when even some of the Pagan oracles were silent, and indications of the decay and weakening of their powers were by their impotence made manifest. Plutarch in his book on the "Cessation of Oracles," makes mention of the voice which, near Paxos, the pilot of a vessel heard in the spring of the nineteenth year of the Emperor Tiberius, crying out, "Great Pan is dead." Now we know that in the spring of that year, and possibly on the afternoon of that very day, our Divine Lord overcame death by dying, conquered Satan, and opened the gates of everlasting life to mankind. Can we be surprised that after that victory on the first Good Friday, the power of the Evil One was largely and surely curbed?

Second Sight, indications of the existence of which have already been given, appears to be a power or property of seeing beforehand events which are still in the future, and such sight claimed by several[145] is said to belong to many persons in Scotland. In a "Description of the Western Isles," a popular writer of the last century somewhat amplified the definition. He maintained as follows: "The Second Sight is a singular faculty of seeing an otherwise invisible object, without any previous means used by the person that sees it for that end; the vision makes such a lively impression upon the seers, that they neither see nor think of anything else, except the vision, as long as it continues; and then they appear pensive or jovial, according to the object which was represented to them." He further points out generally that when persons gifted with Second Sight "actually behold something unusual, the eyelids of the person are erected, and the eyes continue staring until the object vanish." In the case of a certain person in the Island of Skye, "when he sees a vision, the inner part of his eyelids turns so far upwards, that after the object disappears, he must draw them down again with his fingers." The same writer maintains that the property of Second Sight does not necessarily descend in a family, as some persons hold and assert. "I know several parents," he writes, "who are endowed with it, but their children not, and vice versa; neither is it acquired by any previous compact. And, after a strict inquiry, I could never learn from any among them that this faculty was communicable any way whatsoever."

Several volumes have been written on the subject, and examples almost without number provided.

In John Aubrey's "Miscellanies"[146] is recorded a remarkable escape from death of Dr. William Harvey, the celebrated discoverer of the circulation of the blood through Second Sight:--"When Dr. Harvey, one of the Physicians' College in London, being a young man (in 1695), went to travel towards Padua, he went to Dover with several others, and showed his pass as the rest to the Governor there. The Governor told him that he must not go, but he must keep him prisoner. The Doctor desired to know 'for what reason? how he had transgressed?' 'Well, it was his will to have it so.' The pacquet boat hoisted sail in the evening, which was very clear, and the doctor's companions in it. There ensued a terrible storm, and the pacquet boat and all the passengers were drowned. The next day the sad news was brought to Dover. The Doctor was unknown to the Governor both by name and face; but the night before the Governor had a perfect vision of Dr. Harvey in a dream, who came to pass over to Calais, and that he had a warning to stop him. This the Governor told the Doctor the next day. The Doctor was a pious, good man, and has several times directed this story to some of my acquaintance."

The following, from a rare and curious volume of the last century,[147] containing nearly two hundred cases, authenticated mainly by ministers of the Scotch Establishment, is a good example:--

"Alexander Macdonald, of Kingsborough (when living in the possession of Aird, in the remote end of Trotternish), dreamed that he saw a reverend old man come to him, desiring him to get out of bed, and get his servants together, and make haste to save his fields of corn, as his whole cattle, and his tenants' cattle also, had got out of the fold, and were in the middle of a large field behind the house. He awaked and told his wife, with whom he consulted whether he would rise or not; and she telling him it was but a dream, and not worth noticing, advised him to lie still, which he obeyed; but no sooner fell asleep, than the former old man appeared to him, and seemed angry, by telling Mr. Macdonald (then of Aird), he the old man was very idle, in acquainting him of the loss he would or had by this time sustained by his cattle, and seemed not to heed what he said, and so went off. Mr. Macdonald awaking the second time, told his wife, but she would not allow him, and ridiculed him for noticing the folly of a confused dream; so that, after attempting to get up, he was, at his wife's persuasion, prevailed upon to lie down again; and falling asleep, it being now near break of day, the old gentleman appeared to him a third time, with a frowning countenance, and told him he might now lie still, for that the cattle were now surfeited of his corn, and were lying in it; and that it was for his welfare that he came to acquaint him so often, as he was his grand-uncle by his father; and so went off. He awaking in about an hour thereafter, arose and went out, and actually found his own and his tenants' cattle lying in his corn, after being tired of eating thereof; which corn, when comprised, the loss amounted to eight bolls of meal."

Two quite recent cases of Second Sight are here given, and are each somewhat remarkable. Both have been furnished to the Editor by those who knew the cases, and the accuracy of each has been vouched for by trusty and courteous correspondents.

The first has reference to the murder of a policeman at Cardiff:--"An inquest was formally opened on the body of William Perry, a constable of the Cardiff police force, who was fatally stabbed on Tuesday by a butcher, named Jones. The medical evidence went to show that the murderer was in a very excited state at the time, but was neither insane nor suffering from delirium tremens. The further hearing was adjourned. The 'Western Mail' says:--The deceased man Perry was a well-known and very efficient officer. He joined the borough police force on the 5th of July, 1865, and from that time had always conducted himself in a praiseworthy manner, having attained to the position of a first-class constable some time ago. Previous to 1865 he was employed in the Merthyr division of the county police. He was 36 years of age. The superstitious will probably feel interested in the following story, which our reporter heard last night from the lips of the widow herself. Strange as it may seem, it is no less strange than true; and mournful as the circumstance is in itself, those who believe in the efficacy of dreams as prognosticators of future events, will perhaps derive some gratification from it. On Sunday night Mrs. Perry (who resides at Melrose-cottage, Heath-street, Canton), had a dream, which but too faithfully predicted the sad tragedy of yesterday. In the midst of her sleep she saw, to use her own words, a large crowd following her husband down the Cowbridge-road, in the direction of the Westgate hotel, where the murder was committed. She saw, in the horror of her dream, a knife plunged into the breast of her husband, and drawn out again, blood-stained and grimy, by some cruel but unknown hand. She saw, too, the murdered form of her husband borne away, and little thought, when brooding over her awful dream, that it was a 'dark presage,' and the precursor of what was soon to be a terrible reality. The dream occasioned her great uneasiness, but she mentioned it to no one until the dreadful tidings of her husband's death reached her yesterday morning, when the circumstance forced itself vividly upon her recollection." (A.D. 1873.)

The second example is equally remarkable:--"A singular case of Second Sight is reported from the neighbourhood of Marlborough. A labourer named Duck, employed by Mr. Dixon, of Mildenhall Warren Farm, was in charge of a horse and water-cart on the farm, when the animal took fright and knocked him down. The wheel went over his chest, and the injuries he received were such that his death occurred shortly afterwards. However, the singular part of the story remains to be told. Duck resided at Ramsbury, and immediately after the accident Mr. Dixon despatched a woman to acquaint his wife of the fact. On arriving at her home the messenger found her out gathering wood; but shortly afterwards a girl who was her companion arrived, and, without being told of what had occurred, volunteered the statement that 'Ria (Mrs. Duck) was unable to do much that morning, that she had been very much frightened, having seen her husband in the wood. Shortly afterwards Mrs. Duck returned, without any wood, and, being informed by a neighbour that a woman from Mildenhall Woodlands wished to see her, ejaculated immediately, 'My David's dead, then.' Inquiry has since been made by Mr. Dixon of the woman, and she positively asserts that she saw her husband in the wood, and said, 'Holloa, David, what wind blows you here, then?' and that he made no reply. Mr. Dixon inquired what time this occurred, and she replied about 10 o'clock, the hour at which the fatal accident took place." (A.D. 1874.)

Before this chapter is closed, the following account, which created the deepest impression in the town and neighbourhood of Devizes, is embodied in terms which plainly enough set forth its point and purpose. It is an awful example of God's summary judgment, recorded by the local authorities both as a memorial of the Supernatural and as a warning to all:--

"The Mayor and Corporation of Devizes avail themselves of the stability of this building [the Market Cross,] to transmit to future times the record of an awful event which occurred in the Market Place in the year 1753, hoping that such record may serve as a salutary warning against the danger of impiously invoking Divine vengeance, or of calling on the Holy Name of God to conceal the devices of falsehood and fraud:

"On Thursday, the 25th of January, 1753, Ruth Pierce, of Potterne in this county, agreed with three other women to buy a sack of wheat in the market, each paying her due proportion towards the same. One of these women, in collecting the several quotas of money, discovered a deficiency, and demanded of Ruth Pierce the sum which was wanting to make good the amount. Ruth Pierce protested that she had paid her share, and said: She wished she might drop down dead if she had not. She rashly repeated the awful wish; when, to the consternation and terror of the surrounding multitude, she instantly fell down and expired, having the money concealed in her hand."

The narrative of this solemn event was by order of the authorities recorded on a tablet and hung up in the Market house (a row of sheds near the Cross). When the building was taken down,

Rev. Frederick George Lee, D.C.L.

Mr. Halcombe, who kept the Bear Inn, in order that the remembrance might not be lost, caused it to be inscribed on the pediment of a couple of pillars which stood opposite his inn, supporting the sign of the Bear.

The sign was removed in 1801, and a few years after Lord Sidmouth having presented to the town the New Cross, which forms the central ornament of the Market Place, the Mayor and Corporation "availed themselves," to use their own language, "of the stability of the new structure to transmit to future time a record of the awful death of Ruth Pierce in hope that it might serve as a salutary warning against the practice of invoking the Sacred Name to conceal the devices of falsehood and fraud."

And now to conclude this portion of the subject. Each example already recorded has, no doubt, told its own story sufficiently well. Some cases may appear to certain minds to be as trivial as they certainly are, to others, marvellous and inexplicable; other examples, again, cannot fail to leave a deep impression on the reader, as well from the remarkable character of the presentiments and dreams themselves, as from the reasonable testimony by which their truth is supported by persons of repute and credibility. The Editor has intentionally avoided the making of comments, either prolix or the reverse, preferring to present to the reader each recorded narrative, as received or obtained by himself, without dissertations, theories, or explanations.

END OF VOLUME I

FOOTNOTES:

1. "Westminster Review," July, 1872.
2. Acts xvii. 27.
3. The idea of the eternal enters largely into the stock arguments of unbelief; for it is through the asserted "eternity of matter" that the unbeliever shifts away the ideas of creation and a creator.
4. Articles of Religion, No. 1, Book of Common Prayer.
5. Christianity, as we know, exhorted men and women to the care of the aged, the suffering, and the infirm. Our Blessed Saviour's promise, regarding the gift of a cup of cold water and its reward, was not forgotten. Christian love resisted and cast out Pagan selfishness. Hospitals were built where the diseases of the poor might be cured; where the sore distress of hopeless pain and slow wasting-away might be soothed; and asylums were provided where the weak and imbecile might be tended. Now if the Pagan theories of "scientific people" are applied, the chief duty of physicians in the future will be to poison their patients. Such a conception would be ludicrous were it not so utterly revolting.
6. A writer in an influential organ of opinion connected with the American Church puts forth the following vigorous protest:--

"It is quite as well that we should be accustomed to the logical consequences of some of our philosophies. The tradition of Christianity is so strong upon the most 'advanced' of our wise men that it holds them back from the carrying-out of their principles. But here and there is one, and we should all be thankful to him who is so intellectually constituted that he must carry 'a law' to its issue, and by the issue let us see the nature of the law. The hint of what may be is given in the revival of the advocacy of suicide for the wretched, and the putting to death of the helpless. Naturalism carried out comes to that conclusion. Mr. Herbert Spencer had been patiently laying down principles which scores who think they think are accepting, without the slightest idea, on his part apparently or on theirs, that they are simple savagery and pure Paganism, and that the man who dines off his aged mother has been acting on them, though Mr. Spencer's name had never been heard in his native speech.

"In some sense of the supernatural, in some faith in the unseen, in some feeling that man is not of this world, in some grasp on the Eternal God, and on an eternal, supernatural, and supersensuous life, lies the basis of all pity and mercy, all help and comfort and patience and sympathy among men. Set these aside, commit us only to the natural, to what our eyes see and our hands handle; and while we may organize society scientifically, and live according to 'the laws of nature,' and be very philosophical and very liberal, we are standing on the ground on which every pack of wolves gallops.

"One may safely say, 'If you will show me, on any principle of naturalism, or any rule of what you shallowly in these days call 'philosophy,' on any law of nature, why I should not strangle my deaf and dumb child, smother my paralytic father, or drown my hopelessly insane wife, then I will turn materialist also.' We are far from believing that these gentlemen know how they have been undermining the foundations of civilized and social life. A lurid glare cast across these speculations, like this English discussion of Euthanasia, may startle some whom Mr. Tyndall's discussion of the scientific absurdity of prayer might not startle, though both are locked in one, and stand or fall together. But however it be, we are sure that man will find that society stands on supernatural ground, that the Family and the Nation are divine, and that 'Naturalism,' modified or disguised as it may be, is only isolated savagery--'every man for himself, and the weakest to the wall.'"

7. A writer in the "Church Journal" of New York puts the case well and fairly as follows:-- "The scientific people have taken up the lost weapons of bigoted theological polemics, and assail with the rough sides of their tongues and pens any man who calls for further evidence, or presumes to bring their assumptions to the test of examination. But having no more reverence for the unsustained dicta of Sir Charles Lyell, Mr. Proctor, or Professor Tyndall, than for the same sort of dicta from a Middle Age monk, we shall go on calling for proof. Our credulity is incapable of saying 'we know' about a thing of which, when we examine, nobody 'knows' anything, except that some scientific man asserts it in his book.

"We are not 'enemies to science;' we only want science, and not guesses. And the thoroughly unscientific, uncritical, and credulous way in which men like Mr. Proctor are declaring 'we know' about things of which they know nothing, is one of the greatest obstacles with which science has to contend."

8. "La Croix de Migné vengée de l'incrédulité du siècle." Published at Paris, in 1829.

9. "Account of the Miraculous Events at Rome in the years 1792 and 1793." Published in London, by Keating and Brown, Duke Street, Grosvenor Square.

10. Hume's "Essays and Treatises on Various Subjects," second edition, vol. ii. p. 122. London, 1784.

11. Ibid. vol. ii. p. 133.

12. Take for example the subject of meteoric stones. Marked changes with regard to a belief in these, have existed in the past. The scholar can testify that antiquity is undoubtedly in favour of their existence. Plutarch, for example, in his "Life of Lysander," describes a celebrated aerolite which fell in Thrace, and History testifies unmistakably to similar events--more particularly to the preservation of such in ancient temples. Yet it was not until the year 1803, when meteoric stones fell at L'Aigle in Normandy, that the Academy of Sciences in Paris appointed a committee to investigate the case, and their report determined the question. Mr. W. G. Nevill, F.G.S., of Gresham Street, City, London, comprises the above in the following testimony to facts which appeared in the "Standard," of Feb. 25, 1873. "With reference to a paragraph headed 'An Exercise of Credulity' in your paper of the 24th instant, allow me to offer a few observations, as the circumstance narrated therein of the fall of an aerolite on board the Seven Stones light-vessel, as narrated by the crew, is of extreme interest. The men in the light-vessel service are carefully selected by the elder brethren of the Trinity House and trained to make observations on the weather and record them in books at the time, which books are received as evidence in the Admiralty Court. Their account agrees in the main with the details given in other cases. My father, Mr. W. Nevill, of Godalming, has a collection of specimens of 226 distinct falls of such bodies. These take place in all parts of the world. I believe only one instance has before been recorded in England. That occurred at Wold Cottage, Thwing, Yorkshire, on Dec. 13, 1795. One of the earliest recorded falls took place at Guisheim, in Alsace, during a battle, Nov. 7, 1492, and was preserved in the neighbouring church. A large shower of stones took place at L'Aigle, in north of France, on April 26, 1803 (not very far from the Seven Stones). These stones are of a grey ashy colour and invariably coated with black enamel; other meteorites are composed of solid native iron, and are sometimes of large size, as the one at Bitburg in Rhenish Prussia, which weighed several tons."

13. "Athenæum," for March 12, 1859, p. 350.

14. Testimonies to the Supernatural amongst Christian writers are abundant. The following may be instanced as a few concerning such events, both in the second and third centuries:--Justin Martyr, Ap. ii. cap. vi.; Dial. cum Tryph. cap. xxxix. and lxxxii.; Irenæus, ii. 31 and v. 6; Tertullian "Apolog." cap. 23, 27, 32, 37; "Origen against Celsus," book i. p. 7 and book vii. pp. 334-335, Ed. Spencer; Dionysius of Alexandria, in "Eccl. Hist." of Eusebius, vi. 40; Minucius Felix Octav. p. 361, Ed. Paris, 1605; S. Cyprian, "De Idol. Vanit." p. 14.

15. S. John xiv. 12.

16. "Hist. Eccles." cap. v. Chronicon. p. 82.

17. The following version by Dio. Cassius, translated from the "Annals" of Baronius, affords no slender testimony to the account by Eusebius given in the text:--"When the barbarians would not give them battle, in hopes of their perishing by heat and thirst, since they had so surrounded them that they had no possible means of getting water; and when they were in the utmost distress from sickness, wounds, sun, and thirst, and could neither fight nor retreat, but remained in order of battle and at their posts in this parched condition, suddenly clouds gathered, and a copious rainfall, not without the mercy of God. And when it first began to fall, the Romans, raising their mouths towards heaven, received it upon them; next, turning up their shields and helmets, they drank largely out of them, and gave to their horses. And when the barbarians charged them, they drank as they fought, and numbers of them were wounded.... And while they were thus incurring heavy loss from the assault of the enemy, because most of them were engaged in drinking, a violent hailstorm and much lightning were discharged upon the enemy. And thus water and fire might be seen in the same place falling from heaven, that some might drink refreshment and others be burnt to death."--Dion. Cass. "Hist." lxxi. p. 805.

18. The treatise of Apollinaris, it should be added, is lost; and there seems to be some ground for believing that a particular Legion bore the name "Thundering" as far back as the days of Augustus. This latter assertion, however, even if proved, cannot set aside the leading facts recorded in the text.

19. "Life of Marcus Antonius," chap. xxiv.

20. "Historia Romana," lxi. 8.

21. Mosheim's "Ecclesiastical History" (Ed. Stubbs), vol. i. pp. 99-101. London, 1863.

22. "Two Essays on Scripture Miracles and on Ecclesiastical," by J. H. Newman, pp. 273-4, Second Edition. London, 1870.

23. Socrates, Philostorgius, Gelasius, and Nicephorus declare that the Cross was in the sky. Sozomen, too, on the authority of Eusebius, makes a similar statement. So likewise does Rufinus.

24. This standard was known by the name of the "Labarum"--a word the etymology of which is very uncertain. It was a pole plated with gold, upon which was laid horizontally a cross-bar, so as to form the figure of a cross. The top of the perpendicular shaft was adorned with a golden crown, ornamented with precious stones. In the middle of this crown was a monogram representing the name of Christ by the two Greek initial letters X and P. A purple veil of a square figure hung from the cross-bar, which was likewise spangled with jewels. Gretser, "De Cruce," Lib. i. cap. iv.

25. S. John v. 20.

26. Liber cont. Hær. c. xxxi.

27. Daniel ix. 20-27.

28. These miraculous interventions are testified to by S. Gregory Nazianzen, S. Chrysostom, and S. Ambrose, as well as by Rufinus, Socrates, Sozomen, and Theodoret. They are also recorded by Philostorgius the Arian, and by Ammianus the Pagan. Bishop Warburton published a volume entitled "Julian" in proof of their miraculous character, and they are acknowledged as such by Bishop Halifax on p. 23 of his "Discourses."

29. Those who testify to the truth of this miracle are firstly a Christian prelate, Victor Vitenus, "Hist. Pers." sec. Vandal, iii. p. 613, whose words are translated above; the Emperor Justinian (who declares that he had seen some of the sufferers, "Codex Justin." Lib. I. Tit. xxx. Ed. 1553); the Greek historian, Procopius of Cæsarea, who asserts that their tongues were cut off as low down as their throat, and that he had conversed with them, Lib. I. "De Bell. Vand." cap. viij. and x. 1. Æneas of Gaza, a Platonic philosopher, who, having examined their mouths, remarked that he was not so much surprised at their being able to talk, as at their being able to live. He saw them at Constantinople. Mosheim, amongst Protestants, and Dodwell, the nonjuror, amongst English writers, frankly admit the miracle. The most lucid and exhaustive account, however, may be found in Section ix. of Dr. J. H. Newman's "Essays on Miracles," pp. 369-387 (Second edition, London, 1870), where the ancient evidence is set forth at length.

30. On this subject a volume has recently been published, entitled "The Tongue not Essential to Speech: with Illustrations of the Power of Speech in the African Confessors." By the Hon. Edward Twistleton. London: 1873. This book has been carefully and exhaustively criticized in "The Month," for September, 1873. It will be sufficient here to remark that the modern scientific objections to this miracle, that, because in a certain case, by the skill of an operator, a tongue was so removed with marked dexterity in recent times, therefore the power of speech retained by the African Confessors was an ordinary event, are objections at once inconsequential and invalid.

31. "De Civitate Dei," Lib. xxii. p. 8.

32. "Epist. Sti. Greg.;" "Hist. Bed." Lib. i. c. xxxj.

33. Vide "Sti. Bernardi Vita," in loco, published by Mabillon.

34. They were examined on the spot, by virtue of a Commission from John III. King of Portugal, and were generally acknowledged, not only by Europeans, but also by native Mahometans and Pagans. The important and conclusive testimony of three Protestant writers--Hackluyt, Baldens, and Tavernier--is set forth in Bouhours' "Life of Francis Xavier," which our own poet, John Dryden, translated and published.

35. S. Matthew xv. 22-28.

36. S. Mark iii. 11. Ibid. iii. 15, 22-30.

37. S. Mark v. 2-15. See also S. Luke viii. 26-40. Instances of such power bestowed and exercised over unclean or deaf and dumb spirits may be found in the following:--S. Mark vi. 13; vii. 25-30; ix. 17-29. S. Luke iv. 33-37; ix. 38-42; xi. 14-26. Acts v. 12, 16; xvi. 16-18; xix. 13-20; xxviii. 3-6.

38. One of the most distinguished physicians in London recently assured the Editor that, in his judgment, numerous peculiar and remarkable cases both of epilepsy and madness could only be duly and rationally accounted for by the Christian theory of possession; and he himself declared that if the Church's spiritual powers on the one hand, and the virtue of faith on the other, were more commonly put into practice than they are, many cures, by God's blessing, might be looked for.

39. "The History of Cornwall," by Fortescue Hitchins, Esq., in 2 vols. 4to. Helston, 1824. Vol. ii. pp. 548-51.

40. The parish of Little Petherick is six miles north of S. Columb, and three due south from Padstow.

41. Bishop Seth Ward, D.D.--Editor.

42. "No minister or ministers shall ... without the license and direction (mandatum) of the Bishop ... attempt upon any pretence whatsoever either of possession or obsession, by fasting or prayer, to cast out any devil or devils, under pain of the imputation of imposture or cosenage, and deposition from the ministry."--Canons of 1604, No. 72.

43. Mr. Hawker quotes from the Diary of Mr. Ruddle for July 10th, 1665, the following triumphant entry:--"How sorely must the infidels and hereticks of this generation be dismayed when they know that this Black Death, which is now swallowing its thousands in the streets of the great city [London] was foretold six months agone, under the exorcisms of a country minister, by a visible and suppliant ghost! And what pleasures and improvements do such deny themselves who scorn and avoid all opportunity of intercourse with souls separate, and the spirits, glad and sorrowful, which inhabit the unseen world."--pp. 123-4.

44. In the act of exorcism, of course it is not necessary that the exorcist be a clergyman, in other words, in holy orders. An "exorcist" technically so called, when formally ordained, is only in "minor" and not in "holy" or "sacred orders." Any Christian layman, with faith and a hearty desire and readiness to abide by the rules of the Church, can perform the act of exorcism, if no duly-ordained exorcist can be had; just as a layman (in the absence of a priest), can validly baptize. By baptism the "old man" is cast out, and the work of regeneration formally effected. By exorcism, some evil spirit or devil is expelled from a person possessed, in the Name of our Adorable Redeemer, Who triumphed over death and hell, and Who delegated Divine powers to the Church which He instituted. "It belongs to an exorcist," writes a distinguished Western divine, "by exorcisms to deliver energumens and catechumens from the vexations of demons."--"Axioms concerning the Sacraments," No. lxviii. of Augustinus Hunnæus. On this point, the same theologian, sometime Professor of Theology at Louvain, writes thus:--"In adults catechism, whereby the doctrine of faith is delivered, ought to precede baptism; but exorcism, whereby evil spirits are expelled, and the senses opened to the perception of the mysteries of Salvation, ought to precede catechism. Both, as well catechism as exorcism, pertain to the office of a priest; but in catechizing he uses the ministry of a reader: in exorcism that of an exorcist."--"Axioms concerning the Sacraments," No. xii.

45. This clergyman, whose name the Editor is not at liberty to mention, is known to many to be "a discerner of spirits." He is now a dignitary of the English Church in the colonies.

46. "The same has been attested to myself by M. Denison, nephew to the celebrated Morand, whom I saw at that time at Maubuisson-les-Pontoise. He ran the same career as his uncle, and was also distinguished for his merit. F. G. P."

47. Deut. x. 8; Numb. vi. 22-26, a form which the Christian Church has adopted and retained.

48. Heb. vii. 7.

49. Another version of this conversation gives the report as follows: "And should I die unjustly and undeservedly, my lord, in that case, you, my lord, shall soon die too, and follow me; yea within the compass of a year."--MS. Letter of Very Rev. Dr. Husenbeth.

50. "That dead dog Arrowsmith" stands in another version of this portion of the narrative.--Editor.

51. They went in company with Thomas Cutler and Elizabeth Dooley. The above facts were formally authenticated by the parents of Lamb, as also by the Rev. Thomas Sadler, of Trafford, near Manchester; and the Rev. J. Craythorne, of Garswood. A friend who resides in Lancashire informs the Editor that this miracle is firmly believed by thousands (A.D. 1873).

52. It was on this day that formal and sufficient testimonies were put into writing of the fact of the cure narrated above; and duly signed by those who from their own personal knowledge could testify to the truth of the same.

53. The event recorded above, Arrowsmith's sufferings and death, and its details are taken from Dod's "Church History," Challoner's "Memoirs of Missionary Priests," vol. ii. pp. 130-146; a "Relation of the Death of E. Arrowsmith," published A.D. 1630; a Latin MS. of his life, preserved at Douay; and special traditional information given to the Editor by the late Very Rev. Dr. Husenbeth, Provost of Northampton.

54. This wonderful mystery is frequently represented in Christian Art, both with beauty and effect.

55. See a rare and remarkable pamphlet, by Mr. De Lisle, with etchings by J. R. Herbert, R.A., now out of print, containing an account of his visit to the subject of this miraculous occurrence. London: Dolman, 1841.

56. The following is the full title of the volume from which the above narrative and the extracts given are taken:--"Louise Lateau of Bois d'Haine, her Life, her Ecstasies, and her Stigmata." A medical study, by Dr. F. Lefebvre. Translated from the French. Edited by Rev. J. Spencer Northcote, D.D., President of S. Mary's College, Oscott. To which the following explanatory note may be added:--The name of Dr. Lefebvre is sufficient guarantee of the importance of any work coming from his pen. During twenty years that he has filled the chair of General Pathology and Therapeutics in the University of Louvain he has gained a world-wide reputation by his investigations in the wide and, to a great extent, unexplored field of medical research. Add to this moral qualities of the first order, and ardent zeal in the cause of religion, and

Glimpses of the Supernatural Volumes I & II

we have a character which commands our admiration and esteem in the highest degree. The book, translated into English under the superintendence of Dr. Northcote, is a medical inquiry into the case of Louise Lateau, the Belgian stigmatizata. The medical features of the case are all that Dr. Lefebvre proposes to treat, leaving, of course, to the proper ecclesiastical authorities the theological investigation. An abridged account of this case has been published, entitled "Louise Lateau, the Ecstatica of Bois d'Haine," by Dr. Lefebvre, translated from the French by J. S. Shepard. London: Richardson and Son. 1872.

57. This account was written in 1874.

58. Affidavits of the truth of the above narrative have been made by the physician and clergyman who witnessed the miraculous intervention, as also by the person more immediately concerned--Miss Collins.

59. Among the spectators were the following: Mr. R. Tobin and family, Mr. John Sullivan and wife, Mr. C. D. O'Sullivan and wife, Mr. J. A. Donahue and wife, Mr. George Hooper and wife, Mrs. Emmet Doyle, Mr. D. J. Oliver, and many others. Dr. Polactri was standing by Miss Collins's bedside, taking notes on the condition of the patient. He confessed the case was beyond the reach of medical science. Her head moved from side to side with the intensity of her agony, and her tongue was parched and swollen.

60. Mr. D. J. Oliver writes from San Francisco, in a private letter, as follows: "I was awe-stricken whilst beholding the miracle. I know both the young girls, and the account is correct in every particular, except that the stigmata was on both sides of the hands and feet, and not on one side only. I spent an hour with them last evening, and saw them at communion at early mass this morning."

61. The account up to this point is copied from a Letter to Miss F. T. Bird, dated September 3, 1809, by Mr. Woodford, an eminent surgeon of Taunton, who attended Mary Wood upon her accident.

62. Certain stated prayers and devotional exercises continued throughout nine days.

63. The authentic documents of the examination, and of the whole process of the cure, are contained at length in a work entitled "The Miraculous Cure of Winifred White," by the Rev. John Milner, D.D., published by Grace of Dublin, and reprinted, on several occasions and in different forms, in England. It may be added that Winifred White departed this life on the 13th of January, 1824, nineteen years after her cure. She died of consumption.

64. A well-known clergyman of the Church of England.

65. The account from which the above was compiled was a formal and authentic statement of the Curé de S. Martin, at Metz (A.D. 1865).

66. The account given above is taken from a small tractate entitled "The Miracle of Metz, wrought by the Blessed Sacrament, June 14, 1865," translated from the French, by Lady Georgiana Fullerton. With the imprimaturs of His Grace the Archbishop of Westminster and the Bishop of Metz. London: Burns and Co., 1865.

67. See a series of most interesting letters, entitled "Is God amongst us?" by a Clergyman of the Church of England, published in the "Union" newspaper, for 1857, vol. ii. pp. 262, 329-330. London: Painter.

68. "The Measure of Christian Sorrow for the Departed," a Sermon preached at the funeral of Mary Lisle Phillipps de Lisle, by the Rev. Henry Collins, M.A. Loughborough: J. H. Gray, 1860, pp. 11-13.

69. "Indulgenced prayers are prayers to the recital of which is attached by the Church the grant of indulgences. By indulgences Catholics understand a remission of sin, that is, of all those temporal pains which God inflicts for sin committed by His servants after baptism; and the Church teaches that the power of remission was conferred by Jesus Christ when He said to the Apostles, 'Whatsoever ye shall loose on earth, shall be loosed in Heaven.'" S. Matt. xvi. 19.

70. An anonymous seventeenth-century writer reasons as follows:--"To know things aright and perfectly is to know the causes thereof. A definition doth consist of those causes which give the whole essence, and contain the perfect nature of the thing defined; where that is therefore found out, there appears the very clear light. If it be perfect, it is much the greater; though if it be not fully perfect, yet it giveth some good light. For which respect, though I dare not say I can give a perfect definition in this matter, which is hard to do even in known things, because the essential form is hard to be found, yet I do give a definition which may at the least give notice and make known what manner of persons they be of whom I am to speak:--A witch is one that worketh by the Devil, or by some devilish or curious art, either hurting or healing, revealing things secret, or foretelling things to come, which the Devil hath devised to entangle and snare men's souls withal unto damnation. The Conjurer, the Enchanter, the Sorcerer, the Diviner, and whatsoever other sort there is, are indeed encompassed within this circle. The Devil doth (no doubt) after divers sorts and divers forms, deal in these. But no man is able to show an essential difference in each of them from

the rest. I hold it no wisdom or labour well spent to travel much therein. One artificer hath devised them all."

71. "Thou shalt not suffer a witch to live."--Exodus xxii. 18. "Neither shall ye use enchantment."--Levit. xix. 26. "Regard not them which have familiar spirits, neither seek after wizards, to be defiled by them."--Ibid. ver. 31. "When thou art come into the land which the Lord thy God giveth thee, thou shalt not learn to do after the abominations of those nations. There shall not be found among you any one that maketh his son or his daughter to pass through the fire, or that useth divination, or an observer of times, or an enchanter, or a witch, or a charmer, or a consulter with familiar spirits, or a necromancer. For all that do these things are an abomination unto the Lord: and because of these abominations the Lord thy God doth drive them out from before thee."--Deut. xviii. 9-12. Of Manasseh is recorded, that "He caused his children to pass through the fire in the valley of the son of Hinnom: also he observed times, and used enchantments, and used witchcraft, and dealt with a familiar spirit, and with wizards."--2 Chron. xxxiii. 6. Lastly, S. Paul mentions "witchcraft" amongst such "works of the flesh" as "adultery, fornication, heresies, drunkenness, and murders."--Galat. v. 19-21.

72. Many of the heathens cordially defended magic and Necromancy. For example, Asclepiades, who lived in the time of Pompey the Great, cured diseases by magic, enjoining upon his patient, in the case of the falling sickness, to bind upon his arm a Cross with a Nail driven into it. Julianus, the magician, is reported to have driven the plague out of Rome by magical power. Apuleius, a disciple of Plato, wrote at length on magic. To him may be added Marcellus and Alexander Trallian. Pliny asserts in very plain language that Necromancy was so prevalent in his day, but was condemned by the wisest, that it was classed with treason and poisoning. And it is notorious that magic was long used as a convenient though inefficient weapon against Christianity.--Vide, likewise, Livy i. 20, and Strabo, lib. vi.

73. "Fuga Satanæ. Exorcismus, ex sacrarum Litterarum fontibus, pioɋ S. Ecclesiæ Instituto exhaustus. Authore Petro Antonio Stampa, Sacerdote Clavenense. Cum privilegio. Venetiis. M.D.C.V. Apud Sebastianum Combis."

74. "Touching the antiquity of Witchcraft, we must needs confess that it hath been of very ancient time, because the Scriptures do testify so much, for in the time of Moses it was very rife in Egypt. Neither was it then newly sprung up, being common, and grown into such ripeness among the nations, that the Lord, reckoning by divers kinds, saith that the Gentiles did commit such abominations, for which He would cast them out before the children of Israel."--"What a Witch is, and the Antiquities of Witchcraft," A.D. 1612.

75. See note to this effect on page 152.

76. The following passage, from a sermon by the late Canon Melville, bears out the above statement:--"It is unnecessary for us to inquire what those arts may have been in which the Ephesians are said to have greatly excelled. There seems no reason for doubting that, as we have already stated, they were of the nature of magic, sorcery, or witchcraft; though we cannot profess accurately to define what such terms might import. The Ephesians, as some in all ages have done, probably laid claim to intercourse with invisible beings, and professed to derive from that intercourse acquaintance with, and power over, future events. And though the very name of witchcraft be now held in contempt, and the supposition of communion with evil spirits scouted as a fable of what are called the dark ages, we own that we have difficulty in believing that all which has passed by the names of magic and sorcery may be resolved into sleight of hand, deception, and trick. The visible world and the invisible are in very close contact: there is, indeed, a veil on our eyes, preventing our gazing on spiritual beings and things, but we doubt not that whatsoever passes upon earth is open to the view of higher and immaterial creatures. And as we are sure that a man of piety and prayer enlists good angels on his side and engages them to perform towards him the ministrations of kindness, we know not why there cannot be such a thing as a man whose wickedness has caused his being abandoned by the Spirit of God, and who, in this his desertion, has thrown open to evil angels the chambers of his soul, and made himself so completely their instrument, that they may use him in the uttering or working strange things, which shall have all the air of prophecy or miracle."--"Sermons on certain of the less prominent facts and references in Sacred Story." By Henry Melville, D.D. In two volumes. London: Rivingtons, 1872. Vol. i. pp. 57, 58.

77. The above definitions are taken from the literary productions of certain of the most recent "philosophers" and "thinkers" already referred to in the text.

78. "The works of the flesh are manifest, which are these: adultery, fornication, uncleanness, lasciviousness, idolatry, witchcraft, hatred, variance, emulations, wrath, strife, seditions, heresies, envyings, murders, drunkenness, revellings, and such like." Galat. v. 19-21.

79. This took place in England in the year 1736, in the teeth of the protests of many, who felt that a modification of laws founded on an explicit principle of Scripture would have been both

wiser and safer than their total and absolute abolition. Amongst others, Mr. John Wesley wrote and preached to this effect. Quite recently a distinguished Liberal statesman remarked that if the practices of the so-called "Spiritualists" still developed, as for some time they had been developing, some re-enactment of the laws against Witchcraft might become necessary. It certainly seems one-sided and unfair that ignorant women should be punished for "fortune-telling," and that the paid professional mediums should go scot free.

80. The following bears out the remarks in the text:--"The influence of Christianity upon magic could not be small; material changes would undoubtedly be brought about through its influence.... At the epoch of Christ's appearance, faith in demons, and particularly in evil spirits, was not only general amongst the heathen, but also among the Jews to an incredible extent; and unbounded powers, even as great as those of the Divinity, were ascribed to them, which not only were supposed to influence the mind, but also Nature and physical life."--Ennemoser's "History of Magic." Translated by W. Howitt. London, 1854. Vol. i., pp. 340, 341. One particular fact may be here put upon record, as being, to say the least, more than remarkable: To the Roman Emperor Augustus, who, according to Suidas and Nicephorus, sent to a renowned Oracle to inquire what successor he should have, it was answered, "The Hebrew Child, Whom all the gods obey, drives me hence." No other response was vouchsafed.

81. The Editor is indebted to the Rev. Dr. Littledale for the following note:--"There is an authorized Form of Exorcism in the Greek 'Euchologion.' It begins with the Trisagion, and Psalms, Domine exaudi, Dominus regit me, Dominus illuminatio mea, Exurgat Deus, Miserere, Domine ne in furore, and Domine exaudi precem. Then follows the Consolatory Canon, with a long Hymn addressed to our Blessed Lord, the Blessed Virgin Mary, and All Saints. At the close of this the priest anoints the patient, saying a brief prayer over him, and so the office closes." See also Appendix to Chapter iii. pp. 138-148.

82. John Selden, in his "Table Talk," in the article upon "Devils," somewhat scoffingly asserts that the Roman Catholics affirm that "the Protestants the Devil hath already, and the Papists are so holy, he dares not meddle with them."

83. "The Question of Witchcraft debated." By John Wagstaffe. London: 1669. Second edition, 1671.

84. "A True Discourse upon the Matter of Martha Brossier, of Romorantin," translated out of French into English, by Abraham Hartwell. London: imprinted for John Wolfe. 1599.

85. "The Copy of a Letter describing the Wonderful Worke of God in delyviring a maydene within the city of Chester from a horrible kind of torment or sicknesse, 16 February anno 1564." Imprinted at London for John Judely, dwelling in Little Britayne Street beyond Aldersgate, 23 March 1564.

86. "A Briefe and True Discourse, contayning the certayne possession and dispossession of seven persons in one familie, in Lancashire." By George More, Minister and Preacher of the Word, and now (for bearing witness unto this, and for justifying the rest,) a prisoner at the Clinks, where he hath continued almost for two yeares. A.D. 1600.

87. It is asserted by several authorities that no less than three thousand persons were executed for Witchcraft during that dark period of heretical pravity, the Great Rebellion. Now, as "Rebellion," according to the express assurance of the Prophet Samuel (1 Sam. xv. 23) "is as the sin of Witchcraft," no hearty believer in God's revelation can be at all surprised to find that both Witchcraft and Rebellion in an atmosphere of heresy flourished together, under that odious tyrant and hypocritical fanatic, Oliver Cromwell: when the altar was thrown down and both King and Archbishop were murdered.

88. "An Antidote against Atheism: or an Appeal to the Natural Faculties of the Mind of Man." By Henry More, Fellow of Christ's College, Cambridge. 1655.

89. "Cases of Conscience concerning Evil Spirits personating Men." By Increase Mather. Printed at Boston, and reprinted in London for John Dutton at the Raven in the Poultry, 1693.

90. "Sadducismus Triumphatus: a Full and Plain Evidence concerning Witches and Apparitions." By Joseph Glanville, Chaplain in Ordinary to King Charles II. London: 1726.

91. A careful deposition as to the above facts was made before the Justices of the Peace mentioned, who added the following formal attestation: "The aforesaid passages [i.e. occurrences] were some of them seen by us, and some other remarkable ones, not here set down, were upon the examination of several witnesses taken on oath before us.

"(Signed)
Robert Hunt.
John Carey."

92. "The Surey Demoniack; or, an Account of Satan's Strange and Dreadful Actings in and about the Body of Richard Dugdale of Surey, near Whalley in Lancashire." London: 1697.

93. The following curious extract from a "Coventry News-Letter," dated Nov. 2, 1672,

Rev. Frederick George Lee, D.C.L.

certainly tells a wonderful story, in some respects not unlike that recorded in the text. It serves at all events to show what were the popular notions concerning occurrences which, to say the least, were very remarkable; and it is reprinted here verbatim:--

"All our wonder here about is employ'd at the strange condition of a maid neare us, one Elizabeth Tibbots of about 18 yeares of age liveing with her unkle one Thomas Crofts at a place cal'd Hust (?) in ye parish of Stonely (Stoneleigh) about two miles hence. Ye maid for about this 3 weekes past has bene taken with strange fitts in which shee has vomitted up severall things incredible, as first severall Peble stones neare as big as eggs, knives, sissers, peices of glass some of them two or 3 Inches square, peices of Iron, an Iron Bullet of at least 8 Inches round, and 2 pound & halfe weight, a black drinking pot of neare halfe a pint, peices of cloth & wood, a pockett pistoll, a paire of Pincers, Bottoms of yarne and severall other things many whereof are now at our majors, and have bene evidently seene to come out at her mouth, by many credible witnesses, nor should I my selfe venture to give you this Relation, which seemes soe unlike truth, had I not my selfe beene an eye wittness, with my most cunning observation of soe much of it, that I am confirmed in ye beleife of the whole, all which is imputed to some diabollicall practices of one Watson a strang kind of an Emperick, to whom shee was some tyme a Patient, who had it seemes soe wrought with her as that shee had promis'd him marriage, & to goe with him (though shee knew not whither,) But afterwards refused it. Immediately upon which shee fell into these fitts, yet has shee her respites, dureing which shee appears reasonable well, & I have heard her discourse very rationally of her selfe & condition, a full account whereof would be too long to give; 'tis said that for these 4 or 5 dayes past (in which tyme I have not seene her) somewhat appeares to her in ye shape of a dogg. Now, whether shee be bewicht or whether shee be a witch, or whether ye Divell be in her, (as well as some others of her sex,) I know not, but that what I have told you seemed to ye most vigilant eye to be infallibly true is not doubted, so that if it be not really soe, I can onely say the Divell's in't, who you perhaps may fancy to be in him that gives you this seemingly incredible Relation, which be pleased to accept for better, for worse from," &c.

94. "Witchcraft further Displayed." London: Printed for E. Curl at the Dial and Bible. 1714.

95. In the "Overseer's Accounts" for the parish of S. Giles, Northampton, there is an item for the purchase of faggots for the purpose of burning a witch. A.D. 1705.

96. "An Account of the Tryals, Examination, and Condemnation of Ellinor Shaw & Mary Phillips (Two Notorious Witches) at Northampton Assizes on Wednesday the 7th of March, 1705, for Bewitching a Woman & Two children, Tormenting them in a Sad and Lamentable Manner till they Dyed. With an account of their strange Confessions about their Familiarity with the Devil, and How They Made a wicked Contract with him to be revenged on several Persons, by Bewitching their Cattel to Death, &c. And several other Strange and Amasing Particulars." London: Printed for F. Thorne, near Fleete-street.

97. The following "Letter" from Mr. Ralph Davis, of Northampton, addressed to Mr. William Simons, merchant in London, is reprinted almost verbatim, certain passages, by reason of their extreme coarseness, being alone suppressed. It was published by Thorne, of Fleet Street, in 1705, and had a very large circulation. It is entitled "The Northamptonshire Witches:"--

"According to my word Promise in my last I have sent you here Inclosed a faithful Account of the Lives and Conversations of the two notorious Witches that were Executed on the North side of our town on Saturday the 17th instant, and indeed considering the extraordinary Methods these wicked women used to accomplish their Diabolical Art, I think it may merit your Reception, and the more since I understand you have a friend near Fleete Street who being a Printer may make use of it in order to oblige the Publick; which take as followeth; viz:--

"To proceed in order, I shall first begin with Ellinor Shaw (as being the most notorious of the two) who was Born at Cotterstock within a small Mile of Oundle in Northamptonshire, of very obscure Parents, who not willing, or at least not able, to give their Daughter any manner of Education, she was left to shift for her self at the age of 14 years; at which time she got acquainted with a Partener in Wickedness, one Mary Phillips, Born at Oundle aforesaid, with whom she held a frindly Correspondence for several years together, and work'd very hard for a Livelihood; but when she arriv'd to the age of 21 she began to be a very lude [lewd] sort of a Person ... which wicked and loathsom Actions were not only talked of in the Town of Cotterstock where she was Born but at Oundle, Glapthorne, Benefield, Southwick and several Parts adjacent; and that as well by Children of four or five years of Age as persons of riper years; so that by degrees her Name became so famous or rather infamous that she could hardly peep out of her Door but the Children would point at her in a Scoffing manner ... [so] that she Swore she would be revenged on her enemies tho' she pawn'd her Soul for the Purchase; and then Mary Phillips being her Partner in Knitting and Bedfellow also, who was as bad as herself in the Vices aforesaid, she communicated her Thoughts to her, relating to a Contract with the Devil, in order to have the Wills of those who Slandered them.... In fine as these two Harlots agreed in their other Wickedness so they were resolv'd to go

Hand in Hand in this, and consequently go to the Devil together for Company, but out of a Hellish kind of Civility he saved them that Trouble at present, for ... he immediately waited upon 'em to obtain his Booty on Saturday the 12th of February 1704 about 12 a Clock at Night according to their own Confessions, appearing in the shape of a black tall Man, at whose approach they were very much startled at first, but taking Ellinor Shaw by the Hand he spoke thus--Says he, Be not afraid, of me for I am one of the Creation as well as your selves, having power given me to bestow it on whom I please, and do assure you that if you will pawn your Souls to me for only a Year and two Months I will for all that time assist you in whatever you desire. Upon which he produced a little piece of Parchment on which by their Consents having prick't their Fingers' ends, he wrote the Infernal Covenants in their own Blood which they signed with their own Hands and the same Night.... In the Morning he told them they were now as substantial Witches as any were in the world, and that they had power by the assistance of the Imps that he would send them to do what Mischief they pleased.

"I shall not trouble you with what is already mention'd in the Tryals of these two persons because it is in print by your Friend already but only instance what was omitted in that as not having room here to contain it altogether but as to their general confessions after their Condemnations, take as followeth:--

"The day before they were Executed, Mr. Danks the Minister visited them in Prison, in order if possible to bring them to a State of Repentance, but seeing all pious Discourse prov'd ineffectual, he desired them to tell him what mischeivous Pranks they had Play'd and what private Conference they had with the Devil from time to time, since they had made that fatal Bargain with him: To which Ellinor Shaw with the Consent of the other told him that the Devil in the Shape of a tall black Man appear'd several times to them and at every visit would present them with new Imps some of a Red Coulour others of a Dun and the third of a black Colour and that ... by the Assistance of these Hellish Animals they often Kill'd Men Women and Children to the great surprise of all the towns thereabouts; she further adding that it was all the Delight they had to be doing such wicked Actions and they had Kil'd by their Inchantments and Witchcraft in the space of nine Months time 15 children eight Men and six Women tho' none was suspected of being Bewitch'd but those two Children, said the Woman, that they Dy'd for; and that they had Bewitch'd to Death in the same Space of Time 40 Hoggs of several poor People, besides 100 Sheep, 18 Horses, and 30 Cows, even to the utter Ruin of several Families: As to their particular Intreagues and waggish tricks I have not Room to enumerate, they are so many; only some remarkable Feats they did in Prison which was thus, viz:--one Day Mr. Laxon and his wife coming by the Prison had the Curiosity to look through the Grates and seeing of Ellinor Shaw told her that now the Devil had left her in the Lurch, as he had done the rest of his Servants; upon which the said Ellinor was observ'd to Mutter strangely to herself in an unknown Language for about two Minutes; at the end of which Mr. Laxon's Wife's Cloathes were all turn'd over her head Smock and all in a most strange manner ... notwithstanding all the Endeavours her Husband could use to keep her Cloathes in order; at which the said Ellinor having Laughed Heartily and told her She had prov'd her Lyer, her Cloathes began to come to their right order again. The keeper of the Prison having one Day Threatened them with Irons, they, by their Spells, caused him to Dance almost an Hour Naked in the Yard to the Amazement of the Prison: nay, such Pranks were Play'd by them during their Confinement that no one durst give them an ill Word, insomuch that their Execution was the more hastened in the regard of their frequent Disturbances and great Mischief they did in several places of the Town notwithstanding their Imprisonment.

"They were so hardened in their Wickedness that they Publickly boasted that their Master (meaning the Devil) would not suffer them to be Executed: but they found him [a] Lyer; for on Saturday Morning being the 17th instant they were carried to the Gallows on the Northside of the Town whither numerous Crowds of people went to see them Die, and being come to the place of Execution the Minister repeated his former pious endeavours to bring them to a sense of their Sins but to as little purpose as before: for instead of calling on God for Mercy nothing was heard from them but D----g and Cursing. However a little before they were ty'd up; at the request of the Minister, Ellinor Shaw confessed not only the Crime for which she Dyed, but openly declared before them all how she first became a Witch, as did also Mary Phillips; and being desired to say their Prayers they both set up a very loud Laughter, calling for the Devil to come and help them in such a Blasphemous manner as is not fit to Mention, so that the Sherif seeing their presumptious Impenitence caused them to be Executed with all the Expedition possible; even while they were Cursing and raving; and as they liv'd the Devil's true Factors so they resolutely Dyed in his service, to the Terror [of] all People who were eye-Witnesses of their dreadful and amazing Exits.

"So that being Hang'd till they were almost Dead the Fire was put to the Straw, Faggots and other Combustable matter till they were Burnt to Ashes. Thus Liv'd and thus Dyed two of the most notorious and presumptious Witches that ever were known in this Age.

"To conclude: I heartly wish that these wretched Women's Sad and Lamentable Fates may be a warning to all Proud, Lustful and Malicious Persons whatsoever, least they be brought Step by Step before they are aware unto the Devil's Slaughterhouse of Confusion and Misery to all Eternity.

"I am promised a Copy of the Sermon that was Preached by Mr. Danks at the Church of All Saint's the next day after the said Witches were Executed (being Sunday) upon that very Occasion, which I hope to send you by the next Post.

"I am Sir, Your humble Servant, Ralph Davis."

98. "A Full and Impartiall account of the Discovery of Sorcery and Witchcraft, practised by Jane Wenham," etc. London: 1712.

99. "Sadducismus Debellatus: or a True Narrative of the Sorceries and Witchcraft exercised by the Devil and his Instruments upon Mrs. Christian Shaw in the county of Renfrew, in the West of Scotland, from August 1696 to April 1697, &c." Collected from the Records. London: Newman and Bell, 1698.

100. "Another Brand Plucked out of the Burning: or More Wonders of the Invisible World." London: 1700.

101. "Saddvcismus Triumphatus," pp. 20-37.

102. Two remarkable works for and against what was termed "Judiciall Astrologie," were published in the latter years of Queen Elizabeth's reign. One, attacking the system, from the pen of John Chamber, Prebendary of Windsor and Fellow of Eton College (London: John Harrison, Paternoster Row, 4to., Lambeth Library, 78 F. 22); the other defending it, in reply to the above, by Sir Christopher Heydon, Knt., printed at Cambridge, by John Legat, printer to the University in 1603 (Lambeth Library, 78 F. 12). The former is a treatise of very considerable vigour and power of reasoning: the latter is somewhat laboured, eminently pedantic, overburdened with tedious and irrelevant quotations, and altogether very inferior from a literary point of view.

103. In almost all Heathen or Pagan countries, Witchcraft, Necromancy and Sorcery are recognized and established institutions.

104. There was a notorious sorcerer and reputed necromancer in King James the First's reign, a certain Dr. Lamb. In Baxter's "Certainty of the World of Spirits" (A.D. 1691), he records a curious instance of Lamb's miraculous performances. This sorcerer, meeting two of his acquaintances in the street, they, expressing a wish to witness some example of his spiritual skill, were invited to his house. There they were conducted to an inner room, where to their intense surprise they saw a growing-tree spring up slowly in the middle of the room. [It may be here remarked that the Oriental jugglers and sorcerers work a similar manifestation of their powers, often witnessed and frequently described.--Editor.] In a moment, as this record informs us, there appeared three diminutive men, who with little axes felled the tree; and then the doctor dismissed his guests, who had been duly impressed by his powers. On that very night, however, a tremendous hurricane arose, causing the house of one of the guests to rock from side to side, with every probability that the house would fall, and bury him and his wife in its ruins. The wife in an agony of fear inquired, "Were you not at Dr. Lamb's to-day?" The husband admitted that it was true that he had been. "And did you not bring something away from his house?" The husband confessed that he had done so. When the little men were felling the tree, he had picked up some of the chips and put them into his pocket. Nothing, therefore, as his wife pointed out, remained to be done but to produce these chips, and get rid of them as fast as possible. When this was done, the tempest ceased, and the rest of the night was perfectly calm. It may be added that this sorcerer became so odious, because of his necromancy and other infernal practices, that in 1640 the populace rose upon him and tore him to pieces in the streets; while, thirteen years afterwards, a woman who had been in his service was apprehended upon a charge of Witchcraft, was tried on what seems to have been very strong and conclusive evidence, found guilty, and in expiation of her crime was executed at Tyburn. [The contemporary literature extant, relating to this case of Lamb and his servant, would fill a large volume.--Editor.]

105. These persons are reported and reputed to be professional mediums, and are said to be very largely patronized by people of all ranks and classes, more especially the higher.

106. "Report on Spiritualism." Examination of the Master of Lindsay, p. 215. London: Longman, 1871.

107. Genesis iii. 1; Revelation xii. 9; Ibid. xx. 2.

108. The Editor, while avoiding the reproduction of examples which are tolerably well known, has generally aimed at setting forth cases which have not yet been put into print; though in some records which follow, a few have been selected which have already been published, in order that one example, at least, of all the particular kinds of warning and dreams, may be here presented to the reader.

109. Genesis xx. 3; Ibid. xxxi. 11, and (to Laban) ver. 31. As to Pharaoh's dream of a coming famine, see Genesis xli.

110. Numbers xii. 6; 1 Kings iii. 5-15; Daniel vii. to the end of the book. S. Matthew, 1-20; Ibid. ii. 12 (as to S. Joseph), ver. 13. and verses 19 and 20; Ibid, xxvii. 19.

111. Two valued correspondents respectively write as follows:--"One could relate many such family incidents as you suggest, but everyone shrinks from allowing them to be verified by name. I imagine that this reticence arises from the natural dread and dislike to having what is sacred to one's own faith and feelings submitted to the ridicule of sceptical and rationalistic minds."

Another:--"I send you the enclosed--a record of the supernatural appearance which is always seen immediately prior to the death of the head of our family. But I do not wish it printed; and absolutely forbid the mention either of place or person, lest it should be identified, which might cause annoyance to our friends."

112. De Anima, c. 45-47.

113. Ibid.

114. De Opificio Dei, sæc. xviii.

115. Epist. Sti. Cypriani, lxiii.

116. Epist. Sti. Basilii, cxx.

117. Opera Thom. Aquin., Tom. ii., Quæst. xcv., Art. vi.: Tom. iii., Quæst. lxxx., Art. vii.

118. "The Philosophy of Sleep." By Macknish.

119. The Rev. George R. Winter, M.A., Vicar of Swaffham and Rural Dean, thus most obligingly writes to the Editor (A.D. 1874):--"The story of the Dream is popularly believed, and there was a good foundation for it. In the upper portion of the windows of the north aisle is some old painted glass, which is supposed to represent the man and his family; but the chief monument of his identity is a piece of old carving representing a pedlar with a pack on his back, and also his dog, forming part of the westernmost stalls of the choir. This, I believe, was at one time in the north aisle, which the man is supposed to have built." The dream is related at length in Blomfield's "History of Norfolk."

120. The above was written at Alton Towers, Cheadle, on the 23rd of October, 1842, and duly signed by Mr. William Talbot, a relation of John, Earl of Shrewsbury.

121. "The account here given of the Dream which occurred in Cornwall, is, as I personally testify, true and accurate. (Signed) Rachel L. Lee (daughter of the late Benjamin Tucker, of Trematon Castle, Esquire, and daughter-in-law of the late Rev. T. T. Lee, Vicar of Thame), Kentons, near Henley-on-Thames, May 14th, 1873."

122. A friend who provided the above example writes to the Editor:--"I knew the family, and the circumstance of Mr. Perring's singular dream; and can certainly testify to its truth."

123. From a Letter dated Nov. 1, 1872, in the handwriting of the Widow of the Clergyman in question, kindly communicated to the Editor by the Rev. Theodore J. Morris, Vicar of Hampton in Arden, near Birmingham.

124. The following document was drawn up about thirteen years ago, and given to the Editor with the above account by an Oxford friend:--

"This is to certify that in 1840 I dreamt the Dream about the strange man coming to the front door and forcing himself in; and that seven years afterwards, that is in 1847, what I had seen in my dream occurred in London, when, having heard knocks at the door when I was alone in the house, I saw the man outside the door whom I had seen in my dream seven years before."

"Hannah Green.

"Wootton, Oxfordshire, August 5, 1861."

125. "Notes and Queries," Sept. 24, 1853.

126. "I have carefully read the account which you have so nicely written out from my own and my brother's Letters; and have also twice read the same to my mother and brother. Both join with me in testifying to its absolute truth and perfect accuracy. Our account was taken down from the lips of the Rector of ---- himself. We, indeed, have reason to believe in the Supernatural."

127. The Rector of Phillack and Gwithian, near Hayle in Cornwall, is the Rev. Frederick Hockin, M.A. and Rural Dean.

128. He is described as "Wilfred D. Speer, Esq., of West End Lodge, Thames Ditton, a magistrate for the County of Surrey, and a captain in the Militia of that county."

129. "Statement of the Circumstances attending the Death of Wilfred D. Speer, Esq., with copies of Testimony and Correspondence." London, Ontario: John Cameron, Dundas Street, West, 8vo. pp. 12, 1867.

130. "If my dream come true, I am certainly approaching my latter end, and have only a little time longer in this world." Attested copy of Captain Wilfred Speer's Letter, given to the Editor by the Rev. John Richardson, of Warwick.

131. He was shot dead on the night of the 17th of June, 1867, on board a steamboat on the Missouri.

132. The following Letter has been received by the Editor from the dignitary in question:--

"Nov. 6, 1874. Rev. and dear Sir, I only wish that my name should not be published. The statement, as written out by me, is entirely at your service.... To the Rev. Dr. Lee."

133. It seems that as a matter of fact there is no tunnel near the scene of the accident, but a long, level line of railway, very near the margin of the sea. At least so a correspondent who knows the locality well has informed me.--Editor.

134. "Having made enquiries regarding the fact of Tinley's remarkable dream, which seemed to foreshadow his death by the well-known accident, I can testify to the truth that he had such a dream, and that he regarded it as a sign of coming death.

"A. Rutherford, Wolverhampton.

"July 14, 1874."

135. Sir Roger Tichborne, Knt. of Tichborne, flourished in the reign of Henry II. He married Mabella, daughter and sole heiress of Ralph de Lamerston, in the Isle of Wight.

136. Sir Henry Tichborne, born in 1756, married in 1778 Elizabeth Plowden, and had seven sons, viz. 1. Henry, 2. Benjamin, 3. Edward, 4. James, 5. John, 6. George, and 7. Roger. His eldest son Henry, who married Anne, daughter of Sir Thomas Burke, had seven daughters, viz. 1. Eliza, 2. Frances, 3. Julia, 4. Mary, 5. Katherine, 6. Lucy, and 7. Emily.

137. "Staffordshire Chronicle," July, 1835.

138. Lysons in his "Magna Britannia," vol. vi. describing the parish of South Tawton, about five miles from Okehampton, co. Devon, says:--"Oxenham, in this parish, gave name to an ancient family who possessed it, at least from the time of Henry III. to the death of William Long Oxenham, Esq., in 1814." The mansion, as the Editor learns, has long been occupied as a farm-house. It may here be added that it is believed that Drake's friend, Captain John Oxenham, who lost his life in an engagement with the Spaniards in South America (A.D. 1575), was a member of this family. Mr. Canon Kingsley, in "Westward-Ho," has introduced the omen of a Bird with a white breast in connection with this gentleman.

139. "A True relation of an Apparition in the likeness of a Bird with a White Breast, that appeared hovering over the deathbeds of some of the children of Mr. James Oxenham, of Sale Monachorum, Devon, Gent. Confirmed by Sundry witnesses. London, printed by I. O. for Richard Clutterbuck, and are to be sold at the figure of the Gun in little Britain, near St. Botolph's church. 1641." British Museum, Press-Mark E. 205-9.

A copy of this pamphlet is also to be found amongst Gough's collection in the Bodleian. The British Museum copy contains a curious and very effective engraving, representing the actual appearance of the Bird to a person dying in bed.

140. It is also stated in this pamphlet that the clergyman of the parish had been appointed by the bishop of the diocese to inquire into the truth of these particulars, and that a monument had been put up with his approbation with the names of the witnesses of each apparition of the Bird. The pamphlet states that those who had been sick and had recovered, never saw the apparition. It further came out in the evidence tendered, that the same Bird had appeared to Grace, the grandmother of John Oxenham, who died in 1618.

141. Lysons states that these monumental inscriptions do not now exist either in the church or churchyard of Tawton or Sale Monachorum. But, considering the shameful destruction of monuments in late years by so-called "Church Restorers," this is not to be wondered at.

142. It has been shrewdly and perhaps not untruly observed, that "a genuine and solemn citation may tend to work its own fulfilment in certain minds, who, by allowing the thing to prey upon their spirits, enfeeble the powers of life, and perhaps at the critical date arouse some latent or dormant disease into deadly action."

143. The following is from a MS. note of a member of the Editor's family--George Henry Lee, Lord Litchfield, who was Chancellor of the University of Oxford in the latter part of the last century. Lord Rochester, it should be added, was allied to that family through his mother, Anne, Countess of Rochester, previously the widow of Sir F. H. Lee:--

"Lord Rochester told me of an odd presage that one had of his approaching death in the Lady Warre his mother-in-law's house. The chaplain had dreamt that such a day he should die, but being by all the family put out of the belief of it, he had forgot it till the evening before at supper, there being thirteen at table, according to a fond conceit that one of these must soon die, one of the young ladies pointed to him that he was to die. He, remembering his dream, fell into some disorder; and the Lady Warre reproving him for his superstition, he said he was confident he was to die before morning; but he being in perfect health, it was not much minded. It was Saturday night, and he was to preach the next day. He went to his chamber, sat up late, (as appeared by the burning of his candle,) and he had been preparing his notes for his sermon, but he was found dead in his bed next morning. These things he said made him inclined to believe [that] the soul was a substance distinct from matter, and this often returned into his thoughts."

144. The Registrar-General in his last Report writes thus:--"Seamen will not sail, women will

not wed on a Friday so willingly as on other days of the week. It has been ascertained that out of 4,057 marriages which took place during a certain period in the midland district of England, not two per cent. were celebrated on a Friday, while thirty-two per cent. were entered as having taken place on a Sunday."

145. Jerome Cardan, the strange sixteenth-century physician, who dealt so extensively in horoscopes, and is said to have sought the assistance of spirits, professed to own and exercise some specific and supernatural gifts:--1. The power of throwing his spirit out of his body, by which he could see things at a distance. 2. His faculty of Second Sight, or of seeing whatever he pleased with his eyes, "Oculis, non vi mentis." 3. His dreams, which, as he maintained, uniformly foretold to him what was about to occur, and by which he truly predicted the day of his own death, and 4. his "unerring astrological knowledge."

146. "Miscellanies, collected by J. Aubrey, Esq." London: printed for Edward Castle, 1696.

147. "A Treatise on the Second Sight, Dreams, and Apparitions," by Theophilus Insulanus. Dedicated "To the Honourable Sir Harry Monro, of Foulis, Baronet." Pp. 107-108. Edinburgh: 1763.

Rev. Frederick George Lee, D.C.L.

VOLUME II

CHAPTER VI - SPECTRAL APPEARANCES

"Now a thing was secretly brought to me, and mine ear received a little thereof.
In thoughts from the visions of the night, when deep sleep falleth on men,
Fear came upon me, and trembling, which made all my bones to shake.
Then a Spirit passed before my face; the hair of my flesh stood up:
It stood still, but I could not discern the form thereof: an Image was before mine eyes." - Job iv. 12-16.

Examples of Spectral Appearances are so numerous, and the Editor has collected so many, both ancient and modern, that considerable difficulty has been occasioned in determining which shall here be set forth. The following, chosen from examples, some well known and well authenticated, and others now first published, but equally interesting and important, and coming to the Editor upon very high authority, deserve the best consideration of the reader.

The following record describes what is known as the "Chester-le-Street" Apparition:--

"About the year of Our Lord 1632 (as near as I can remember, having lost my notes and the copy of the letter to Serjeant Hutton, but I am sure that I do most perfectly remember the substance of the story), near unto Chester-in-the-Street, there lived one Walker, a yeoman of good estate, and a widower, who had a young woman to his kinswoman, that kept his house, who was by the neighbours suspected to be with child, and was, towards the dark of the evening one night, sent away with one Mark Sharp, who was a collier, one who digged coals under ground, and one that had been born at Blackburn hundred in Lancashire; and so she was not heard of a long time, and no noise, or little, was made about it. In the winter time after, one James Graham, or Grime, for so in that country they call them, being a miller, and living about two miles from the place where Walker lived, was one night alone very late in the mill grinding corn; and about twelve or one of the clock at night, he came down the stairs from having been putting corn in the hopper; the mill doors being shut, there stood a woman upon the midst of the floor, with her hair about her head, hanging down and all bloody, with five large wounds on her head. He being much affrighted and amazed began to bless himself;[1] and at last asked her who she was, and what she wanted. To which she said, 'I am the spirit of such a woman who lived with Walker, and being got with child by him, he promised to send me to a private place, where I should be well-looked to, till I was brought to bed, and well again; and then I should come again and keep his house. And, accordingly,' said the apparition, 'I was one night sent away with one Mark Sharp, who, upon a moor (naming a place that the miller knew) slew me with a pick, such as men dig coals withal and gave me these five wounds, and after threw my body into a coal-pit hard by, and hid the pick under a bank; and his shoes and stockings being bloody, he endeavoured to wash them; but seeing the blood would not forth, he hid them there.' And the apparition further told the miller that he must be the man to reveal it, or else that she must still appear and haunt him. The miller returned home very sad and heavy, but spoke not one word of what he had seen, but eschewed as much as he could to stay in the mill within night without company, thinking thereby to escape the seeing again of that frightful apparition. But notwithstanding, one night when it began to be dark, the apparition met him again and seemed very fierce and cruel, and threatened him that if he did not reveal the murder she would continually pursue and haunt him; yet, for all this, he still concealed it until S. Thomas' Eve before Christmas; when being soon after sunset walking in his garden, she appeared again, and then so threatened him, and affrighted him, that he promised faithfully to reveal it next morning. In the morning he went to a magistrate, and made the whole matter known with all the circumstances; and diligent search being made, the body was found in a coal-pit, with five wounds in the head, and the pick and shoes and stockings yet bloody; in every circumstance as the apparition had related unto the miller; whereupon Walker and Mark Sharp were both apprehended, but would confess nothing. At the assizes following, I think it was at Durham, they were arraigned, found guilty, condemned and executed; but I could never hear they confessed the fact. There were some that reported the apparition did appear unto the judge, or the foreman of the jury, who was alive in Chester-in-the-Street about ten years ago, as I have been credibly informed, but of that I know no certainty. There are many persons yet alive that can remember this strange murder, and the discovery of it; for it was, and sometimes yet is, as much discoursed of in the north country, as anything that almost hath

Rev. Frederick George Lee, D.C.L.

ever been heard of, and the relation printed, though now not to be gotten. I relate this with the greater confidence (though I may fail in some of the circumstances) because I saw and read the letter that was sent to Serjeant Hutton, who then lived at Goldsburgh in Yorkshire, from the judge before whom Walker and Mark Sharp were tried, and by whom they were condemned, and had a copy of it until about the year 1658, when I had it and many other books and papers taken from me; and this I confess to be one of the most convincing stories, being of undoubted verity, that ever I read, heard, or knew of, and carrieth with it the most evident force to make the most incredulous spirit to be satisfied that there are really, sometimes, such things as apparitions.--William Lumley."[2]

The above account, in which the object of the Spectral Appearance is obvious enough, is taken from the well-known "History of Durham," by that celebrated antiquarian the late Mr. Robert Surtees. It needs no comment, telling as it does so well, in quaint but plain language, its own remarkable story.

The next example to be recorded, the Apparition of the Rev. Mr. Naylor, may be found in Mr. John Nichols' "Literary Illustrations,"[3] and, though less startling than that already given, is certainly not without its own inherent interest:--

"*Part of a Letter from Mr. Edward Walter, Fellow of S. John's College, Cambridge, to his friend in the country, dated 'Dec. 6, 1706.'*

"'I should scarce have mentioned anything of the matter you write about of my own accord; but, since you have given yourself the trouble of an inquiry, I am, I think, obliged in friendship to relate all that I know of the matter; and that I do the more willingly, because I can so soon produce my authority.

"'Mr. Shaw, to whom the apparition appeared, was Rector of Soldern, or Souldern, in Oxfordshire, late of S. John's College aforesaid; on whom Mr. Grove, his old Fellow Collegiate, called July last in his journey to the West, where he stayed a day or two, and promised to see him again on his return, which he did, and stayed three days with him; in that time one night after supper, Mr. Shaw told him that there happened a passage which he could not conceal from him, as being an intimate friend, and one to whom this transaction might have something more relation than another man. He proceeded therefore, and told him that about a week before that time, viz. July the 28th, 1706, as he was smoking and reading in his study about eleven or twelve at night, there came to him the apparition of Mr. Naylor, formerly Fellow of the said College, and dead some years ago, a friend of Mr. Shaw's, in the same garb he used to be in, with his hands clasped before him. Mr. Shaw, not being much surprised, asked him how he did and desired him to sit down, which Mr. Naylor did. They both sat there a considerable time and entertained one another with various discourses. Mr. Shaw then asked him after what manner they lived in the separate state; he answered, Far different from what they do here, but that he was very well. He inquired further, whether there was any of their old acquaintance in that place where he was? he answered, 'No, not one;' and then proceeded and told him that one of their old friends, naming Mr. Orchard, should die quickly, and he himself should not be long after. There was mention of several people's names; but who they were, or upon what occasion, Mr. Grove cannot or will not tell. Mr. Shaw then asked him whether he would not visit him again before that time; he answered, No, he could not; he had but three days allowed him, and farther he could not go. Mr. Shaw said, "Fiat voluntas Domini;" and the apparition left him. This is word for word as Mr. Shaw told Mr. Grove, and Mr. Grove told me.

"'Note.--What surprised Mr. Grove was, that as he had in his journey homewards occasion to ride through Clopton, or Claxton, he called upon one Mr. Clark, Fellow of our College aforesaid and curate there, when inquiring after College news, Mr. Clark told him Arthur Orchard[1] died that week, Aug. 7, 1706, which very much shocked Mr. Grove, and brought to his mind the story of Mr. Shaw afresh. About three weeks ago Mr. Shaw died of apoplexy in the desk, [i. e. when ministering in church,] of the same distemper poor Arthur Orchard died of.

"'Note.--Since this strange completion of matters, Mr. Grove has told this relation, and stands to the truth of it; and that which confirms the narrative is, that he told the same to Dr. Baldiston, the present Vice-Chancellor and Master of Emanuel College, above a week before Mr. Shaw's death; and when he came to the College he was no way surprised as others were.

"'What farthers my belief of its being a true vision and not a dream, is Mr. Grove's incredulity of stories of this nature. Considering them both as men of learning and integrity, the one would not first have declared, nor the other have spread the same, were not the matter serious and real.

"'Edward Walter.'"

The following example of an Apparition in Scotland, unlike those already recorded, carries with it evidences of truth:--

"A gentleman of rank and property in Scotland served in his youth in the army of the Duke of

Glimpses of the Supernatural Volumes I & II

York in Flanders. He occupied the same tent with two other officers, one of whom was sent on some service. One night during his absence, this gentleman while in bed saw the figure of his absent friend sitting on the vacant bed. He called to his companion, who also saw the figure, which spoke to them, and said he had just been killed at a certain place, pointing to his wound. He then requested them on returning to England, to call at a certain agent's house in a certain street, and to procure from him a document of great importance for the family of the deceased. If the agent, as was probable, should deny the possession of it, it would be found in a certain drawer of a cabinet in his room. Next day it appeared that the officer had been shot as he had told them, in the manner and at the time and place indicated. After the return of the troops to England, the two friends walking together one day, found themselves in the street where the agent lived, and the request of their friend recurred to both, they having hitherto forgotten it. They called on the agent, who denied having the paper in question; when they compelled him in their presence to open the drawer of the cabinet, where it was found and restored to the widow."[5]

An authentic record of the "Tyrone," or "Beresford Apparition," will now be given. It created a very great sensation at the time of its occurrence; and the narrative which follows has been pronounced traditionally "true and accurate" by a member of the family:--

"Lord Tyrone and Miss ---- were born in Ireland, and were left orphans in their infancy to the care of the same person, by whom they were both educated in the principles of deism. Their guardian dying when they were each of them about fourteen years of age, they fell into very different hands.

"The persons on whom the care of them now devolved, used every means to eradicate the erroneous principles they had imbibed, and to persuade them to embrace revealed religion, but in vain. Their arguments were strong enough to stagger their former faith. Though separated from each other, their friendship was unalterable, and they continued to regard each other with a sincere and fraternal affection.

"After some years were elapsed, and both were grown up, they made a solemn promise to each other that whichever should die first, would, if permitted, appear to the other, to declare what religion was most approved by the Supreme Being.

"Miss ---- was shortly after addressed by Sir Martin Beresford, to whom she was after a few years married, but a change of condition had no power to alter their friendship. The families visited each other, and often spent some weeks together. A short time after one of these visits, Sir Martin remarked, that when his lady came down to breakfast, her countenance was disturbed, and inquired after her health. She assured him she was quite well. He then asked her if she had hurt her wrist: 'Have you sprained it?' said he, observing a black ribbon round it. She answered in the negative, and added, 'Let me conjure you, Sir Martin, never to inquire the cause of my wearing this ribbon; you will never see me without it. If it concerned you as a husband to know, I would not for a moment conceal it: I never in my life denied you a request, but of this I entreat you to forgive me the refusal, and never to urge me further on the subject.' 'Very well,' said he, smiling; 'since you beg me so earnestly, I will inquire no more.'

"The conversation here ended; but breakfast was scarcely over when Lady Beresford eagerly inquired if the post was come in; she was told it was not. In a few minutes she rang again and repeated the inquiry. She was again answered as at first. 'Do you expect letters?' said Sir Martin, 'that you are so anxious for the arrival of the post?' 'I do,' she answered, 'I expect to hear that Lord Tyrone is dead; he died last Tuesday at four o'clock.' 'I never in my life,' said Sir Martin, 'believed you superstitious; some idle dream has surely thus alarmed you.' At that instant the servant entered and delivered to him a letter sealed with black. 'It is as I expected,' exclaimed Lady Beresford, 'Lord Tyrone is dead.' Sir Martin opened the letter; it came from Lord Tyrone's steward, and contained the melancholy intelligence of his master's death, and on the very day and hour Lady Beresford had before specified. Sir Martin begged Lady Beresford to compose herself, and she assured him she felt much easier than she had done for a long time; and added, 'I can communicate intelligence to you which I know will prove welcome; I can assure you, beyond the possibility of a doubt, that I shall in some months present you with a son.' Sir Martin received this news with the greatest joy.

"After some months Lady Beresford was delivered of a son (she had before been the mother of only two daughters). Sir Martin survived the birth of his son little more than four years.

"After his decease his widow seldom left home; she visited no family but that of a clergyman who resided in the same village; with them she frequently passed a few hours; the rest of her time was spent in solitude, and she appeared determined for ever to banish all other society. The clergyman's family consisted of himself, his wife, and one son, who at the time of Sir Martin's death was quite a youth; to this son, however, she was after a few years married, notwithstanding the disparity of years and the manifest imprudence of a connexion so unequal in every point of view.

Rev. Frederick George Lee, D.C.L.

"Lady Beresford was treated by her young husband with contempt and cruelty, while at the same time his conduct evinced him the most abandoned libertine, utterly destitute of every principle of virtue and humanity. By this, her second husband, she had two daughters; after which such was the baseness of his conduct that she insisted on a separation. They parted for a few years, when so great was the contrition he expressed for his former conduct, that, won over by his supplications, promises, and entreaties, she was induced to pardon, and once more to reside with him, and was in time the mother of a son.

"The day on which she had lain-in a month being the anniversary of her birthday, she sent for Lady Betty Cobb (of whose friendship she had long been possessed), and a few other friends, to request them to spend the day with her. About seven, the clergyman by whom she had been christened, and with whom she had all her life been intimate, came into the room to inquire after her health. She told him she was perfectly well, and requested him to spend the day with them; for, said she, 'This is my birthday. I am forty-eight to-day.' 'No, madam,' answered the clergyman, 'you are mistaken; your mother and myself have had many disputes concerning your age, and I have at last discovered that I was right. I happened to go last week into the parish where you were born; I was resolved to put an end to the dispute; I searched the register, and find that you are forty-seven this day.' 'You have signed my death warrant,' she exclaimed; 'I have then but a few hours to live. I must therefore entreat you to leave me immediately, as I have something of importance to settle before I die.'

"When the clergyman had left her, Lady Beresford sent to forbid the company coming, and at the same time to request Lady Betty Cobb and her son (of whom Sir Martin was the father, and who was then about twenty-two years of age), to come to her apartment immediately. Upon their arrival, having ordered the attendants to quit the room, 'I have something,' she said, 'of the greatest importance to communicate to you both before I die, a period which is not far distant. You, Lady Betty, are no stranger to the friendship which subsisted between Lord Tyrone and myself: we were educated under the same roof and in the same principles of deism. When the friends, into whose hands we afterwards fell, endeavoured to persuade us to embrace Revealed Religion, their arguments, though insufficient to convince, were powerful to stagger our former feelings, and to leave us wavering between the two opinions: in this perplexing state of doubt and uncertainty, we made a solemn promise to each other that whichever died first should (if permitted) appear to the other, and declare what religion was most acceptable to God; accordingly, one night, while Sir Martin and myself were in bed, I suddenly awoke and discovered Lord Tyrone sitting by my bedside. I screamed out and endeavoured to awake Sir Martin. "For Heaven's sake," I exclaimed, "Lord Tyrone, by what means or for what reason came you hither at this time of night?" "Have you then forgotten our promise?" said he; "I died last Tuesday at four o'clock, and have been permitted by the Supreme Being to appear to you to assure you that the Revealed Religion is true, and the only religion by which we can be saved. I am further suffered to inform you that you will soon produce a son, who it is decreed will marry my daughter; not many years after his birth Sir Martin will die, and you will marry again, and to a man by whose ill-treatment you will be rendered miserable: you will have two daughters and afterwards a son, in childbirth of whom you will die in the forty-seventh year of your age." "Just Heavens!" I exclaimed, "and cannot I prevent this?" "Undoubtedly," returned the spectre; "you are a free agent, and may prevent it all by resisting every temptation to a second marriage; but your passions are strong, you know not their power; hitherto you have had no trials. More I am not permitted to reveal, but if after this warning you persist in your infidelity, your lot in another world will be miserable indeed." "May I not ask," said I, "if you are happy?" "Had I been otherwise," he replied, "I should not have been permitted to appear to you." "I may, then, infer that you are happy?" He smiled. "But how," said I, "when morning comes, shall I know that your appearance to me has been real, and not the mere representation of my own imagination?" "Will not the news of my death be sufficient to convince you?" "No," I returned, "I might have had such a dream, and that dream accidentally come to pass. I will have some stronger proofs of its reality." "You shall," said he, and waving his hand, the bed curtains, which were crimson velvet, were instantly drawn through a large iron hoop by which the tester of the bed was suspended. "In that," said he, "you cannot be mistaken; no mortal arm could have performed this." "True," said I, "but sleeping we are often possessed of far more strength than when awake; though waking I could not have done it, asleep I might; and I shall still doubt." "Here is a pocket-book; in this," said he, "I will write my name; you know my handwriting." I replied, "Yes." He wrote with a pencil on one side of the leaves. "Still," said I, "in the morning I may doubt; though waking I could not imitate your hand, asleep I might." "You are hard of belief," said he. "Touch would injure you irreparably; it is not for spirits to touch mortal flesh." "I do not," said I, "regard a slight blemish." "You are a woman of courage," said he, "hold out your hand." I did; he struck my wrist: his hand was cold as marble; in a moment the sinews shrunk up, every nerve withered. "Now," said he, "while you live let no mortal eye behold that wrist: to see it is sacrilege." He stopped; I turned to him again; he was gone.

"'During the time I had conversed with him my thoughts were perfectly calm and collected; but the moment he was gone I felt chilled with horror, the very bed moved under me. I endeavoured, but in vain, to awake Sir Martin; all my attempts were ineffectual, and in this state of agitation and terror I lay for some time, when a shower of tears came to my relief and I fell asleep.

"'In the morning Sir Martin arose and dressed himself as usual, without perceiving the state the curtains remained in. When I awoke I found Sir Martin gone down; I arose, and having put on my clothes, went to the gallery adjoining the apartment and took from thence a long broom (such as cornices are swept with); by the help of this I took down with some difficulty the curtains, as I imagined their extraordinary position might excite suspicion in the family. I then went to the bureau, took up my pocket-book, and bound a piece of black ribbon round my wrist. When I came down, the agitation of my mind had left an impression on my countenance too visible to pass unobserved by my husband. He instantly remarked it, and asked the cause; I informed him Lord Tyrone was no more, that he died at the hour of four on the preceding Tuesday, and desired him never to question me more respecting the black ribbon, which he kindly desisted from after. You, my son, as had been foretold, I afterwards brought into the world, and in little more than four years after your birth your lamented father expired in my arms. After this melancholy event I determined, as the only probable chance to avoid the sequel of the prediction, for ever to abandon all society, to give up every pleasure resulting from it, and to pass the rest of my days in solitude and retirement. But few can long endure to exist in a state of perfect sequestration: I began an intimacy with a family, and one alone; nor could I foresee the fatal consequences which afterwards resulted from it. Little did I think their son, their only son, then a mere youth, would form the person destined by fate to prove my destruction. In a very few years I ceased to regard him with indifference; I endeavoured by every possible way to conquer a passion, the fatal effects of which I too well knew. I had fondly imagined I had overcome its influence, when the evening of one fatal day terminated my fortitude and plunged me in a moment down that abyss I had so long been meditating how to shun. He had often solicited his parents for leave to go into the army, and at last obtained permission, and came to bid me adieu before his departure. The instant he entered the room he fell upon his knees at my feet, told me he was miserable, and that I alone was the cause. At that moment my fortitude forsook me, I gave myself up as lost, and regarding my fate as inevitable, without further hesitation consented to a union, the immediate result of which I knew to be misery, and its end death. The conduct of my husband after a few years amply justified a separation, and I hoped by these means to avoid the fatal sequel of the prophecy: but won over by his reiterated entreaties, I was prevailed upon to pardon and once more reside with him, though not till after I had, as I thought, passed my forty-seventh year.

"'But alas! I have this day heard from indisputable authority that I have hitherto lain under a mistake with regard to my age, and that I am but forty-seven to-day. Of the near approach of my death then I entertain not the slightest doubt; but I do not dread its arrival; armed with the sacred precepts of Christianity I can meet the King of Terrors without dismay, and without fear bid adieu to mortality for ever.

"'When I am dead, as the necessity for concealment closes with my life, I could wish that you, Lady Betty, would unbind my wrist, take from thence the black ribbon, and let my son with yourself behold it.' Lady Beresford here paused for some time, but resuming the conversation she entreated her son would behave himself so as to merit the high honour he would in future receive from a union with the daughter of Lord Tyrone.

"Lady B. then expressed a wish to lay down on the bed and endeavour to compose herself to sleep. Lady Betty Cobb and her son immediately called her domestics and quitted the room, having first desired them to watch their mistress attentively, and if they observed the smallest change in her, to call instantly.

"An hour passed and all was quiet in the room. They listened at the door and everything remained still, but in half an hour more a bell rang violently; they flew to her apartment, but before they reached the door, they heard the servants exclaim, 'Oh, she is dead!' Lady Betty then bade the servants for a few minutes to quit the room, and herself with Lady Beresford's son approached the bed of his mother; they knelt down by the side of it; Lady Betty lifted up her hand and untied the ribbon,--the wrist was found exactly as Lady Beresford had described it, every sinew shrunk, every nerve withered.

"Lady Beresford's son, as had been predicted, is since married to Lord Tyrone's daughter. The black ribbon and pocket-book were formerly in the possession of Lady Betty Cobb, Marlborough Buildings, Bath, who, during her long life, was ever ready to attest the truth of this narration, as are, to the present hour, the whole of the Tyrone and Beresford families."[6]

Three remarkable examples of Spectral Appearances must now be given, because of their inherent interest and corresponding likeness. The first is recorded by Glanville, a learned and pious author already referred to; the second is the case of Dr. Ferrar, and the third that of the "Wynyard Ghost Story."

(I.) Glanville tells a story regarding the appearance of a spirit in fulfilment of a promise made during lifetime, which is full of point and purpose. It runs thus. The substance, not the exact words, of the narrative are here given:--In the seventeenth century there lived two friends, Major George Sydenham of Dulverton in the county of Somerset, and Captain William Dyke of the same county. They were both reputed to be unbelievers in the Christian religion, if not avowed atheists. During the civil wars they had each served under the Parliamentary generals, and took an active part on the side of the rebels.

Having held many discussions both on the subject of religion and irreligion, they eventually argued out the fact of the immortality of the soul, which each felt disposed to deny: and finally they agreed between themselves that whichever of them died first, should (if such a possibility existed,) appear on the third day after death to the survivor in Major Sydenham's summer-house at Dulverton, and enlighten him as to the existence of a future state of rewards and punishments.

In due course Major Sydenham died; and Captain Dyke, in company with a cousin of his own, a celebrated physician, who was attending a sick child at Major Sydenham's house, but who knew nothing of the matter in hand, arrived there. Captain Dyke and his relative Dr. Dyke, the physician, occupied the same bedroom. The latter was surprised to hear the captain ask of the servant for two of the largest candles that could be obtained, and sought an explanation. The captain then informed him of his promise to Major Sydenham, and of his own determined resolution to fulfil it. Dr. Dyke urged with considerable force that as there was no warrant for making such engagements, they were to be regarded as unquestionably wrong; and pointed out, firstly, that evil spirits might take advantage of the situation, and secondly, that such a tempting of the Almighty was altogether wrong.

"This may be all very true," responded Captain Dyke, "but as I faithfully promised to go, go I will. If you will come and sit up with me, well and good: and I shall be grateful. But if not, I shall certainly go alone."

Then, placing his watch on the table, he waited until half-past eleven; when taking up the candles, he walked up and down in close proximity to the entrance of the summer-house, until two o'clock, without either seeing or hearing anything extraordinary.

Upon this he formed two conclusions; either that the soul perished with the body, or that the laws of the spiritual world forbade his friend Major Sydenham abiding by his pledge.

Six weeks afterwards, however, Captain Dyke and his relation the physician had occasion to go to Eton, where one of the sons of the former was to be placed at the college. They lodged at the S. Christopher's Inn, occupying different sleeping-rooms. On the last morning of their stay, Captain Dyke was unusually late, and when he entered the doctor's room was like a man struck with madness, his eyes staring, his knees refusing to support him, and his whole appearance altered.

"What is the matter?" asked Dr. Dyke.

"I have seen the major," replied the captain; "for if ever I saw him in my life, I certainly saw him just now."

Upon the doctor pressing for details, Captain Dyke gave the following account:--"After it was first light this morning, someone pulled back the curtains of my bed suddenly, and I saw the major exactly as I had seen him in life. 'I could not,' he said, 'come at the time appointed, but I am here now to tell you that there is a God, a very just and terrible God, and that if you do not turn over a new leaf you will find it so.' He then disappeared."

It is said, finally, that Captain Dyke's truthfulness was so notorious, as to preclude the possibility of doubting his relation of the occurrence. Furthermore, the apparition and warnings of his departed friend exercised a visible effect on his character and life, which latter was prolonged for two years; during which period he is said to have had the words then spoken to him always sounding in his ears.

(II.) The celebrated Nicholas Ferrar, of Little Gidding, (who, in the seventeenth century, lived a most retired, religious, and pious life,) had a brother, a physician in London. This physician made a compact with his eldest and favourite daughter that whichever of them died first should, if happy, appear to the other. This compact is said to have proved the subject of many conversations and religious discussions between father and child. The latter is reported to have been very averse to making any such agreement; but being overcome by arguments as to the reasonableness of such a course (if permitted by a gracious and merciful God) at last consented. After this she married and settled with her husband at Gillingham Lodge, in the county of Wiltshire. Here she was prematurely confined; and during her illness, one night by mistake took poison, and died quite suddenly. That very night her spirit appeared to her father in London, the curtains of whose bed she drew back, and with a sweet but mournful expression looked upon him, and then gradually faded away. In fact, and as a test of the objective reality of his daughter's apparition, Dr. Ferrar, deeply impressed by the occurrence, announced the death of his daughter to his family two days before he received intelligence of it by the then tardy post.

(III.) John Cope Sherbroke and George Wynyard appear in the "Army List" of 1785, the one as a captain and the other lieutenant in the 33rd Regiment,--a corps which some years after had the honour to be commanded by the Hon. Arthur Wellesley, subsequently Duke of Wellington. The regiment was then on service in Canada, and Sherbroke and Wynyard, being of congenial tastes, had become great friends. It was their custom to spend in study much of the time which their brother officers devoted to idle pleasures. According to a narration[7] resting on the best authority now attainable, they were one afternoon sitting in Wynyard's apartment. It was perfectly light, the hour was about four o'clock: they had dined, but neither of them had drunk wine, and they had retired from their mess to continue together the occupations of the morning. It ought to have been said that the apartment in which they were had two doors in it, the one opening into a passage and the other leading into Wynyard's bedroom. There was no other means of entering the sitting-room, so that any person passing into the bedroom must have remained there unless he returned by the way he entered. This point is of consequence to the story.

"As these two young officers were pursuing their studies, Sherbroke, whose eyes happened accidentally to glance from the book before him towards the door which opened to the passage, all at once observed a tall youth of about twenty years of age whose appearance was that of extreme emaciation. Struck with the presence of a perfect stranger, he immediately turned to his friend, who was sitting near him, and directed his attention to the guest who had thus strangely broken in upon their studies. As soon as Wynyard's eyes were turned towards the mysterious visitor his countenance became suddenly agitated. 'I have heard,' says Sir John Sherbroke, 'of a man's being as pale as death, but I never saw a living face assume the appearance of a corpse except Wynyard's at that moment.' As they looked silently at the form before them--for Wynyard, who seemed to apprehend the import of the appearance, was deprived of the faculty of speech, and Sherbroke, perceiving the agitation of his friend, felt no inclination to address it--as they looked silently upon the figure it proceeded slowly into the adjoining apartment, and in the act of passing them cast its eyes with an expression of somewhat melancholy affection on young Wynyard. The oppression of this extraordinary presence was no sooner removed than Wynyard, seizing his friend by the arm, and drawing a deep breath as if recovering from the suffocation of intense astonishment and emotion, muttered in a low and almost inaudible tone of voice, 'Great God, my brother!' 'Your brother!' repeated Sherbroke, 'what can you mean? Wynyard, there must be some deception; follow me;' and immediately taking his friend by the arm, he preceded him into the bedroom, which, as before stated, was connected with the sitting-room, and into which the strange visitor had evidently entered. It has already been said that from this chamber there was no possibility of withdrawing but by the way of the apartment, through which the figure had certainly never returned. Imagine then the astonishment of the young officers when, on finding themselves in the chamber, they perceived that the room was perfectly untenanted. Wynyard's mind had received an impression at the first moment of his observing him, that the figure whom he had seen was the spirit of his brother. Sherbroke still persevered in strenuously believing that some delusion had been practised. They took note of the day and hour in which the event had happened, but they resolved not to mention the occurrence in the regiment, and gradually they persuaded each other that they had been imposed upon by some artifice of their fellow-officers, though they could neither account for the means of its execution. They were content to imagine anything possible rather than admit the possibility of a supernatural appearance. But though they had attempted these stratagems of self-delusion, Wynyard could not help expressing his solicitude with respect to the safety of the brother whose apparition he had either seen or imagined himself to have seen; and the anxiety which he exhibited for letters from England, and his frequent mention of his brother's health, at length awakened the curiosity of his comrades, and eventually betrayed him into a declaration of the circumstances which he had in vain determined to conceal. The story of the silent and unbidden visitor was no sooner bruited abroad than the arrival of Wynyard's letters from England were welcomed with more than usual eagerness, for they promised to afford the clue to the mystery which had happened among themselves.

"By the first ships no intelligence relating to the story could have been received, for they had all departed from England previously to the appearance of the spirit. At length, the long wished-for vessel arrived; all the officers had letters except Wynyard. They examined the several newspapers, but they contained no mention of any death or of any other circumstance connected with his family that could account for the preternatural event. There was a solitary letter for Sherbroke still unopened. The officers had received their letters in the mess-room at the hour of supper. After Sherbroke had broken the seal of his last packet, and cast a glance on its contents, he beckoned his friend away from the company, and departed from the room. All were silent. The suspense of the interest was now at its climax; the impatience for the return of Sherbroke was inexpressible. They doubted not but that letter had contained the long-expected intelligence.

"After the interval of an hour, Sherbroke joined them. No one dared inquire the nature of his correspondence; but they waited in mute attention, expecting that he would himself touch upon the subject. His mind was manifestly full of thoughts that pained, bewildered, and oppressed him. He drew near to the fire-place, and leaning his head on the mantlepiece, after a pause of some moments, said in a low voice to the person who was nearest him, Wynyard's brother was dead. 'Dear John, break to your friend Wynyard the death of his favourite brother.' He had died on the day and at the very hour on which the friends had seen his spirit pass so mysteriously through the apartment.

"It might have been imagined that these events would have been sufficient to have impressed the mind of Sherbroke with the conviction of their truth, but so strong was his prepossession against the existence or even the possibility of any preternatural intercourse with the spirits of the departed, that he still entertained a doubt of the report of his senses, supported as their testimony was by the coincidence of sight and event. Some years after, on his return to England, he was with two gentlemen in Piccadilly, when on the opposite side of the street he saw a person bearing the most striking resemblance to the figure which had been disclosed to Wynyard and himself. His companions were acquainted with the story, and he instantly directed their attention to the gentleman opposite, as the individual who had contrived to enter and depart from Wynyard's apartment without their being conscious of the means.

"Full of this impression, he immediately went over and addressed the gentleman. He now fully expected to elucidate the mystery. He apologized for the interruption, but excused it by relating the occurrence which had induced him to the commission of this solecism in manners. The gentleman received him as a friend. He had never been out of the country, but he was the twin brother of the youth whose spirit had been seen.

"From the interesting character of this narration--the facts of the vision occurring in daylight, and to two persons; and of the subsequent verification of likeness by the party not previously acquainted with the subject of the vision, it is much to be regretted that no direct report of particulars had come to us. There is all other desirable authentication for the story, and sufficient evidence to prove that the two gentlemen believed and often told nearly what is here reported.

"Dr. Mayo makes the following statement on the subject: 'I have had opportunities of inquiring of two near relations of this General Wynyard, upon what evidence the above story rests. They told me that they had each heard it from his own mouth. More recently a gentleman, whose accuracy of recollection exceeds that of most people, had told me that he had heard the late Sir John Sherbroke, the other party in the ghost story, tell it in much the same way at the dinner-table. A writer in 'Notes and Queries' for July 3, 1858, states that the brother, not twin-brother, whose spirit appeared to Wynyard and his friend, was John Otway Wynyard, Lieutenant in the 3rd Regiment of Foot-guards, who died on the 15th of October, 1785. As this gentleman writes with a minute knowledge of the family history, this date may be considered as that of the alleged spiritual incident.

"In 'Notes and Queries' for July 2nd, 1859, appeared a correspondence, giving the strongest testimony then attainable to the truth of the Wynyard ghost story. A series of queries on the subject being drawn up at Quebec, by Sir John Harvey, Adjutant-General of the forces in Canada, was sent to Colonel Gore of the same garrison, who was understood to be a survivor of the officers who were with Sherbroke and Wynyard at the time of the occurrence, and Colonel Gore explicitly replied to the following effect: He was present at Sydney, in the island of Cape Breton, in the autumn of 1785 or 1786, when the incident happened. It was in the then new barrack, and the place was blocked up by ice so as to have no communication with any part of the world. He was one of the first persons who entered the room after the apparition was seen. The ghost passed them as they were sitting at coffee, between eight and nine in the evening, and went into G. Wynyard's bed closet, the window of which was putt[i]ed down. He next day suggested to Sherbroke the propriety of making a memorandum of the incident, which was done. 'I remember the date, and on the 6th of June our first letters from England brought the news of John Wynyard's death, [which had happened] on the very night they saw his apparition.' Colonel Gore was under the impression that the person afterwards seen in one of the streets of London, by Sherbroke and William Wynyard, was not a brother of the latter family, but a gentleman named (he thought) Hayman, noted for being like the deceased John Wynyard, and who affected to dress like him."

So much for these records and testimonies. The following, now to be narrated, not altogether unlike them, and producing a good result on the person who witnessed the apparition, is of almost equal interest:--

"Lord Chedworth[8] had living with him the orphan daughter of a sister of his, a Miss Wright, who often related this circumstance: Lord Chedworth was a good man, and seemed anxious to do his duty, but, unfortunately, he had considerable intellectual doubts as to the existence of the soul in another world. He had a great friendship for a gentleman, whom he had known from his boyhood, and who was, like himself, one of those unbelieving mortals that must have ocular demonstration for everything. They often met, and often, too, renewed the subject so interesting to both; but neither could help the other to that happy conviction which was honestly wished for by each.

"One morning Miss Wright observed on her uncle joining her at breakfast, a considerable gloom of thought and trouble displayed on his countenance. He ate little, and was unusually silent. At last, he said, 'Molly' (for thus he familiarly called her), 'I had a strange visitor last night. My old friend B---- came to me.'

"'How?' said Miss Wright, 'did he come after I went to bed?'

"'His spirit did,' said Lord Chedworth, solemnly.

"'Oh! my dear uncle, how could the spirit of a living man appear?' said she, smiling.

"'He is dead, beyond doubt,' replied his lordship; 'listen, and then laugh as much as you please. I had not entered my bedroom many minutes when he stood before me. Like you, I could not but think that I was looking on the living man, and so accosted him; but he answered, "Chedworth, I died this night at eight o'clock; I come to tell you, that there is another world beyond the grave; and that there is a righteous God Who judgeth all."'

"'Depend upon it, uncle, it was only a dream!' But while Miss Wright was thus speaking a groom on horseback rode up the avenue, and immediately after delivered a letter to Lord Chedworth, announcing the sudden death of his friend. Whatever construction the reader may be disposed to put upon this narrative, it is not unimportant to add that the effect upon the mind of Lord Chedworth was as happy as it was permanent. All his doubts were at once removed, and for ever."

The well-known Lyttelton Ghost Story may now be fitly recorded. It created a great and widespread interest at the time of its occurrence, and was criticised and commented upon by many. Several versions of it have already appeared in print, and they seem to vary in certain unimportant details. The Editor, instead of writing out what has already appeared, prefers to set forth at length various documents containing independent evidence of the truth of the several apparitions, which by the courtesy and kindness of the present accomplished bearer of the title, he is enabled to embody verbatim in this volume, having been permitted to transcribe them from the originals in Lord Lyttelton's possession.

The subject of this narrative was the son of George, Lord Lyttelton, who was alike distinguished for the raciness of his wit and the profligacy of his manners. The latter trait of his character has induced many persons to suppose the apparition which he asserted he had seen, to have been the effect of a conscience quickened with remorse and misgivings, on account of many vices. The probability of the narrative[9] has, consequently, been much questioned; but two gentlemen, one of whom was at Pitt Place, the seat of Lord Lyttelton, and the other in the immediate neighbourhood, at the time of his lordship's death, bore ample testimony to the veracity of the whole affair. The several narratives of the singular occurrence correspond in material points; and the following are the circumstantial particulars written by the gentleman who was at the time on a visit to his lordship:--

"I was at Pitt Place, Epsom, when Lord Lyttelton died; Lord Fortescue, Mrs. Flood, and the two Miss Amphletts were also present. Lord Lyttelton had not long been returned from Ireland, and frequently had been seized with suffocating fits; he was attacked several times by them in the course of the preceding month, while he was at his house in Hill Street, Berkeley Square. It happened that he dreamt, three days before his death, that he saw a fluttering bird, and afterwards a woman appeared to him in white apparel and said to him, 'Prepare to die, you will not exist three days!' His lordship was much alarmed, and called to a servant from a closet adjoining, who found him much agitated and in a profuse perspiration; the circumstance had a considerable effect all the next day on his lordship's spirits. On the third day, while his lordship was at breakfast with the above personages, he said, 'If I live over to-night I shall have jockied the ghost, for this is the third day.' The whole party presently set off for Pitt Place, where they had not long arrived before his lordship was visited by one of his accustomed fits. After a short interval he recovered. He dined at five o'clock that day, and went to bed at eleven, when his servant was about to give him rhubarb and mint-water, but his lordship perceiving him stir it with a toothpick, called him a slovenly dog, and bade him go and fetch a teaspoon; but on the man's return he found his Master in a fit, and the pillow being placed high, his chin bore hard upon his neck, when the servant, instead of relieving his master on the instant from his perilous situation, ran in his fright and called out for help, but on his return he found his lordship dead.

"In explanation of this strange tale it is said that Lord Lyttelton acknowledged, previously to his death, that the woman he had seen in his dream was the 'mother' of the two Misses Amphletts mentioned above, whom, together with a third sister then in Ireland, his lordship had seduced and prevailed on to leave their parent, who resided near his country residence in Shropshire. It is further stated that Mrs. Amphlett died of grief through the desertion of her children at the precise time when the female vision appeared to his lordship. The most surprising part of the story, because the most difficult of explanation, yet remains to be related. On the second day Miles Peter Andrews, one of Lord Lyttelton's most intimate friends, left the dinner-party at an early hour, being called away upon business to Dartford, where he was the owner of certain powder-mills. He had all along professed himself one of the most determined sceptics as to the vision, and therefore ceased to think of it. On the third night, however, when he had been in bed about half an hour, and still remained, as he imagined, wide awake, his curtains were suddenly pulled aside, and Lord Lyttelton appeared before him in his robe-de-chambre and night-cap. Mr. Andrews gazed at his visitor for some time in silent wonder, and then began to reproach him for so odd a freak in coming down to Dartford Mills without any previous notice, as he hardly knew how on the emergency to find his lordship the requisite accommodation. 'Nevertheless,' said Andrews, 'I will get up and see what can be done for you.' With this view he turned aside to ring the bell; but on looking round again he could see no signs of his strange visitor. Soon afterwards the bell was rung for his servant, and upon his asking what had become of Lord Lyttelton, the man, evidently much surprised at the question, replied that he had seen nothing of him since they had left Pitt Place. 'Psha, you fool,' exclaimed Mr. Andrews, 'he was here this moment at my bedside.' The servant, more astonished than ever, declared that he did not well understand how that could be, since he must have seen him enter; whereupon Mr. Andrews rose, and having dressed himself, searched the house and grounds, but Lord Lyttelton was nowhere to be found. Still, he could not help believing that his friend, who was fond of practical jokes, had played him this trick for his previously expressed scepticism in the matter of the dream. But he soon viewed the whole affair in a different light. About four o'clock on the same day an express arrived from a friend with the news of Lord Lyttelton's death, and the whole manner of it, as related by the valet to those who were in the house at the time. In Mr. Andrews's subsequent visits to Pitt Place, no solicitations could ever induce him to sleep there; he would invariably return, however late, to the Spread Eagle Inn, at Epsom, for the night."

REMARKABLE DREAM OF THOMAS, LORD LYTTELTON.[10]
"On Thursday, the 25th of November, 1779, Thomas, Lord Lyttelton, when he came to breakfast, declared to Mrs. Flood, wife of Frederick Flood, Esq., of the kingdom of Ireland, and to the three Miss Amphletts, who were lodged in his house in Hill Street, London (where he then also was), that he had had an extraordinary dream the night before. He said he thought he was in a room which a bird flew into, which appearance was suddenly changed into that of a woman dressed in white, who bade him prepare to die. To which he answered, 'I hope not soon, not in two months.' She replied, 'Yes, in three days.' He said he did not much regard it, because he could in some measure account for it; for that a few days before he had been with Mrs. Dawson when a robin-redbreast flew into her room.
"When he had dressed himself that day to go to the House of Lords, he said he thought he did not look as if he was likely to die. In the evening of the following day, being Friday, he told the eldest Miss Amphlett that she looked melancholy; but, said he, 'You are foolish and fearful. I have lived two days, and, God willing, I will live out the third.'
On the morning of Saturday he told the same ladies that he was very well, and believed he should bilk the ghost. Some hours afterwards he went with them, Mr. Fortescue, and Captain Wolseley, to Pitt Place, at Epsom; withdrew to his bed-chamber soon after eleven o'clock at night, talked cheerfully to his servant, and particularly inquired of him what care had been taken to provide good rolls for his breakfast the next morning, stepped into his bed with his waistcoat on, and as his servant was pulling it off, put his hand to his side, sunk back and immediately expired without a groan. He ate a good dinner after his arrival at Pitt Place, took an egg for his supper, and did not seem to be at all out of order, except that while he was eating his soup at dinner he had a rising in his throat, a thing which had often happened to him before, and which obliged him to spit some of it out. His physician, Dr. Fothergill, told me Lord Lyttelton had in the summer preceding a bad pain in his side, and he judged that some gut vessel in the part where he felt the pain gave way, and to that he conjectured his death was owing. His declaration of his dream and his expressions above mentioned, consequential thereon, were upon a close inquiry asserted to me to have been so, by Mrs. Flood, the eldest Miss Amphlett, Captain Wolseley, and his valet-de-chambre Faulkner,[11] who dressed him on the Thursday; and the manner of his death was related to me by William Stuckey, in the presence of Mr. Fortescue and Captain Wolseley, Stuckey being the servant who attended him in his bed-chamber, and in whose arms he died.
"Westcote.[12]
"February the 13th, 1780."

Lord Lyttelton is also asserted to have appeared to Mr. Andrews, his friend and boon companion, at the time of his lordship's sudden and mysterious death. Of this fact testimony is furnished by Mr. Plumer Ward, M.P., in his "Illustrations of Human Life," from which (vol. i. p. 165) the following narrative is taken:--

"I had often heard much and read much of Lord Lyttelton's seeing a ghost before his death, and of himself as a ghost appearing to Mr. Andrews; and one evening, sitting near that gentleman, during a pause in the debates in the House of Commons, I ventured to ask him whether there was any and what truth in the detailed story so confidently related. Mr. Andrews, as perhaps I ought to have expected, did not much like the conversation. He looked grave and uneasy, and I asked pardon for my impertinent curiosity. Upon this he good-naturedly said, 'It is not a subject I am fond of, and least of all in such a place as this; but if you will come and dine with me, I will tell you what is true and what is false.' I gladly accepted the proposal, and I think my recollection is perfect as to the following narrative:--'Mr. Andrews in his youth was the boon-companion, not to say fellow-rake, of Lord Lyttelton, who, as is well known, was a man distinguished for abilities, but also for a profligacy of morals which few could equal. With all this he was remarkable for what may be called unnatural cowardice in one so determinedly wicked. He never repented, yet could never stifle his conscience. He never could allow, yet never could deny, a world to come, and he contemplated with unceasing terror what would probably be his own state in such a world if there was one. He was always melancholy with fear, or mad in defiance; and probably his principal misery here was, that with all his endeavours, he never could extinguish the dread of an hereafter.... Andrews was at his house at Dartford when Lord Lyttelton died at Pitt Place, Epsom, thirty miles off. Andrews' house was full of company, and he expected Lord Lyttelton, whom he had left in his usual state of health, to join them the next day, which was Sunday. Andrews himself feeling much indisposed on the Saturday evening, retired early to bed, and requested Mrs. Pigou, one of his guests, to do the honours of the supper-table. He admitted that, when in bed, he fell into a feverish sleep, but was waked between eleven and twelve by somebody opening his curtains. It was Lord Lyttelton in a night-gown and cap, which Andrews recognized. He also plainly spoke to him, saying he was come to tell him all was over. The world said he informed him there was another state, and bade him repent, &c. That was not so. And I confine myself to the exact words of this relation.

"'Now it seems that Lord Lyttelton was fond of horse-play, or what we should call mauvaise plaisanterie; and, having often made Andrews the subject of it, the latter had threatened him with manual chastisement next time it occurred. On the present occasion, thinking this annoyance renewed, he threw the first thing he could find, which were his slippers, at Lord Lyttelton's head. The figure retreated towards a dressing-room which had no ingress or egress except through the bed-chamber, and Andrews, very angry, leapt out of bed, to follow it into the dressing-room. It was not there. Surprised, he returned to the bedroom, which he strictly searched. The door was locked on the inside, yet no Lord Lyttelton was to be found. He was astonished, but not alarmed, so convinced was he that it was some trick of Lord Lyttelton, who, he supposed, had arrived, according to his engagement, but after he, Andrews, had retired. He therefore rang for his servant, and asked if Lord Lyttelton was not come. The man said, "No." "You may depend upon it," replied he, out of humour, "he is somewhere in the house, for he was here just now, and is playing some trick." But how he could have got into the bedroom with the door locked puzzled both master and man. Convinced, however, that he was somewhere in the house, Andrews, in his anger, ordered that no bed should be given him, saying he might go to an inn, or sleep in the stables. Be that as it may, he never appeared again, and Andrews went to sleep.

"'It happened that Mrs. Pigou was to go to town early the next morning. What was her astonishment, having heard the disturbance of the night before, to hear on her arrival about nine o'clock that Lord Lyttelton had died the very night he was supposed to have been seen. She immediately sent an express to Dartford with the news; upon the receipt of which, Andrews, (quite well, and remembering accurately all that had passed,) swooned away. He could not understand it, but it had a most serious effect upon him, so that--to use his own expression--he "was not his own man again for three years."'

"Such is the celebrated story; stript of its ornamentations and exaggerations; and for one, I own, if not convinced that this was a real message from Heaven, which certainly I am not, I at least think the hand of Providence was seen in it; working upon the imagination, if you please, and therefore suspending no law of Nature (though that after all is an ambiguous term), but still Providence, in a character not to be mistaken."

The following remarkable occurrence of the Spectral Appearances of two persons, one recently dead and the other a canonized saint of the Roman Catholic Church, which occurred about thirty years ago, is now published for the first time. It is known as "The Weld Ghost Story:"--

"Philip Weld was a younger son of Mr. James Weld of Archer's Lodge, near Southampton, and a nephew of the late Cardinal Weld, the head of that ancient family, whose chief seat is Lulworth Castle in Dorsetshire.[13] He was sent by his father in 1844 to S. Edmund's college, near

Rev. Frederick George Lee, D.C.L.

Ware in Hertfordshire, for his education. He was a boy of great piety and virtue, and gave not only satisfaction to the masters of studies, but edification to all his fellow-students. It happened that on April 16, 1846, a play-day or whole holiday, the President of the college gave the boys leave to boat upon the river at Ware.

"In the morning of that day Philip Weld had been to the Holy Communion at the early celebration of Mass, having just finished his retreat. In the afternoon of the same day he went with his companions and some of the masters to boat on the river as arranged. This sport he enjoyed very much. When one of the masters remarked that it was time to return to the college, Philip asked whether they might not have one more row. The master consented, and they rowed to the accustomed turning-point. On arriving there, and in turning the boat, Philip accidentally fell out into a very deep part of the river; and, notwithstanding that every effort was made to save him, was drowned.

"His dead body was brought back to the college, and the Very Rev. Dr. Cox, the President, was immensely shocked and grieved. He was very fond of Philip; but what was most dreadful to him was to have to break this sad news to the boy's parents. He scarcely knew what to do, whether to write by post, or to send a messenger. At last he determined to go himself to Mr. Weld at Southampton. So he set off the same evening, and, passing through London, reached Southampton the next day, and drove from thence to Archer's Lodge, Mr. Weld's residence.

"On arriving there and being shown into his private study, Dr. Cox found Mr. Weld in tears. The latter, rising from his seat and taking the doctor by the hand, said, 'My dear sir, you need not tell me what you are come for. I know it already. Philip is dead. Yesterday I was walking with my daughter Katharine on the turnpike road, in broad daylight, and Philip appeared to us both. He was standing on the causeway with another young man in a black robe by his side. My daughter was the first to perceive him. She said to me, "Look there, papa: there is Philip." I looked and saw him. I said to my daughter, "It is Philip, indeed; but he has the look of an angel." Not suspecting that he was dead, though greatly wondering that he was there, I went towards him with my daughter to embrace him; but a few yards being between us, while I was going up to him a labouring man, who was walking on the same causeway, passed between the apparition and the hedge, and as he went on I saw him pass through their apparent bodies, as if they were transparent. On perceiving this I at once felt sure that they were spirits, and going forward with my daughter to touch them, Philip sweetly smiled on us, and then both he and his companion vanished away.'"

"The reader may imagine how deeply affected Dr. Cox was on hearing this remarkable statement. He of course corroborated it by relating to the afflicted father the circumstances attendant on his son's death, which had taken place at the very hour in which he appeared to his father and sister. They all concluded that he had died in the grace of God, and that he was in happiness, because of the placid smile on his face.[14]

"Dr. Cox asked Mr. Weld who the young man was in the black robe who had accompanied his son, and who appeared to have a most beautiful and angelic countenance, but he said that he had not the slightest idea.

"A few weeks afterwards, however, Mr. Weld was on a visit to the neighbourhood of Stonyhurst in Lancashire. After hearing Mass one morning in the chapel, he, while waiting for his carriage, was shown into the guest-room, where, walking up to the fireplace, he saw a picture above the chimney-piece, which, as it pleased God, represented a young man in a black robe with the very face, form, and attitude of the companion of Philip as he saw him in the vision, and beneath the picture was inscribed 'S. Stanislaus Kostka,'[15] one of the greatest saints of the Jesuit order, and the one whom Philip had chosen for his patron saint at his Confirmation. His father, overpowered with emotion, fell on his knees, shedding many tears, and thanking God for this fresh proof of his son's blessedness. For in what better company could he be than in that of his patron saint, leading him, as it were, into the presence of his Creator and his Saviour, from the dangers and temptations of this state of exile to a condition of endless blessedness and happiness?"[16]

This is, perhaps, one of the most remarkable and best-authenticated recent cases of Spectral Appearances which has ever been narrated. The various independent testimonies dove-tailing together so perfectly, centre in the leading supernatural fact--the actual apparition in the daytime of a person just departed this life by sudden death, seen not by one only, but by two people, simultaneously; and seen in company with the spirit of a very holy and renowned saint, the chosen patron of the youth who had just been drowned. A more clear and conclusive example of the Supernatural it would be impossible to obtain.

The following case in certain particulars is not unlike that just recorded; for two persons, at a distance of many hundred miles apart, saw the Apparition of their departed relative who had just died in Australia:--

"Circumstances, in the year 1848," writes a correspondent of the Editor, "induced me to allow my youngest daughter to leave England, in order to join a son of mine in Australia, who had left home about five years previously, to seek his fortune in that country. In England, at home, he had every opportunity of making his way in life, and settling advantageously, but had availed himself of none that had offered. After leaving school, he was placed under a private tutor's care, and duly entered at Oxford. There he did nothing, or next to nothing, and left without taking any degree. Soon after this, at his own suggestion, in company with a friend, whose acquaintance he had made at the university, an acquaintance which eventually ripened into a warm friendship, he went to Australia; and he did not go empty-handed. A sum of money was placed to his credit with a colonial bank in the city of London having agencies in that colony, and nothing was left undone to secure for him a good start in his self-chosen and new life. I ought to add here that my own wish always had been that he should remain at home, and, after receiving orders, become vicar of a parish, the patronage of which was in the gift of a relation. Man proposes, but God disposes.

"In Australia, as was not otherwise than I myself had anticipated, the manner of life was utterly unlike that to which he had been accustomed. Ill-luck and want of success met him at every turn, as we afterwards found out; and not only did want of success meet him, but he had to undergo privations and hardships, which eventually weakened a constitution never too strong.

"At the time that I consented to my daughter going out, much of the above was unknown to us. He had written complaining of ill-health and weakness, and she, with great self-denial and sisterly devotion, resolved to go. She went with the understanding that she was soon to return. Just before she started, the mail brought us unexceptionally bad news of her brother's weak state of health, written by his college friend.

"About six weeks after her departure, I was sitting musing in my arm-chair, on a summer afternoon, close to the window of my library, which looked out upon a lawn, to the left of which were three large and overspreading cedar-trees. All of a sudden I saw the life-like apparition of my son standing below the cedar-trees. He looked very pale, thin, and careworn, much altered, but my very son. He gazed at me intently, and with a mournful gaze, for about the space of two minutes. I could not speak--I could not move--I could not take my eyes off him. I seemed riveted to the spot; and, of course, I was at once convinced of the fact that he had died. Then he seemed gradually to fade away. It was weeks before I could get the thoughts of his appearance out of my mind; and nothing that the members of my family could say served to remove the impression so indelibly stamped upon it of our loss.

"Some months afterwards, we received letters from my daughter (just landed) and his other friends in Australia announcing his decease. He had died somewhat suddenly, having expressed the most anxious desire to see me before his death--a desire repeated again and again, and regarding which he seemed to be unquiet.

"The most remarkable feature yet to be told in the circumstance was this,--that my daughter, who was reposing in the ladies' cabin of the ship, on her way to Australia, saw the apparition of her brother come into the cabin, move round it by a strange motion, and then, after looking at herself with a strained and mournful look, glide out again.

"Events afterwards showed that these appearances, both on shipboard and at my own home, occurred at or about the very time of my dear boy's death. And nothing will convince me that the record here set down is not one of the most remarkable and undoubted examples of supernatural apparitions. May God Almighty join us all together again, after these earthly separations, in His heavenly kingdom!"

The following example, which has already appeared in print, is authenticated by a personal acquaintance of the Editor, who has kindly written him a Letter on the subject. It was first given to Dr. William Gregory,[17] who published it about twenty-three years ago. It is said to have occurred in 1849:[18]--

"An officer occupied the same room with another officer in the West Indies. One night he awoke his companion, and asked him if he saw anything in the room, when the latter answered that he saw an old man in the corner whom he did not know. 'That,' said the other, 'is my father, and I am sure he is dead.' In due time news arrived of his death in England at that very time. Long afterwards the officer took his friend who had seen the vision to visit the widow, when, on entering the room, he started, and said, 'That is the portrait of the old man I saw.' It was, in fact, the portrait of the father, whom the friend had never seen except in the vision."

"This story," writes Dr. Gregory, "I have on the best authority; and everyone knows that such stories are not uncommon. It is very easy, but not satisfactory, to laugh at them as incredible ghost stories; but there is a natural truth in them, whatever they may be."

Examples of Apparitions at the time of Death to friends and relations are, however, so numerous that a considerable number might readily be printed. Here are two, well and duly authenticated.

The following statement is vouched for by the person signing the same:--

"In the summer of 1816, my father and mother having retired to bed about nine o'clock, the

Rev. Frederick George Lee, D.C.L.

latter was about to draw down the blind, when she observed the figure of a female approaching their house by a footpath which communicated with the village. Thinking the circumstance unusual, she waited till the figure approached sufficiently near to discern its features, when she exclaimed to my father, 'Why, here is my sister B----; what can have induced her to come here at this time of the evening?' She was about to prepare to go downstairs to inquire the cause of such a visit at that late time of night, when my mother observed the figure retracing its steps in the same direction by which it had come. The following morning, early, intelligence was brought to my mother that her sister B---- died at the same hour at which her apparition appeared to my mother. This is a simple statement of facts.

"Signed by the son of the person to whom the apparition appeared.
"C. J. Hanmer.
"33, Henley Street, Camp Hill, Birmingham."

The following is another statement of facts vouched for by those who formally testify to its truth:--

"One evening in the autumn of the year 1868, my wife retired to bed early. On my entering the bedroom about midnight, I found her wide awake, and in a very excited state. On inquiring the cause, she state that she believed most firmly she had seen our old friend Mrs. G----, then residing at a distance, whom we believed to be in perfect health. My wife gave a minute description of her dress, which I had remembered to have seen her wear, and at the same time stated that when the apparition appeared to her, every object in the bedroom was strangely but distinctly visible. Of course I tried to allay my wife's excitement by assuring her that she was suffering from the effects of an unpleasant dream, but I failed to shake her conviction that she had seen the spirit of our friend.

"Nothing occurred during the next day, but on the following we received a letter from a relative, stating that Mrs. G---- had died the night before about twelve o'clock.

"It appears that Mrs. G----, while in her garden, was observed to fall upon one of the flower beds. Having been taken to her room, medical aid was promptly procured, but without avail: she remained unconscious from that time until the moment of her death, which occurred about twelve o'clock the same evening.

"(Signed) C. L. Hanmer,
Catherine Hanmer
(Wife of the above).
"Branch Dispensary, Camp Hill, Birmingham,
Oct. 18, 1872."

The following Account of the Apparition of a murdered man, near the place of his death, is very remarkable. It has been published, though in another form, in Australia, and is there generally accepted as true. The version given below is from those who are thoroughly competent to furnish a true and faithful account of a very impressive narrative:--

"In Australia, about twenty-five years ago, two graziers, who had emigrated from England, and entered into partnership, became, as was generally believed, possessed of considerable property, by an unlooked-for success in their precarious but not unprofitable occupation. One of them all of a sudden was missed, and could nowhere be found. Search was made for him in every quarter, likely and unlikely, yet no tidings of him or his whereabouts could be heard.

"One evening, about three weeks afterwards, his partner and companion was returning to his hut along a bye-path which skirted a deep and broad sheet of water. The shadows of twilight were deepening, and the setting sun was almost shut out by the tall shrubs, brushwood, and rank grass which grew so thick and wild. In a moment he saw the crouching figure of his companion, apparently as real and life-like as could be, sitting on the ground by the very margin of the deep pond, with his left arm bent, resting on his left knee. He was about to rush forward and speak, when the figure seemed to grow less distinct, and the ashen-coloured face wore an unusually sad and melancholy aspect; so he paused. On this the figure, becoming again more palpable, raised its right arm, and, holding down the index finger of the right hand, pointed to a dark and deep hole, where the water was still and black, immediately beside an overhanging tree. This action was deliberately done, and then twice repeated, after which the figure, growing more and more indistinct, seemed to fade away.

"The grazier was mortally terrified and alarmed. For a while he stood riveted to the spot, fearing either to go forward or backward; while the silence of evening and the strange solitude, now for the first time in his Australian life thoroughly experienced, overawed him completely. Afterwards he turned and went home. Night, which came on soon, brought him no sleep. He was restless, agitated, and disquieted.

"The next morning, in company with others, the pool was dragged, and the body of his partner discovered, in the very spot towards which the figure of the phantom had twice pointed. It had been weighted and weighed down by a large stone attached to the body; while from the same spot was recovered a kind of axe or hatchet, with which the murder had evidently been committed. This was identified as having belonged to a certain adventurer, who, on being taxed and formally charged with the murder, and found to be possessed of certain valuable documents belonging to the murdered man, eventually confessed his crime, and was executed.

"This incident, and its supernatural occurrences, made a deep impression; and, having been abundantly testified to, in a court of justice, as well as in common and general conversation, is not likely to be soon forgotten in the neighbourhood of Ballarat, in Australia, where it occurred."

Here, of course, the purpose of the Apparition was obvious enough; and the end attained was as just and proper as it was true and righteous; for "whoso sheddeth man's blood, by man shall his blood be shed."

The following example of the appearance of the spirit of a dying woman to her children, who were at a distance of some hundreds of miles from her, is a plain unvarnished narrative of facts. It is now published for the first time.

"A lady and her husband (who held a position of some distinction in India) were returning home (A.D. 1854) after an absence of four years, to join a family of young children, when the former was seized in Egypt with an illness of a most alarming character; and, though carefully tended by an English physician and nursed with the greatest care, grew so weak that little or no hope of her recovery existed. With that true kindness which is sometimes withheld by those about a dying bed, she was properly and plainly informed of her dangerous state, and bidden to prepare for the worst. Of a devout, pious, and reverential mind, she is reported to have made a careful preparation for her latter end, though no clergyman was at hand to minister the last sacrament, or to afford spiritual consolation. The only point which seemed to disturb her mind, after the delirium of fever had passed away, was a deep-seated desire to see her absent children once again, which she frequently expressed to those who attended upon her. Day after day, for more than a week, she gave utterance to her longings and prayers, remarking that she would die happily if only this one wish could be gratified.

"On the morning of the day of her departure hence, she fell into a long and heavy sleep, from which her attendants found it difficult to arouse her. During the whole period of it she lay perfectly tranquil. Soon after noon, however, she suddenly awoke, exclaiming, 'I have seen them all: I have seen them. God be praised for Jesus Christ's sake!' and then slept again. Towards evening, in perfect peace and with many devout exclamations, she calmly yielded up her spirit to God Who gave it. Her body was brought to England, and interred in the family burying-place.

"The most remarkable part of this incident remains to be told. The children of the dying lady were being educated at Torquay under the supervision of a friend of the family. At the very time that their mother thus slept, they were confined to the house where they lived, by a severe storm of thunder and lightning. Two apartments on one floor, perfectly distinct, were then occupied by them as play and recreation rooms. All were there gathered together. No one of the children was absent. They were amusing themselves with games of chance, books, and toys, in company of a nursemaid who had never seen their parents. All of a sudden their mother, as she usually appeared, entered the larger room of the two, pausing, looked for some moments at each and smiled, passed into the next room, and then vanished away. Three of the elder children recognized her at once, but were greatly disturbed and impressed at her appearance, silence, and manner. The younger and the nursemaid each and all saw a lady in white come into the smaller room, and then slowly glide by and fade away."

The date of this occurrence, September 10, 1854, was carefully noted, and it was afterwards found that the two events above recorded happened almost contemporaneously. A record of the event was committed to paper, and transcribed on a fly-leaf of the family Bible, from which the above account was taken and given to the Editor of this book in the autumn of the year 1871, by a relation of the lady in question, who is well acquainted with the fact of her spectral appearance at Torquay, and has vouched for the truth of it in the most distinct and formal manner. The husband, who was reported to have been of a somewhat sceptical habit of mind, was deeply impressed by the occurrence. And though it is seldom referred to now, it is known to have had a very deep and lasting religious effect on more than one person who was permitted directly to witness it.[19]

A personal acquaintance of the Editor, whom he has had the pleasure of knowing for twenty years, most kindly furnishes the following example:--

"In the winter of 1872-3 I was afflicted with a long and severe illness, so severe indeed, that for six weeks I was hovering between life and death. A nurse of great knowledge and intelligence was in attendance on me; she had been brought up as a Socinian, and was entirely careless as to religious belief. At the same time she was wholly devoted to her duties, and most attentive and assiduous in the same. Two days after her arrival she was sitting up in the adjoining room, the folding-doors between which and the room where I was lying being open, and lights were burning in each apartment. It had struck two o'clock a.m., and from my critical position she was unwilling either to sleep or to secure temporary rest. On looking up at that moment she perceived a form bending over me. The figure was that of an aged person with attenuated features, straggling grey hair, and thin clasped hands, which were placed in the attitude of prayer. For a while she thought it was someone who had entered the room; but, after gazing at it intently, she was smitten with a strange awe, and stood watching it attentively for at least five minutes, when it gradually faded away and disappeared.

"On the first opportunity she mentioned this strange occurrence to the people of the house, when she heard for the first time that my father had been lying dangerously ill at his own residence, more than a hundred miles away. At the time of my own and my father's sickness, my dangerous state, for medical and prudential reasons, was not communicated to him, and my illness was made light of, fearing the bad effect upon himself. That it was his Spirit which then appeared seems undoubted: for at two o'clock p.m. a relation came to see me from the City where my father had lived, to break to me the sad news of his decease. He had departed this life exactly at the period when his apparition in the attitude of prayer had been seen by my attendant. These facts were not made known to me until some time afterwards."[20]

The following story, no less interesting and impressive, appears in "The Life and Times of Lord Brougham, written by Himself," published a few years ago by Messrs. Blackwood and Co.:--

"'A most remarkable thing happened to me--so remarkable that I must tell the story from the beginning. After I left the High School [in Edinburgh], I went with G----, my most intimate friend, to attend the classes in the University. There was no divinity class, but we frequently in our walks discussed and speculated upon many grave subjects--among others, on the immortality of the soul, and on a future state. This question and the possibility, I will not say of ghosts walking, but of the dead appearing to the living, were subjects of much speculation; and we actually committed the folly of drawing up an agreement, written with our blood, to the effect that whichever of us died first should appear to the other, and thus solve any doubts we had entertained of the "life after death." After we had finished our classes at the College, G---- went to India, having got an appointment there in the Civil Service. He seldom wrote to me, and after the lapse of a few years I had almost forgotten him; moreover, his family having little connection with Edinburgh, I seldom saw or heard anything of them, or of him through them, so that all the old schoolboy intimacy had died out and I had nearly forgotten his existence. I had taken, as I have said, a warm bath; and while in it and enjoying the comfort of the heat after the late freezing I had undergone, I turned my head round towards the chair on which I had deposited my clothes, as I was about to get out of the bath. On the chair sat G----, looking calmly at me. How I got out of the bath I know not, but on recovering my senses I found myself sprawling on the floor. The apparition, or whatever it was that had taken the likeness of G----, had disappeared. The vision produced such a shock that I had no inclination to talk about it, or to speak about it even to Stuart; but the impression it made upon me was too vivid to be easily forgotten; and so strongly was I affected by it, that I have here written down the whole history with the date, 19th December, and all the particulars as they are now fresh before me. No doubt I had fallen asleep; and that the appearance presented so distinctly to my eyes was a dream, I cannot for a moment doubt, yet for years I had had no communication with G----, nor had there been anything to recall him to my recollection; nothing had taken place during our Swedish travels either connected with G---- or with India, or with anything relating to him or to any member of his family. I recollected quickly enough our old discussion, and the bargain we had made. I could not discharge from my mind the impression that G---- must have died, and that his appearance to me was to be received by me as a proof of a future state.' This was on December 19, 1799. In October, 1862, Lord Brougham added as a postscript:--'I have just been copying out from my journal the account of this strange dream: certissima mortis imago! And now to finish the story, begun about sixty years since. Soon after my return to Edinburgh there arrived a letter from India announcing G----'s death! and stating that he had died on the 19th of December.'"

The following example of the apparition of a departed friend is, for reasons which will be apparent from the narrative, not unlike the three curious, but independent cases already recorded in the early part of the present chapter, and not altogether unlike that told by the late Lord Brougham. It comes directly to the Editor from the pen of the person who saw the spectral appearance:--

"I was sitting in my library one evening, towards the close of summer, somewhat late. The shadow of evening had been deepening for some time, for the sun had long gone down; and the expansive valley beyond and below my sloping garden was white with mist. Within, beyond the heavy folds of the curtains which hung beside a single and rather small and open window, there was a grey darkness which almost enshrouded the corners of the room on either side. I had been musing and meditating on a variety of subjects, theological, metaphysical, and moral, for more than an hour; while I reposed in a low arm-chair on one side of the fire-place.

"All of a sudden I saw what seemed to be an elongated perpendicular cloud of foggy-looking grey smoke, collected in the right-hand corner of the room. I could not comprehend what it was. While looking steadily at it, and rubbing my eyes (doubting for a moment whether I was awake or asleep), it seemed to form itself, by a kind of circular rolling motion of the smoke or luminous mist, into a human shape. There, before me, came out slowly, as it were, face, head, body, arms, hands and feet--at first a little indistinct in detail, but eventually so self-evident and clear that it was impossible to doubt the fact--of a figure, which a moment or two afterwards was developed into the exact and unmistakeable form of an old fellow-student at Oxford, who had died soon after we left that university, and of whom I had heard nothing whatever since the day of his death about seven years previously,[21] to that moment. Appearing just as he had lived, though death-like and ashen, he looked at me with a fixed and strangely-vacant stare, which appeared to grow alternately vivid and piercing, and dull and nebulous. I seemed to feel the air all at once chill and unearthly; and an indescribable sensation came over me which I had never experienced either before or afterwards. I felt almost paralyzed, and yet not altogether terrified. The form of my old college companion (who had been a very upright, devout and religious man) in a moment smiled at me, and raising his hand, pointed for a few seconds upwards. At this action a very bright mist, not exactly a light, but a luminous mist, seemed to hover over him. I tried to speak, but could not. My tongue clave to the roof of my mouth. Then, protecting myself with the sign of the Cross, and a mental invocation of the Blessed Trinity, I sheltered my eyes with my right hand for a few seconds, and then looking up again saw the apparition become more and more indistinct and soon altogether fade away.

"This is my ghost story, and I have always connected the appearance with arguments and conversations which, against aggressive objectors, used to be held at Oxford in defence of the Christian doctrines of the Resurrection of the Body and the Immortality of the Soul, in which my dead friend took so intelligent and earnest a part."

Not less interesting is the following account of a Spectral Appearance which occurred in the latter part of the afternoon of a bright autumnal day, well authenticated, and here set forth for the first time:--

"The widow of a well-known Bristol merchant was, in 1856, acting as lady housekeeper to a Berkshire clergyman. One of her sons was an officer in the Indian army, and serving in the Madras Presidency. It was his custom to write to his mother by every fortnightly mail. He had not missed doing so with punctual regularity.

"One evening, however, between six and seven, in the month of October of the above year, the lady in question was walking on the lawn before the house, in company with the curate of the parish, a well-known Oxford man, when all of a sudden both of them saw what appeared to be a dog-cart containing three men drive along the lane which skirted the lawn and flower-garden, and which was separated from it by a closely-cut box-hedge, so low as to admit of those who were walking in the garden seeing with ease and distinctness any person approaching the house in a vehicle. It was driven in the direction of the carriage entrance, and, from the sound, appeared to have entered the court-yard of the house. One of the persons in it, he who sat behind, half rose, and looking towards his mother and the clergyman, smiled, and waved his right hand as a greeting. He looked very pale and ashy; otherwise there was nothing remarkable in his appearance. Both most distinctly observed the action just mentioned. Immediately on seeing it, the lady exclaimed with marked feeling and excitement, 'Good heavens! why, there's Robert.' She at once rushed through a passage of the house, which led directly to the court-yard, only to find to her amazement and perplexity that no carriage nor dog-cart had arrived, and that the large gates of the house were, as usual, locked and fastened, and moreover had not been opened.

"The impression this remarkable incident made was deep and great. No doubt whatever existed in the minds of those who had seen and heard the passing vehicle, that the form on the seat behind was the son of the lady in question. She consequently felt confident that some harm had happened to him, became miserable, and was inconsolable. No remarks or reasoning to the contrary, several of which were attempted, produced the slightest effect. A deep gloom settled over her. The sequel can soon be narrated. In the course of a few weeks the mail viâ Southampton, most anxiously looked for, brought two letters to the lady in question, one intimating that her son had been suddenly struck with a most severe fever, was delirious and in great danger; the other intimating his death. This latter occurred on the very day at which the appearance in question was seen, but at a slightly different time."

With the following example, as strange in itself as it is painfully interesting, this part of the subject will be brought to a close. It is only right to add that a version of the incident which now follows has already appeared in one of Mr. Henry Spicer's interesting volumes:--

"A young German lady of rank, still alive to tell the story, arriving with her friends at one of the most noted hotels in Paris, an apartment of unusual magnificence on the first floor was apportioned to her use. After retiring to rest, she lay awake a long while contemplating, by the dim light of a night lamp, the costly ornaments in the room, when suddenly the folding doors opposite the bed, which she had locked, were thrown open, and amid a flood of unearthly light there entered a young man in the dress of the French navy, having his hair dressed in the peculiar mode à la Titus. Taking a chair, and placing it in the middle of the room, he sat down, and took from his pocket a pistol of an uncommon make, which he deliberately put to his forehead, fired, and fell back dead. At the moment of the explosion, the room became dark and still, and a low voice said softly, 'Say an Ave Maria for his soul.'

"The young lady fell back, not insensible, but paralyzed with horror, and remained in a kind of cataleptic trance, fully conscious, but unable to move or speak, until at nine o'clock, no answer having been given to repeated calls of her maid, the doors were forced open. At the same moment, the powers of speech returned, and the poor young lady shrieked out to her attendants that a man had shot himself in the night, and was lying dead on the floor. Nothing, however, was to be seen, and they concluded that she was suffering from the effects of a dream.

"A short time afterwards, however, the proprietor of the hotel informed a gentleman of the party that the terrible scene witnessed by the young lady had in reality been enacted only three nights previously in that very room, when a young French officer put an end to his life with a pistol of a peculiar description, which, together with the body, was then lying at the Morgue, awaiting identification. The gentleman examined them both, and found them exactly correspond with the description of the man and the pistol seen in the apparition. The Archbishop of Paris, Monseigneur Sibour, being exceedingly impressed by the story, called upon the young lady; and, directing her attention to the words spoken by the mysterious voice, urged her to embrace the Roman Catholic faith, to whose teaching, as His Grace asserted, it pointed so clearly."

The various examples of Spectral Appearances now given (and they might have been largely augmented) may certainly serve to provide cases, so inherently striking and conclusive in themselves, as to leave little or no doubt of their intrinsic truth. Making every allowance for unintentional misconceptions and exaggeration in the record of them, putting aside mere rhetorical ornaments and literary additions, it seems quite impossible, being guided by the ordinary rules of evidence, not to admit the force and value of such striking facts as the above. In the cases already set forth, it is quite irrational to maintain that the disturbed imagination or wild fancy of the persons who are said to have seen the Apparitions were the sole foundations of the things seen; more especially as in some instances the Appearances were beheld by two or more persons at the same time, and often the same form presented itself to different people upon different occasions. It may be that some own a power of seeing disembodied spirits, which is not possessed by others, and it is tolerably certain that the large majority of people have never beheld anything of the sort. But this, after all, is but negative testimony. That which is positive, covering, it may be, a small area, is of considerable value and importance in aiding those who are open to conviction in coming to a reasonable conclusion. For existing positive evidence cannot be rudely and arrogantly set aside, when found to be, as in the case under consideration, so completely in harmony with many of the plain and specific statements of Holy Scripture, with the express testimony of the Fathers of the Christian Church, and the almost universal tradition of mankind in every age.

CHAPTER VII - HAUNTED HOUSES AND LOCALITIES

"Nations civilized as well as uncivilized: barbarians of the rudest type, and Christians of the highest and deepest spirituality, have always believed that certain localities were the haunts of unquiet spirits." - Richard H. Froude.

Many who are unaffected by the demoralizing and degrading materialistic theories of life, which are now enunciated by some who name themselves, and whom their flattering admirers style "philosophers," will not be unwilling to allow that a considerable amount of evidence[22] is in existence, indicating that certain localities are troubled by the presence of evil spirits, who from time to time manifest their powers, or sometimes appear to mankind in forms which give a shock to those who are enabled or permitted to perceive them.

If Christian tradition be accepted, a belief in the official ministry of unfallen spirits,--"the armies of the Living God,"--will be held, firmly[23] and intelligibly, as a most reasonable and beautiful part of Almighty God's revelation, Who "has ordained and constituted the services of angels and men in a wonderful order." So, by consequence, the existence and action of fallen angels, the Legions of Satan, and of spirits,[24] who, at the particular judgment following immediately upon death, have merited the swift and righteous condemnation of an all-just Judge, will be fully admitted.

The power, activity, and malice of Satan is apparent from numerous statements in Holy Scripture; and most Christian writers who have dealt with the subject of evil spirits have maintained that their power and influence are unquestionably greater in some localities than others. It is commonly held, that in lonely deserts, on lofty mountains, where the feet of men seldom tread, as well as in the mines of the earth,[25] and in vast forests where desolation reigns, the powers of the Devil and his angels, being unchecked and uncurbed by the positive energizing activity of Christianity, are vast. So, likewise, the universal instinct of mankind has maintained that there are certain places in which the appearances of unquiet or lost souls might be reasonably looked for, rather than in others. Deserted houses and lonely roads, where crimes of violence and special wickedness have been perpetrated; deep mines,[26] localities, unblessed by Holy Church, where the bodies of Christians have been placed to moulder away, instead of in God's holy acre, the consecrated churchyard; battlefields, where it may be that so many have been cut off in deadly sin--

"Unhouseled, disappointed, unanealed,"

have each and all been regarded as the fitting haunts of disquieted and wandering spirits.

On this point Southey, in "The Doctor," with much force thus writes:--"The popular belief that places are haunted where money has been concealed (as if, where the treasure was and the heart had been, there would the miserable soul be also), or where some great and undiscovered crime has been committed, shows how consistent this is with our natural sense of fitness."

On a collateral detail of this subject (the constant and malignant activity of evil spirits), Mr. John Wesley, a thorough believer in the Supernatural, put forth his faith and convictions with singular force and lucidity, plainly maintaining the reality and importance of all those explicit statements of Holy Scripture which so directly and practically bear on the point under treatment.

"Let us consider," wrote Wesley, "what may be the employment of unholy spirits from death to the resurrection. We cannot doubt but the moment they leave the body, they find themselves surrounded by spirits of their own kind, probably human as well as diabolical. What power God may permit these to exercise over them we do not distinctly know. But it is not improbable [that] He may suffer Satan to employ them as he does his own angels, in inflicting death or evils of various kinds on the men that know not God. For this end they may raise storms by sea or by land; they may shoot meteors through the air; they may occasion earthquakes; and in numberless ways afflict those whom they are not suffered to destroy. Where they are not permitted to take away life, they may inflict various diseases; and many of these, which we may judge to be natural, are undoubtedly diabolical. I believe this is frequently the case with lunatics. It is observable that many of these, mentioned in the Scripture, who are called 'lunatics' by one of the Evangelists, are termed 'demoniacs' by another. One of the most eminent physicians I ever knew, particularly in cases of insanity, the late Dr. Deacon, was clearly of opinion that this was the case with many, if not with most lunatics. And it is no valid objection to this, that these diseases are so often cured by natural means; for a wound inflicted by an evil spirit might be cured as any other, unless that spirit were permitted to repeat the blow. May not some of these evil spirits be likewise employed, in conjunction with evil angels, in tempting wicked men to sin, and in procuring occasions for them? Yea, and in tempting good men to sin, even after they have escaped the corruption that is in the World. Herein, doubtless, they put forth all their strength, and greatly glory if they conquer."[27]

Although some may maintain that this passage is perhaps wanting in theological exactness, there can be little doubt that, with much force, it truly and eloquently embodies the belief of all Christian people, and gives a simple and forcible explanation of Scripture statements regarding the active and untiring energy of the legions of Hell.

Again, the Marquis de Marsay, a pious French Protestant writer of the last century, whose collected works were issued about the year 1735, sets forth from his own point of view a theory regarding the nature and character of spirits, which because it bears directly on the subject of Haunted Localities, and in some respects follows the teaching of the schoolmen, it may be well to quote here:--

"I believe," he writes, "that there are three kind of spirits, which return to this World, after the death of their bodies. The spirits of such as are in a state of condemnation, and which are in a very miserable condition, hover about, and haunt the places where they have committed their evil deeds and iniquities. They remain at these places by divine permission, and do all the evil they can; whilst, at the same time, they suffer intolerable torments and are malignant. Some of this kind of spirits occasionally make themselves visible.... The second kind of spirits are those which roam about, because they seek to free themselves from their state of purification[28] by other means than by resignation to Divine Justice; hence they seek help from those that fear God, and in so doing, withdraw themselves from the Divine Order.... These are not evil spirits, but such as are still in their self-will, and therefore refuse to yield to the Divine Order, by voluntarily submitting themselves to the punishment imposed upon them.... The third kind of spirits, or rather souls that reappear, are those, whose punishment is to be at some certain place in this world, because they have satisfied their passions in that place, and lived according to their lusts in an idolatrous manner; for that which now causes a man lust and pleasure, must hereafter serve as his pain and punishment. Of this we have several instances; amongst others, that of a pious man, who after his death appeared to his daughter, who was likewise a pious person, and after conversing with her some time on his state, began to turn pale, to tremble, and be much distressed; and said to his daughter that the time was now arrived when he must go and remain for a time in his grave, with his putrefying and corrupting corpse; and that this happened to him every day, because in his life-time he had had too much affection and tenderness for his body."

The dissertations of the schoolmen, and of certain English writers of the seventeenth century, are not unlike the above.[29] So, too, are several of their most reasonable deductions and conclusions. In fact, Dr. Joseph Hall, sometime Bishop of Exeter (A.D. 1627-1641, and afterwards of Norwich, from 1641 until 1656), maintained that many souls, guilty both of deadly sin (duly repented of during life), and of venial sin, in which not improbably they died, might have to suffer, by lingering, unsatisfied, because away from their Creator, and about the places where they sinned in their lifetime, until their temporal punishment was complete; a theory which though from the pen of one suspected of favouring Puritanism, is very like that embodied in the faith and practice of the Universal Church.

However this may be, at all events there is scarcely a locality in which some old tradition as regards Haunted Houses and Places does not exist; and which is not more or less accepted and believed in even now. A general rejection of the Supernatural may be the case with many, and a shallow desire not to be thought superstitious or over-credulous by more, are obvious reasons why some traditions have become weakened and others obscure. But putting aside all such, half-lost, forgotten, or fading away, and making every allowance for exaggeration and hyperbole, the facts which can still be testified to by credible witnesses, the evidence which is even now on record, coupled with that innate sentiment of awe, so common to many, and often strengthened by a sound religious belief, which gives point to old traditions, are sufficient to induce the calm and the unprejudiced not too hastily to disavow the existence of a principle of almost universal acceptance with mankind, and which neither the lame and limping logic of the sceptic, nor the imperfectly marshalled facts and random conclusions of the materialist can, in the long run, either weaken or destroy.

The following curious record, a fair example of numerous others, may now be suitably set forth:--

"Elizabeth, the third daughter of Sir Anthony Cooke (preceptor to Edward VI.) married Sir Thomas Hobby, of Bisham Abbey in Berkshire, and accompanied him to France, when as ambassador to Queen Elizabeth he went thither. On his death abroad in 1566 Lady Hobby brought his corpse home to Bisham, where he was buried in a mortuary chapel. She afterwards married John, Lord Russell. By her first husband she had a son, who when quite young is said to have entertained the greatest dislike and antipathy to every kind of learning; and such was his resolute repugnance to acquiring the art of writing that in a fit of obstinacy he would wilfully and deliberately blot his writing-books in the most slovenly manner. Such conduct so vexed and angered his mother, who was eminently intellectual, and like her three sisters, Lady Burleigh, Lady Bacon, and Lady Killigrew, an excellent classical scholar, that she beat him again and again on the shoulders and head, and at last so severely and unmercifully that he died.

"It is commonly reported that, as a punishment for her unnatural cruelty, her spirit is doomed to haunt the house where this cruel act of manslaughter was perpetrated. Several persons have seen the apparition, the likeness of which, both as regards feature and dress, to a pale portrait of her ladyship in antique widow's weeds still remaining at Bisham, is said to be exact and lifelike. She is reported to glide through a certain chamber, in the act of washing blood stains from her hands. And on some occasions the apparition is said to have been seen in the grounds of the old mansion.

"A very remarkable occurrence in connection with this narrative, took place about thirty years ago. In taking down an old oak window-shutter of the latter part of the sixteenth century, a packet of antique copy-books of that period were discovered pushed into the wall between the joists of the skirting, and several of these books on which young Hobby's name was written, were covered with blots, thus supporting the ordinary tradition."[30]

Creslow in Buckinghamshire,[31] like so many old manor-houses, has its ghost story. It is said to be the disturbed and restless spirit of a lady, which haunts a certain sleeping chamber in the oldest portion of the house. She has been seldom seen but often heard only too plainly by those who have ventured to sleep in this room, or to enter it after midnight. She appears to come up from the old groined crypt, and always enters by the door at the top of the nearest staircase. After entering she is heard to walk about, sometimes in a gentle, stately manner, apparently with a long silk train sweeping the floor. Sometimes her motion is quick and hurried, her silk dress rustling violently as if she were engaged in a desperate struggle.

This chamber, though furnished as a bedroom, is seldom used, and is said to be never entered without trepidation and awe. Occasionally, however, some persons have been found bold enough to dare the harmless noises of the mysterious intruder; and many are the stories current in Buckinghamshire respecting such adventures. The following will suffice as a specimen, and may be depended on as authentic:--

"About the year 1850, a gentleman, not many years ago High Sheriff of the county, who resides some few miles' distance from Creslow, rode over to a dinner-party; and, as the night became exceedingly dark and rainy, he was urged to stay over the night if he had no objection to sleep in the haunted chamber. The offer of a bed in such a room, so far from deterring him, induced him at once to accept the invitation. He was a strong-minded man of a powerful frame and undaunted courage, and like so many others, entertained a sovereign contempt for all haunted chambers, ghosts, and apparitions. The room was prepared for him. He would neither have a fire nor a night-light, but was provided with a box of lucifers that he might light a candle if he wished. Arming himself in jest with a cutlass and a brace of pistols, he took a serio-comic farewell of the family and entered his formidable dormitory.

"In due course, morning dawned; the sun rose, and a most beautiful day succeeded a very wet and dismal night. The family and their guests assembled in the breakfast-room, and every countenance seemed cheered and brightened by the loveliness of the morning. They drew round the table, when the host remarked that Mr. S--, the tenant of the haunted chamber, was absent. A servant was sent to summon him to breakfast, but he soon returned, saying he had knocked loudly at his door, but received no answer, and that a jug of hot water left there was still standing unused. On hearing this, two or three gentlemen ran up to the room, and, after knocking and receiving no answer, opened it and entered. It was empty. Inquiry was made of the servants; they had neither seen nor heard anything of him. As he was a county magistrate, some supposed that he had gone to attend the Board which met that morning at an early hour. But his horse was still in the stable; so that could not be. While they were at breakfast, however, he came in, and gave the following account of his last night's experiences:--'Having entered my room,' said he, 'I locked and bolted both the doors, carefully examined the whole room, and satisfied myself that there was no living creature in it but myself, nor any entrance but those which I had secured. I got into bed, and, with the conviction that I should sleep soundly as usual till six in the morning, was soon lost in a comfortable slumber. Suddenly I was awakened, and, on raising my head to listen, I certainly heard a sound resembling the light soft tread of a lady's footstep, accompanied with the rustling as of a silk gown. I sprang out of bed, and having lighted a candle, found that there was nothing either to be seen or heard. I carefully examined the whole room. I looked under the bed, into the fire-place, up the chimney, and at both the doors, which were fastened just as I had left them. I then looked at my watch, and found it was a few minutes past twelve. As all was now perfectly quiet again, I put out the candle, got into bed, and soon fell asleep. I was again aroused. The noise was now louder than before. It appeared like the violent rustling of a stiff silk dress. A second time I sprang out of bed, darted to the spot where the noise was, and tried to grasp the intruder in my arms. My arms met together, but enclosed nothing. The noise passed to another part of the room, and I followed it, groping near the floor to prevent anything passing under my arms. It was in vain, I could feel nothing. The sound died at the doorway to the crypt, and all again was still. I now left the candle burning, though I never sleep comfortably with a light in my room, and went to bed again, but certainly felt not a little perplexed at being unable to detect the cause of the noise, nor to account for its cessation when the candle was lighted.'"

So that this gentleman's experience (and as to ghosts, he was a sceptic) only served to strengthen the old and unbroken tradition. Of its foundation nothing very certain is known. The general facts, however, are commonly received.

Another example, unusually curious, relating to the Castle at York, is taken from the "Memoirs of Sir John Reresby:"--

"One of my soldiers being on guard about eleven in the night at the gate of Clifford Tower, the very night after the witch was arraigned, he heard a great noise at the Castle; and, going to the porch, he saw there a scroll of paper creep from under the door, which, as he imagined by moonshine, turned first into the shape of a monkey, and thence assumed the form of a turkey-cock, which passed to and fro by him. Surprised at this, he went to the prison, and called the under-keeper, who came and saw the scroll dance up and down, and creep under the door, where there was scarce an opening of the thickness of half-a-crown. This extraordinary story I had from the mouth both of one and the other."[32]

An account of the haunting of Spedlin's Tower was furnished to me by a Scotch friend, who asserts and vouches for the authenticity of the tradition:--

"Spedlin's Tower, the scene of one of the best accredited and most curious ghost stories perhaps ever printed, stands on the south-west bank of the Annan, in Dumfriesshire. The ghost story is simply this:--Sir Alexander Jardine, of Applegarth, in the time of Charles II., had confined in the dungeon of his tower of Spedlin's, a miller named Porteous, suspected of having wilfully set fire to his own premises. Sir Alexander being soon after suddenly called away to Edinburgh, carried the key of the vault with him, and did not recollect or consider his prisoner's case till he was passing through the West Port, where, perhaps, the sight of the warder's keys brought the matter to his mind. He immediately sent back a courier to liberate the man, but Porteous had, in the meantime, died of hunger.

"No sooner was he dead, than his ghost began to torment the household, and no rest was to be had within Spedlin's Tower by day or by night. In this dilemma, Sir Alexander, according to old use and wont, summoned a whole legion of ministers to his aid; and by their strenuous efforts, Porteous was at length confined to the scene of his mortal agonies, where, however, he continued to scream occasionally at night, 'Let me out, let me out, for I'm deein' o' hunger!' He also used to flutter against the door of the vault, and was always sure to remove the bark from any twig that was sportively thrust through the key-hole. The spell which thus compelled the spirit to remain in bondage was attached to a large black-lettered Bible, used by the exorcists, and afterwards deposited in a stone niche, which still remains in the wall of the staircase; and it is certain that, after the lapse of many years, when the family repaired to a newer mansion (Jardine Hall), built on the other side of the river, the Bible was left behind, to keep the restless spirit in order. On one occasion, indeed, the volume requiring to be rebound, was sent to Edinburgh; but the ghost, getting out of the dungeon, and crossing the river, made such a disturbance in the new house, hauling the baronet and his lady out of bed, &c., that the Bible was recalled before it reached Edinburgh, and placed in its former situation. The good woman who told Grose this story in 1788, declared that should the Bible again be taken off the premises, no consideration whatever should induce her to remain there a single night. But the charm seems to be now broken, or the ghost must have become either quiet or disregarded, for the Bible is at present kept at Jardine Hall."

Another example from Scotland now follows, all the more remarkable, because it is still asserted that in a certain part of the mansion unusual voices, and supernatural footsteps are said to be still heard, a fact to which the late Mr. Hope Scott often testified:--Sir Walter Scott relates a striking occurrence which happened to him at the time Abbotsford was in the course of erection. Mr. Bullock was then employed by him to fit the castle up with proper appurtenances, when during that person's absence in London the following extraordinary circumstance took place:--In a letter to Mr. Terry in the year 1818 Scott wrote:--"The night before last we were awakened by a violent noise like drawing heavy boards along the new part of the House. I fancied something had fallen and thought no more about it. This was about two in the morning. Last night at the same witching hour the same noise recurred. Mrs. S., as you know, is rather timbersome; so up I got with Beardy's broadsword under my arm,

> 'Sat bolt upright
> And ready to fight.'

But nothing was out of order; neither could I discover what occasioned the disturbance." Now, strangely enough on the morning that Mr. Terry received this letter he was breakfasting with Mr. Erskine (afterwards Lord Kinneder) and the chief subject of their conversation was the sudden death of Mr. Bullock, which on comparing dates must have happened on the same night and as near as could possibly be ascertained at the same hour, these disturbances occurred at Abbotsford. One might be induced to maintain that some drunken workmen or disorderly persons were on the premises, but this method for accounting for the coincidence will at once be exploded on reading the following passage from Scott to the same gentleman:--"Were you not struck with the fantastical coincidence of our nocturnal disturbance at Abbotsford with the melancholy event that followed? I protest to you that the noise resembled half-a-dozen men hard at work pulling up boards and furniture, and nothing could be more certain than that there was nobody on the premises at the time."

The following account of a haunted locality is from the pen of a scholarly and accomplished clergyman[33] in the diocese of Ripon:--"Some years ago I was residing in a village about eleven miles from York, and one mile and a half from another village, in which was the Post Office for the surrounding district. Whenever I had reason to suppose a letter was lying there for me, I used to anticipate the delivery of it on the following morning, by calling for it myself in the evening before. One night, in the latter end of November, I was going, for this purpose, along the path through the fields, and when I was midway between the two villages, I passed through a little hand-gate, and after going about twenty yards from it, I was startled and alarmed by a succession of the most horrible shrieks that can possibly be conceived. They seemed scarcely human, though I felt at the time that they were certainly uttered by some man or woman, imitating the piercing scream of a hog when the fatal knife is being plunged into its throat. The panic that seized me vanished in a moment, as the thought instantaneously flashed across my mind that I was being made the victim of some ploughman's joke. Being armed, as I then invariably was, with a particularly tough and stout cudgel, I ran back to the little hand-gate on tip-toe, intending to take condign vengeance on some rustic, whom I felt sure I should find crouching down behind the low hedge. Just as I reached the hand-gate, the sounds suddenly ceased, and to my utmost astonishment I could see no one, although it was quite impossible for any person within the distance of two or three hundred yards to have escaped my observation. The full moon was shining brightly, with the very thinnest of fleecy clouds before her face, which did not obscure her light, but only made the whole country distinctly visible in every direction, from the absence of all strongly-defined shadow. Then, again, I must confess, an unaccountably superstitious awe crept over me, and, instead of pursuing my intended route, I returned to my own home.

"On the following morning, when reflecting on what had happened, I began to take a philosophical and reasonable view of the singular occurrence. In passing through the little gate I might, as I thought, have left it ajar, and that soon after it lost its nice equilibrium, and swung back to its accustomed resting-place. The hinges might have given a creaking sound, which the lonely solitude of the night had intensely magnified in my imagination. So much for the philosophical view. I then determined that I would put this view to the proof, and see if I could by any means get the gate to produce any noise similar to what I fancied I had heard. This was the reasonable view. I took care, however, to put my determination into practice at the earliest period of the evening, just, in fact, as the daylight had departed. Accordingly I was at the little gate between five and six o'clock, but in spite of all kinds of efforts it would make no sign, but swung backwards and forwards on its hinges with noiseless smoothness. In the midst of my experiments a very intelligent man, a Gardener by calling, came up. He was a resident of my own village, but had been working in the other village, and was then returning home from his day's labour. He expressed some surprise at seeing me there at that time of the evening, and I gave him a brief account of the reason. 'Well, sir,' said he; 'if you will walk back with me, I will tell you something more about that little hand-gate.' I consented immediately, and he said to me as follows: 'Some years ago, when we were all children at home, my mother had been to the other village, where she remained till night; on her return homewards, just as she passed through the little gate, she saw some kind of figure lying close by it, huddled together in a strange, mysterious manner. She was horror-stricken, and fled from the spot as fast as possible. On reaching her own cottage, she flung open the door, and fell fainting on the ground before her astonished and frightened children. When she came to herself, and was asked what had caused her evident terror, she told what she had seen, and where she had seen it. She could, however, give no definite description of the figure she had seen. She could only say, "It was something hideous." But never could she be induced to pass that place again after night-fall, as long as she lived.' 'Well,' said I, 'this is a very remarkable coincidence.' 'Yes,' said he, 'but I will tell you something more remarkable still. About forty years ago the land between the two villages was unenclosed. It was nothing more than a wild, uncultivated common. One night, about that period, as the villagers were going to bed, loud and piercing shrieks were heard coming from the common. Some of the men dressed themselves hastily, with the intention of going and seeing what was taking place. Some woman, as it seemed to them, was evidently being ill-treated. They set off on their kindly-intentioned errand, but as the sounds completely ceased, and the night was very dark, they thought it impossible to reach the exact spot where their services might be required. They went to bed, and slept soundly. On the following morning one of them was going to work at the other village, and as he passed over the common he was almost distilled to a jelly with the effect of fright at the appalling sight that suddenly met his gaze. A woman was lying before him, huddled up on the ground, quite dead, with her throat cut from ear to ear. She had evidently been murdered, on the preceding night. Who she was, whence she came, why or by whom she had been murdered, was never known, and probably never will be in this world. When, a short time after this dreadful event, the common was enclosed, it so happened that the little hand-gate was put up close to the spot where the woman's lifeless body was found.'

"He finished his narrative. I thanked him for it, and internally resolved never, if I could help it, to pass through those fields alone in the gloom of night, on any account whatever. I scrupulously kept my resolve."

The celebrated case of the Haunted Room in the Jewel House of the Tower of London created great interest, about fifty-five years ago. Additional interest and importance have been given to it by the publication of the following authentic account of Mr. E. Lenthal Swifte,[34] which in simple but forcible language tells its own story:--

"I have often purposed to leave behind me a faithful record of all that I know personally of this strange story.... Forty-three years have passed, and its impression is as vividly before me as on the moment of its occurrence.... In 1814 I was appointed keeper of the Crown Jewels in the Tower, where I resided with my family until my retirement in 1852. One Saturday night in October, 1817, about 'the witching hour,' I was at supper with my then wife, our little boy, and her sister, in the sitting room of the Jewel House, which--then comparatively modernized--is said to have been 'the doleful prison' of Anne Boleyn, and of the ten bishops whom Oliver Cromwell piously accommodated therein.... The room was, as it still is, irregularly shaped, having three doors and two windows, which last are cut nearly nine feet deep into the outer wall; between these is a chimney-piece projecting far into the room, and (then) surmounted with a large oil picture. On the night in question the doors were all closed; heavy and dark cloth curtains were let down over the windows, and the only light in the room was that of two candles on the table.... I sate at the foot of the table, my son on my right hand, his mother fronting the chimney-piece, and her sister on the opposite side. I had offered a glass of wine and water to my wife, when, on putting it to her lips, she paused and exclaimed, 'Good God, what is that?' I looked up, and saw a cylindrical figure like a glass tube, seemingly about the thickness of my arm, and hovering between the ceiling and the table. Its contents appeared to be a dense fluid, white and pale azure, like to the gathering of a summer cloud, and incessantly rolling and mingling within the cylinder. This lasted about two minutes, when it began slowly to move before my sister-in-law, then following the oblong shape of the table, before my son and myself; passing behind my wife it paused for a moment over her right shoulder (observe, there was no mirror opposite to her in which she could then behold it). Instantly she crouched down, and, with both hands covering her shoulder, she shrieked out, 'Oh, Christ! it has seized me.' Even now, while writing, I feel the fresh horror of that moment. I caught up my chair, struck at the wainscot behind her, rushed upstairs to the other children's room, and told the terrified nurse what I had seen.... Neither my sister-in-law nor my son beheld this 'appearance.'... I am bound to add that shortly before this strange event some young lady residents in the Tower had been, I know not wherefore, suspected of making phantasmagorical experiments at their windows, which, be it observed, had no command whatever on any windows in my dwelling. An additional sentry was accordingly posted so as to overlook any such attempt. Happening, however, as it might, following hard at heel the visitation of my household, one of the night sentries at the Jewel Office was, as he said, alarmed by a figure like a huge bear issuing from underneath the door. He thrust at it with his bayonet, which stuck in the door, even as my chair dinted the wainscot. He dropped in a fit, and was carried senseless to the guard-room. His fellow-sentry declared that the man was neither asleep nor drunk, he himself having seen him the moment before awake and sober. Of all this I avouch nothing more than that I saw the poor man in the guard-house prostrated with terror,

Glimpses of the Supernatural Volumes I & II

and that in two or three days the fatal result, be it of fact or fancy, was that he died. Let it be understood that to all which I have herein set forth as seen by myself, I absolutely pledge my faith and my honour.--Edmund Lenthal Swifte."

Another statement, regarding another apparition in the same part of the Tower, stated by Mr. Offor to have been produced by some instrument, but which latter assertion is pronounced impossible by Mr. Lenthal Swifte, also sufficiently illustrates the facts embodied in it:--

"Before the burning of the armouries there was a paved yard in front of the Jewel House, from which a gloomy and ghost-like doorway led down a flight of steps to the Mint. Some strange noises were heard in this gloomy corner; and on a dark night at twelve the sentry saw a figure like a bear cross the pavement and disappear down the steps. This so terrified him that he fell, and in a few hours after, having recovered sufficiently to tell the tale, he died. It was fully believed to have arisen from phantasmagoria.... The soldier bore a high character for bravery and good conduct. I was then in my thirtieth year, and was present when his body was buried with military honours in the Flemish burial ground, St. Catherine's.

"George Offor."

On this, however, Mr. Swifte thus writes:--

"When on the morrow I saw the unfortunate soldier in the main guard-room, his fellow sentinel was also there, and testified to having seen him on his post just before the alarm, awake and alert, and even spoken to him. Moreover, as I then heard the poor man tell his own story, the figure did not cross the pavement and disappear down the steps of the sally-port; but issued from underneath the Jewel Room door--as ghostly a door, indeed, as ever was opened to or closed on a doomed man; placed, too, beneath a stone archway as utterly out of the reach of my young friends' apparatus (if any such they had) as were my windows. I saw him once again on the following day, but changed beyond my recognition; in another day or two--not 'in a few hours'--the brave and steady soldier, who would have mounted a breach or led a forlorn hope with unshaken nerves, died at the presence of a shadow, as the weakest woman might have died.

"Edmund Lenthal Swifte."

The case of a Haunted House in Northamptonshire may now follow:--

"A house at Barby,[35] a small village about eight miles from Rugby, was reputed to be haunted, and this under the following circumstances:--An old woman of the name of Webb, a native of the place, and above the usual height, died on March 3, 1851, at two A.M. aged sixty-seven. Late in life she had married a man of some means, who having predeceased her, left her his property, so that she was in good circumstances. Her chief and notorious characteristic, however, was excessive penuriousness, being remarkably miserly in her habits; and it is believed by many in the village that she thus shortened her days. Two of her neighbours, women of the names of Griffin and Holding, nursed her during her last illness, and her nephew, Mr. Hart, a farmer in the village, supplied her temporal needs; in whose favour she had made a will, by which she bequeathed to him all her possessions.

"About a month after the funeral Mrs. Holding, who, with her uncle, lived next door to the house of the deceased (which had been entirely shut up since the funeral), was alarmed and astonished at hearing loud and heavy thumps against the partition wall, and especially against the door of a cupboard in the room wall, while other strange noises, like the dragging of furniture about the rooms (though all the furniture had been removed), and the house was empty. These were chiefly heard about two o'clock in the morning.

"Early in the month of April a family of the name of Accleton, much needing a residence, took the deceased woman's house, the only one in the village vacant, and bringing their goods and chattels, proceeded to inhabit it. The husband was often absent, but he and his wife occupied the room in which Mrs. Webb had died, while their daughter, a girl about ten years of age, slept in a small bed in the corner. Violent noises in the night were heard about two o'clock, thumps, tramps, and tremendous crashes, as if all the furniture had been collected together, and then violently banged on to the floor. One night at two A.M. the parents were suddenly awakened by the violent screams of the child, 'Mother, mother, there's a tall woman standing by my bed, a-shaking her head at me!' The parents could see nothing, so did their best to quiet and compose the child. At four o'clock they were again awakened by the child's screams, for she had seen the woman again; in fact she appeared to her no less than seven times, on seven subsequent nights.

"Mrs. Accleton, during her husband's absence, having engaged her mother to sleep with her one night, was suddenly aroused at the same hour of two by a strange and unusual light in her room. Looking up she saw quite plainly the spirit of Mrs. Webb, which moved towards her with a gentle appealing manner, as though it would have said, 'Speak, speak!'

"This spectre appeared likewise to a Mrs. Radbourne, a Mrs. Griffiths, and a Mrs. Holding. They assert that luminous balls of light hovered about the room during the presence of the spirit, and that streams of light seemed to go up towards a trap-door in the ceiling, which led to the roof of the cottage. Each person who saw it testified likewise to hearing a low, unearthly, moaning noise,--'strange and unnatural-like,' but somewhat similar in character to the moans of the woman in her death-agony.

"The subject was, of course, discussed; and Mrs. Accleton suggested that its appearance might not impossibly be connected with the existence of money hoarded up in the roof, an idea which may have arisen from the miserly habits of the dead woman. This hint having been given to and taken by her nephew, Mr. Hart, the farmer, he proceeded to the house, and with Mrs. Accleton's personal help made a search. The loft above was totally dark, but by the aid of a candle there was discovered, firstly, a bundle of writings, old deeds, as they turned out to be, and afterwards a large bag of gold and bank-notes, out of which the nephew took a handful of sovereigns, and exhibited them to Mrs. Accleton. But the knockings, moanings, strange noises, and other disturbances did not cease upon this discovery. They did cease, however, when Mr. Hart, having found that certain debts were owing by her, carefully and scrupulously paid them. So much for the account of the Haunted House at Barby. The circumstances were most carefully investigated by Sir Charles Isham, Bart., and others, the upshot of which was that the above facts were, to the complete satisfaction of numerous enquirers, completely verified."

The following comes to the Editor from Scotland:--

"There is, without a doubt, a 'Haunted Room' in Glamis Castle. Access to it now is cut off by a stone wall, and none are supposed to know where it is, except Lord Strathmore, his eldest son, and the Factor on the estate. This wall was built some years ago by the present proprietor. Strange, weird, and unearthly noises have been heard from time to time by numbers, and these by many persons wholly unprepared for the same. The following statement is from the lips of a lady who was sleeping in the castle one night, and who knew nothing of the reputation of the house:--She was undressing to retire for the night, when all of a sudden she was alarmed by a most violent noise, which made her fancy that one of the walls of the house had fallen. She rushed out into the passage, but no one but herself had been aroused by it. So she went back, and slept until morning. She mentioned the circumstance at breakfast, but the subject was evidently an unpleasant one. The conversation was at once changed, and she received a hint to take no further notice of it. Some members of the family cannot bear the subject to be alluded to, and repel all inquiries."

"There is no doubt," writes another correspondent, "about the reality of the noises at Glamis Castle. On one occasion, some years ago, the head of the family with several companions was determined to investigate the cause one night, when the disturbance was greater and more violent and alarming than usual. His lordship went to the Haunted Room (before it was walled up), opened the door with the key, and dropped back in a dead swoon into the arms of his companions; nor could he be ever induced to open his lips on the subject afterwards.

"On another occasion a lady and her child were staying for a few days at the castle. The child was asleep in an adjoining dressing-room, and the lady, having gone to bed, lay awake for a while. Suddenly a cold blast stole into the room, extinguishing the night-light by her bedside, but not affecting the one in the dressing-room beyond, in which her child had its cot. By that light she saw a tall mailed figure pass into the dressing-room from that in which she was lying. Immediately thereafter there was a shriek from the child. Her maternal instinct was aroused. She rushed into the dressing-room, and found the child in an agony of fear. It described what it had seen as a giant, who came and leant over its face.

"An accomplished antiquarian, who has investigated this subject, writes as follows:--There is a tradition that in olden times, during one of the frequent feuds between the Lindsays and the Ogilvies, a large number of the latter, in flying from their enemies, came to Glamis, and claimed hospitality. The master of the castle did not like to deny them the protection of his castle walls. He therefore admitted them; and on plea of hiding them, is reported to have put them into this out-of-the-way chamber. There he let them starve, and it is said that their bones lie there unto this day, the bodies never having been buried. This may have been the sight which startled the late Lord Strathmore on entering the haunted room--a large number of skeletons lying in the various parts of the place was a sight calculated to startle any man. And these are declared to be peculiarly revolting. Some had apparently died in the act of gnawing the flesh off their own arms."

The Editor is indebted to Henry Cope Caulfeild, Esq., of Clone House, St. Leonard's, for the following:--

"The account here set forth was recently told to me by a Captain S----living near Cardiff, South Wales.

"A few miles from Cardiff, on the Monmouth road, there is a narrow spot held in awe by the peasantry; for a murder was committed there years ago, and it is said to be haunted by unquiet spirits.

"The brother of my friend, an officer in the army, who has seen active service in India, was returning with his wife in a dog-cart, some few months ago, from a dinner with some friends in the country a few miles from Cardiff. It was late in the night; and as they entered the narrow part of the road just mentioned, they heard the sound of wheels behind them. They looked back, and saw the lights of a carriage, and to avoid being overtaken and passed in such a narrow road, Captain S---- whipped his horse, and tried to keep well in front. Presently the sounds of wheels ceased; and to their great surprise, indeed consternation, they all of a sudden saw the lights and heard the wheels of a carriage some distance on in front of them. It was evidently the same; and yet it had never passed them! It seemed to stop at the side of the road, and Captain S---- drove his dog-cart past the strange carriage. He and his wife saw in it a dim light; there were people in it, and they seemed to be without heads! Mrs. S---- was paralysed with terror; her husband told his brother that he would rather face a battery of artillery than go through the horror of that moment; and the horse evidently was in sympathy with them, for he went like one mad.

"It appears that the very same spectral figures had been seen by a country surgeon when passing the same place; and that the land-owners in those parts had cut down trees, and clipped and altered the appearance of the hedges on each side of the road, in order to get rid, if possible, of the ghastly horror, and of the hold which it has upon the popular mind. The appearance of the carriage and its occupants, in a dim, hazy light, was to the last degree unearthly and spectral."

A correspondent of the Editor furnishes him with the following:--

"A brother of mine, a man who is the last person in the world to believe over much, or to be in the least degree superstitious, wishing to be near a particular town, and yet within easy reach of the permanent country residence of his greatest friend, was induced (A.D. 1862) to take over the remainder of the lease of an old-fashioned furnished mansion in Cheshire, where he, with his wife, children, and servants, in due course, went to reside. He was advised to take the place as well because of the reasonableness of the rent--for it was spacious and comfortably furnished--as by the recommendation of the London house-agents, a well-known firm in the West End, with whom the letting of it rested.

"Soon after the arrival of the family and servants, the latter protested again and again that they were disturbed almost every night by a continual 'tramp, tramp, tramp' of heavy footsteps up the stairs, and along the narrow passage, out of which were the doors which led to their bedrooms. They would have it that the house was haunted. The sounds were sometimes so loud and alarming that, as one of the servants remarked, 'It seemed like a regiment of foot soldiers marching over creaking boards.' Complaints were made to my brother, who merely said that the noises must be the result of wind under the joists, or of rats, and he laughed at the whole affair. Some of the servants gave warning, and left. Still the sounds went on: not always, and every night, but, with certain cessations, from time to time.

"In the autumn of the year 1863, a lady, her daughter of fourteen, and a maid, came to stay in the House; and as the former was somewhat of an invalid, a suite of rooms in the west wing, each communicating with the other, was apportioned to them. The second night after their arrival, the lady in question, suddenly awaking, saw in her bedroom a luminous cloud, which gradually appeared to be formed into the shape of an old man, with a most painfully depressing countenance, full of the deepest sorrow, and wearing a large full-bottomed wig. She tried to raise herself in bed, to see if it were not the effect of her half-waking fancy, or the result of a disturbed dream, but could not. The room, in which there was no natural light, seemed to be partially but quite sufficiently illuminated; and she felt confident that a spectre was before her. She gazed at it for some minutes, three at least, hearing the ticking of her watch, and counting the seconds. There the apparition stood, and seemed to be making an effort to speak, while a strange, dull, inarticulate groan seemed to come up as from the floor. Upon this, seeing the bell-rope hanging within the folds of the curtains at her right hand, she braced herself up to seize it and give it a most violent pull. Immediately she did this, the face of the figure bore an expression of anger, and by degrees it faded away. The bell, which hung some distance away, was heard by no one, and she was compelled to lie alone, for she feared to rise (though the apparition did not reappear) until the church clock near struck four, when, the morning having broken, she rose, and dressed herself.

"In the morning, before she had said a word, her daughter, on meeting her, said, 'Oh, mamma, an old man in a great wig tramped through my room twice in the night. Who could it have been?'

"The lady being so impressed by these occurrences, which her host and hostess would persist in saying were only the result of her own fancy, determined on leaving in the course of a few days (as she afterwards stated). On the following night, she slept with a night-light, and the door into her maid's room open. But the noise of tramping, which had been hitherto heard only in the servants' wing of the house, which was opposite, was now heard in the east side of it. 'Tramp, tramp, tramp!'

the sounds were heard constantly, without cessation; so much so that the master of the house, my brother, rose suddenly that very night, thinking that thieves had broken in, and rushed out to the east passage. But all in a moment, they stopped; nothing was to be heard, nothing seen; all was still. This occurred again and again.

"The lady left as arranged. The noises ceased for a while, and then began once more. It was with difficulty that any of the servants could be induced to remain, believing that the house was haunted.

"About ten months afterwards, my brother having forgotten all about the supposed spectre and the noises, had been out for the day, and returned home in a dog-cart, some time after midnight, in company with his groom. Only the housekeeper had remained out of bed, as his return was quite uncertain. The horse and trap were put up, both the servants had gone to their rooms, and my brother was taking some refreshment in the housekeeper's apartment, by the light of the fire, when all of a sudden, a loud and decisive rap was heard at the door. Thinking, of course, that it was one of the servants, he replied, 'Come in.' Before the words were out of his mouth, the door opened, and the apparition of the old man in a large wig stood before him. My brother was paralysed with terror for a while. He could not speak; he tried hard, as he says, but his mouth was dry and his tongue motionless. 'Good God!' he exclaimed at length, 'am I awake or asleep, in my senses or gone mad?' The motionless figure, whose face was intensely sad, looked at him beseechingly. 'In God's Name, what do you want, or what can I do for you?' 'Too late! nothing,' was the mournful, but somewhat inarticulate response. And with that the spectre suddenly vanished away. At this moment a strong, loud, piercing, bitter wail, as of the voice of a woman, broke the awful silence. It seemed to come from the courtyard outside, and was repeated again and again round the upper part of the house. The scream was said to be like nothing human. The servants heard it, my sister-in-law was awoke by it, and the groom and housekeeper, with the others, as a consequence, came rushing downstairs. My brother, who is as brave and bold as he is remarkable for common sense, does not now dispute the reality of haunted houses.

"A few months afterwards, he and his left. And after he had given up possession, he was informed, on good and credible authority, that tradition confidently asserted the mansion to have been the residence of a disreputable Dutch hanger-on of William of Orange, who is represented to have violently made away with one of his mistresses in that very house, in a room which overlooked the park, now a disused lumber-room, at the east end of the old mansion."[36]

An American clergyman, of what is commonly termed "the Protestant Episcopal Church," sent the following, which, as he writes, "went the round of the newspapers," and for the truth of which he himself vouches:--

"Few positions in life can be imagined more disagreeable than that of being imprisoned in a haunted cell in a police station. 'The New Orleans Times' tells a most unpleasant story of a ghost-infested cell in the Fourth Precinct police station in that city. It appears that several years ago 'a little old woman,' named Ann Murphy, committed suicide by hanging herself in this cell; and since that event no fewer than thirteen persons have attempted to destroy themselves in a similar manner; four of these attempts being attended with fatal results. One of those lately cut down before life was extinct was a girl named Mary Taylor, who, on recovering consciousness, declared that while lying on the floor of the cell she was aroused by a little old white woman in a faded calico dress, with no stockings and down-trodden slippers, with a faded handkerchief tied round her head. Her faded dress was bound with a sort of reddish-brown tape, and her hand was long, faded, and wrinkled, while on the fourth finger of her left hand was a plain, thin gold ring. 'This little woman,' said the girl, 'beckoned me to get up, and impelled me by some mysterious power to tear my dress in strips, place one of the strips round my neck, and tie the other to the bars. I lifted my feet from the floor, and fell. I thought I was choking, a thousand lights seemed to flash before my eyes, and I forgot all until I found myself in the room with the doctors and police bending over me. It was not until then that I really comprehended what I had done, and was, I believe, under a kind of trance or influence at the time, over which I had no control.' Mary Taylor had never heard of the suicide of Ann Murphy, whose appearance, according to the police, tallied exactly with the description given by the girl. Others having complained in a like manner of the ghostly occupant of the cell, the police, to test the real facts of the case, placed a night lodger who had just arrived in the city in this cheerful apartment. Being thoroughly tired and worn out, he fell asleep immediately, but shortly afterwards rushed into the office in a state of terrible alarm. He, too, had been visited by the little old woman, and wisely declined to sleep another hour in the station."

The following case, as may be seen from an attestation at its conclusion, is likewise well authenticated:--

"An English clergyman, who was seeking a residence in a northern Scottish city about ten years ago, had his attention accidentally called to an old-fashioned, pleasant-looking detached house, of some size and convenience, which had been for some time vacant, about a mile and a-half from the city. It had considerable grounds round it well timbered, a high-walled garden, and was in many respects both commodious and comfortable. One attraction, likewise, was the extremely moderate rent which was asked for it. So he secured a lease of it for a short term of years. He and his family and servants came up from England in due course, and took up their abode in it. They were not there long before it soon became evident, to some of them at least, that the house was haunted. Noises of the most extraordinary character were heard in various parts. Sometimes there came the sound of heavy footsteps on the stairs. At others there were knocks, both violent and gentle, at the doors, none of which could be accounted for. At midnight, on several occasions, there was a constant, uninterrupted sound in one room, as if a large sledgehammer (having been wrapped in a blanket folded several times), was steadily and regularly struck against the wall, at the head of the bed in the room, by some particularly powerful arms. 'Thump, thump, thump,' it sounded, as though lifted and directed with tremendous force; and this noise often lasted, with only slight intermission, for two or three hours. On other occasions persons on the stairs or in the passages felt the air move, and heard the creaking of the floor close to them, as if someone invisible were passing quickly by. One night, between twelve and two, the master and mistress of the family were awakened by a loud and startling noise, as if all the shutters of the windows of the house had been suddenly and simultaneously burst open with the greatest violence. The crash was literally tremendous; and each believed that thieves were breaking in. So the clergyman, seizing a large presentation sword which hung on the wall of the landing, unsheathed it, and went downstairs with a light, expecting to face the intruders. He first examined the dining-room (from whence the noise seemed chiefly to come), but everything was just as usual. No shutter was open; no cupboards forced. So, too, in hall and library. Nothing was moved. Then he descended into the large cellars; but there, likewise, everything was untouched, and nothing unusual was seen. A large retriever dog, which lay at the foot of the front stairs, however, was greatly agitated, trembled and howled. But still nothing was to be seen. Perfect silence reigned. So the clergyman and his wife returned to their sleeping-room, only to hear, all of a sudden, precisely the same strange noise repeated about ten minutes after their return, with, if anything, even greater violence.

It was currently reported, and commonly believed by several residents thereabouts, that many years previously, the cast-off mistress of a Scotch nobleman, having been handed over to a physician and university professor for marriage, and the latter having received from the nobleman in consideration of the marriage the gift of the house and lands in question, subsequently murdered the woman, for whom he had conceived a special dislike, and buried her body on the premises. This story, with slight but unimportant variations, was told by several; and it is quite certain that a young female Scotch servant, who once lived in the house, following the sound of heavy footsteps up to an attic in the front portion of the house, which she had pledged herself to do when next she heard them, fell down in a swoon or fit at the top of the stairs; from that moment lost her reason, and is now in a lunatic asylum, near the City in question. These are facts testified to by those who know the circumstances.[37] As to the general accuracy of the foregoing, the Editor is enabled, on the testimony of several, to pledge his word thereto.

I am indebted for the following narrative to a friend,[38] who in her own words has given all the details of another remarkable example of a Haunted House:--

"Monsieur de Goumoëns, a magistrate, or a gentleman holding a high judicial position at Berne in Switzerland, a man of undoubted and well-established character for personal courage, as well as for moral rectitude, related to my father, Mr. Caulfeild of Bath, with whom he was on the most intimate terms of personal friendship, the following circumstance, at once so extraordinary and so painful, which had come within the precincts of his own house, as to drive him from his place of residence. The account was given to my father in the year 1829, when he was residing with his family at Berne. Noises and disturbances had been frequently heard in M. de Goumoëns' bedroom, as of footsteps, the opening and shutting of drawers, and of an escritoire when papers were shuffled about. The heavy curtains of the large old four-posted bed were drawn and undrawn by no human hand, and were sometimes suddenly flung up on to the top of the bed; while the sound of the flapping of the wings of some very large bird was often heard. All these and other sounds so disturbed M. de Goumoëns and his wife, that the health of the latter began perceptibly and seriously to fail. Examinations of the house made by himself, in conjunction with the police, and special investigations of the bedroom and other adjoining apartments, afforded no solution whatsoever of the mystery. At length Madame de Goumoëns' maid gave warning to leave her service, complaining that her sleep and peace were completely broken by these supernatural occurrences. While consulting together as to what could be done, and hesitating as to whether they might not be compelled to leave the place, the strange sounds became louder than ever. One night they were suddenly aroused by hearing sharp cries of distress from one of their children, a little boy, who slept in their room, and who in great terror called out fretfully again and again, 'Let me alone; let me alone; don't you hurt me!' as he pointed into vacancy. This particular event was the last straw which broke the camel's back, and led the child's parents to determine on leaving the house immediately.

"I may add that on a subsequent and more searching examination of the house, one room was found to be both locked and fastened up; regarding the character of which the owner was somewhat reticent. However, the boarding before the door, which had been papered over, was removed, the keys were forthcoming, and the room was carefully examined. On the shutters being opened, it was found just as it had been left since its occupation by a previous tenant, who had gone by the sobriquet of 'the Black Styger.' He was a nobleman of bad reputation, and had committed suicide in that very apartment by blowing out his brains; the traces of which with blood were found scattered both on wall and floor. It was generally believed that his disturbed spirit haunted the place."

One of the most singular recent examples, testified to by two independent eye-witnesses, now deserves to be reproduced. The appearance of a large spectral bird is thus recorded by Mr. Henry Spicer in one of his curious and thoughtfully written volumes entitled "Strange Things amongst Us:"--

"Captain Morgan, a gentleman of the highest honour and veracity, and who certainly was not over-gifted with ideality, arrived in London one evening in 18--, in company with a friend, and took up his lodgings in a large old-fashioned house of the last century, to which chance had directed them. Captain Morgan was shown into a large bed-chamber, with a huge four-posted bed, heavy hangings, and altogether that substantial appearance of good, solid respectability and comfort which associated itself with our ideas of the wealthy burghers and merchants of the time of Queen Anne and the first George, when so many strange crimes of romantic daring or of deep treachery stained the annals of the day, and the accursed thirst for gold, the bane of every age, appeared to exercise its most terrific influence.

"Captain Morgan retired to bed, and slept, but was very soon awaked by a great flapping of wings close beside him, and a cold, weird-like sensation such as he had never before experienced spread through his frame. He started, and sat upright in bed; when an extraordinary appearance declared itself in the shape of an immense black bird, with outstretched wings, and red eyes flashing as it were with fire.

"It was right before him and pecked furiously at his face and eyes so incessantly, that it seemed to him a wonder that he was enabled, with his arms and the pillow, to ward off the creature's determined assaults. During the battle it occurred to him that some large pet bird belonging to the family had effected its escape, and been accidentally shut up in the apartment.

"Again and again the creature made at him with a malignant ferocity perfectly indescribable; but though he invariably managed to baffle the attack, he noticed that he never once succeeded in touching his assailant. This strange combat having lasted several minutes, the gallant officer, little accustomed to stand so long simply on the defensive, grew irritated, and leaping out of bed, dashed at his enemy. The bird retreated before him. The captain followed in close pursuit, driving his sable foe, fluttering and fighting, towards a sofa which stood in the corner of the room. The moonlight shone full into the chamber, and Morgan distinctly saw the creature settle down, as if in terror, upon the embroidered seat of the sofa.

"Feeling now certain of his prey he paused for a second or two, then flung himself suddenly upon the black object, from which he had never removed his gaze. To his utter amazement it seemed to fade and dissolve under his very fingers. He was clutching the air; and in vain he searched, with lighted lamp, every nook and corner of the apartment, unwilling to believe that his senses could be the victims of so gross a delusion--no bird was to be found. After a long scrutiny the baffled officer once more retired to rest, and met with no further disturbance.

"While dressing in the morning, he resolved to make no allusion to what he had seen, but to induce his friend, on some pretext, to change rooms with him. That unsuspecting individual readily complied, and the next day reported, with much disgust, that he had had to contend for possession of the chamber with the most extraordinary and perplexing object[39] he had ever encountered, to all appearance a huge black bird, which constantly eluded his grasp, and ultimately disappeared, leaving no clue to its mode of exit."[40]

And with this, the present chapter is closed. Numerous other cases of Haunted Localities might have been provided; some which have long been in print, others which have been heard from the lips of those whose experience and good faith testify to the truth of their narratives. In so many examples collected, almost every one owns certain features in common: and all in some measure are alike. Repetition, by consequence, becomes wearisome. The cases here put on record, therefore, while sufficiently diversified, serve abundantly to set forth the reality of those facts, to a brief record of which this chapter has been devoted.

CHAPTER VIII - MODERN SPIRITUALISM

"Now the Spirit speaketh expressly that, in the latter times, some shall depart from the Faith, giving heed to seducing spirits and doctrines of devils." - 1 Tim. iv. 1.

"Many believe that the final assault upon Christianity will be made by the enemies of God, bonded and compacted together into an universal kingdom. It may be, as some have held, that another Incarnation shall take place; and that the Enemy of souls will be permitted to assume man's nature. Anyhow, we are told that Antichrist shall reign. Thousands, deluded by false miracles and lying wonders, will become his subjects, his willing votaries; and own him as their king. His worship will be an adroit counterfeit of the worship of the True God--his kingdom a parody of the Catholic Church; while its doctrines will be at once so attractive and delusive to fallen man as that the predicted Apostasy will be great and widespread." - Sermons on Antichrist.

When, in a country where for at least twelve centuries the Christian Religion has been accepted, and by which that country has received unknown blessings both temporal and spiritual, schools of thought arise, in which Historical Christianity is not simply patronized, but put out of court, the phenomenon is both portentous and noteworthy. That this is so at the present time in England with many, need scarcely be pointed out. The scepticism which has deluged the Continent, coming upon a people whose religious convictions had been so seriously disturbed by the Reformation, and whose conceptions of objective political truth had been so ruthlessly disorganized by the events of the Commonwealth and the Revolution of 1688, has found the ground well prepared for a scattering of the seeds of doubt. Abroad they were sown some generations ago, and brought forth deadly fruit. The French Revolution and its horrors followed as a matter of course. Events before our eyes tell in very plain language that our own turn has at last come.[41] The day of trial is now upon us. True, the vulgarity of the eighteenth-century unbelievers is not at present so manifestly apparent; though it exists amongst certain active leaders of the lower classes with whom scepticism is popular. But the tone and temper of public opinion, the bold utterances of serials and newspapers, the public political policy now in vogue and popular, the too general understanding that Christianity is to be as far as possible ignored in legislation--all indicate the steady and rapid progress of sceptical liberalism.

The Broad Church party in the established communion has done much, and will no doubt do much more, to eliminate the Supernatural from the minds of its admirers and of the people of England. Disliking dogma, its teaching, when the fog which surrounds it allows that teaching to be partly comprehended, is of the earth earthy. It dovetails in with the low material views and carnal desires of the money-grubbing many. Its ideal of bliss, not always wrapped up in philosophical jargon (and therefore sometimes intelligible), is simply commercial prosperity and temporal wealth; eating and drinking, marrying and giving in marriage, comfort, material pleasure and ease; the conquest of Nature by scientific research and progress; an enjoyment of the present and only the present; and a complete banishment of the old-world theology--useful, it may have been, in times gone by, when the World was being educated; but now to be thrown aside as lumber, worn out and valueless. In place of that Historical Christianity accepted since the days of S. Augustine of Canterbury, we are promised doubt, disbelief, a refined as well as an unrefined intellectual Paganism; and in the end--though such an end may not now be contemplated by all members of that ecclesiastical school--a positive rejection of the distinct nature of God.

At present, of course, the figure is decently draped. Its ugly proportions and hateful outline are not apparent. Its admirers have to accommodate themselves with some skill to the strong prejudices of the age; to tolerate systems which they contemn, to carry out the silent but certain operation of destruction, under the hypocritical desire of assisting mankind to complete the work of temporal progress.

All this is before us and around us, if we would but note it. And this being so, the state of thought and of society, as few can fail to observe, is eminently calculated to afford those who disbelieve in the Supernatural, good opportunities of advance in the direction of negations. On the other hand, the presence amongst us of a sect of persons who call themselves "Spiritualists," and whose notorious words and works may be noted and criticized, is full of moment and importance. Spiritualism, when first it appeared and took shape, was treated with contempt. The facts urged by its supporters were denied; the manifestations almost universally disbelieved in. It was declared to be the work of acute knaves, or the offspring of idle and imaginative dreamers. Public writers treated it with scornful contempt. Reports of its strange proceedings and extraordinary developments were knowingly and deliberately suppressed. It was hastily hustled off the public stage, refused a hearing, and denied a defence. This policy, however convenient to its promoters, has failed. Sneers have not killed it. Its ideas and theories have been recently reduced to a formal system, while its votaries have increased to an extent scarcely credited. Christians and non-Christians, Roman Catholics, Church-of-England people and Protestants, have ranged themselves under its banner, and accept and propagate its views. To some the existence of spurious coin proves the value of the true; and the portents of these latter times are surely full of warning and value.

At all periods, it should be observed, certain classes of leaders of men's thoughts have succeeded in banishing the Supernatural from the field of human action. For example, Thucydides, representing the World exclusively in its natural aspect, did this. He had neither ear nor eye for the marvellous. In recent times, from the period of Locke to the beginning of the present century, a similar course was adopted by a very influential school of writers, remarkable for their careful dismissal of the miraculous, both from ken and consideration. To such, the World was a machine, wound up once for all by its Author, and needing no further application of that power which appeared to have spent itself, so to speak, in the act of creation. Like S. Peter's "scoffers," "walking after their own lusts," they practically declared, "since the fathers fell asleep, all things continue as they were from the beginning of creation."[42]

But, of course, such a state of thought could only be transitory. The universal convictions of man's conscience, and the most earnest desires of his heart, produced a reversion of opinion. The very dogmatic philosophers soon found themselves at sea. Reason and Imagination were starved, while the Understanding was profoundly flattered. This has so turned out, not once, nor twice, but continually. Scepticism has followed Superstition, and Superstition Scepticism. Wherever the Catholic Religion, having once been had, has been deliberately cast out and denied, there, as in Scotland at the present day, Superstition is more than ordinarily widespread and rampant. The Gnosticism and Manichæism of the early Christian era have reproduced themselves in later times; while Materialism has lived side by side with that Superstition which, on the surface, it seemed so necessary for the same Materialism to deny.

The following faithful account of the rise of the modern system of Spiritualism is borrowed from a contemporary record:--

"In December, 1847, a respectable farmer and his family, named Fox, settled in a house at Hydesville, a hamlet near Newark, in the State of New York. They were troubled from the first with noises, which in January, 1848, assumed the definite character of knockings, like that of a hammer. Two children, since so famous as the Misses Fox, felt something heavy, like a dog, lie on their feet when in bed, and one of them felt as if a cold hand were passed over her face. The knockings went on increasing in violence, and at length it was observed, on some occasion when Farmer Fox tried the windows to see if they could be caused by the wind, that the knockings exactly answered the rattle accidentally made by the moving sash. This suggested the idea of inviting the noises, or rather the beings who caused them, to reply by rapping, on repetition of the letters of the alphabet, to questions put to them. This was first tried at a place called Rochester, with which the family were connected, whence the term 'Rochester knockings' came into use. The experiment succeeded perfectly, and this was the origin of 'spirit-rapping,' which has since grown into a regular system. The neighbours being called in, the affair soon thickened and developed into a 'movement.' The rappings revealed a murder which had taken place in the house when in other hands. Public meetings were called, committees of ladies formed to examine the children, and prevent the possibility of deception. Similar phenomena began to show themselves in various parts of the country, and under yet more extraordinary conditions. Raps were heard on all sorts of objects-- ceilings, tables, chairs, &c., and it was discovered that certain persons were better fitted than others to communicate with the spirits, to whom these noises were now attributed. Such persons were called mediums, a name with which the World is now sufficiently familiar, and when they were present, tables and chairs would move about and rise from the ground. Many other astonishing things became common, as drawing and music, executed under this strange influence, by persons who knew nothing of these arts."

As to its principles and policy, no better nor fairer exposition of them can be had than from the various publications which are so largely and generally circulated. From a pamphlet written with some system[43] by Mr. T. Grant of Maidstone, the following extracts, explanatory of the now formulated principles of Modern Spiritualism, are made:--

"TABLE OF MEDIA.
Outward.
1. Vibratory Medium.
2. Motive Medium.
3. Gesticulating Medium.
4. Tipping Medium.
5. Pantomimic Medium.
6. Impersonating Medium.

Inward.
7. Pulsatory Medium.
8. Manipulating Medium.
9. Neurological Medium.
10. Sympathetic Medium.
11. Clairlative Medium.
12. Homo-motor Medium.

Onward.
13. Symbolic Medium.
14. Psychologic Medium.
15. Psychometric Medium.
16. Pictorial Medium.
17. Duodynamic Medium.
18. Developing Medium.

Upward.
19. Therapeutic Medium.
20. Missionary Medium.
21. Telegraphic Medium.
22. Speaking Medium.
23. Clairvoyant Medium.
24. Impressional Medium.

"The Outward stratum includes all kinds of mediumship in which spirits act only on the physical organism, first using simply the electrical or magnetic emanations from the medium and others in the room to produce movements of objects, or concussions called rappings, and to control matter in various ways; and secondly, using portions or the whole of the medium's body by direct action of spirits upon the bodily organs, the medium's spirit being more or less passive, and not taking part in the performance....

"Vibratory Mediumship. I have often met with instances in my experience, and multitudes of persons are sometimes attacked together, with variations in accordance with individual character. The physical excitement and convulsive phenomena often witnessed at revival meetings are chiefly of this kind....

"The Motive Medium comes next in order; he furnishes the magnetic power by which spirits are enabled to move tables and other material objects....

"The third class is Gesticulating Mediumship, which appears to be a development of the vibratory. It is exhibited by the sect of 'Shakers' of the present day in the initiatory stage of their development, and was a form of mediumship common amongst the prophets of the Cevennes, the votaries of S. Vitus, and in most religious excitements.

"Tipping Mediumship follows next, and this again is a step in advance from the Motive mediumship, the movements of tables and other objects being so regulated by the intelligence of spirits as to produce telegraphic communications....

"Pantomimic media belong to the fifth class; they are made, by the controlling or guardian spirit, to put themselves in various postures, so as to represent any peculiarity belonging to spirit-friends who are standing by, wishing to make their presence known and to communicate. Lecturers on electro-biology produce, to some extent, the same effects.

"The last in this stratum is the Impersonating Mediumship, which is a development from the Pantomimic. In this case the communicating spirit enters and takes full possession of the medium's body, whilst his own spirit stands aside."

The writer then passes on to consider what he terms the "Inward stratum," thus:--

"First we have Pulsatory Mediumship, in which the medium receives communications from spirits and answers to mental questions by means of pulsations, like tiny raps, on different parts of

Rev. Frederick George Lee, D.C.L.

the body, or by sounds heard only by himself. These manifestations, although very convincing to the medium himself, afford but little satisfaction to anybody else.

"Manipulating Mediumship, which follows, is in fact Curative Mesmerism, in which, however, the will of the mesmeriser is strengthened and guided by spirits. Dr. Newton, of America, who visited Maidstone in 1870 and made several interesting and permanent cures, is a most remarkable and successful medium of this class, many of his cures having, indeed, all the appearance of miracles.

"In the next form of mediumship, the Neurological, the spirit impresses thoughts upon the brain, and the medium puts them into words; thus the communications partake of the peculiarities of the medium, and if the medium is impressed to write, he does so in his own handwriting and mode of diction and spelling.

"Next comes Sympathetic Mediumship, which is an extension of the Neurologic, but in which the spirits enter more intimately into sympathy with the medium. Both of these last are transitional forms of mediumship, and not very reliable until carefully developed.

"In Clairlative Mediumship, which succeeds in order, scenes of the past are clearly reproduced, or original scenes pictured to the mind, as in dreams and visions.[44]

"The last of this Inward group is called the Homo-motor medium, one who is in perfect sympathy and under the complete control of one individual spirit only, who, in fact, appears to live a second life on earth in union with him."

And then he defines and discusses the "Onward stratum":--

"We begin with Symbolic Mediumship, in which the interior vision is opened by spiritual aid, and the medium sees in a vision the almost exact pre-figurations of things which will occur at some future time, or which do in reality now exist, either in germ or in full or partial development.

"The second in this group, Psychologic Mediumship, is a very important form. A medium of this class is one who is in a condition to be impressed by a sympathetic spirit with any set of ideas which he desires to represent. It is sometimes done in a pictorial form, when the medium clearly sees and describes scenes which appear to the vision, such as the appearance and movements of an army, a landscape, a congregation in a cathedral, and so forth....

"The Psychometric Medium has the power of feeling and correctly describing the characteristics of persons with whose spheres he or she is brought into sympathy or contact. The power is generally exercised by placing to the forehead, the perceptive region of the brain, anything which has been intimately connected with the person, as a piece of his hair, his handwriting, or a well-worn article of dress. Some will thus read a sealed letter or the mottoes enclosed in nuts....

"Pictorial Mediumship differs from the Symbolic chiefly in the circumstance that the things seen and described by the medium do not in reality exist as material facts, but are only representations, prefiguring or bodying-forth a spiritual or psychical truth....

"The next is the Duodynamic Medium, a word signifying two powers, he being capable of exhibiting two or more forms of mediumship at the same time. These compound media, maturely developed, are said to be comparatively rare.

"The last in this Onward stratum is the Developing Medium, through whom spirits can very usefully assist in developing the mediumistic faculty in others. They have the power of harmonising the influences which affect them, and of rendering media passive to the action of the spirits who are seeking the control of their organisms."

As regards the "Upward stratum," the following definitions are given:--

"The Therapeutic Medium is one who effects the cure of many diseases through the sympathetic power of seeing and describing minutely the disorganized parts of the body, and directing the necessary treatment; sometimes the manipulating mediumship is added, when the medium not only sees the source of mischief, but also makes curative mesmeric passes at the same time.

"Next, we have the Missionary Medium, who is irresistibly compelled to go, without knowing why or whither, wherever the spirit guides him. Under this controlling influence, media have been made to travel nearly all over the civilized world, generally without purse or scrip, or any personal knowledge of the places; the spirits raising up friends and helpers at every step as they are required." Writing of a Missionary Medium known to himself, Mr. Grant adds the following:--"I am acquainted with a medium of this class in Maidstone, who is too weak in body to walk far in his ordinary state, yet, under this influence, he is often made to walk long distances without feeling fatigue, at the most unreasonable hours of day or night, and he has several times been instantaneously transported from one place to another, miles apart."

"Speaking mediumship," writes the author quoted, "is a most useful and instructive faculty.... In most cases speakers have to be entranced, that is, their spirits have to be removed from the body for a time, in order to give the acting spirit full control; but when this has to be done the medium is but little advanced from the personating mediumship, which is one of the successive stages which a fully-developed speaking medium generally passes through. Many of our most celebrated and effective preachers and speakers have been, or are, really speaking media, under the guidance of spirits, without its being suspected or understood even by themselves. This is, indeed, 'inspiration.'

"The Clairvoyant Medium follows next in order, and is in advance of the telegraphic, because he is able to see the scenes that are actually transpiring at the time in another place, no matter how far distant.

"The Impressional Medium is generally one who has advanced through the neurologic, sympathetic, clairlative, and psychologic phases, and thus become so easily and thoroughly impressible by his guardian spirit that the medium appears to live a double life, the conditions and circumstances of both states of existence finding a ready expression through his organism at all times without his being entranced, the spiritual existence becoming as much as the physical his normal state." pp. 7-18.

The acts and deeds of Mr. Daniel Home, a Scotchman, and of the Davenport brothers, Americans, who figure very prominently as mediums in the authentic records of the spiritualists, are tolerably well known by report to many. From America, where the signs were first noticed, they came eastwards to England and the European continent, in which places the spiritual manifestations were even more remarkable than those which had occurred and been testified to in the West. Under the direction of a medium, people sat round a table, and by a silent invocation of spirits, by "willing"[45] that they should come, they came, and produced the following amongst other equally strange phenomena.[46] Large tables rose to the ceiling, floating in the atmosphere with a sort of undulating motion, and coming down again to the floor without noise; sprigs of flowers were torn off and presented to people by the spirit; accordions and other musical instruments were played without any visible hand holding or moving them; luminous stars and streaks of light appeared in various places, while "spirit hands" were seen and felt as palpably as mortal flesh and blood could be; answers to questions made, were given by a system of raps or by spelling out words on a child's alphabet placed on the floor. Thus conversations, sometimes sensible, but frequently trivial and absurd,[47] were held with the spirits summoned. Spirit hands, using material pens, ink and paper, wrote answers to queries; quoted verses from known authors, or put down original poems. In some cases the narratives published were anonymous, and only authenticated by witnesses who privately testified to the newspaper-editors their accuracy. But in some instances persons of repute and ability came forward in support of their correctness.[48] Dr. Gully of Malvern, for example, publicly testified that he had seen Mr. Home float about a room for several minutes, and guaranteed the accuracy of the facts set forth in a most remarkable fashion in an early number of the "Cornhill Magazine." A well-known clergyman of the High Church party in the Church of England, gives his testimony to the truth and strangeness of certain appearances and manifestations, in the following communication to the Editor of this volume:--

"I was staying in the north of England with the Rev. ----, in 1850. During my visit a well-known medium (at that period a clergyman of the diocese of London) spent the evening with us. Eight or ten other people were there at the same time. 'Table-turning' was the subject of a long and animated discussion, in which those who accepted the facts and those who rejected them were about equally divided. There was nothing to be done, therefore, but to test the question. This was determined on. A circular table about four feet in diameter, of considerable size and weight, was used. Seven people sat round it, joining their hands on the table, and after conjointly willing that it should turn itself in one direction or be turned, for about twelve minutes, it began to vibrate strangely and then slowly to move. At first its motion was in circles, then it moved from side to side of the room with dash and rapidity. Afterwards it was strangely tilted on the other side. On one occasion later on, it rose several inches from the ground, and remained suspended in the air for nearly two minutes. As to the facts, no one could dispute them. Afterwards a variety of questions were put, to which the table replied by knocking on the floor. It was agreed beforehand that one knock should stand for 'No', two for 'Yes.' An alphabet was produced, and words in response were spelled out. Some of the queries were trivial, some arithmetical, some momentous. The answers were usually accurate, sensible, and intelligible, but not always so. After questions had been put concerning the future state, heaven, hell, purgatory, the happiness of the good and the punishment of the wicked, a question was asked, 'Where did the spirit now answering dwell when on earth?' The name of a place in Devonshire was spelled out. This reply greatly interested a clergyman present, who some fifteen years previously had been curate in that county. It was followed by another:--'What was the name of the person whose spirit is here?' Then the table spelt out, by means of the alphabet, the name of a yeoman who had died impenitent and blaspheming at the period before referred to. This was sufficient for me," writes the above correspondent; "what I had heard and seen convinced me that necromancy was practised. I left the house, protecting myself by the sacred sign, convinced of the sin of the practice. And though I had been a spectator and not an actor, I made a resolution, which I have scrupulously kept, never to see nor sanction such

Rev. Frederick George Lee, D.C.L.

proceedings again."

Another somewhat similar example is here recorded. A clergyman of the Church of England, intimately known to the Editor of this volume, supplies the following remarkable narrative regarding the action and authors of Spiritualistic manifestations:--"Being a perfect and total sceptic as to the supernatural character of so-called 'Spiritualism,' and believing that the results asserted to be produced by its votaries were brought about by pre-arranged trickery and the deception of confederates, I for a long time declined to be present at, or to take part in, a séance, though earnestly pressed to do so. However, circumstances led me to attend one in the year 1862, at a house in Notting Hill Square, London, in the month of October. Prior to the operations, which were managed and conducted by a 'medium,' I was invited to examine both the room where the séance was to be held, and the table by which the operations were to be conducted. Conversations, held by a well-known spiritualist, were to be carried on, (by means of an alphabet, raps and knockings,) with the spirits who were presumed to be present, and who were declared to have miraculously moved the table round which, for some time, seven persons, including myself, had been sitting. The room was about ten feet in height, and in the centre was a gas chandelier of three lights, all of which were burning. During the sitting, after the table had made several most remarkable gyrations, tilting one side of itself upwards and downwards at an angle of at least forty-five degrees, at the command of the chief operator it slowly ascended from the floor to the height of at least seven feet, viz. the bottom of the pendent gaselier. Its plane having caused the lamp glasses to rattle by contact, the table then with a strange throbbing and vibration and slow movement began to descend. We had all removed our chairs, to give room for its ascent, and standing close to the walls around, saw it slowly come down to its place. I was so shocked and horrified at what I beheld, and now so firmly convinced that the remarkable actions we had witnessed were the result of the invocation and intervention of evil spirits, that I declined, in language most positive and unmistakable, to have any further part in such unlawful performances. When further attempts were made to obtain fresh manifestations, taking from my neck a small silver crucifix, which had been blessed by a high ecclesiastical dignitary, I made a mental act of faith in the Blessed Trinity, and holding the small crucifix in my closed hand, placed my hand clasping it on the table, saying mentally, 'If this be the work of evil spirits, may God Almighty, for Christ's sake, stop it!' The moment I did this, the table, which had been moving about strangely in several directions, and by varied singular motions, became suddenly and at once motionless. Nor could it be made to stir afterwards. Being perfectly convinced that such operations were of the nature of Necromancy, forbidden by the Church, as Scripture plainly testifies, I made an earnest exhortation to those in the room, after the last manifestation, not to cooperate in such deeds any further. Some maintained by rather blasphemous arguments that Spiritualism was destined to, and would soon, take the place of Christianity; and were kind enough to pity my ignorance, narrowness, prejudice, and sectarianism, to which I made no reply. I then left."

From another source (a well-known country gentleman in one of the midland counties) has been obtained a series of questions and answers which were put, given, and taken down in the year 1856, at a gathering at which the practice of table-turning and spirit invocation was tested by those whose conviction, in the main, regarding them, as the Editor is informed, agrees with that of the correspondents already quoted. Similar strange phenomena occurred on this occasion likewise:--

"Are you a Spirit who inhabited this earth? Yes.
How long have you been dead? No reply.
Have you been dead years? No.
Months? No.
Weeks? No.
Days? Yes.
How many? Five days.
Do you mean five days? Yes.
Did you live in this neighbourhood? Yes.
Did you know any at this table? Yes.
Will you point them out? Yes. (It then crossed the room three times violently and stopped before three persons.)
Will you spell your name? Yes. R---- J----[49] (the way he always spelt it).
Are you happy? No answer.
Can we do you any good? No.
Was the Baptist religion true? No.
Will you spell the true religion? Yes--Saients.
Is there a middle state of souls? Yes.
Will the end of the World be soon? Yes.

Will it be the end of the World or the end of wickedness? The end of wickedness? Yes.
Will the World be destroyed by water? No.
By fire? No.
Will it be partly destroyed by fire? Yes.
Shall any of us see the Last Day? Yes.
In how many years? Twenty-five years.
Will the Last Judgment be then? No.
Will that be the Millennium? Yes.
Will Enoch and Elijah come again? Yes.
Will the Jews be restored? Yes.
Will Russia conquer England? Yes.
Will it be in the reign of Queen Victoria? No.
In the reign of her successor? Yes."

The testimony of Mr. Crookes, the discoverer of a new metal, and a Fellow of the Royal Society, may here be suitably recorded. Unlike some other so-called "scientific investigators," he is reported to have resolved upon a careful and thorough examination of the spiritualistic phenomena. He is said to have maintained originally that, even if the alleged facts were true, he might be able to explain them by some natural law. Accordingly he thoughtfully pursued his inquiries and investigations over a series of years, taking unusual care to render deception out of the question and impossible. The result has been given to the public in the "Quarterly Journal of Science" for January, 1874,[50] from which the following quotations are made:--

"The phenomena I am prepared to attest are so extraordinary and so directly oppose the most firmly-rooted articles of scientific belief--amongst others, the ubiquity and invariable action of the law of gravitation--that, even now, on recalling the details of what I witnessed, there is an antagonism in my mind between reason, which pronounces it to be scientifically impossible, and the consciousness that my senses, both of touch and sight--and these corroborated, as they were, by the senses of all who were present--are not lying witnesses when they testify against my preconceptions. But the supposition that there is a sort of mania or delusion which suddenly attacks a whole roomful of intelligent persons who are quite sane elsewhere, and that they all concur to the minutest particulars in the details of the occurrences of which they suppose themselves to be witnesses, seems to my mind more incredible than even the facts they attest" (pp. 77-78).

Under the heading of "The Phenomena of Percussive and other Allied Sounds," he makes reference to the raps and knocks of various kinds made and heard in different places, "in a living tree, on a sheet of glass, on a stretched iron wire, on a stretched membrane, a tambourine, on the roof of a cab, and on the floor of a theatre," and where no known law, and no contrivance or trickery, could afford any clue to their cause. He then inquires whether the sounds thus heard are the result of some blind, irrational, hidden material force obeying the Laws of Nature. His conclusion, however, was that the varied phenomena being evidently governed by intelligence, a thinking being must have been concerned in their origination. "The intelligence," he maintains, "is sometimes of such a character as to lead to the belief that it does not emanate from any person present." The movement of heavy substances at a distance from the medium is then discussed, and Mr. Crookes thus writes:--

"On three successive evenings a small table moved slowly across the room, under conditions which I had specially pre-arranged, so as to answer any objections which might be raised to the evidence" (p. 84).

Again:--"On five separate occasions a heavy dining-table rose between a few inches and one and a half feet off the floor, under special circumstances which rendered trickery impossible. On another occasion a heavy table rose from the floor in full light, while I was holding the medium's hands and feet. On another occasion the table rose from the floor, not only when no person was touching it, but under conditions that I had pre-arranged, so as to assure unquestionable proof of the fact" (p. 85).

Once more:--

"On one occasion I witnessed a chair, with a lady sitting on it, rise several inches from the ground. On another occasion, to avoid the suspicion of this being in some way performed by herself, the lady knelt on the chair in such manner that its four feet were visible to us. It then rose about three inches, remained suspended for about ten seconds, and then slowly descended. At another time two children, on separate occasions, rose from the floor with their chairs, in full daylight, under (to me) most satisfactory conditions; for I was kneeling and keeping close watch upon the feet of the chair, and observing that no one might touch them" (p. 85).

Respecting another class of phenomena, said to be common enough with Modern Spiritualists, which appeal to the sense of sight, under the head of "Luminous Appearances," Mr.

Rev. Frederick George Lee, D.C.L.

Crookes thus writes:--

"Under the strictest test conditions I have seen a solid self-luminous body, the size and nearly the shape of a turkey's egg, float noiselessly about the room, at one time higher than anyone present could reach standing on tip-toe, and then gently descend to the floor. It was visible for more than ten minutes, and before it faded away it struck the table three times, with a sound like that of a hard, solid body. During this time the medium was lying back, apparently insensible, in an easy-chair.

"I have seen luminous points of light darting about and settling on the heads of different persons; I have had questions answered by the flashing of a bright light a desired number of times in front of my face. I have seen sparks of light rising from the table to the ceiling, and again falling upon the table, striking it with an audible sound. I have had an alphabetical communication given by luminous flashes occurring before me in the air, whilst my hand was moving about amongst them. I have seen a luminous cloud floating upwards to a picture. Under the strictest test conditions, I have more than once had a solid, self-luminous crystalline body placed in my hand by a hand which did not belong to any person in the room. In the light, I have seen a luminous cloud hover over a heliotrope on a side-table, break a sprig off, and carry the sprig to a lady; and on some occasions I have seen a similar luminous cloud visibly condense to the form of a hand, and carry small objects about" (p. 87).

Two pages later on the following occurs:--

"I was sitting next to the medium, Miss Fox, the only other persons present being my wife and a lady relative, and I was holding the medium's two hands in one of mine, whilst her feet were resting on my feet. Paper was on the table before us, and my disengaged hand was holding a pencil. A luminous hand came down from the upper part of the room, and after hovering near me for a few seconds, took the pencil from my hand, rapidly wrote on a sheet of paper, threw the pencil down, and then rose up over our heads, gradually fading into darkness" (p. 89).

And then Mr. Crookes testifies that not only spirit-hands, but spectres or spirit-persons in their entirety, were seen:--

"In the dusk of the evening, during a séance with Mr. Home at my house, the curtains of a window about eight feet from Mr. Home were seen to move. A dark, shadowy, semi-transparent form like that of a man was then seen by all present standing near the window, waving the curtain with his hand. As we looked, the form faded away and the curtain ceased to move. The following is a still more striking instance. As in the former case, Mr. Home was the medium. A phantom form came from a corner of the room, took an accordion in its hand, and then glided about the room playing the instrument. The form was visible to all present for many minutes, Mr. Home also being seen at the same time. Coming rather close to a lady who was sitting apart from the rest of the company, she gave a slight cry, upon which it vanished" (p. 90).

In conclusion Mr. Crookes sets forth five current theories with regard to these and similar phenomena; one of which theories is clearly expressed in the following sentence. These supernatural manifestations, he asserts, some maintain to be "the actions of Evil Spirits or Devils, personifying who or what they please, in order to undermine Christianity and to ruin men's souls" (p. 96). Such a definition, it may be added, is in perfect accordance with ordinary experience, the testimony of Scripture, the action and teaching of the living Church, as well as a fulfilment of express and definite prophecies regarding "the latter days."

CHAPTER IX - MODERN SPIRITUALISM (CONTINUED)

"Superstition, in its grossest form, is the worship of Evil Spirits." - John Henry Newman.

"Let no man deceive you by any means: for that day shall not come, except there come a falling away first, and that Man of Sin be revealed, the Son of Perdition, who opposeth and exalteth himself above all that is called God, or that is worshipped.... Whose coming is after the working of Satan, with all power and signs and lying wonders, and with all deceivableness of unrighteousness in them that perish; because they received not the love of the Truth that they might be saved. And for this cause God shall send them a strong delusion that they should believe a lie." - 2 Thess. ii. 3-11.

"The greatest intellectual triumph that can be achieved by the Devil is gained when men are prepared to believe that he is not." - Sermons, Rev. T. T. Lee (A.D. 1796).

More recently the manifestations have been still further developed. From the "Spiritual Magazine" the following is quoted:--

"The séance was held by appointment. Our object being that of investigation, we limited the number to three, and, I must add, used every precaution we could think of to preclude the possibility of self-deception; we likewise guarded against any possible preparatory arrangement. Accordingly, we changed from the library to the dining-room. We were soon seated at a heavy square table. Twenty minutes passed without any manifestation; then came gentle raps, followed by the table being lifted, tilted, and gently vibrated. Then raps were heard simultaneously in different and opposite parts of the room. At my suggestion, the lamp was partly turned down, when a cold current of air was felt to pass over our hands and faces. A pause ensued. The dining-room table leaf standing in the corner of the room then commenced to vibrate, and one of the leaves being taken from the stand, was passed between Mr. Home and the table at which we were seated. It was then raised straight up, and passing vertically over my friend, gently touched him; in passing over me, it struck me on the crown of the head, but so gently, that I could hardly realize it to be the heavy leaf of the dining-room table; the touch nevertheless caused the leaf to vibrate all but sonorously. I name this to prove how delicately balanced and suspended in the air the leaf of the table must have been to have produced the vibration. It then passed over to the right, touching my shoulders, and finally was placed upon the table at which we were seated. The distance the leaf was carried I compute at nearly twelve yards (allowing for the circuit made), and at an elevation of six feet. A small round table was then moved from the corner of the room, and placed next to my friend; and in reply to his question 'who it was,' he received the answer, audible to us all, 'Pa, Pa,--dear--darling Pa.' An arm-chair behind my friend, and at a distance of three yards, was raised up straight into the air, carried over our heads, and placed upon the dining-room table to my left, a voice clearly and loudly repeating the words, 'Papa's chair.' We then observed the wooden box of the accordion being carried from the extreme corner of the room up to my friend. In passing my right hand, I passed my hand under and over the box, as it travelled suspended in the air to my front. I did this to make sure of the fact of its being moved by an invisible agency, and not by means of mechanical aid.... The accordion was then taken from Mr. Home, carried about in the room, and played. Voices were distinctly heard; a low whispering, and voices imitating the break of a wave on the shore. Finally, the accordion placed itself upon the table we were seated at, and two luminous hands were distinctly seen resting on the keys of the instrument. They remained luminously visible for from twenty to thirty seconds, and then melted away. I had, in the meantime, and at the request of my friend, taken hold of the accordion; whilst so held by me, an invisible hand laid hold of the instrument, and played for two or three minutes what appeared to me to be sacred music. Voices were then heard, a kind of murmuring or low whistling and breathing; at times in imitation of the murmur of the waves of the sea, at other times more plaintively melodious. The accordion was then a second time taken by an invisible power, carried over our heads, and a small piece of sacred music played,--then a hymn, voices in deep sonorous notes singing the hallelujah. I thought I could make out three voices, but my friend said he could speak to four. A jet of light then crossed the room, after which a star or brilliantly illuminated disk, followed by the appearance of a softly luminous column of light, which moved up between me and my friend. I cannot say that I could discern any distinct outline. The luminous column appeared to me to be about five to six feet high, the subdued soft light mounting from it half illumining the room. The column or luminous appearance then passed to my right, and a chair was moved and placed next to me. I distinctly heard the rustling as of a silk dress. Instinctively I put my hand forward to ascertain the presence of the guest, when a soft hand seized my hand and wrist. I then felt that the skirt of a dress had covered my knees. I grasped it; it felt like thick silk, and melted away as I firmly clenched my hand on it. By this time I admit I shuddered. A heavy footstep then passed to my right, the floor vibrating to the footfall; the spirit-form now walked up to the fire-place, clapping its hands as it passed me. I then felt something press against the back of my chair; the weight was so great, that as the form leaned on my shoulder, I had to bend forward under the pressure. Two hands gently pressed my forehead; I noticed a luminous appearance at my right; I was kissed, and what to me at the time made my very frame thrill again, spoken to in a sweet, low, melodious voice. The words uttered by the spirit were distinctly heard by all present. As the spirit-form passed away, it repeated the words, 'I kissed you, I kissed you,' and I felt three taps on each shoulder, audible to all present, as if in parting to reimpress me with the reality of its presence. I shuddered again, and, in spite of all my heroism, felt very 'uncanny.' My friend now called our attention to his being patted by a soft hand on his head. I heard a kiss, and then the words, 'Papa, dear papa.' He said his left hand was being kissed, and that a soft, child-like hand was caressing him. A cloud of light appeared to be standing at his left."

Another example, from the same publication, deserves to be put on record:--

"The first group of the manifestations (I use the term 'group' to mark the characteristic difference of the phenomena on each occasion,) occurred at a friend's house at Great Malvern. Those present had only incidentally met; and, owing to a prohibition being laid upon Mr. Home by his medical man against trying his strength, no séance was attempted. I name this as characteristic. Raps in different parts of the room, and the movement of furniture, however, soon told the presence of the invisibles. The library in which the party had met communicated with the hall; and the door having been left half open, a broad stream of light from the burners of the gas-lamp lit up the room. At the suggestion of one of the party, the candles were removed. The rapping, which had till then been heard in different parts of the room, suddenly made a pause, and then the unusual phenomena of the appearance of spirit-forms manifested itself. The opening of the half-closed door was suddenly darkened by an invisible agency, the room becoming pitch dark. Then the wall opposite became illumined, the library now being lit up by a luminous element, for it cannot be described otherwise. Between those present and the opposite and now illumined wall two spirit-forms were seen, their shadowy outline on the wall well defined. The forms moved to and fro. They made an effort to speak; the articulation, however, was too imperfect to permit of the meaning of the words to be understood. The darkening which had obscured the half-closed door was then removed, and the broad light from the hall lamp reappeared, looking quite dim in comparison with the luminous brilliancy of the light that had passed away. Again the room became darkened, then illumined, and a colossal head and shoulders appeared to rise from the floor, visible only by the shadow it cast upon the illumined wall. What added to the interest was the apparent darkening and lighting up of the room at will, and that repeatedly, the library door remaining half open all the while. The time occupied by these phenomena was perhaps five to ten minutes, the manifestations terminating quite abruptly."

A correspondent of the same serial gives the following facts:--

"On the 1st October, 1865, I attended a séance at 13, Victoria Place, Clifton, where the younger Mrs. Marshall, the well-known medium from London, was staying.

"I had previously prepared, as a test, a series of written questions inserted in a book and numbered consecutively; my wife, who was present, was by the usual method put in communication with the spirit of her mother, and the following are a few of the results. It is important to observe that no clue was given to the medium, or to the others present, as to the nature of the answer required, the questions being put in the following form:--'Will you answer the question No. 33?' &c., and as the answers were occasionally given in a different form from what was anticipated, though still quite correctly, these two facts taken together conclusively prove, as it appears to me, that the answers were neither the result of any knowledge on the part of the medium, nor any 'reflex action' from the mind of the interrogator.

"The spirit having been requested to answer the question numbered 33, viz.:--'Will you spell the name of the place where we lived when you left this state?' The reply, spelt through the alphabet, was 'Aust.'

"Question No. 34 having been put in the same manner, viz.:--'Where was your body buried?' The reply was, 'Saint George's.'

"No. 35.--'While your body was lying in the coffin, was anything put in the hand?'[51] Reply,

'Yes.'

"No. 36.--'What was it?' Reply, 'A sprig of myrtle.'

"No. 37.--'By whom was it put there?' Reply, 'Thomas Bowman.'

"No. 38.--'Who else were present at the time?' Reply, 'Ann, Tommy and Mary Bowman Bryant.'

"Many other replies were given of an equally satisfactory character, but I must not further trespass on your space. I would merely remark that the answers in each case were quite correct, and that the events referred to occurred upwards of forty years since."

Again, Mr. James Howell, of 7, Guildford Road, Brighton, writes as follows in the "Spiritual Magazine" for November, 1867:--

"When I was at the Marshalls' last summer, a circumstance, unknown to anyone present save myself, was made known to me by unaccountable means. The name of a young lady who suffered and died from spinal complaint in the year 1843 was correctly spelled out, and the date of her death given. I was most intimately acquainted with her. She was good, pious, and highly intellectual. To her I owe my knowledge of the French language, and my love of its literature. I was not thinking of her at the time; in fact, she was furthest from my thoughts; yet her name--a very uncommon one, you will admit--was given correctly, 'Aletta V----.' Now I am honest enough to confess that a million guesses would not have guessed that name. I was astounded and affected; for it brought back to my mind a rush of thoughts, happy and sad, of those evenings when I sat by her bedside listening to her sweet voice, and imbibing the original thoughts which sprang, not only from a well-stored mind, but one instinct with genius. Twenty-three years had elapsed from the time of her death; she had often promised to communicate with me from the spirit-world, if it was possible, and now that promise was fulfilled, even in the presence of others."

And once more, the same writer gives the following record of facts:--

"I paid a visit on Monday, July 2nd, to Mrs. Parks, of Cornwall Terrace, Regent's Park, then staying at 7, Bedford Square. Miss Purcell, the medium, went with me; and we three had some strong and wonderful manifestations. The table was turned about merrily, and once whirled round in mid-air. It became as animated as a living being; it even ran about when not a single being touched it. Knockings were heard all over the room; in chairs, in tables, under the floor, and along the wainscot. We had great trouble to keep the tables from being smashed.

"During the evening, the 'Blue Bells of Scotland' and 'Marlbrook s'en va-t-en guerre' were knocked out on the table in a beautiful and correct manner, the table beating and dancing admirable time to each tune. At a previous séance a well-known tune was knocked out, and my wife was requested to dance, the spirits stating that the table should accompany her; but as we could not induce her to do so, we lost the promised pas de deux between a human being and a table. At my request the table also gave a series of knocks, viz. the footman's, the postman's, the tax-gatherer's, and the countryman's, which were perfect, and caused us much amusement. In one part of the room there appeared a silvery, bluish star, shining brilliantly. Mrs. Parks, strange to say, could not see it, but to the medium and myself it was clearly visible, at the same time too; and a brilliant member of the stellar creation it was, coming and going like those of the sky, when for a moment a veil of clouds passes over them."

The conviction that such acts and deeds are the work of evil spirits is put on record in the same serial, a formal organ of the Spiritualists, in the following narrative:--

"Mr. and Mrs. C---- attend a séance at which the spirit of 'a darling child' is manifestly present. They attend a second séance, and through the same medium they are confirmed in the conviction of the real presence of their child. Mr. C---- then finds that he is himself a medium, and forthwith he purchases a small table for the exercise of his power.

"His first experiment proves to him beyond a doubt that an intelligent being, though invisible, is with him; but he speedily begins to suspect that whatever the character may have been of the spirit which first manifested to him through another medium, this, which is now communicating through himself, is an evil spirit. On his 'wishing it to walk to the dining-room, it started at once.' He was struck by its heavy tread, 'so very unlike the footfalls of a young child,' and he exclaimed, 'This is not the spirit of my child, if so, I want no other manifestation.' Becoming more and more suspicious of the character of this particular visitant, he said, 'If thou art not the spirit of my child, march out of the house.' 'The table did, indeed, march, making a noise like the loud and well-measured footfalls of a heavy dragoon--literally shaking everything in the room.'

"This gentleman then adjured the spirit in a variety of forms, and asked if it was not a bad spirit? and it said, 'Yes!' Then he said, 'Accursed devil! by the living God I adjure thee to speak the truth! Has the spirit of my child ever been put in communication with myself or her mother through this or any other table?' The 'accursed devil' said, 'No, never!' Then, after similar assurances, Mr. C---- made up his mind to believe the devil; and he closed his experiments with an auto-da-fé, by breaking up and burning the table!"

Rev. Frederick George Lee, D.C.L.

Mr. Chevalier, who was the first witness called before the committee appointed by the Dialectical Society, gives the following personal version of this experiment, 20th July, 1869. He stated that he had had seventeen years' experience of Spiritualism, but it was not till 1866 that he commenced experimenting on tables. He obtained the usual phenomena, such as raps and tiltings and answers to questions. On one occasion, the answer which was given being obviously untrue, the witness peremptorily inquired why a correct answer had not been given, and the spirit in reply said, "Because I am Beelzebub." Mr. Chevalier, in continuation, said, "I continued my experiments until I heard of the 'Spiritual Athenæum.' About that time I lost a child, and heard my wife say she had been in communication with its spirit. I cautioned her, and yet was anxious to communicate also. I placed one finger on the table; it moved, and the name of the child was given. It was a French name. I told a friend of mine what had happened, but was laughed at by him; he however came, sceptic as he was. I placed one hand on the table asking mental questions, which were all answered. He then asked where my child went to school, not knowing himself, and the answer 'Fenton' was given; this also was correct. Frequently after this, I obtained manifestations in French and English, and messages as a child could send to a parent. At my meals I constantly rested my hand on a small table, and it seemed to join in the conversation. One day the table turned at right angles, and went into the corner of the room. I asked, 'Are you my child?' but obtained no answer. I then said, 'Are you from God?' but the table was still silent. I then said, 'In the Name of the Father, Son, and Holy Spirit, I command you to answer--are you from God?' One loud rap, a negative, was then given. 'Do you believe,' said I, 'that Christ died to save us from sin?' The answer was 'No!' 'Accursed spirit,' said I, 'leave the room.' The table then walked across the room, entered the adjoining one and quickened its steps. It was a small tripod table. It walked with a sidelong walk. It went to the door, shook the handle, and I opened it. The table then walked into the passage, and I repeated the adjuration, receiving the same answer. Fully convinced that I was dealing with an accursed spirit, I opened the street door, and the table was immediately silent; no movement or rap was heard. I returned alone to the drawing-room, and asked if there were any spirits present. Immediately I heard steps like those of a little child outside the door. I opened it, and the small table went into the corner as before, just as my child did when I reproved it for a fault. These manifestations continued until I used the adjuration, and I always found that they changed or ceased when the Name of God was mentioned. One night, when sitting alone in my drawing-room, I heard a noise at the top of the house; a servant who had heard it came into the room frightened. I went to the nursery and found that the sounds came from a spot near the bed. I pronounced the adjuration and they instantly ceased. The same sounds were afterwards heard in the kitchen, and I succeeded in restoring quiet as before.

"Reflecting on these singular facts, I determined to inquire further and really satisfy myself that the manifestations were what I suspected them to be. I went to Mrs. Marshall, and took with me three clever men, who were not at all likely to be deceived. I was quite unknown; we sat at a table, and had a séance: Mrs. Marshall told me the name of my child. I asked the spirit some questions, and then pronounced the adjuration. We all heard steps, which sounded as if someone was mounting the wall; in a few seconds the sounds ceased, and although Mrs. Marshall challenged again and again, the spirits did not answer, and she said she could not account for the phenomenon. In this case, I pronounced the adjuration mentally; no person knew what I had done. At a séance, held at the house of a friend of mine, at which I was present, manifestations were obtained, and, as I was known to be hostile, I was entreated not to interfere. I sat for two hours a passive spectator. I then asked the name of the spirit, and it gave the name of my child. 'In the Name of the Father, Son, and Holy Ghost,' said I, 'are you the spirit of my child?' It answered, 'No!' and the word 'Devil' was spelled out."

Dr. Edmunds: "How were the names spelled out?"

Mr. Chevalier: "The legs rapped when the alphabet was called over. Mrs. Marshall used the alphabet herself, and the table rapped when her pencil came to the letters. My opinion of the phenomena is that the intelligence which is put in communication with us is a fallen one. It is the Devil, the Prince of the Powers of the air. I believe we commit the crime of Necromancy when we take part in these spiritual séances."

We obtain from these extracts, which might be multiplied thirty-fold from the authorized publications of the Spiritualists, some idea of the nature of their séances and proceedings. Our own statement at the outset has been more than justified as regards its moderation and accuracy from the examples provided in the extracts in question. "Necromancy" has been well defined to be "The art of communicating with devils and of doing surprising things by means of their aid; particularly that of calling up the dead and extorting answers from them." Now this, it seems clear, in one form or another, is precisely that which is carried on by a considerable and increasing section[52] of people in America, in England, on the Continent, and elsewhere. It is practised mainly by persons who were such extreme Protestants in previous times that, having almost altogether denied the Supernatural, they have been reluctantly won over to a belief in it by communion with evil spirits. Father Perrone, the distinguished Jesuit, has calculated that upwards of two thousand treatises have been published in defence of the system of these manifestations during the past fifteen years. It has been pointedly remarked by an English clergyman, of those people who once, like the ancient Sadducees, rejected the idea of the existence of spirits, but who now have accepted the Spiritualistic theory, that "they have given up believing in nothing, and have taken to believe in the Devil."[53] And this epigrammatic saying is hardly too pointed. According to Perrone, the modern professors of divination frankly allow that the phenomena have passed through three phases. First, that of Mesmerism; secondly, artificial Somnambulism and Clairvoyance; and thirdly, Spiritualism, properly so called. He gives five reasons for maintaining his theory of diabolical agency with regard to the same. 1. From the nature of the phenomena. 2. From its effects. 3. From the manner in which Mesmerism operates. 4. From the malice and wickedness of the agent, who frequently utters anti-Christian and blasphemous doctrines; and lastly, 5. from the frank and candid admission of the mediums or operators themselves.

In most cases it may be safely assumed that evil spirits personify the souls of the departed. That such spirits are the deadly foes of man so long as he is in his period of probation, may, for all Catholic Christians, be also assumed. That such spirits, moreover, constantly represent the departed as continually desiring the hand of Death to fall upon their earthly friends, in order, as is implied or stated, that a future of unclouded light and everlasting happiness may speedily link them together, can be seen from a careful study of the records of Spiritualism. Some of the facts already set forth teach this. The principle that men, whether good or bad, righteous or unrighteous, will all be certainly saved, and be for ever hereafter in bliss, is the practical heresy[54] that Spiritualism in its theological aspect has most openly taught, and still continues to teach. "Spiritualism," writes Mr. William Howitt, a convert to it from Quakerism, "rejects the doctrine of eternal damnation as alike injurious to God and man. Injurious to God's noblest attributes, repugnant to the principles of justice, and unavailing in men as a motive to repentance.... Spiritualism knows that there are isolated passages in the Gospels and in the words of our Saviour capable of being made to bear an appearance favouring the doctrine of eternal punishment, but it knows that the original terms bear no such latitude, and when Christ says there is a state 'where the worm dieth not, and the fire is not quenched,' it admits the state, but denies that any of God's creatures will continue in that state a minute longer than is necessary to purge the foulness of sin and the love of sin out of their spiritual constitutions. Were the solution of this supposed difficulty much harder than it is, Spiritualism would place the love of God and the love of Christ, and all the great and gracious attributes of God and His Saviour--justice and truth and wisdom, and a charity more immeasurable than God Himself recommends to mankind, confidently and courageously against so horrible and senseless a doctrine."

Now, though Spiritualism be ignored by the press, Universalism, its own offspring, is constantly and persistently maintained. Spiritualism also flatly denies the great Christian doctrine of the Resurrection of the body:--

"Spiritualism teaches, on the authority of Scripture and of all spirit-life, that there is no such thing as death: it is but a name given to the issue of the soul from the body. To those in bodies who witness this change, the spirit is invisible, and they only see a body which ceases all its living functions, has lost that intelligence which during so-called 'life' emanated from it, and lies stiff and cold, and to all appearance dead. But even the body is not dead. There is a law of life even in what is called dead matter, which is perpetually changing its particles and converting them into mere black earth and water, and hence into all the articles necessary for the physical life--corn, meat, wine, all foods, all fruits. The same law immediately begins to operate in the dead body, and, if unobstructed, speedily resolves it back into earth, and then forms this again into food and clothing and fresh enveloping forms for fresh human beings. The whole of the universe is in perpetual action, and the ever-revolving wheel of physical is subserving the perpetual evolution of spiritual life."[55]

And again:--

"The Church of England and Spiritualism accord, but not in the doctrine of the resurrection of the body. The spirits all assert with S. Paul, that the body which rises from the death-bed is the spiritual body, and that the soul needs no other, much less an earthly body, in its spirit-home--that, in fact, nothing of the earth can ever enter heaven. That if the spirits of just men are made perfect, they can be nothing more, and no addition of anything belonging to this earth can add to their happiness, freedom, power, and perfection, but on the contrary. That so far from receiving at some indefinite and, probably, very distant period, their earthly bodies back again, they are continually, as they advance, casting off the subtler particles of matter that have interpenetrated their spiritual bodies."[56]

With regard to the influence of the Protestant Reformation on that temper of mind and habit of thought which have led sceptics and those whose faith has been overturned by the blasphemies of Calvin or the immoral principle of the Lutheran systems and their offshoots, to become votaries of Spiritualism, we cannot do better than put on record Mr. Howitt's deliberate judgment, expressed in language which, however painful to read in some parts, is at once forcible and pertinent:--

"By the denial of the intermediate states, the Protestant Reformers perpetrated a more monstrous outrage on the Divine justice, and more frightfully libelled the Divine mercy, than by the broadest stretch of imagination one would have thought it possible. By this arbitrary extinction of some of the loveliest regions of creation, by this wiping out of vast kingdoms of God's tolerance and goodness by the sponge of Protestant reaction, God's whole being was blackened, and every one of His eternal attributes dislocated and driven pell-mell into the limbo of Atheism. I say Atheism, for such a God could not possibly exist as this Protestant theory would have made Him--a God with less justice than the most stupid country squire ever established in the chair of magistracy; with less mercy than an inquisitor or a torturer with his red-hot pincers and iron boots. These atrocities were but the work of moments, but this system made the God of love and the Father of Jesus Christ sitting in endless bliss amid a favoured few, whilst below were incalculable populations suffering the tortures of fires which no period even of millions of years should extinguish, and that without any proportion whatever to the offences of the sufferers! All who were not 'spirits of just men made perfect' were, according to this doctrine, only admissible to this common hell, this common receptacle of the middling, bad, and the most bedevilled of devils! Never could any such monstrous, foul, and detestable doctrine issue from any source but that of the hearts of fiends themselves. None but devils could breed up so black a fog of blasphemy to blot out the image of a loving and paternal God from the view of His creatures. And yet the mocking devil induced the zealous Protestant fathers to accept this most truly 'doctrine of devils,' as an antidote to Popish error. As some glimmering of the direst consequences of this shutting-up of the middle states of the invisible world began to dawn on the Protestant mind, it set about to invent remedies and apply palliatives, and by a sort of spiritual hocus-pocus, it taught that if the greatest sinners did but call on Christ at the last gasp, they were converted into saints, and found themselves in heaven itself with God and the Lamb. This was only making the matter worse, and holding out a premium for the continuance in every sin and selfishness to the last moment. It was an awful temptation to self-deception presented to human selfishness. Millions, no doubt, have trusted to this wretched Protestant reed.... Yet common sense in others rejected and rejects the cruel deceit. A country poet, writing the epitaph of the blacksmith in my native village, expressed the truth on the Protestant theory of no middle regions:--

'Too bad for heaven, too good for hell,
So where he's gone we cannot tell.'"

And now to conclude this portion of our subject, regarding which not a tenth part of the examples of "Spiritual" manifestations gathered has been given. To have discussed the facts and theories provided on previous pages, would have occupied several chapters. Sufficient, however, is recorded to show that Spiritualism is directly antagonistic to the Christian Religion,[57] to point out the true character of many of the signs and wonders which exist in this nineteenth century, and which testify and witness to old and unchangeable truths. The ministry of "men and of angels in a wonderful order,"[58] the practice of exorcism, the facts of diabolical agency, possession by evil spirits, the sins of Witchcraft and Necromancy, are all more or less intertwined with the Divine Revelation which God has been pleased to give to man. But the Materialism of these latter days is blinding men's eyes, that they cannot see, and successfully destroying their faith in all that is beyond their cramped and narrow temporal range. Intellectual Paganism, and a positive disbelief in the distinct Nature of God, if not openly professed, is indirectly acknowledged; while the Faith of Pentecost, which for generations has regenerated the World, is cast aside as worn out, effete, and valueless. The possibility of miracle is derided; Providence is scouted as the fond dream of an exaggerated human self-love; belief in the power of prayer is asserted to be only a superstition, illustrative of man's ignorance of the scientific conception of law; the hypothesis of absolute invariable law, and the cognate conception of Nature as a self-evolved system of self-existent forces and self-existent matter, are ideas advancing with giant strides. Side by side with all this, however, stand the portentous phenomena referred to here. Let the existence of one course of such facts as those related be granted, and far more follows than the pure Materialist or the Positivist would for a moment allow. Yet none can deny the presence amongst us of such, evil in their essence and mischievous in their operations. The whole cycle represents the works of the Devil and his angels--works opposed at every step in theory by the Truths of Christianity, and in fact by the sacraments of the Church Universal. Man's highest and chiefest duty is to do the Will of the Most High: the practice of the Spiritualists, on the other hand (and let men lay the warning to heart), appears to be an intentional and systematic giving up of their wills to the evil one; an invocation of evil spirits for unlawful purposes, a "willing" for supernatural intervention in things which are not lawful, and a deliberate turning away from Him to Whom all power is given in Heaven and in Earth.

Rev. Frederick George Lee, D.C.L.

APPENDIX TO CHAPTER IX - SPIRITUALISM AND SCIENCE

The following Letter appeared in "The Times" newspaper a few years ago:--

"SIR,--Having been named by several of your correspondents as one of the scientific men who believe in Spiritualism, you will perhaps allow me to state briefly what amount of evidence has forced the belief upon me. I began the investigation about eight years ago, and I esteem it a fortunate thing that at that time the more marvellous phenomena were far less common and less accessible than they are now, because I was led to experiment largely at my own house, and among friends whom I could trust, and was able to establish to my own satisfaction, by means of a great variety of tests, the occurrence of sounds and movements not traceable to any known or conceivable physical cause. Having thus become thoroughly familiar with these undoubtedly genuine phenomena, I was able to compare them with the more powerful manifestations of several public mediums, and to recognize an identity of cause in both by means of a number of minute but highly characteristic resemblances. I was also able, by patient observation, to obtain tests of the reality of some of the more curious phenomena which appeared at the time, and still appear to me, to be conclusive. To go into details as to those experiences would require a volume, but I may, perhaps, be permitted briefly to describe one, from notes kept at the time, because it serves as an example of the complete security against deception which often occurs to the patient observer without seeking for it.

"A lady who had seen nothing of the phenomena asked me and my sister to accompany her to a well-known public medium. We went, and had a sitting alone in the bright light of a summer's day. After a number of the usual raps and movements, our lady friend asked if the name of the deceased person she was desirous of communicating with, could be spelt out. On receiving an answer in the affirmative, the lady pointed successively to the letters of a printed alphabet while I wrote down those at which three affirmative raps occurred. Neither I nor my sister knew the name the lady wished for, nor even the names of any of her deceased relatives; her own name had not been mentioned, and she had never been near the medium before. The following is exactly what happened, except that I alter the surname, which was a very unusual one, having no authority to publish it. The letters I wrote down were of the following kind:--yrnehnospmoht. After the first three--yrn--had been taken down, my friend said, "This is nonsense, we had better begin again." Just then her pencil was at e, and raps came, when a thought struck me (having read of, but never witnessed, a similar occurrence), and I said, 'Please go on, I think I see what is meant.' When the spelling was finished I handed the paper to her, but she could see no meaning in it till I divided it at the first h, and asked her to read each portion backwards, when to her intense astonishment the name 'Henry Thompson' came out, that of a deceased son of whom she had wished to hear, correct in every letter. Just about that time I had been hearing ad nauseam of the superhuman acuteness of mediums who detect the letters of the name the deluded visitors expect, notwithstanding all their care to pass the pencil over the letters with perfect regularity. This experience, however (for the substantial accuracy of which as above narrated I vouch), was and is, to my mind, a complete disproof of every explanation yet given of the means by which the names of deceased persons are rapped out. Of course I do not expect any sceptic, whether scientific or unscientific, to accept such facts, of which I could give many, on my testimony; but neither must they expect me, nor the thousands of intelligent men to whom equally conclusive tests have occurred, to accept their short and easy methods of explaining them.

"If I am not occupying too much of your valuable space I should like to make a few remarks on the misconceptions of many scientific men as to the nature of this inquiry, taking the Letters of your correspondent Mr. Dirks as an example. In the first place, he seems to think that it is an argument against the facts being genuine that they cannot all be produced and exhibited at will; and another argument against them, that they cannot be explained by any known laws. But neither can catalepsy, the fall of meteoric stones, nor hydrophobia be produced at will; yet these are all facts, and none the less so that the first is sometimes imitated, the second was once denied, and the symptoms of the third are often greatly exaggerated, while none of them is yet brought under the domain of strict science; yet no one would make this an argument for refusing to investigate these subjects. Again, I should not have expected a scientific man to state, as a reason for not examining it, that Spiritualism 'is opposed to every known natural law, especially the law of gravity,' and that it 'sets chymistry, human physiology, and mechanics at open defiance;' when the facts simply are that the phenomena, if true, depend upon a cause or causes which can overcome or counteract the action of these several forces, just as some of these forces often counteract or overcome others; and this should surely be a strong inducement to a man of science to investigate the subject.

"While not laying any claim myself to the title of 'a really scientific man,' there are some who deserve that epithet who have not yet been mentioned by your correspondents as at the same time spiritualists. Such I consider the late Dr. Robert Chambers, as well as Dr. Elliotson, Professor William Gregory, of Edinburgh; and Professor Hare, of Philadelphia--all unfortunately deceased; while Dr. Gully, of Malvern, as a scientific physician, and Judge Edmonds, one of the best American lawyers, have had the most ample means of investigation; yet all these not only were convinced of the reality of the most marvellous facts, but also accepted the theory of Modern Spiritualism as the only one which would embrace and account for the facts. I am also acquainted with a living physiologist, of high rank as an original investigator, who is an equally firm believer.

"In conclusion I may say that, although I have heard a great many accusations of imposture, I have never detected it myself; and, although a large proportion of the more extraordinary phenomena are such that, if impostures, they could only be performed by means of ingenious apparatus or machinery, none has ever been discovered. I consider it no exaggeration to say that the main facts are now as well established and as easily verifiable as any of the more exceptional phenomena of nature which are not yet reduced to law. They have a most important bearing on the interpretation of History, which is full of narratives of similar facts, and on the nature of life and intellect, on which physical science throws a very feeble and uncertain light; and it is my firm and deliberate belief that every branch of philosophy must suffer till they are honestly and seriously investigated, and dealt with as constituting an essential portion of the phenomena of human nature.

"I am, Sir, yours obediently,
"ALFRED R. WALLACE."

The following Review, taken from the "Weekly Register" of August 1, 1874, will be read with interest:--

"The May and June numbers of the 'Fortnightly Review' for 1874, contain two remarkable articles by Mr. Wallace, the eminent naturalist. They are entitled--'A Defence of Modern Spiritualism.' His aim in these is to prove the objective reality of its phenomena in the first instance, and then to show that the theory which explains them can be accepted by those who, like himself, entirely disbelieve in a Supernatural order. He points out that Modern Spiritualism is not in any way a survival or revival of old superstitions, but a completely new science. The facts upon which it rests have been known and noted from the earliest beginnings of history, but, owing to the influence of Superstition, were almost universally misinterpreted. Now, at last, these mists are clearing away. We have abundant materials upon which to work, and he looks forward with confidence to the establishment of a satisfactory scientific theory of a future life. Such a theory will be a truly regenerating influence, resting, not on arbitrary beliefs, but on established facts, and will, for the first time, make a true religion possible and a pure morality.

"At the close of the second essay, there is a sketch of the outline of the theory up to the point which it has reached as yet. Of course there is still much which requires to be explained and developed. The science is only in its infancy; but still its principles can be understood and appreciated. It is taken for granted that there are no spirits but human ones, these being the only spirits of which we can have any scientific knowledge. This being assumed, Mr. Wallace proceeds to give a short analysis of human nature, drawn from generalizations from the 'phenomena in their entirety,' and the communications of the spirits themselves. This is contained in four propositions:--

"1. Man is a duality, consisting of an organized spiritual form evolved coincidently with and permeating the physical body, and having corresponding organs and development.

"2. Death is the separation of this duality, and effects no change in the spirit, morally or intellectually.

"3. Progressive evolution of the intellectual and moral nature is the destiny of individuals; the knowledge, attainments, and experience of earth-life forming the basis of spirit-life.

"4. Spirits can communicate through properly-endowed mediums. They are attracted to those they love or sympathise with.... But, as follows from Clause 2, their communications will be fallible, and must be judged and tested just as we do those of our fellow-men.

"From the acceptance of these propositions will result a far purer morality than any which either Religious systems or Philosophy have yet put forth, and with sanctions far more powerful and effective--'For the essential teaching of Spiritualism is that we are all, in every act and thought, helping to build up a "mental fabric" which will be and constitute ourselves more completely after the death of the body than it does now. Just as this fabric is well or ill built will our progress and happiness be aided or retarded. There will be no imposed rewards and punishments; but everyone will suffer the inevitable consequences of a well or ill spent life. The well-spent life is that in which those faculties which concern our personal physical well-being are subordinated to those which regard our social and intellectual well-being and the well-being of others; and that inherent feeling, which is so universal and so difficult to account for, that those latter constitute our higher nature, seems also to point to the conclusion that we are intended for a condition in which the former will be almost wholly unnecessary, and will gradually become rudimentary through disuse, while the latter will receive a corresponding development. This teaching will make a man dread to give way to passion, or falsehood, or a selfish and luxurious life--knowing that the inevitable consequences of such habits are future misery and a long and arduous struggle, in order to develop anew the faculties which had been crippled by long disuse. He will be deterred from crime, knowing that its unforeseen consequences may cause him ages of remorse, and his bad passions perpetual torment, in a state of being in which mental emotions cannot be drowned in the fierce struggles and sensual pleasures of a physical existence. And these beliefs (unlike those of theology) will have a living efficacy, because depending on facts occurring again and again within the family circle, and so bringing home the realities of the future life to the minds of even the most obtuse.' He asks us to 'contrast this system of natural and inevitable reward and retribution, dependent wholly on the proportionate development of our higher mental and moral nature, with the arbitrary system of rewards and punishments dependent on stated acts and beliefs only, as set forth by all dogmatic religions; and who can fail to see that the former is in harmony with the whole order of Nature--the latter opposed to it?' We cannot enter on the religious and moral questions which this brief survey of Mr. Wallace's theory suggests, but we wish to make some remarks on the 'facts' on which it is founded, and his treatment of them. The point that strikes one most in these articles is their evident sincerity. Mr. Wallace has become a believer in Spiritualism in spite of deeply-rooted prejudices against it, and he is anxious to deal thoroughly and impartially with all the facts connected with it as far as he can, without contradicting the first principles of his scientific creed. We can understand this limitation, for we, too, have first principles--first principles of which we are so certain that no seeming contradiction of them by facts could shake our belief. But the difference between our position and his is that our first principles are founded, not on facts of experience, but on a belief that God has spoken to us, and is speaking every day in the Church. Therefore, whatever God has revealed becomes to us as a first principle, which, à priori, cannot contradict facts, and which, as our knowledge increases, we more and more find experimentally to harmonize with them and explain them. But the whole of Mr. Wallace's theory is founded on the assumption that God does not speak--that He, and all that concerns Him, is unknown and unknowable to us; and this assumption rests, he would tell us, on facts--i. e. on his view of the order of Nature. Now, what we wish to point out is, that nothing which thus rests only on experience can, in any true sense, be called a first principle. It is merely a wide generalization, which may, any moment, be displaced by a still wider one. Mr. Lecky, in his 'History of Rationalism,' asserts that the evidence in favour of the reality of witchcraft would be irresistible, were we not convinced, on à priori grounds, that witchcraft is a delusion. Once Mr. Wallace fully shared this conviction, and found himself compelled, in his own words, to 'reject or ignore' all this evidence. Now, Modern Spiritualism has enabled him to accept all these, and other facts of a similar nature; and he expatiates on the relief he feels in being able to open his eyes to a whole host of things which he had hitherto been obliged painfully and laboriously to overlook. There is quite a string of them. Socrates' Demon, the ancient Oracles, all Miracles--those of the Bible, the lives of the Saints, and in the present day, answers to prayer, all the phenomena of Second Sight, Ghosts, and occult disturbances of all sorts. We cannot refer our readers to the articles themselves for the explanations, some of them very curious, of all these things. But we should like to ask whether it may not be possible that there may be some theory yet to be found still more comprehensive than Spiritualism, and which may yield a still deeper joy and relief? The one before us seems to us still to require a considerable amount of reserve, to say no more, in dealing with some of the facts. Professor Huxley objects to the amount of twaddle that is talked by the spirits; but to this Mr. Wallace replies, very justly, we think, that it is no more than we must expect, considering the mental and moral calibre of the majority of mankind; and, consequently, of spirits, who are not much improved by the mere fact of dying, not to mention that of the spiritualists themselves; and we know that the proverb, 'Like attracts like,' is especially applicable to mediums. But we confess that we are surprised when we are told that 'sectarian' spirits continue to maintain special dogmas and doctrines, while yet quite unable to describe themselves as being in any situation which at all corresponds to the orthodox teaching about a future life. We cannot understand what doctrines or dogmas could survive such a désillusionnement, whether agreeable or the reverse, as Mr. Wallace's future life would be to a spirit whose conceptions on the subject had been moulded on any form of Christianity. Nor can we conceive of any motive, except a diabolical maliciousness, which could prompt spirits to wish to keep up such delusions among their surviving friends. And yet Mr. Wallace explains the apparitions of Our Lady, &c., in modern times, as being produced by spirits with strong Catholic predilections, knowing that they would be very efficacious in stimulating the cultus which they prefer. And this is said without any moral comment whatever. Also allowing, as he does, the reality of the apparitions, though only of human origin, in the Bible and lives of the saints, we are at a loss to see how he can say that orthodox notions of heaven are never confirmed by spirits. We should have said that it was precisely by them that most of these had been originated, not to say confirmed. If his spirits are spirits, so are ours, and quite as worthy of credit. These are only a few of the difficulties on the surface of Sceptical Spiritualism. But we have already exceeded our limits. We will only add that we cannot but hope that, Spiritualism being so far an approach to truth that it admits an important class of facts which had lately been very much denied and ignored, may, by the difficulties which they raise, lead some minds to reconsider the position they have taken up with regard to the Supernatural. There is no bridge across the chasm which divides Faith from Unbelief, and yet in this World the edges are so close that it is but a step, and we pass from darkness into light."

Rev. Frederick George Lee, D.C.L.

CHAPTER X - SUMMARY AND CONCLUSION

"The Angel of the Lord tarrieth round about them that fear Him, and delivereth them." - Psalm xxxiv. 7.

"God sees at one view the whole thread of my existence, not only that part of it which I have already passed through, but that which runs forward into all the depths of Eternity. When I lay me down to sleep I recommend myself to His care; when I awake I give myself up to His direction. Amidst all the evils that threaten me, I look up to Him for help, and question not that He will either avert them, or turn them to my advantage. Though I know neither the time nor the manner of the death I am to die, I am not at all solicitous about it: because I am sure that He knows them both, and that He will not fail to comfort and support me under them." - Addison.

"Reverence the angels; shun the demons." - Thomas Scott.

Before a brief summary is made of the contents and purport of this book, an account of a most remarkable event which occurred at Oxford about forty-five years ago may be fitly chronicled. It will be known, in its general outline, by many Oxford men; and was given to the Editor in the month of June, 1854, by a member of Brasenose College, where it had occurred.

In the year 1829, a club, known as the "Hell-Fire Club," consisting of members of the university in statu pupillari,--formed in some respects on the model of that existing in the last century, which met at Medmenham Abbey,--was accustomed to meet twice a week at Brasenose College, in Oxford. Unbelief at that time is said to have taken coarser forms there than is the case now. Then it was less dangerous, because more gross and revolting. The members of the Club, however, were not unsuccessful in their imitation of the blasphemy, drunkenness and other sins which had so notoriously characterized the older society. They met twice a week, and each is reported to have endeavoured to outdo his fellow-member in rampant blasphemy and sceptical daring. The meetings were kept so private, and such judicious care was taken to preserve unity of thought and secrecy amongst the various members, that the College authorities, though partially aware of its existence, were said to be unable to interfere.

On the north side of the College runs a narrow lane, connecting the square in which Brasenose College faces that of All Souls, with Turl Street. Going towards the latter, on the left-hand side stands Brasenose, until it is joined by the north portion of Lincoln College. On the other side is the high garden wall of Exeter College. It is a dreary and dismal-looking thoroughfare at best; and especially so at night. The windows of Brasenose College are of a narrow Jacobean type, protected both by horizontal as well as perpendicular stanchions. The lower windows, being almost level with the street, were further secured by a coarse wire netting.

Towards midnight on a day in December in the year above-named, one of the Fellows of Brasenose College was returning home, when as he approached he saw a tall man apparently draped in a long cloak, and, as he imagined, helping to assist some one to get out of the window. The window belonged to the rooms of one who was reported to be a leading member of the Hell-Fire Club. Being one of the authorities of the College, he instinctively rushed forward to detect what he imagined to be the perpetration of a distinct breach of the rules, when (as he himself afterwards declared) a thrill of horror seized him in a moment, and he felt all at once convinced that it was no human being at whom, appalled and fear-stricken, he looked. As he rushed past he saw the owner of the rooms, as he conceived, being forcibly and strugglingly dragged between the iron stanchions. The form, the features,[59] horribly distorted and stamped with a look of indescribable agony, were vividly before him; and the tall figure seemed to hold the frantic struggler in a strong grasp.

He rushed past, round to the chief entrance, knocked at the gate, and then fell to the ground in a swoon. Just as the Porter opened it, there rose a cry from a crowd of men trooping out from a set of rooms immediately to the right of the Porter's lodge. They were members of the notorious Hell-Fire Club. In the middle of a violent speech, as profane as it is said to have been blasphemous, and with a frightful imprecation upon his lips, a chief speaker (the owner of the rooms) had suddenly broken a blood vessel, and was then lying dead on the floor.

The club in question, it is reported, never met again.[60]

So much on this point. A few words are perhaps needed upon another. It may be held by some that what has already been written on Witchcraft and Necromancy is a melancholy instance of grovelling superstition on the part of its Author.[61] Be it so. He is quite ready to avow his entire belief in the express statements of Holy Scripture, and in the general Christian tradition and teaching on the subject itself and all that is necessarily involved in it. Those who believe in the existence of angels, "the glorious battalions of the living God," and who frankly accept as truth the various records of Holy Scripture, in which their ministry to mankind is set forth, will likewise believe that S. Peter's exhortation to the Early Christians did not simply embody a sentiment but declared a fact, when he wrote: "Be sober, be vigilant, because your adversary the Devil, as a roaring lion, walketh about, seeking whom he may devour."[62]

That the pagan nations owning and serving the Prince of this World, and being supernaturally served by him in return, actively practised magic at the time of our Blessed Saviour's first coming, is generally allowed. And that the Christian writers of early times, more particularly S. Gregory Thaumaturgus, admitted the reality and force of the sorcerers' incantations and powers, is abundantly evident from their words and reasoning. The case of the damsel of Thyatira, "possessed with a spirit of divination," who "brought her masters much gain by soothsaying," clearly establishes this point; and so does the apostle's authoritative action:--"Paul, being grieved, turned and said to the spirit, I command thee in the Name of Jesus Christ to come out of her. And he came out the same hour."[63]

When, three centuries after the Day of Pentecost, the Church of God commenced numbering up her earliest triumphs, the soothsayers, the diviners, and the dealers with evil spirits began to experience her righteous and beneficent power. Constantine, urged to action by those who sat in the seats of the apostles, formally sanctioned the condemnation of magicians; but of course under Julian the Apostate, magic rites were not only still commonly in vogue, but were publicly patronized. Later on, Valentinian re-enacted the laws of Constantine; and under Theodosius the severest penalties were likewise enforced against the practice of magic; and, in truth, against every phase of pagan worship. But a general belief in sorcery and divination remained powerful and active long after the supreme and glorious victory of Christianity in the sixth century; and the manner in which the authorities of the Christian Church met the belief, and, by Sacraments and Sacramentals, aided the faithful to withstand the legions of the Devil and his human allies, is perfectly familiar to the student of history.

The well-known conviction that demons had appeared to mankind under the names of sylvans, gnomes, and fauns was common enough amongst the Romans prior to the revelation of Christianity; while the conviction that these demons had sometimes made women the object of their passion was arrived at by many. Justin Martyr and S. Augustine of Hippo[64] seem to imply something of the sort; and marriage or commerce with demons was a charge frequently made against witches, even from the earliest times.[65] It was said that these demons owned a remarkable attachment to women with beautiful hair,--a belief possibly founded on the passage in S. Paul's First Epistle to the Corinthians,[66] in which he exhorts women to cover their heads "because of the angels." In the middle ages the intercourse of philosophers belonging to certain secret societies with sylphs and salamanders was also believed by many:[67] and, later on, the study of astrology, with its fatalistic theories, and the restoration of the heresies of the Manichees, served to aid in more systematically formulating that belief in witchcraft and the supernatural which was for centuries so universal, and which never could have become so without a sure and solid substratum of fact and truth.

Again, it is impossible to believe that the sorcerers of the Oriental nations have been and are impostors. As regards those of modern Egypt, Mr. Lane, in his interesting volume upon that country,[68] appears to have settled the question by expressing his conviction of the truth and reality of their supernatural performances. And similar conclusions have reluctantly but most certainly been arrived at by those who, with some knowledge and reasonable powers of observation, have witnessed the acts and deeds of the Eastern dealers with evil spirits.

With reference to Egypt, Mr. Lane's statement on the subject stands thus:--

"A few days after my arrival in this country my curiosity was excited on the subject of magic by a circumstance related to me by Mr. Salt, our consul-general. Having had reason to believe that one of his servants was a thief, from the fact of several articles of property having been stolen from his house, he sent for a celebrated Maghrabee magician, with a view of intimidating them, and causing the guilty one, (if any of them were guilty,) to confess his crime. The magician came, and said that he would cause the exact image of the person who had committed the thefts to appear to any youth not arrived at the age of puberty; and desired the master of the house to call in any boy whom he might choose. As several boys were then employed in a garden adjacent to the house, one of them was called for this purpose. In the palm of this boy's right hand, the magician drew with a pen a certain diagram, in the centre of which he poured a little ink. Into this ink he desired the boy steadfastly to look. He then burned some incense, and several bits of paper inscribed with charms;

and at the same time called for various objects to appear in the ink. The boy declared that he saw all these objects, and, last of all, the image of the guilty person; he described his stature, countenance, and dress; said that he knew him; and directly ran down into the garden, and apprehended one of the labourers, who, when brought before the master, immediately confessed that he was the thief."--P. 267.[69]

The performers themselves maintain, that they have been instructed in the art by those who have traditionally received the knowledge step by step, and period by period, from the old "magicians of Egypt;" and some frankly allow, that they themselves are constantly attended and waited on by a familiar spirit, demon, or genius, who actively aids them in their performances, and who is, under certain circumstances, always prepared to do their bidding.

These genii, or "Ginn" as they are called in Egypt, "are said to be of pre-Adamite origin, and in their general properties," remarks Mr. Lane, "are an intermediate class of beings between angels and men, but inferior in dignity to both, created of fire, and capable of assuming the forms and material fabric of men, brutes, and monsters; and of becoming invisible at pleasure. They eat and drink, propagate their species (like or in conjunction with human beings,) and are subject to death."... "The Ginn," continues Mr. Lane, "are supposed to pervade the solid matter of the earth, as well as the firmament, where, approaching the confines of the lowest heaven, they often listen to the conversation of the angels respecting future things, thus enabling themselves to assist diviners and magicians."--P. 222.

In the twentieth chapter of his interesting and attractive volume, he writes:--"I have met with many persons among the more intelligent of the Egyptians who condemn these modern Psylli as impostors, but none who has been able to offer a satisfactory explanation of the most common and most interesting of their performances."--P. 383.

In another part of the book Mr. Lane concludes his chapter on "Magic" thus:--"Neither I nor others have been able to discover any clue by which to penetrate the mystery."[70]

So likewise as regards India,[71] it is impossible to set aside the facts, which are testified to not by one but by hundreds, as to the supernatural powers of the jugglers there. Identical in kind with the performances of the magicians of Egypt before Pharaoh and in the presence of Moses and Aaron, recorded in the Book of Exodus, the secret of the following "tricks" (familiar to any one who has been in India) has been handed down from father to son from the most remote ages; and we have no reason to doubt that the source of the power by which these acts are done is one and the same.

For instance:--The juggler, giving one of the spectators a coin to hold as securely as possible within his hands, after pronouncing incantations in a monotonous voice for some minutes, suddenly stops, still keeping his seat, makes a rapid motion with his right hand, as if in the act of throwing something at the person holding the coin, at the same time breathing with his mouth upon him. Instantaneously the hands of the person taking part in the performance are suddenly distended, while a horrible sensation of holding something cold and disagreeable and nasty, is immediately felt, forcing him to cast away the contents of his palms, which, to the horror and disgust of uninitiated persons, turns out to be, not the coin which before was there, but a live snake coiled up! The juggler then rises, and catching the snake, which is now crawling and wriggling on the ground, takes it by the tail, opens his mouth wide, and allows the snake to drop into it. With deliberation he appears by degrees to swallow it, until the whole, tail and all, completely disappears. He opens his mouth for the spectators to investigate; but nothing is to be seen, neither does the snake appear again.

Here is another instance:--A juggler will be brought to act before, perhaps, many hundreds of people, of all ages, degrees, and religions, including the soldiery of a garrison, in the public yard of a barrack. A guard of soldiers will be placed around him, to prevent either trickery or deception on his part, or interruption from the spectators. A little girl, about eight or nine years old, accompanies the man, who is also provided with a tall, narrow basket, three or four feet high, little more than a foot in width, and open all the way up. The juggler, after some altercation with the child, pretends to get angry, and lashing himself into a fury, seizes hold of the child, and inverts the basket completely over her. Thus placed completely at his mercy, and in spite of her screams and entreaties, he draws his sword, and fiercely plunges it down into the basket, and brings it out dripping with blood--or what apparently is such. The child's screams become fainter and fainter, as again and again the sword is thrust through the basket; and at length they gradually cease, and everything is still. Then follows a critical moment for the supposed murderer: and the exertions of the guard scarcely serve to save him from the excited soldiery. When order is at length obtained, however, the man, raising his bloody sword for an instant, strikes the basket with it, which falls, and reveals--not a murdered child weltering in blood, but an empty space, with no vestige left of the supposed victim. In a few moments the identical little girl comes rushing--from whence no one can tell--to the feet of the performer, with every sign of affection, and perfectly unhurt. Be it observed that these performances commonly take place in India in places where it is impossible for any contrivances or trap-doors to exist, in the centre of court-yards at the various military stations, and before innumerable witnesses.

Again: in Corea and China the practice of Necromancy is said to be almost universal. An intelligent modern writer upon China gives an account, in the following passage, of one mode in which questions are put, and answers obtained, by a kind of divination:--Written communications from spirits are not unfrequently sought for in the following manner: after the presence and desired offices of some spirit are invoked, "two or more persons support with their hands some object to which a pencil is attached in a vertical position, and extending to a table below covered with sand. It is said that the movements of the pencil, involuntary as far as the persons holding it are concerned, but governed by the influences of spirits, describe certain characters which are easily deciphered, and which often bring to light remarkable disclosures and revelations. Many who regard themselves as persons of superior intelligence are firm believers in this mode of consulting spirits."[72]

Here, as illustrating the common principles and course of action which are adopted and followed in all parts of the World by those who seek information by forbidden means, the following may be set forth:--

There is a dreary-looking House in one of the London Squares which is reported to be haunted. And certainly this opinion, as the Editor can testify from a careful personal enquiry, is tolerably current in the neighbourhood. A Lady, curious about the fact, was present on an occasion when certain inquiries were made regarding this House by means of "Planchette,"--the instrument just referred to as so commonly used in China. It is a small board, in shape like a heart, which is made to run on two wheels or castors, and a hole is provided for a pencil so to be placed with its point downward as that, when put upon a sheet of white paper the point may just touch the surface. After the usual invocation or incantation (or whatever it be), the persons who practise modern divination place their hands on the board. Questions are put, and answers given. No one touches the pencil, but the board is so guided, as the Necromancers and Spiritualists assert, that the pencil is made to write intelligible answers to expressed (and sometimes to mere mental) queries. The following, printed verbatim et literatim, are in the handwriting of the lady who witnessed them put and responded to, and are given as a fair specimen of this mode of divination, now so generally practised in England:--

Is any house haunted in B---- Square? Yes.
What killed the two people in the haunted room? Fright.
What frightened them? Spirits.
What kind of spirits? Yourself.
How could any one be afraid of me? Without your body.
Did they see them? Spirits not visible.
How did they know they were there? Thought they saw them.
Did they make them feel them? No.
Then how did the spirits make themselves known--by what means? Mesmeric.
Were you ever there? No.
Why do those spirits haunt that house? Murder was committed there.
Who was murdered, a man or a woman? A woman.
What was the name of the woman? (Writing not intelligible.)
Who murdered her? (Writing not intelligible.)
Is he alive or dead? Dead.
Is it the woman's spirit, or the man's, who haunts the house? Both.
Was the man hung? No.
Was the murder found out while he lived? No.
Are you a bad spirit? Bad.
Is it what the Bible calls "divination" to consult you in this way? Yes.
Is it displeasing to God? Perhaps.
Is it wrong? You know.

It is only right to add that those who made and obtained the foregoing intelligible responses to intelligible questions, for good and sufficient reasons came to hold such practices to be unlawful and wicked, and threw the instrument by which they had been given into the Thames.

On this subject, and all its details, no words of warning could be more forcible than the following, which are quoted, in the hope that some who may have been thoughtlessly induced to adopt the practices of Modern Spiritualism, may be led at once to desist from the same:--

"Although good and evil spirits possess a powerful influence in the government of the World, yet it is strictly forbidden, in the divine laws of the Old and New Testament, to seek any acquaintance with them, or to place ourselves in connection with and relation to them; and it is just as little permitted for citizens of the world of spirits visibly to manifest themselves to those who are still in the present state of existence, without the express command or permission of the Lord. He, therefore, that seeks intercourse with the invisible world sins deeply, and will soon repent of it; whilst he that becomes acquainted with it, without his own seeking and by Divine guidance, ought to beg and pray for wisdom, courage, and strength, for he has need of all these; and let him that is introduced into such a connection, by means of illness, or the aberration of his physical nature, seek by proper means to regain his health, and detach himself from intercourse with spirits."[73]

Yet, with many, and an increasing number, it is to be feared such advice is wholly unheeded. For more than five-and-twenty years the subject of Modern Spiritualism has been under discussion in England, and the facts on which it has been founded have been before the World; but "having eyes men see not, and having ears they hear not." Or, guided by the superficial opinions of those whose one-eyed Materialism tinges so many of their hap-hazard theories, they put aside a consideration of the astonishing phenomena of the system of Spiritualism, and absolutely deny their existence.[74] The age is shallow in its very incredulity. The wisdom of the World is foolishness indeed.

When it is too late, when thousands upon thousands have become the active votaries of Spiritualism, perhaps the bishops and clergy of the Church of England may wake up to some realization of the enormous influence for evil,[75] both dogmatic and moral, which this diabolical system cannot do other than secure, and lift their testimony against it. Mahometanism is not more directly anti-christian. Yet the numbers of those who believe in Spiritualism are daily increasing, and the purblind policy of ignoring its principles and action must very soon come to an end. Of course Materialists and sceptics reasonably doubt; for otherwise their own infallibility would ignominiously collapse. But for Christians, who possess a copy of the "Holy Bible," and are able to read it, doubt seems to me (I write with all due humility) simply inconsequent and irrational.

Here, let us turn from shadow to sunshine, from that which is evil to that which is good; from the "lying wonders" of designing evil spirits, to the glorious manifestations of God Almighty's power in the Christian Church--for the one kind are but reasonable correlatives of the other.

And, for myself, I am free to confess that the evidence in favour of certain of the recent miracles said to have been wrought in the Roman Catholic portion of the One Family of God is not only convincing, but conclusive. Having long given up attributing any value to the slanders and misstatements of Protestant and infidel writers, I have attempted for myself to investigate the principle of action, in the reception of evidence and the decision of authority, which is taken at Rome, with regard to such events and occurrences; and briefly give it as follows:--

The Congregation of Rites, which enquires into all miracles which demand sanction, is presided over by the cardinal-vicar. It consists of twenty-one cardinals of various nations, nine official prelates, nine consulting prelates of various nations, all the fourteen Papal Masters of Ceremonies, fourteen ordinary members, one secretary, one deputy-secretary, and one notary and keeper of the archives--in all seventy people. Four miracles are required to be distinctly proved for Beatification; and two more for Canonization. All these must be proved by eye, and not by ear-witnesses. In miracles where diseases have been cured, it is required, 1st, That the disease must have been of an aggravated nature, and difficult or impossible to be cured; 2ndly, that it was not on the turn; 3rdly, that no medicine had been used, or if it had that it had done no good; 4thly, the cure must be sudden; 5thly, it must be complete and perfect; and 6thly, there must have been no crisis. In the process of examination and enquiry, no step is taken, no doubt propounded, no fact allowed, without many of the members of the Congregation being present: and a printed Report is sent to all who may have been absent. Besides the ordinary cross-examinations, which are always of a most scrutinizing character, it is the sole duty of one of the leading members of the Congregation, the Promotor Fidei, as he is termed, to raise objections, and if possible to disprove every reported miracle. The members of this Congregation are as keen, penetrating and business-like, and have as complete a knowledge of the unconscious delusions of the human heart, as any body of English jurymen. As ecclesiastical scholars they may be truly said to be equal to the same number of English barristers; and the head of the Congregation, for shrewdness, acuteness of intellect, and judicial ability, is equal to any judge in England, who by his interpretation of the law, and his particular sentence in a special case, wills away the life or property of any Englishman. The subject has been treated at length in the great work of Pope Benedict XIV. (A.D. 1740-1758) "On Beatification," &c., as well as in the Decrees of Pope Urban VIII. and Pope Clement XI.; and so sifting and careful has always been the investigation, that Alban Butler asserts, on the authority of Daubenton, that an English gentleman (not a Roman Catholic) being present and seeing the process of several miracles, maintained them to have been completely proved and perfectly incontestable, but was astonished beyond measure at the scrupulosity of the scrutiny when authoritatively informed that not one of those which he had heard discussed had been allowed by the Congregation to have been sufficiently proved.

Father Perrone, the distinguished living theologian, also asserts that having shown the formal process for certain miracles to a lawyer of some eminence (not a Roman Catholic) who after examination was perfectly satisfied with both the testimony and the reasoning, the latter declared that they would certainly stand before a British jury; but was mightily astonished on hearing that the Congregation did not consider that evidence to be sufficiently convincing and conclusive.

Similar investigations have been made in England, since the Reformation, and this by ecclesiastical authority. For example: in the year before his translation to the see of Norwich (i. e. in 1640), Dr. Joseph Hall, then Bishop of Exeter, made a strict and judicial inquiry into all the circumstances of the sudden and miraculous cure of a cripple at S. Madron's Well, in Cornwall, and the following is the recorded conviction of this pious prelate:--"The commerce which we have with the good spirits is not now discerned by the eye, but is, like themselves, spiritual. Yet not so, but that even in bodily occasions we have many times insensible helps from them; in such a manner as that by the effects we can boldly say, 'Here hath been an angel, though we see him not.' Of this kind was that (no less than miraculous) cure which at S. Madron's, in Cornwall, was wrought upon a poor cripple, John Trelille, where (besides the attestation of many hundreds of neighbours), I took a strict and personal examination in that last Visitation which I ever did or ever shall hold. This man, that for sixteen years together was fain to walk upon his hands, by reason of the close contraction of the sinews of his legs, (upon three admonitions in a dream to wash in that well) was suddenly so restored to his limbs, that I saw him able to walk and get his own maintenance. I found here was neither art nor collusion: the thing done, the author invisible."[76]

Now, whatever may be thought of the principles enunciated in Mr. Lecky's[77] volumes on "The Rise and Influence of Rationalism," none can deny either the marvellous faculty exhibited for gathering and marshalling facts; while some portions of his thoughtful reflections do but put into luminous language thoughts and convictions which find a cordial response from many.

The following remarkable passage is singularly true and accurate in its estimate of an unmistakeable historical fact, viz., that the Oxford movement to a great extent left out of consideration[78] the continued existence of modern miracles in the Christian Church. Mr. Lecky writes thus:--"At Oxford these narratives (i. e. the record of patristic and mediæval miracles) hardly exercised a serious attention. What little influence they had was chiefly an influence of repression; what little was written in their favour was written for the most part in the tone of an apology, as if to attenuate a difficulty rather than to establish a creed. This was surely a very remarkable characteristic of the Tractarian movement, when we remember the circumstances and attainments of its leaders, and the great prominence which miraculous evidence had long occupied in England. It was especially remarkable when we reflect that one of the great complaints which the Tractarian party were making against modern theology was, that the conception of the Supernatural had become faint and dim, and that its manifestations were either explained away or confined to a distant past. It would seem as if those who were most conscious of the character of their age were unable, in the very midst of their opposition, to free themselves from its tendencies."--Vol. i. pp. 165-166.

It must be allowed that there is some amount of truth in this temperately-made charge. Whatever else may have been pressed forward, and with success, it is obvious that the active energy of the Supernatural has been kept somewhat in the background. At all events it has not been made too prominent. Even in books of devotion, adapted from Roman Catholic sources, examples of miracles have been omitted; and so the golden threads which were so rudely broken three centuries and a half ago, are still in the mire; for few have cared to gather them up once more and weave them into a perfect whole. That work has still to be done. Not until there be what a modern writer terms "daring faith"--faith which can move mountains--should the work be attempted.

And now, fully alive to its imperfections, I bring my book to its close.

It has been briefly shown herein what a great influence the materialistic speculations of a few bold and over-confident writers have recently exercised on current thought. At the same time the presence of the Supernatural in Church History has been made perfectly manifest, and abundant sources pointed out from which additional examples may readily be gathered for consideration by those who may desire to gather them. Side by side, however, with that which in the Supernatural order is good and beneficial to man, energizes that which is evil. There are angels and there are demons. There is light and there is darkness. Numberless armies of glorious spirits, as the Divine Revelation tells us,[79] stand, rank by rank and order by order, as the bright ornaments of the City of God. Their subtlety, their quickness of penetration, their extensive knowledge of natural things, are undoubtedly perfect in proportion to the excellency of their being, inasmuch as they are pure intelligences, perfect from the Hand of their Maker. They know the concerns of mortal men.[80] They are our protectors, our patrons, our guides. For us they lift up their prayers to God, and they are

Rev. Frederick George Lee, D.C.L.

near us in our trials and temptations. Their motion is swift as thought, their activity inconceivable. As they are the friends of mankind by God's decree, so specially do they become the guardians of the regenerate and the particular protectors of the innocent and young. And their beneficent actions are not altogether unknown. The old records tell of their charity; man's experience testifies to their presence. And, furthermore, for man's behoof in his time of trial, and for his eternal advantage hereafter, were given those powers and properties which belong to the Church by the grace and efficacy of the Sacraments.

Yet, on the other hand, until the number of the Elect is accomplished, the Enemy of Souls, the Prince of the Powers of the Air, is permitted to wield an alarming influence; while too often the natural man, with his will free, wills to remain his servant. Yea; and even the baptized, too. For by Witchcraft, Sorcery, and Necromancy Satan still works, men being his direct agents and slaves. Sometimes in one form, sometimes in another, he dupes those who seek him; while his legions suggest to men's minds evil thoughts, paint dangerous objects to the imagination, frequently direct the active current of the human heart to sin, and finally turn round and accuse their captives at the tribunal of God the Judge of all. So must it be to the end, for this life is man's time of probation.

Of Dreams and Warnings, Omens and Presentiments, much has been written. Each example must be considered on its own merits; for perhaps no coherent theory will sufficiently cover and explain all the instances here already adduced.

So, too, with Spectral Appearances and Haunted Localities. While experience testifies to the facts recorded, such Glimpses of the Supernatural may be well left to tell their own story, to leave their own impression, and set forth their own teaching. To those who possess the grace and habit of faith they will not seem over-strange, for as Hamlet remarked to his friend--

*"There are more things in Heaven and Earth, Horatio,
Than are dreamt of in our philosophy."*

As I prepare to lay down my pen, I cannot but notice and put on record what amid "the triumphs of Science," so frequently start up to confront us, viz. the sad records of calamity brought to notice, and the gloomy scenes of deepest misery which are yet so frequently depicted. "Woe is me!" is man's wail still. But with many the Supernatural, as we too well know, is bidden to stand aside. The Catholic Religion is written of as antiquated, out of date, and effete. The truth of the Christian Revelation is openly denied. Yet may not the terrible disasters of which we hear, and the miserable calamities which so constantly occur along the path of "human progress" and "scientific triumph," be permitted by God Almighty as an intelligible and richly deserved rebuke to lofty looks and the impious and blasphemous thoughts of the proud?[81]

Man's life in this country is certainly not longer than it was eight or ten centuries ago. He dies as he died. Nor is the race of Englishmen sturdier, finer, or better grown than of old. The tombs of the Crusaders tell us this. Look at the stately figures of the Fitzalans in Bedale Church, or at those of the Marmions in that of Tanfield, and it may be that in this practical particular deterioration instead of progress should be more fittingly and faithfully recorded. As is obvious enough, Science, with all the boasting of its adherents, can, after all, effect but little. True it is that wonderful discoveries are made in the Realms of Nature. Operations untraced before, are now accurately apprehended; and secrets, long hidden, are triumphantly brought to light. One might imagine from the random confidence of some (as guides more shallow than safe), that Science had discovered an appliance for every human weakness, an antidote to every physical evil or disease, an unfailing specific against every want and woe. Yet, after all its researches and with all its supposed discoveries (for many may have been known and lost), never were failures so great or misfortunes so heavy. The ugly iron ship of the present day, hideous in form and appearance, yet constructed with all the obtainable skill of modern science, at an enormous sacrifice of expense, fitted with life-boats and patent scientific life-preservers, divided into compartments, after due calculations (on a scientific method), suddenly goes down, where a fisherman of six centuries ago, in his wooden skiff, would have ridden a storm securely, and becomes an iron coffin for five or six hundred corpses, rotting where the seaweed grows. Again, War, with scientific appliances--in the invention and preparation of which the great nations are active rivals--marches over a great country, defended by the highest military art and strength, and in a few short months reduces its people to spoliation, tribute, and shame. Less than a century ago, nearly a twenty years' struggle would have been made, ere such a sudden and sweeping contest could have been so securely sealed.

Human Art may do something, and Science may effect more: but how frequently some little flaw or casualty defeats all! The boastings of Science, consequently, become vain and vapid: its works lie in the dust. Past ages have had their pride humbled; as Tyre and Alexandria and Babylon too eloquently tell. When God, by the insolence of intellect, is thrust aside, He sometimes, nevertheless, mercifully but efficiently reminds men that He is. When the Supernatural is deliberately denied and scornfully rejected, suffering may serve to open the eyes of the blind and make the dumb to speak. The general tendency in these days is to worship Mind, Intelligence, and Power, for Might, with too many, is Right. Literary jargon setting forth this duty may be constantly read. The wisest action for the truly wise is to turn away from such; for the noblest and proudest ambition of a Christian's life should consist in being humble worshippers of Him the One Author of the Supernatural and the Natural, Whose only power is infinite, Whose knowledge and wisdom are boundless, and Whose abiding love and mercy are over all His works.

Rev. Frederick George Lee, D.C.L.

APPENDIX TO CHAPTER X - THE CLAIMS OF SCIENCE AND FAITH

By my friend Mr. Hawker's obliging kindness I am enabled to publish the following remarkable Letter:--
"To Mr. S. J----, Merchant, Plymouth.
"MY DEAR NEPHEW,--You ask me 'to put into one of my nutshells' the pith and marrow of the controversy which at this time pervades the English mind as to the claims of Science and Faith. Let me try: The material universe--so the sages allege--is a vast assemblage of atoms or molecules--'motes in the sunbeam' of Science, which has existed for myriads of ages under a perpetual system of evolution, restructure, and change. This mighty mass is traversed by the forces electrical, or magnetic, or with other kindred names; and these by their incessant and indomitable action are adequate to account for all the phenomena of the world of matter, and of man. The upheaval of a continent; the drainage of a sea; the creation of a metal; nay, the origin of life, and the development of a species in plant, or animal, or man; these are the achievements of fixed and natural laws among the atomic materials, under the vibration of the forces alone. Thus far the vaunted discoveries of Science are said to have arrived. Let us indulge them with the theory that these results, for they are nothing more, are accurate and real. But still, a thoughtful mind will venture to demand whence did these atoms derive their existence? and from what, and from whom, do they inherit the propensities wherewithal they are imbued? And tell me, most potent seigniors, what is the origin of these forces? And with whom resides the impulse of their action and the guidance of their control? 'Nothing so difficult as a beginning.' Your philosopher is mute! he has reached the horizon of his domain, and to him all beyond is doubt, and uncertainty, and guess. We must lift the veil. We must pass into the border-land between two Worlds, and there inquire at the Oracles of Revelation touching the Unseen and Spiritual powers which thrill through the mighty sacrament of the visible Creation. We perceive, being inspired, the realms of surrounding space peopled by immortal creatures of air--

> *'Myriads of spiritual things that walk unseen,*
> *Both when we wake and when we sleep.'*

These are the existences, in aspect as 'young men in white garments,' who inhabit the void place between the Worlds and their Maker, and their God. Behold the battalions of the Lord of Hosts! the Workers of the sky! the faithful and intelligent Vassals of God the Trinity! We have named them in our own poor and meagre language 'the Angels,' but this title merely denotes one of their subordinate offices--messengers from on high. The Gentiles called them 'Gods,' but we ought to honour them by a name that should embrace and interpret their lofty dignity as an intermediate army between the kingdom and the throne; the Centurions of the stars, and of men; the Commanders of the forces and their Guides. These are they that, each with a delegated office, fulfil what their 'King invisible' decrees; not with the dull, inert mechanism of fixed and natural law, but with the unslumbering energy and the rational obedience of spiritual life. They mould the atom; they wield the force; and, as Newton rightly guessed, they rule the World of matter beneath the silent Omnipotence of God.
"'And he dreamed, and behold a ladder set up on the earth, and the top of it reached to Heaven; and behold the angels of God ascending and descending on it. And behold the Lord stood above it.'--Genesis xxviii. 12. Tolle, Lege, my dear nephew.

"Your affectionate uncle,
"R. S. HAWKER.
"Morwenstow Vicarage, Cornwall."

THE END

FOOTNOTES:

1. Here in Mr. Surtees' record is a remarkable example of the pious and devout use of the sacred Sign of the Cross, which, having been universal amongst all classes before the Reformation, was continued by many for long generations afterwards, and the use of which since the Catholic Revival in the English Church has become common.

2. "History of Durham," by Robert Surtees, Esq.: under "Chester-le-Street." Vol. ii. pp. 147-148.

3. "Nichols' Literary Illustrations." Vol. iv. p. 119, et seq. London, 1822.

4. Arthur Orchard, of S. John's College, Cambridge, B.A. 1662; M.A. 1666; B.D. 1673.

5. "Letters on Animal Magnetism," by Dr. W. Gregory, p. 487. London, 1851.

6. A member of the noble family of Beresford thus wrote (A.D. 1873) to a friend of the Editor, with reference to the above narrative:--"The tradition in our family is entirely in favour of the truth of the Spectral Appearance, and the account which I have read, and return, is in my opinion a true and faithful narration of it."

7. The record of this came to the Editor, through a friend, from the late Rev. W. Hastings Kelke, M.A., sometime Rector of Drayton Beauchamp, in the county of Bucks.

8. The barony of Chedworth was conferred upon John Howe, Esq., of Chedworth, co. Gloucester, on May 12, 1741. He had two sons, John Thynne, the nobleman referred to in the above account, and Henry Frederick, who in turn succeeded him in the title. His daughter Mary married Alexander Wright, Esq., whose daughter Mary Wright is the lady mentioned in the above narrative. Miss Wright's cousin John inherited as fourth baron, but died unmarried, Oct. 29, 1804, when the peerage became extinct.

9. Another narrative of this remarkable event, which substantially corresponds with those given in the text above is provided here. In certain respects there are discrepancies, and just those kinds of discrepancies which might reasonably have been looked for in accounts drawn up by different hands; but in the main facts, regarding which there can be no reasonable doubt, there is a remarkable and notable identity in all the leading features: "Two nights before, on Lord Lyttelton retiring to bed, after his servant was dismissed and his light extinguished, he had heard a noise resembling the fluttering of a dove at his chamber window. This attracted his attention to the spot; when, looking in the direction of the sound, he saw the figure of an unhappy female whom he had seduced, and who, when deserted, had put a violent end to her own existence, standing in the aperture of the window from which the fluttering sound had proceeded. The form approached the foot of the bed, the room was preternaturally light, the objects of the chamber were distinctly visible. Raising her hand and pointing to a dial which stood on the mantlepiece of the chimney, the figure, with a severe solemnity of voice and manner, answered to the appalled and conscience-stricken man that at that very hour, on the third day after the visitation, his life and his sins would be concluded, and nothing but their punishment remain, if he availed himself not of the warning to repentance which he had thus received. The eye of Lord Lyttelton glanced upon the dial; the hand was on the stroke of twelve: again the apartment was involved in total darkness--the warning spirit disappeared, and bore away at her departure all the lightness of heart and buoyancy of spirit, ready flow of wit, and vivacity of manner, which had formerly been the pride and ornament of the unhappy being to whom she had delivered her tremendous summons. Such was the tale that Lord Lyttelton delivered to his companions. They laughed at his superstition, and endeavoured to convince him that his mind must have been impressed with this idea by some dream of a more consistent nature than dreams generally are, and that he had mistaken the visions of his sleep for the visitation of a spirit. He was consoled, but not convinced; he felt relieved by their distrust, and on the second night after the appearance of the spectre, he retreated to his apartment with his faith in the reality of the transaction somewhat shaken; and his spirits, though not revived, certainly lightened of somewhat of their oppression. On the succeeding day the guests of Lord Lyttelton, with the connivance of his attendant, had provided that the clocks throughout the house should be advanced an hour; by occupying the host's attention during the whole day with different and successive objects of amusement, they contributed to prevent his discovering the imposture. Ten o'clock struck: the nobleman was silent and depressed. Eleven struck, the depression deepened, and now not even a smile, or the slightest movement of his eye indicated him to be conscious of the efforts of his associates, as they attempted to dispel his gloom. Twelve struck. 'Thank God! I am safe,' exclaimed Lord Lyttelton, 'the ghost was a liar after all. Some wine, there. Congratulate me,

my friends; congratulate me on my reprieve. Why, what a fool I was to be cast down by so idle and absurd a circumstance! But, however, it is time for bed. We'll be up early and out with the hounds to-morrow. By my faith, it's half-past twelve, so good night!' and he returned to his chamber convinced of his security, and believing that the threatened hour of peril was now past. His guests remained together to await the completion of the time so ominously designated by the vision. A quarter of an hour had elapsed: they heard the valet descend from his master's room. It was just twelve. Lord Lyttelton's bell rang violently. The company ran in a body to his apartment. The clock struck one at their entrance, the unhappy nobleman lay extended on the bed before them, pale and lifeless, and his countenance terribly convulsed."

In his "Memoirs," Sir Nathaniel Wraxall has the following relating to this occurrence:--

"Dining at Pitt Place, about four years after the death of Lord Lyttelton, in the year 1783, I had the curiosity to visit the bed-chamber, where the casement window, at which Lord Lyttelton asserted the dove appeared to flutter, was pointed out to me; and at his stepmother's, the Dowager Lady Lyttelton's in Portugal Street, Grosvenor Square, who being a woman of very lively imagination, lent an implicit faith to all the supernatural facts which were supposed to have accompanied or produced Lord Lyttelton's end. I have frequently seen a painting which she herself executed in 1780, especially to commemorate the event: it hung in a conspicuous part of her drawing-room. There the dove appears at the window, while a female figure, habited in white, stands at the foot of the bed, announcing to Lord Lyttelton his dissolution. Every part of the picture was faithfully designed after the description given to her by the valet-de-chambre who attended him, to whom his master related all the circumstances."

10. Copied from a paper in the autograph of Lord Westcote, entitled "Remarkable Circumstances attending the Death of Thomas, Lord Lyttelton," which the present Lord Lyttelton most courteously entrusted to the Editor of this volume, together with several other original documents relating to the same, as follows:--1. Extract from Mr. Plumer Ward's "Illustrations of Human Life," vol. i. p. 165. 2. Written account given by Sir Digby Neave, bart., to Lord Lyttelton in 1860. 3. MS. containing Mr. George Fortescue's testimony, signed S. L. 4. The following declaration:--"Chiswick, May 6th, 1867. Miles Peter Andrews told me the story of Lord Lyttelton's appearance to him, driving with me at Wingerworth, many years ago.--Anna Hunloke."

11. Lord Lyttelton's valet made the following statement:--"That Lord Lyttelton made his usual preparations for bed; that he kept every now and then looking for his watch; that when he got into bed, he ordered his curtains to be closed at the foot. It was now within a minute or two of twelve by his watch; he asked to look at mine, and seemed pleased to find it nearly keep time with his own. His lordship then put them both to his ear, to satisfy himself if they went. When it was more than a quarter after twelve by our watches, he said, 'This mysterious lady is not a true prophetess, I find.' When it was near the real hour of twelve, he said, 'Come, I'll wait no longer; get me my medicine, I'll take it, and try to sleep.' I just stepped into the dressing-room to prepare the physic, and had mixed it, when I thought I heard my lord breathing very hard. I ran to him, and found him in the agonies of death."--"Gentleman's Magazine," vol. lxxxv. part i. p. 598, A.D. 1815.

12. In Boswell's "Life of Samuel Johnson" (vol. iv. p. 313) the Doctor is recorded to have said, "It is the most extraordinary occurrence in my days. I heard it from Lord Westcote, his uncle. I am so glad to have evidence of the spiritual world, that I am willing to believe it."

13. "James Weld, Esq., seventh son of Thomas Weld, Esq., of Lulworth Castle, was born April 30, 1785, married July 15, 1812, the Hon. Juliana Anne, daughter of Robert Edward, tenth Lord Petre, and has had issue, 1. Henry, 2. Francis, a priest, 3. Philip, died 1846; 1. Anna Maria, 2. Katharine, 3. Agnes, a nun, 4. Charlotte."--See Burke's "Landed Gentry," vol. ii. art. "Weld of Lulworth Castle."

14. The Right Rev. Monsignor Patterson, the present President of S. Edmund's college (A.D. 1872), kindly informs me that there is a memorial brass in front of the sanctuary of the chapel of that society, on which is figured a floriated cross, rising out of waves, with a label appended to it,-- "Lord save me."

15. S. Stanislaus Kostka was born on Oct. 28, 1550, his parents being John and Margaret Kostka, Polish nobles of wealth and repute. Miraculous signs foreshadowed his birth; and the holiness and purity of his early years betokened in a marked manner the favour of God towards this child. In his fourteenth year he went to Vienna to finish his studies at the Jesuit college. Here, his saintliness was so manifested forth by his conduct, that the Fathers said, "We have in our seminary an angel under the form of Stanislaus." Many miraculous favours are said to have been bestowed upon him by the hands of saints and angels, too numerous and lengthy to be recorded. He commenced his noviciate in the Jesuit college at Rome; where, after a short but edifying sojourn, he joyfully departed this life, aged 18 years, on the morning of August 15, 1568.

16. Mr. de Lisle, of Garendon Park, Leicestershire, in communicating to me the above narrative, writes as follows:--"I send you my account of the apparition of Philip Weld, according to

my promise. I received it back this morning (July 17, 1872) from the Benedictine Convent at Athenstone, in Warwickshire, where my daughter Gwendoline is a nun, and where one of the Miss Welds, a cousin of Philip, is also a nun. She approves the accuracy of my account, and has added a paper with a few notes, which I inclose along with my own article, and from which you can correct mine so far as needed. I add here my affirmation that the above recorded narrative is a true and faithful account of what the Very Rev. Dr. Cox, then President of S. Edmund's College, related to me and to Mrs. de Lisle in February, 1847." The Editor is also greatly indebted to the Very Rev. Alfred Weld, S.J., for his courteous Letters upon the subject of the above narrative, as likewise to the Rev. E. J. Purbrick, S.J.

17. "Letters on Animal Magnetism," by Dr. W. Gregory, pp. 448-489. London, 1851.

18. "The Apparition or Spectral Appearance of my friend's father to him in the West Indies-- the old gentleman having died in England, and the fact of two officers having seen it simultaneously, shows that it could not have been the result of their imagination, but that it was an objective appearance; in fact, the dead man's immortal spirit, indicating to one once bound by Nature's ties to the living witness of it, that the separation of soul and body had taken place. It is firmly believed by the family, who, however, all shrink from making their names public. So, my dear doctor, you must be content with this."--E. M. C., Cambridge, July 15, 1873.

19. "The narrative of the spectral appearance of a lady at Torquay, forwarded to Dr. F. G. Lee at his special request, is copied from, and compared with that in, the family Bible of H. A. T. Baillie-Hamilton by the undersigned,

"C. Margaret Balfour,

Mary Baillie-Hamilton.

Witness, J. R. Grant.

"Princes Street, Edinburgh,

October 7, 1871."
20. "The above is a correct and truthful statement.

"Witness my hand and seal.

John Gill Godwin.
Illustration.

"76, Warwick Street,

South Belgravia, Nov. 6, 1874."
21. Special enquiry, made since the above was penned, shows conclusively that this appearance was seen exactly seven years after the date of death.--Editor.

22. The Editor is in no degree concerned with Paganism or Pagan superstitions, nor has he gathered præ-Christian examples. Yet such will have been numerous to the ordinary student of classical history. The Haunted House of Damon, mentioned by Plutarch, will be familiar to many.

23. The following is the original of a most beautiful verse in Bishop Ken's well-known "Evening Hymn," either mutilated in the worst of taste in most hymn-books, or else altogether eliminated and suppressed:--

"You, my best guardian, while I sleep

Close to my bed your vigils keep;

Your love angelical instil,

Stop all the avenues of ill."

24. "What do we know of the World of Spirits? Little or nothing, beyond what Faith and Revelation afford. Still we know that they surround us; that they hover over us; that they accompany us whithersoever we go; and that even in the innermost tabernacle of the soul they penetrate and have their being. Good spirits and bad are around us; good spirits to aid us, to waft our lame and imperfect prayers to heaven, and to protect us in the hour of temptation or peril. 'He shall give His angels charge over thee, lest thou dash thy foot against a stone.' Bad angels, too, are

around us and against us, percolating through every avenue of the soul, inflaming the imagination, warping the judgment, tainting the will, and too often, alas! perverting it to perdition. Bad angels are around us, even within the protecting sanctuary of God's Church, when summoned, permitted there by the subdued and corrupted will of man. Bad angels are around us in every walk and rank and condition and event of life: we see them not, but they hover over us and around us, and they penetrate within the mysterious precincts of the soul, by many a foul and unholy thought, by many an evil suggestion to sin. And they triumph, and they gibber in their unholy glee whenever they tempt and prevail. They triumph, and they laugh the insulting laugh whenever they steep to the lips in sin an unhappy mortal, and fasten upon him the mocking thought and determination of a deathbed repentance. That is their battle ground, the battle ground of victory. The standard of deceit is then triumphant: the captive is delivered bound into their hands to do with as they list, to be tormented according to the refinement of their infernal pleasure. 'He shall be delivered unto the tormentors.'"--Rev. Edward Price.

25. This belief prevails extensively in Sweden, Germany, and Switzerland.

26. The souls of the dead, or spirits of some sort, are constantly heard and not unfrequently seen in mines. A Shropshire miner informed the Editor that, of his own knowledge, he had heard supernatural sounds of moanings and mutterings underground, and had seemed to feel the passing spirits as they swept by. On one occasion, after the violent and sudden death of a comrade, the noises were unusually loud; while the horses employed underground would stand trembling and covered with perspiration whenever the spirits were heard.

27. "The Life of the Rev. John Wesley, M.A., by Robert Southey, Esq.," vol. ii. p. 370. London: 1858.

28. In many places on the continent, especially in France and Spain, it was the custom to pray for departed souls, suffering (as their needful purification was incompleted) in any particular locality. Dr. Neale gives an example of this, occurring in a prayer which he saw printed and hung up in a church at Braganza in Spain, which ran thus:--"We pray, likewise, for the souls which are suffering in any place by the particular chastisement of God." And the following is translated from a French Prayer-Book of the last century:--"Have mercy, O Lord God, good and pitiful, on the souls of those who are being chastised for their transgressions in the flesh, in those places where Thou willest them to suffer;" an evident reference in both cases to troubled spirits which haunt definite spots.

29. When the tone of thought in Shakspeare's day is compared with that in our own, the contrast between the accurate and explicit religious statements regarding the Supernatural, with the shallow and cynical scepticism of modern writers, can hardly be put down to the credit of the Modern. At all events those who claim to range themselves on the side of the Ancient and the True may be permitted to do so. Nothing could more forcibly set forth the current belief of the sixteenth century than the following well-known utterance of the Ghost in "Hamlet":--

"I am thy Father's spirit;
Doom'd for a certain time to walk the night,
And for the day confined to fast in fires,
Till the foul crimes done in my days of nature
Are burnt and purged away. But that I am forbid
To tell the secrets of my prison-house,
I could a tale unfold whose lightest word
Would harrow up thy soul, freeze thy young blood,
Make thy two eyes, like stars, start from their spheres,
Thy knotted and combined locks to part,
And each particular hair to stand on end,
Like quills upon the fretful porcupine:
But this eternal blazon must not be
To ears of flesh and blood."

"Hamlet," pp. 22-23. Oxford: 1873.

30. The Editor is indebted to the late Revs. W. Hastings Kelke and H. Roundell of Buckingham, for the above curious example. It was intended to have been published some years ago in "The Records of Bucks."

31. For an accurate account by the late Rev. W. Hastings Kelke of this curious and interesting old mansion, the property of Lord Clifford of Chudleigh, see "The Records of Bucks," vol. i. pp. 255-267. Aylesbury, 1858.

32. "Memoirs of Sir John Reresby," p. 238.

33. The Rev. Joseph Jefferson, M.A., Vicar of North Stainley, near Ripon, who sent me the above--unaltered, and printed just as it was written--on the 2nd of June, 1873.

34. "Notes and Queries," vol. x. second series, Sept. 8, 1860, pp. 192-193, and Sept. 22, 1860, p. 236.

35. Barby is a parish in the Hundred of Fawsley, in the county of Northampton, a little more than five miles from Daventry. It contains between six and seven hundred inhabitants.

36. "Your account, as about to be printed, is true and exact, as to all the facts of the haunted house at ----, which came within my own personal knowledge. Don't mention names, or we shall perhaps be damaging the property, and lay ourselves open to an action at law. I may add that the late Bishop of Chester Dr. Graham. is said to have furnished a mutual friend, the late Master of Trinity, with similar accounts, which had taken place before I knew the place, verifying to an A B C the old and, no doubt, perfectly true tradition. It is strange enough I know, but it is true.--Yours, &c., H. S. B., November, 1874."

37. The wife of the clergyman above alluded to, wrote to the Editor as follows:--"Having read the account which you contemplate publishing, I can testify of my own personal knowledge that it is neither understated nor exaggerated, but is in all its details strictly true and accurate.--June, 1874."

38. Miss S. F. Caulfeild, author of "Avenele," "Desmond," &c.

39. It seems that other places are reported to be haunted by appearances of Birds. A correspondent informs the Editor that this is the case with an old House in Dorsetshire, not far from Poole, where a wingless bird is sometimes seen. The same is said of a mansion in Essex, as another correspondent declares. In one room in an old house in Dean Street, Soho, likewise, several persons have seen a large raven, three times the size of an ordinary raven, perched on the tester of the old-fashioned bed. The inmates of the house, in 1854, whose family had had the lease for eighty years, are said to have been so accustomed to seeing it (though they knew it to be spectral) that they were undisturbed by its frequent appearance. Dr. Neale's story as follows (not unlike the examples already given), is very singular. Regarding it he wrote:--"It comes to me with a weight of evidence, which, strange as is the tale, I cannot disbelieve. Three friends, not very much distinguished by piety, had been dining together at the residence of one of them in Norfolk. After dinner they went out and strolled through the churchyard. 'Well,' said a clergyman, one of the three, 'I wonder, after all, if there is any future state or not?' They agreed that whichever died first should appear to the others and inform them. 'In what shape shall it be?' asked one of the friends. At that moment a flight of crows arose from a neighbouring field. 'A crow is as good a shape as any other,' said the clergyman; 'if I should be the first to die, I will appear in that.' He did die first; and some time after his death, the other two had been dining together, and were walking in the garden afterwards. A crow settled on the head of one of them, stuck there pertinaciously, and could only be torn off by main force. And when this gentleman's carriage came to take him home, the crow perched on it, and accompanied him back."

40. "Strange Things Amongst Us." By Henry Spicer. 2nd ed., pp. 100-102. London: Chapman & Hall, 1864.

41. The following is taken from a small volume which has been gratuitously circulated very widely amongst the clergy and laity. It bears a Christian title, but is altogether anti-Christian from end to end:--

"The unwise, idolatrous, early Christian priests, in their admiration of Christ, exalted him in their imagination to be God Himself, forgetting the Creator God, and exalting in their foolish imagination his Blessed Mother as the Mother of God--folly that has been widely perpetuated down to these days. Oh, foolish churches, how great has been your folly, how widely you have departed from the truth; therefore how little you have been able to cope with the wicked heart of man!

"In like manner as the Israelites, from the crucifixion down to these days, have erred in disbelieving the Messiah-ship of Christ, so the spurious churches have, during many ages, exalted Christ in their imagination to be God. The Israelites and the spurious churches being equal in their great error--the one refusing to acknowledge him as the long-promised Messiah, the other exalting him in their imagination as being the Messiah, the Holy Ghost, and God the Creator also; the Israelites refusing to give any glory to Christ, the spurious churches madly rushing, in their ancient antagonism towards the Jews, to the opposite extreme, by robbing, in their imagination, God the Creator of His Glory, and giving all glory to the Messiah, to the great grief of the Messiah.

"Now clearly understand, oh ye nations of the whole world! it was not God who was born out of the Virgin Mary, and who was crucified, but the before holy angel Christ--understand this, and the Holy Scriptures will be plain to your comprehension--Christians have erred greatly during so many generations, in like manner as the followers of Mahomet and of Buddah have erred--errors that were carelessly accepted by powerful rulers, evil and ignorant, and forced upon the priests and the people, generation after generation. The time is at hand, even knocking at the door, when your understanding shall be made clear, and neither the professing followers of Christ, nor of Buddah, nor of Mahomet, nor the unwise of other sects, will continue in their many errors."--"Christ is Coming," pp. 135-6.

"Yet to-day, if one dare question the value of Christianity, what a howl is raised from one end of Christendom to the other! We say so advisedly, for it is the howl of fear.... Though Christianity to-day declines and is losing power and vigour, yet in its day it hath done great and glorious good in the work of human redemption. It was an advance upon the religions which preceded it."--"What of the Dead? An Address by Mr. J. J. Morse, in the Trance State," p. 5. London: J. Burns. 1873.

42. 2 St. Peter iii. 3, 4.

43. "A Scientific View of Modern Spiritualism: a Paper read by Mr. T. Grant to the Maidstone and Mid-Kent Natural History and Philosophical Society on Tuesday, Dec. 31, 1872." London: J. Burns.

44. A remarkable example of this has been courteously given to me by Mr. Thomas Bosworth, of 198, High Holborn, as follows:--"Some seven or eight years ago there appeared in one of the newspapers a story to the following effect:--A commercial firm at Bolton, in Lancashire, had found that a considerable sum of money which had been sent to their bank by a confidential clerk, had not been placed to their credit. The clerk remembered the fact of taking the money, though not the particulars, but at the bank nothing was known of it. The clerk, feeling that he was liable to suspicion in the matter, and anxious to elucidate it, sought the help of spirit medium. The medium promised to do her best. Having heard the story, she presently passed into a kind of trance. Shortly after she said, 'I see you on your way to the bank--I see you go into the bank--I see you go to such and such part of the bank--I see you hand some papers to a clerk--I see him put them in such and such a place under some other papers--and I see them there now.' The clerk went to the bank, directed the cashier where to look for the money, and it was found; the cashier afterwards remembering that in the hurry of business he had there deposited it. A relation of mine saw this story in a newspaper at the time, and wrote to the firm in question, the name of which was given, asking whether the facts were as stated. He was told in reply that they were. That gentleman who was applied to, having corrected one or two unimportant details in the above narration, wrote on November 9, 1874:--'Your account is a correct one. I have the answer of the firm to my enquiry at home now.'"

45. The term "willer" and "necromancer" are used as identical by Easterns as well as by the aborigines of New Zealand.

46. There have been published "Rules to be Observed for the Spirit Circle," "framed under the Direction and Impression of Spirits," by Emma Hardinge, from which the following points are gathered. Firstly, there is a definition, and it is stated that "the Spirit Circle is the assembling together of a given number of persons for the purpose of seeking communion with the spirits who have passed away from Earth into the higher world of souls." A leading direction enjoins the inquiring votaries to "Avoid strong light, which by producing excessive motion in the atmosphere, disturbs the manifestations. A very subdued light is the most favourable for any manifestations of a magnetic character, especially for spiritual magnetism." "Strongly positive persons of any kind" and "the dogmatical" should not be admitted. Furthermore, these "Rules" contain the following:--

"Spirit control is often deficient, and at first almost always imperfect. By often yielding to it, your organism becomes more flexible and the spirit more experienced; and practice in control is absolutely necessary for spirits as well as mortals. If dark and evil-disposed spirits manifest to you, never drive them away, but always strive to elevate them and treat them as you would mortals under similar circumstances. Do not always attribute falsehoods to 'lying spirits,' or deceiving mediums. Many mistakes occur in the communion of which you cannot always be aware. Strive for Truth, but rebuke Error gently, and do not always attribute it to design, but rather to mistake, in so difficult and experimental a stage of the communion as mortals at present enjoy with spirits."

47. The kind of communication made to those who first consult the spirits, is just of that nature calculated to allure the superficial, the frivolous, the uninformed, triflers, and seekers after novelties; and to lead them on to a more frequent intercourse and a deeper kind of communion.

48. Dr. J. G. Davey, M.D., of Northwoods, Bristol, writes as follows:--"I have satisfied myself not only of the mere abstract truth of Spiritualism, but of its great and marvellous power for good, both on moral and religious grounds. The direct and positive communications vouchsafed to me from very many near and dear relatives and friends, said to be dead, have been of the most pleasing yet startling character."--Report on Spiritualism, p. 232. London: Longmans, 1871.

49. This person, whose name was most accurately given, had died five days previously. He was a servant on the estate, and had belonged to the sect of the Anabaptists.

50. "Notes of an Enquiry into the Phenomena called Spiritualism, during the years 1870-73." By William Crookes, F.R.S.

51. "The reader who has not been in the habit of attending séances should be informed that the peculiar phraseology of some of the questions is rendered necessary by the fact that if you ask the spirits, 'Where did you die?' or 'Where were you buried?' they will sometimes tell you that it was not they who died and were buried, but merely the external shell or material covering of the real man."--Note by the Editor of the "Spiritual Magazine."

52. "There is scarcely a city or a considerable town in Continental Europe, at the present moment, where Spiritualists are not reckoned by hundreds if not by thousands; where regularly established communities do not habitually meet for spiritual purposes: and they reckon among them individuals of every class and avocation."--"Scepticism and Spiritualism." In a letter to the "Spiritual Magazine," dated May 4th, 1867, Judge Edmunds, of America, estimated the number of Spiritualists in the United States at ten millions. "In London, ten years ago," writes Mr. R. Dale Owen, "there was but a single Spiritual paper; to-day there are five."--"The Debatable Land," p. 175. London: Trübner, 1871.

53. The Rev. John Edwards, jun., M.A., Vicar of Prestbury, near Cheltenham.

54. "We do not, either by faith or works, earn Heaven, nor are we sentenced, on any Day of Wrath, to Hell. In the next world we simply gravitate to the position for which, by life on earth, we have fitted ourselves; and we occupy that position because we are fitted for it."--"The Debatable Land," by R. Dale Owen, p. 125. London, 1871.

55. Howitt's "What Spiritualism has Taught," p. 8.

56. Howitt's "What Spiritualism has Taught," p. 10.

57. "Spiritualism is avowedly opposed to the Christian Religion. 'The Creed of the spirits' is published in the shape of a little tract, one of those called 'Seed Corn,' which active agents love to distribute gratuitously wherever readers can be found, and these are its clauses: 'I believe in God'--'I believe in the immortality of the human soul'--'I believe in right and wrong'--'I believe in the communion of spirits as ministering angels.' Nothing more. Those well-intending persons, therefore--and we believe that among Protestants there are many--who go to séances out of curiosity, and who are sometimes heard to say that if Spiritualism be true it must therefore be right, should be warned that they are lending countenance to persons in whose writings the doctrines of the Trinity and the Divinity of our Lord Jesus Christ are emphatically denied--the Holy Ghost scoffed at in words too blasphemous for repetition, our Blessed Lady insulted, and the whole fabric of Religion attacked and undermined; and whether this is done by spirits who actually manifest themselves for the purpose of leading people astray, or by impostors who work upon the credulity of their audience, the thing can have but one origin, and that is the same as that of any other work by which the Arch-enemy seeks to close the heart of man against the True Faith. It is time therefore to use other weapons than that of ridicule against the baneful and, we fear, widely increasing delusion."--"Tablet," September 6, 1873.

58. Collect for the Feast of S. Michael and All Angels, "Book of Common Prayer."

59. "The soul has a kind of body of a quality of its own."--Tertull. cont. Marc. lib. v. cap. xv.

60. This account is current, with slender and unimportant variations, at Oxford; or at all events was current in my days there (A.D. 1850-1854), and on what could not be regarded as other than good authority. One version is already in print--that given by Mr. William Maskell, at pp. 108-112 of his curious and interesting book, "Odds and Ends," London, 1872. He seems to imply that it was the late Archdeacon of Cleveland, the Ven. Edward Churton, who saw the spectral apparitions in Brasenose Lane; but the Archdeacon belonged to Christ Church, and, as his son, the Rev. W. R. Churton, of Cambridge, informs me, was not resident at Oxford at the time of the occurrence. More

probably it was the Archdeacon's brother, the Rev. T. T. Churton, sometime Fellow of Brasenose.

61. As to the universality of the belief in Witchcraft, the reader may consult Herder's "Philosophy of History," bk. viii. ch. 2. And as regards the convictions of some of the leading minds of Europe in times past on the subject, Mr. Leckey in his "History of Rationalism" (vol. i. p. 66), makes the following candid admission: "It is, I think, impossible to deny that the books in defence of the belief are not only far more numerous than the later works against it, but that they also represent far more learning, dialectic skill, and even general ability. For many centuries the ablest men were not merely unwilling to repudiate the superstition; they often pressed forward earnestly and with the most intense conviction to defend it. Indeed, during the period when Witchcraft was most prevalent there were few writers of real eminence who did not, on some occasion, take especial pains to throw the weight of their authority into the scale. Thomas Aquinas was probably the ablest writer of the thirteenth century, and he assures us that diseases and tempests are often the direct acts of the devil; that the devil can transport men at his pleasure through the air; and that he can transform them into any shape. Gerson, the Chancellor of the University of Paris, and, as many think, the author of 'The Imitation,' is justly regarded as one of the master intellects of his age; and he, too, wrote in defence of the belief. Bodin was unquestionably the most original political philosopher who had arisen since Machiavelli, and he devoted all his learning and acuteness to crushing the rising scepticism 'on the subject of witches.'"

62. 1 S. Peter v. 8.
63. Acts xvi. 16-18.
64. Apologia, cap. v. De Civit. Dei, lib. xv. cap. xxiii.
65. 1 Cor. xi. 10.
66. Ibid. xi. 15.

67. Luther, following the current tradition of his day, believed that the Devil could beget children on the bodies of women; and declared that he himself had personally come across, and was well acquainted with, one of the Devil's offspring. So too did Erasmus believe the fact of such generation. It is a tradition in the Catholic Church, that the last and great Antichrist--the final Antichrist--may be born of such an alliance. Of course Mahomet was a great Antichrist; for though he borrowed certain Christian features and adopted many Jewish notions and Rabbinical traditions in his system, yet he plainly and undoubtedly fulfilled the prophetic statement of S. John the Divine--"He is Antichrist, who denieth the Father and the Son." (1 S. John ii. 22.) Mahomet's great and leading heresy is expressed in the following dogmatic assertion of the Koran: "God neither begetteth nor is begotten." Now no system has more pertinaciously, successfully, and for so long a time opposed Christianity than Mahometanism--not even Arianism. But modern "Liberalism," so called, as still developing amongst ancient Christian nations, promises even to outstrip the system of Mahomet, and to be as blighting and baneful in its results.

68. "An Account of the Manners and Customs of the Modern Egyptians." By E. W. Lane. 5th edition. London: 1860.

69. See the whole of this chapter, which is full of information and interest. It gives a record of several other similar examples.

70. In No. 117 of the "Quarterly Review," there is a criticism on Mr. Lane's account of these necromancers; but the facts recorded by him are neither satisfactorily accounted for nor successfully explained away.

71. My brother-in-law, Captain Ostrehan, of the Bombay Staff Corps, Sir Alfred Slade, Bart., and the Rev. Dr. Dunbar, chaplain to Bishop Claughton, have furnished me with remarkable examples of the power of Oriental necromancers.

72. Nevins' "China and the Chinese," p. 167. New York, 1868.

73. "Theory of Pneumatology," by J. H. Jung-Stilling, pp. 136-137. London: Longmans, 1834.

74. Dr. Sexton in his "Defence of Modern Spiritualism" (London: J. Burns), a tractate written with ability and frankness, remarks that "it is too late in the day to sneer at this matter with a sort of self-complacency, which seems to say, 'You are a poor deluded creature: behold my superior wisdom; I don't believe in such nonsense.' Here are the facts, and we demand in the true spirit of Science to know what is to be done with them. If you have any theory by which they can be explained, let us hear it, in order that we may judge of its merits; if you have not, we are all the more justified in clinging to our own." And, again, referring to the inquiries of a certain Dr. Hare in America, he writes:--"The question with Dr. Hare was--Did the phenomena occur, and, if so, were they produced by the direct action of those persons in whose presence they took place? The nonsensical notions mooted by unscientific opponents, and which are still urged with as much gravity as though they had been made the subject of mathematical demonstration, that electricity, magnetism, odic, or psychic forces are the agents by which the manifestations are produced, he knew well enough could not bear a moment's investigation. Electricity cannot move tables, nor in fact act at all without cumbrous apparatus. Magnetism cannot give intelligent responses to

questions, and odic force and its twin brother psychic are probably as imaginary as the philosopher's stone; and even if their existence could be proved beyond the shadow of a doubt, they could not in the slightest degree help us to the solution of the great problem of the cause of the phenomena designated Spiritual."

75. A thoughtful writer, and one who is evidently far-seeing and awake to the danger, recently made the following pertinent remarks in the Church Review:--

"The presence of Superstition is always the sign of a wandering from the true path; the excess of Superstition almost invariably the precursor of great intellectual and religious changes, if not absolute convulsions. Before the great crash of Paganism the necromancers and practisers of curious arts were carrying on an unusually brisk trade among the Romans. We all know how prevalent was the belief in witches, wizards, and astrology at the time immediately preceding the (so-called) Reformation. Before the French Revolution the sect founded by Cagliostro and Lorenza Feliciani, which professed a knowledge of the ancient arts of the Egyptians, found great numbers of followers. And have we not a sign of a national mental crisis in our own day in the prevalence of 'Spiritualism,' which is the form which necromancy at present takes? There may be many people who are utterly unaware how large a number of their fellow-countrymen, and especially of their countrywomen, believe in Spiritualism, and attend séances. Those who do so are not usually very fond of parading their belief, because they have a lurking suspicion that they may get laughed at; but this very reserve makes the bond between the votaries of Spiritualism so much the stronger. It is no exaggeration to say that the practice of dealing with familiar spirits is on the increase in Great Britain at the present moment." (A.D. 1873.)

76. "On the Invisible World," by Joseph Hall, D.D., &c., book i. sec. 8. Father Christopher Davenport, better known as "Sancta Clara," in one of his most remarkable treatises, "Paralipomena Philosophica de Mundo Peripatetico," chap. iv. p. 68 (A.D. 1652), confirms the account in the text of the above-named Bishop of Exeter, giving all the details of this particular miraculous cure. It seems that both the Well and Chapel of S. Madron were constantly visited by the faithful during the first part of the seventeenth century, especially in the month of May and on the feast of Corpus Christi.

77. "History of the Rise and Influence of the Spirit of Rationalism in Europe," by W. E. H. Lecky, M.A. Fourth edition in two volumes. London, 1870.

78. Dr. Newman will, of course, be excepted; for his remarkable Dissertation prefixed to the translation of Fleury's "History" is known to many, more especially in its new form,--a volume already referred to at length in chap. ii. pp. 35-36. It is certainly quite unjust to include the Tractarian school amongst those who are referred to by Mr. Lecky in the following passage:--"At present nearly all educated men receive an account of a miracle taking place in their own day, with an absolute and even derisive incredulity which dispenses with all examination of the evidence."--Vol. i. p. 1. Though many are reticent, and many more shrink from publicity and rude criticism, it is known that the direct influence of the Miraculous and Supernatural is by no means unknown in the Church of England.

79. Job xxv. 5.

80. See a most remarkable Letter from the pen of my friend the Rev. R. S. Hawker, of Morwenstow, on "The Claims of Science and Faith," standing as an Appendix to this Chapter, in which the office of the angels is referred to.

81. Mr. Mill, who is now dead, wrote that "this World was a bungled business in which no clear-sighted man meaning himself apparently, and modestly. could see any signs either of wisdom or of God." Mr. Matthew Arnold, son of Dr. Arnold of Rugby, has written that "the existence of God is an unverifiable hypothesis." A third writer maintains that the "great duty" of the philosophers "should be to eliminate the idea of God from the minds of men," a sentiment not unlike that of Mr. Congreve, already quoted on p. 19 of vol. i.; while a popular publication, circulated by thousands amongst the lower classes, declares that the mission of its Editors is "to teach men to live without the fear of God; to die without the fear of the Devil; and to attain salvation without the Blood of the Lamb."

www.ingramcontent.com/pod-product-compliance
Ingram Content Group UK Ltd.
Pitfield, Milton Keynes, MK11 3LW, UK
UKHW041436180426
11947UKWH00007B/483